Programming Google App Engine with Java

Dan Sanderson

Beijing · Boston · Farnham · Sebastopol · Tokyo

Programming Google App Engine with Java

by Dan Sanderson

Copyright © 2015 Dan Sanderson. All rights reserved.

Printed in the United States of America.

Published by O'Reilly Media, Inc., 1005 Gravenstein Highway North, Sebastopol, CA 95472.

O'Reilly books may be purchased for educational, business, or sales promotional use. Online editions are also available for most titles (*http://safaribooksonline.com*). For more information, contact our corporate/institutional sales department: 800-998-9938 or *corporate@oreilly.com*.

Editors: Meghan Blanchette and Brian Anderson	**Proofreader:** Charles Roumeliotis
Acquisition Editor: Mike Loukides	**Indexer:** Judy McConville
Production Editors: Colleen Lobner and Kara Ebrahim	**Interior Designer:** David Futato
Copyeditor: Jasmine Kwityn	**Cover Designer:** Ellie Volckhausen
	Illustrator: Rebecca Demarest

July 2015:   First Edition

Revision History for the First Edition
2015-06-26:   First Release

See *http://oreilly.com/catalog/errata.csp?isbn=9781491900208* for release details.

The O'Reilly logo is a registered trademark of O'Reilly Media, Inc. *Programming Google App Engine with Java,* the cover image of a Comoro cuckoo roller, and related trade dress are trademarks of O'Reilly Media, Inc.

978-1-491-90020-8

[LSI]

Table of Contents

Preface

On the Internet, popularity is swift and fleeting. A mention of your website on a popular news site can bring 300,000 potential customers your way at once, all expecting to find out who you are and what you have to offer. But if you're a small company just starting out, your hardware and software aren't likely to be able to handle that kind of traffic. You've sensibly built your site to handle the 30,000 visits per hour you're actually expecting in your first six months. Under heavy load, such a system would be incapable of showing even your company logo to the 270,000 others that showed up to look around. And those potential customers are not likely to come back after the traffic has subsided.

The answer is *not* to spend time and money building a system to serve millions of visitors on the first day, when those same systems are only expected to serve mere thousands per day for the subsequent months. If you delay your launch to build big, you miss the opportunity to improve your product by using feedback from your customers. Building big early risks building something your customers don't want.

Historically, small companies haven't had access to large systems of servers on day one. The best they could do was to build small and hope that meltdowns wouldn't damage their reputation as they try to grow. The lucky ones found their audience, got another round of funding, and halted feature development to rebuild their product for larger capacity. The unlucky ones, well, didn't.

These days, there are other options. Large Internet companies such as Amazon.com, Google, and Microsoft are leasing parts of their high-capacity systems by using a pay-per-use model. Your website is served from those large systems, which are plenty capable of handling sudden surges in traffic and ongoing success. And because you pay only for what you use, there is no up-front investment that goes to waste when traffic is low. As your customer base grows, the costs grow proportionally.

Google's offering, collectively known as Google Cloud Platform, consists of a suite of high-powered services and tools: virtual machines in a variety of sizes, multiple forms of reliable data storage, configurable networking, automatic scaling infrastructure, and even the big data analysis tools that power Google's products. But Google Cloud Platform does more than provide access to Google's infrastructure. It encapsulates best practices for application architecture that have been honed by Google engineers for their own products.

The centerpiece of Google Cloud Platform is Google App Engine, an application hosting service that grows automatically. App Engine runs your application so that each user who accesses it gets the same experience as every other user, whether there are dozens of simultaneous users or thousands. Your application code focuses on each individual user's experience. App Engine takes care of large-scale computing tasks—such as load balancing, data replication, and fault tolerance—automatically.

The scalable model really kicks in at the point where a traditional system would outgrow its first database server. With such a system, adding load-balanced web servers and caching layers can get you pretty far, but when your application needs to write data to more than one place, you face a difficult problem. This problem is made more difficult when development up to that point has relied on features of database software that were never intended for data distributed across multiple machines. By thinking about your data in terms of Cloud Platform's model up front, you save yourself from having to rebuild the whole thing later.

Often overlooked as an advantage, App Engine's execution model helps to distribute computation as well as data. App Engine excels at allocating computing resources to small tasks quickly. This was originally designed for handling web requests from users, where generating a response for the client is the top priority. Combining this execution model with Cloud Platform's task queue service, medium-to-large computational tasks can be broken into chunks that are executed in parallel. Tasks are retried until they succeed, making tasks resilient in the face of service failures. The execution model encourages designs optimized for the parallelization and robustness provided by the platform.

Running on Google's infrastructure means you never have to set up a server, replace a failed hard drive, or troubleshoot a network card. You don't have to be woken up in the middle of the night by a screaming pager because an ISP hiccup confused a service alarm. And with automatic scaling, you don't have to scramble to set up new hardware as traffic increases.

Google Cloud Platform and App Engine let you focus on your application's functionality and user experience. You can launch early, enjoy the flood of attention, retain customers, and start improving your product with the help of your users. Your app grows with the size of your audience—up to Google-sized proportions—without having to rebuild for a new architecture. Meanwhile, your competitors are still putting out fires and configuring databases.

With this book, you will learn how to develop web applications that run on Google Cloud Platform, and how to get the most out of App Engine's scalable execution model. A significant portion of the book discusses Google Cloud Datastore, a powerful data storage service that does not behave like the relational databases that have been a staple of web development for the past decade. The application model and the datastore together represent a new way of thinking about web applications that, while being almost as simple as the model we've known, requires reconsidering a few principles we often take for granted.

A Brief History of App Engine

If you read all that, you may be wondering why this book is called *Programming Google App Engine* and not *Programming Google Cloud Platform*. The short answer is that the capabilities of the platform as a whole are too broad for one book. In particular, Compute Engine, the platform's raw virtual machine capability, can do all kinds of stuff beyond serving web applications.

By some accounts (mine, at least), App Engine started as an early rendition of the Cloud Platform idea, and evolved and expanded to include large-scale and flexible-scale computing. When it first launched in 2008, App Engine hosted web applications written in Python, with APIs for a scalable datastore, a task queue service, and services for common features that lay outside of the "container" in which the app code would run (such as network access). A "runtime environment" for Java soon followed, capable of running web apps based on Java servlets using the same scalable infrastructure. Container-ized app code, schemaless data storage, and service-oriented architecture proved to be not only a good way to build a scalable web app, but a good way to make reliability a key part of the App Engine product: no more pagers.

App Engine evolved continuously, with several major functionality milestones. One such milestone was a big upgrade for the datastore, using a new Paxos-based replication algorithm. The new algorithm changed the data consistency guarantees of the API, so it was released as an opt-in migration (including an automatic migration tool). Another major milestone was the switch from isolated request handlers billed by CPU usage to long-running application instances billed by instance uptime. With the upgraded execution model, app code could push "warm-up" work to occur outside of user request logic and exploit local memory caches.

Google launched Compute Engine as a separate product, a way to access computation on demand for general purposes. With a Compute Engine VM, you can run any 64-bit Linux-based operating system and execute code written in any language compiled to (or interpreted by) that OS. Apps—running on App Engine or otherwise—can call into Compute Engine to start up any number of virtual machines, do work, and either shut down machines when no longer needed or leave them running in traditional or custom configurations.

App Engine and Compute Engine take different approaches to provide different capabilities. But these technologies are already starting to blend. In early 2014, Google announced Managed VMs, a new way to run VM-based code in an App Engine-like way. (This feature is not fully available as I write this, but check the Google Cloud Platform website (*http://cloud.google.com*) for updates.) Overall, you're able to adopt as much of the platform as you need to accomplish your goals, investing in flexibility when needed, and letting the platform's automaticity handle the rest.

This book is being written at a turning point in App Engine's history. Services that were originally built for App Engine are being generalized for Cloud Platform, and given REST APIs so you can call them from off the platform as well. App Engine development tools are being expanded, with a new universal Cloud SDK and Cloud Console. We're even seeing the beginnings of new ways to develop and deploy software, with integrated Git-based source code revision control. As with any book about an evolving technology, what follows is a snapshot, with an emphasis on major concepts and long-lasting topics.

The focus of this book is building web applications using App Engine and related parts of the platform, especially Cloud Datastore. We'll discuss services currently exclusive to App Engine, such as those for fetching URLs and sending email. We'll also discuss techniques for organizing and optimizing your application, using task queues and offline processes, and otherwise getting the most out of Google App Engine.

Using This Book

Programming Google App Engine with Java focuses on App Engine's Java runtime environment. The Java runtime includes a complete Java 7 JVM capable of running bytecode produced by the Java compiler, as well as that produced by compilers for other languages that target the JVM. App Engine is a J2EE standard servlet container, and includes the standard libraries and features for Java web development. You can even deploy your apps as WAR files.

App Engine supports three other runtime environments: Python, PHP, and Go. The Python environment provides a fast interpreter for the Python programming language, and is compatible with many of Python's open source web application frameworks. The PHP environment runs a native PHP interpreter with the standard library and many extensions enabled, and is capable of running many off-the-shelf PHP applications such as WordPress and Drupal. With the Go runtime environment, App Engine compiles your Go code on the server and executes it at native CPU speeds.

The information contained in this book was formerly presented in a single volume, *Programming Google App Engine*, which also covered Python. To make it easy to find the information you need for your language, that book has been split into language-specific versions. You are reading the Java version. *Programming Google App Engine with Python* covers the same material using the Python language, as well as Python-specific topics.

We are considering PHP and Go versions of this book as a future endeavor. For now, the official App Engine documentation (*https://cloud.google.com/appengine/docs*) is the best resource for using these languages on the platform. If you're interested in seeing versions of this book for PHP or Go, let us know by sending email to *bookquestions@oreilly.com*.

The book is organized so you can jump to the subjects that are most relevant to you. The introductory chapters provide a lay of the land, and get you working with a complete example that uses several features. Subsequent chapters are arranged by App Engine's various features, with a focus on efficient data storage and retrieval, communication, and distributed computation. Project life cycle topics such as deployment and maintenance are also covered.

Cloud Datastore is a large enough subject that it gets multiple chapters to itself. Starting with Chapter 6, datastore concepts are introduced alongside Java APIs related to those concepts. We also dedicate a chapter to JPA (Chapter 10), a standard interface and portability layer for accessing data storage and modeling data objects, which you can use with Cloud Datastore.

Here's a quick look at the chapters in this book:

Chapter 1, Introducing Google App Engine
A high-level overview of Google App Engine and its components, tools, and major features, as well as an introduction to Google Cloud Platform as a whole.

Chapter 2, Creating an Application
An introductory tutorial in Java, including instructions on setting up a development environment, using template engines to build web pages, setting up accounts and domain names, and deploying the application to App Engine. The tutorial application demonstrates the use of several App Engine features—Google Accounts, the datastore, and memcache—to implement a pattern common to many web applications: storing and retrieving user preferences.

Chapter 3, Configuring an Application
A description of how App Engine handles incoming requests, and how to configure this behavior. This introduces App Engine's architecture, the various features of the frontend, app servers, and static file servers. We explain how the frontend routes requests to the app servers and the static file servers, and manages secure

connections and Google Accounts authentication and authorization. This chapter also discusses quotas and limits, and how to raise them by setting a budget.

Chapter 4, Request Handlers and Instances

A closer examination of how App Engine runs your code. App Engine routes incoming web requests to request handlers. Request handlers run in long-lived containers called instances. App Engine creates and destroys instances to accommodate the needs of your traffic. You can make better use of your instances by writing threadsafe code and enabling the multithreading feature. You can organize your app's architecture into modules, individually addressible collections of instances each running their own code and configuration.

Chapter 5, Using Modules

Modules let you build your application as a collection of parts, where each part has its own scaling properties and performance characteristics. This chapter describes modules in full, including the various scaling options, configuration, and the tools and APIs you use to maintain the modules of your app.

Chapter 6, Datastore Entities

The first of several chapters on Cloud Datastore, a scalable object data storage system with support for local transactions and two modes of consistency guarantees (strong and eventual). This chapter introduces data entities, keys and properties, and Java APIs for creating, updating, and deleting entities from App Engine.

Chapter 7, Datastore Queries

An introduction to Cloud Datastore queries and indexes, and the Java APIs for queries. This chapter describes the features of the query engine in detail, and how each feature uses indexes. The chapter also discusses how to define and manage indexes for your application's queries. Advanced features like query cursors and projection queries are also covered.

Chapter 8, Datastore Transactions

How to use transactions to keep your data consistent. Cloud Datastore uses local transactions in a scalable environment. Your app arranges its entities in units of transactionality known as entity groups. This chapter attempts to provide a complete explanation of how the datastore updates data, and how to design your data and your app to best take advantage of these features.

Chapter 9, Datastore Administration

Managing and evolving your app's datastore data. The Cloud Console, SDK tools, and administrative APIs provide a myriad of views of your data, and information about your data (metadata and statistics). You can access much of this information programmatically, so you can build your own administration panels. This chapter also discusses how to use the Remote API, a proxy for building administrative tools that run on your local computer but access the live services for your app.

Chapter 10, The Java Persistence API

A brief introduction to the Java Persistence API (JPA), how its concepts translate to the datastore, how to use it to model data schemas, and how using it makes your application easier to port to other environments. JPA is a Java EE standard interface. App Engine also supports another standard interface known as Java Data Objects (JDO), although JDO is not covered in this book. This chapter covers Java exclusively.

Chapter 11, Using Google Cloud SQL with App Engine

Google Cloud SQL provides fully managed MySQL database instances. You can use Cloud SQL as a relational database for your App Engine applications. This chapter walks through an example of creating a SQL instance, setting up a database, preparing a local development environment, and connecting to Cloud SQL from App Engine. We also discuss prominent features of Cloud SQL such as backups, and exporting and importing data. Cloud SQL complements Cloud Datastore and Cloud Storage as a new choice for persistent storage, and is a powerful option when you need a relational database.

Chapter 12, The Memory Cache

App Engine's memory cache service ("memcache"), and its Java APIs. Aggressive caching is essential for high-performance web applications.

Chapter 13, Fetching URLs and Web Resources

How to access other resources on the Internet via HTTP by using the URL Fetch service. Java applications can call this service using a direct API as well as via Java standard library calls.

Chapter 14, Sending and Receiving Email Messages

How to use App Engine services to send email. This chapter covers receiving email relayed by App Engine by using request handlers. It also discusses creating and processing messages by using tools in the API.

Chapter 15, Sending and Receiving Instant Messages with XMPP

How to use App Engine services to send instant messages to XMPP-compatible services (such as Google Talk), and receive XMPP messages via request handlers. This chapter discusses several major XMPP activities, including managing presence.

Chapter 16, Task Queues and Scheduled Tasks

How to perform work outside of user requests by using task queues. Task queues perform tasks in parallel by running your code on multiple application servers.

You control the processing rate with configuration. Tasks can also be executed on a regular schedule with no user interaction.

Chapter 17, Optimizing Service Calls

A summary of optimization techniques, plus detailed information on how to make asynchronous service calls, so your app can continue doing work while services process data in the background. This chapter also describes AppStats, an important tool for visualizing your app's service call behavior and finding performance bottlenecks.

Chapter 18, Managing Request Logs

Everything you need to know about logging messages, browsing and searching log data in the Cloud Console, and managing and downloading log data. This chapter also introduces the Logs API, which lets you manage logs programmatically within the app itself.

Chapter 19, Deploying and Managing Applications

How to upload and run your app on App Engine, how to update and test an application using app versions, and how to manage and inspect the running application. This chapter also introduces other maintenance features of the Cloud Console, including billing. The chapter concludes with a list of places to go for help and further reading.

Conventions Used in This Book

The following typographical conventions are used in this book:

Italic

Indicates new terms, URLs, email addresses, filenames, and file extensions.

`Constant width`

Used for program listings, as well as within paragraphs to refer to program elements such as variable or function names, databases, data types, environment variables, statements, and keywords.

`Constant width bold`

Shows commands or other text that should be typed literally by the user.

`Constant width italic`

Shows text that should be replaced with user-supplied values or by values determined by context.

This icon signifies a tip, suggestion, or general note.

 This icon indicates a warning or caution.

Safari® Books Online

 *Safari Books Online* is an on-demand digital library that delivers expert content in both book and video form from the world's leading authors in technology and business.

Technology professionals, software developers, web designers, and business and creative professionals use Safari Books Online as their primary resource for research, problem solving, learning, and certification training.

Safari Books Online offers a range of plans and pricing for enterprise, government, education, and individuals.

Members have access to thousands of books, training videos, and prepublication manuscripts in one fully searchable database from publishers like O'Reilly Media, Prentice Hall Professional, Addison-Wesley Professional, Microsoft Press, Sams, Que, Peachpit Press, Focal Press, Cisco Press, John Wiley & Sons, Syngress, Morgan Kaufmann, IBM Redbooks, Packt, Adobe Press, FT Press, Apress, Manning, New Riders, McGraw-Hill, Jones & Bartlett, Course Technology, and hundreds more. For more information about Safari Books Online, please visit us online.

How to Contact Us

Please address comments and questions concerning this book to the publisher:

O'Reilly Media, Inc.
1005 Gravenstein Highway North
Sebastopol, CA 95472
800-998-9938 (in the United States or Canada)
707-829-0515 (international or local)
707-829-0104 (fax)

We have a web page for this book, where we list errata, examples, and any additional information. You can access this page at *http://bit.ly/program-google-java*.

You can download extensive sample code and other extras from the author's website at *http://www.dansanderson.com/appengine*.

To comment or ask technical questions about this book, send email to *bookquestions@oreilly.com*.

For more information about our books, courses, conferences, and news, see our website at *http://www.oreilly.com*.

Find us on Facebook: *http://facebook.com/oreilly*

Follow us on Twitter: *http://twitter.com/oreillymedia*

Watch us on YouTube: *http://www.youtube.com/oreillymedia*

Acknowledgments

I am indebted to the App Engine team for their constant support of this book since its inception in 2008. The number of contributors to App Engine has grown too large for me to list them individually, but I'm grateful to them all for their vision, their creativity, and their work, and for letting me be a part of it.

Programming Google App Engine, from which this book is derived, was developed under the leadership of Paul McDonald and Pete Koomen. Ryan Barrett provided many hours of conversation and detailed technical review. Max Ross and Rafe Kaplan contributed material and provided extensive review to the datastore chapters. Thanks to Matthew Blain, Michael Davidson, Alex Gaysinsky, Peter McKenzie, Don Schwarz, and Jeffrey Scudder for reviewing portions of the first edition in detail, as well as Sean Lynch, Brett Slatkin, Mike Repass, and Guido van Rossum for their support. For the second edition, I want to thank Peter Magnusson, Greg D'alesandre, Tom Van Waardhuizen, Mike Aizatsky, Wesley Chun, Johan Euphrosine, Alfred Fuller, Andrew Gerrand, Sebastian Kreft, Moishe Lettvin, John Mulhausen, Robert Schuppenies, David Symonds, and Eric Willigers.

Substantial effort was required to separate the original book into two books. My thanks to Mike Fotinakis for reviewing the Python version, and to Amy Unruh and Mark Combellack for reviewing the Java version.

Thanks also to Sahala Swenson, Steven Hines, David McLaughlin, Mike Winton, Andres Ferrate, Dan Morrill, Mark Pilgrim, Steffi Wu, Karen Wickre, Jane Penner, Jon Murchinson, Tom Stocky, Vic Gundotra, Bill Coughran, and Alan Eustace.

At O'Reilly, I'd like to thank Michael Loukides, Meghan Blanchette, and Brian Anderson for giving me this opportunity and helping me see it through to the end, three times over.

I dedicate this book to Google's site reliability engineers. It is they who carry the pagers, so we don't have to. We are forever grateful.

CHAPTER 1

Introducing Google App Engine

Google App Engine is a web application hosting service. By "web application," we mean an application or service accessed over the Web, usually with a web browser: storefronts with shopping carts, social networking sites, multiplayer games, mobile applications, survey applications, project management, collaboration, publishing, and all the other things we're discovering are good uses for the Web. App Engine can serve traditional website content too, such as documents and images, but the environment is especially designed for real-time dynamic applications. Of course, a web browser is merely one kind of client: web application infrastructure is well suited to mobile applications, as well.

In particular, Google App Engine is designed to host applications with many simultaneous users. When an application can serve many simultaneous users without degrading performance, we say it *scales*. Applications written for App Engine scale automatically. As more people use the application, App Engine allocates more resources for the application and manages the use of those resources. The application itself does not need to know anything about the resources it is using.

Unlike traditional web hosting or self-managed servers, with Google App Engine, you only pay for the resources you use. Billed resources include CPU usage, storage per month, incoming and outgoing bandwidth, and several resources specific to App Engine services. To help you get started, every developer gets a certain amount of resources for free, enough for small applications with low traffic.

App Engine is part of Google Cloud Platform, a suite of services for running scalable applications, performing large amounts of computational work, and storing, using, and analyzing large amounts of data. The features of the platform work together to host applications efficiently and effectively, at minimal cost. App Engine's specific role on the platform is to host web applications and scale them automatically. App Engine apps use the other services of the platform as needed, especially for data storage.

An App Engine web application can be described as having three major parts: application instances, scalable data storage, and scalable services. In this chapter, we look at each of these parts at a high level. We also discuss features of App Engine for deploying and managing web applications, and for building websites integrated with other parts of Google Cloud Platform.

The Runtime Environment

An App Engine application responds to web requests. A web request begins when a client, typically a user's web browser, contacts the application with an HTTP request, such as to fetch a web page at a URL. When App Engine receives the request, it identifies the application from the domain name of the address, either a custom domain name you have registered and configured for use with the app, or an *.appspot.com* subdomain provided for free with every app. App Engine selects a server from many possible servers to handle the request, making its selection based on which server is most likely to provide a fast response. It then calls the application with the content of the HTTP request, receives the response data from the application, and returns the response to the client.

From the application's perspective, the runtime environment springs into existence when the request handler begins, and disappears when it ends. App Engine provides several methods for storing data that persists between requests, but these mechanisms live outside of the runtime environment. By not retaining state in the runtime environment between requests—or at least, by not expecting that state will be retained between requests—App Engine can distribute traffic among as many servers as it needs to give every request the same treatment, regardless of how much traffic it is handling at one time.

In the complete picture, App Engine allows runtime environments to outlive request handlers, and will reuse environments as much as possible to avoid unnecessary initialization. Each instance of your application has local memory for caching imported code and initialized data structures. App Engine creates and destroys instances as needed to accommodate your app's traffic. If you enable the multithreading feature, a single instance can handle multiple requests concurrently, further utilizing its resources.

Application code cannot access the server on which it is running in the traditional sense. An application can read its own files from the filesystem, but it cannot write to files, and it cannot read files that belong to other applications. An application can see environment variables set by App Engine, but manipulations of these variables do not necessarily persist between requests. An application cannot access the networking facilities of the server hardware, although it can perform networking operations by using services.

In short, each request lives in its own "sandbox." This allows App Engine to handle a request with the server that would, in its estimation, provide the fastest response. For web requests to the app, there is no way to guarantee that the same app instance will handle two requests, even if the requests come from the same client and arrive relatively quickly.

Sandboxing also allows App Engine to run multiple applications on the same server without the behavior of one application affecting another. In addition to limiting access to the operating system, the runtime environment also limits the amount of clock time and memory a single request can take. App Engine keeps these limits flexible, and applies stricter limits to applications that use up more resources to protect shared resources from "runaway" applications.

A request handler has up to 60 seconds to return a response to the client. While that may seem like a comfortably large amount for a web app, App Engine is optimized for applications that respond in less than a second. Also, if an application uses many CPU cycles, App Engine may slow it down so the app isn't hogging the processor on a machine serving multiple apps. A CPU-intensive request handler may take more clock time to complete than it would if it had exclusive use of the processor, and clock time may vary as App Engine detects patterns in CPU usage and allocates accordingly.

Google App Engine provides four possible runtime environments for applications, one for each of four programming languages: Java, Python, PHP, and Go. The environment you choose depends on the language and related technologies you want to use for developing the application.

The Java environment runs applications built for the Java 7 Virtual Machine (JVM). An app can be developed using the Java programming language, or most other languages that compile to or otherwise run in the JVM, such as PHP (using Quercus), Ruby (using JRuby), JavaScript (using the Rhino interpreter), Scala, Groovy, and Clojure. The app accesses the environment and services by using interfaces based on web industry standards, including Java servlets and the Any Java technology that functions within the sandbox restrictions can run on App Engine, making it suitable for many existing frameworks and libraries.

Similarly, the Python, PHP, and Go runtime environments offer standard execution environments for those languages, with support for standard libraries and third-party frameworks.

All four runtime environments use the same application server model: a request is routed to an app server, an application instance is initialized (if necessary), application code is invoked to handle the request and produce a response, and the response is returned to the client. Each environment runs application code within sandbox restrictions, such that any attempt to use a feature of the language or a library that would require access outside of the sandbox returns an error.

You can configure many aspects of how instances are created, destroyed, and initialized. How you configure your app depends on your need to balance monetary cost against performance. If you prefer performance to cost, you can configure your app to run many instances and start new ones aggressively to handle demand. If you have a limited budget, you can adjust the limits that control how requests queue up to use a minimum number of instances.

I haven't said anything about which operating system or hardware configuration App Engine uses. There are ways to figure this out with a little experimentation, but in the end it doesn't matter: the runtime environment is an abstraction *above* the operating system that allows App Engine to manage resource allocation, computation, request handling, scaling, and load distribution without the application's involvement. Features that typically require knowledge of the operating system are either provided by services outside of the runtime environment, provided or emulated using standard library calls, or restricted in sensible ways within the definition of the sandbox.

Everything stated above describes how App Engine allocates application instances dynamically to scale with your application's traffic. In addition to a flexible bank of instances serving your primary traffic, you can organize your app into multiple "modules." Each module is addressable individually using domain names, and can be configured with its own code, performance characteristics, and scaling pattern—including the option of running a fixed number of always-on instances, similar to traditional servers. In practice, you usually use a bank of dynamically scaling instances to handle your "frontend" traffic, then establish modules as "backends" to be accessed by the frontends for various purposes.

The Static File Servers

Most websites have resources they deliver to browsers that do not change during the regular operation of the site. The images and CSS files that describe the appearance of the site, the JavaScript code that runs in the browser, and HTML files for pages without dynamic components are examples of these resources, collectively known as *static files*. Because the delivery of these files doesn't involve application code, it's unnecessary and inefficient to serve them from the application servers.

Instead, App Engine provides a separate set of servers dedicated to delivering static files. These servers are optimized for both internal architecture and network topology to handle requests for static resources. To the client, static files look like any other resource served by your app.

You upload the static files of your application right alongside the application code. You can configure several aspects of how static files are served, including the URLs for static files, content types, and instructions for browsers to keep copies of the files in a cache for a given amount of time to reduce traffic and speed up rendering of the page.

Frontend Caches

All App Engine traffic goes through a set of machines that know how to cache responses to requests. If a response generated by the app declares that another request with the same parameters should return the same response, the frontend cache stores the response for a period of time. If another matching request comes in, the cache returns the stored response without invoking the application. The resources conserved by exploiting frontend caches can be significant.

App Engine recognizes standard HTTP controls for proxy caches. Do a web search for "HTTP cache control" for more information (Cache-Control, Expires). By default, responses from an app have Cache-Control set to no-cache.

The static file servers can also be configured to serve specific cache controls. These are described by a configuration file. (More on that later.)

Cloud Datastore

Most useful web applications need to store information during the handling of a request for retrieval during a later request. A typical arrangement for a small website involves a single database server for the entire site, and one or more web servers that connect to the database to store or retrieve data. Using a single central database server makes it easy to have one canonical representation of the data, so multiple users accessing multiple web servers all see the same and most recent information. But a central server is difficult to scale once it reaches its capacity for simultaneous connections.

By far the most popular kind of data storage system for web applications in the past two decades has been the relational database, with tables of rows and columns arranged for space efficiency and concision, and with indexes and raw computing power for performing queries, especially "join" queries that can treat multiple related records as a queryable unit. Other kinds of data storage systems include hierarchical datastores (filesystems, XML databases) and object databases. Each kind of database has pros and cons, and which type is best suited for an application depends on the nature of the application's data and how it is accessed. And each kind of database has its own techniques for growing past the first server.

Google Cloud Platform offers several kinds of data storage you can use with an App Engine app, including a relational database (Google Cloud SQL). Most scalable apps use Google Cloud Datastore, or as it is known to App Engine veterans, simply "the datastore."[1] The datastore most closely resembles an object database. It is not a join-query relational database, and if you come from the world of relational database–backed web applications (as I did), this will probably require changing the way you think about your application's data. As with the runtime environment, the design of the App Engine datastore is an abstraction that allows App Engine to handle the details of distributing and scaling the application, so your code can focus on other things.

 If it turns out the scalable datastore does not meet your needs for complex queries, you can use Google Cloud SQL, a full-featured relational database service based on MySQL. Cloud SQL is a feature of Google Cloud Platform, and can be called directly from App Engine using standard database APIs. The trade-off comes from how you intend to scale your application. A Cloud SQL instance behaves like a single MySQL database server, and can get bogged down by traffic. Cloud Datastore scales automatically: with proper data design, it can handle as many simultaneous users as App Engine's server instances can.

Entities and Properties

With Cloud Datastore, an application stores its data as one or more datastore *entities*. An entity has one or more *properties*, each of which has a name, and a value that is of one of several primitive value types. Each entity is of a named *kind*, which categorizes the entity for the purpose of queries.

At first glance, this seems similar to a relational database: entities of a kind are like rows in a table, and properties are like columns (fields). However, there are two major differences between entities and rows. First, an entity of a given kind is not required to have the same properties as other entities of the same kind. Second, an entity can have a property of the same name as another entity, but with a different type of value. In this way, datastore entities are "schemaless." As you'll soon see, this design provides both powerful flexibility as well as some maintenance challenges.

Another difference between an entity and a table row is that an entity can have multiple values for a single property. This feature is a bit quirky, but can be quite useful once understood.

Every datastore entity has a unique key that is either provided by the application or generated by App Engine (your choice). Unlike a relational database, the key is not a

---

1 Historically, the datastore was a feature exclusive to App Engine. Today it is a full-fledged service of Google Cloud Platform, and can be accessed from Compute Engine VMs and from apps outside of the platform using a REST API. App Engine apps can access Cloud Datastore using the App Engine datastore APIs and libraries.

"field" or property, but an independent aspect of the entity. You can fetch an entity quickly if you know its key, and you can perform queries on key values.

An entity's key *cannot* be changed after the entity has been created. The entity's kind is considered part of its key, so the kind cannot be changed either. App Engine uses the entity's key to help determine where the entity is stored in a large collection of servers. (No part of the key guarantees that two entities are stored on the same server, but you won't need to worry about that anyway.)

Queries and Indexes

A datastore query returns zero or more entities of a single kind. It can also return just the keys of entities that would be returned for a query. A query can filter based on conditions that must be met by the values of an entity's properties, and can return entities ordered by property values. A query can also filter and sort using keys.

In a typical relational database, queries are planned and executed in real time against the data tables, which are stored just as they were designed by the developer. The developer can also tell the database to produce and maintain indexes on certain columns to speed up certain queries.

Cloud Datastore does something dramatically different. *Every* query has a corresponding index maintained by the datastore. When the application performs a query, the datastore finds the index for that query, locates the first row that matches the query, then returns the entity for each consecutive row in the index until the first row that doesn't match the query.

Of course, this requires that Cloud Datastore know ahead of time which queries the application is going to perform. It doesn't need to know the values of the filters in advance, but it does need to know the kind of entity to query, the properties being filtered or sorted, and the operators of the filters and the orders of the sorts.

Cloud Datastore provides a set of indexes for simple queries by default, based on which properties exist on entities of a kind. For more complex queries, an app must include index specifications in its configuration. The App Engine developer tools help produce this configuration file by watching which queries are performed as you test your application with the provided development web server on your computer. When you upload your app, the datastore knows to make indexes for every query the app performed during testing. You can also edit the index configuration manually.

When your application creates new entities and updates existing ones, the datastore updates every corresponding index. This makes queries very fast (each query is a simple table scan) at the expense of entity updates (possibly many tables may need updating for a single change). In fact, the performance of an index-backed query is not affected by the number of entities in the datastore, only the size of the result set.

It's worth paying attention to indexes, as they take up space and increase the time it takes to update entities. We discuss indexes in detail in Chapter 7.

Transactions

When an application has many clients attempting to read or write the same data simultaneously, it is imperative that the data always be in a consistent state. One user should never see half-written data or data that doesn't make sense because another user's action hasn't completed.

When an application updates the properties of a single entity, Cloud Datastore ensures that either every update to the entity succeeds all at once, or the entire update fails and the entity remains the way it was prior to the beginning of the update. Other users do not see any effects of the change until the change succeeds.

In other words, an update of a single entity occurs in a *transaction*. Each transaction is *atomic*: the transaction either succeeds completely or fails completely, and cannot succeed or fail in smaller pieces.

An application can read or update multiple entities in a single transaction, but it must tell Cloud Datastore which entities will be updated together when it creates the entities. The application does this by creating entities in *entity groups*. Cloud Datastore uses entity groups to control how entities are distributed across servers, so it can guarantee a transaction on a group succeeds or fails completely. In database terms, the datastore natively supports *local transactions*.

When an application calls the datastore API to update an entity, the call returns only after the transaction succeeds or fails, and it returns with knowledge of success or failure. For updates, this means the service waits for all entities to be updated before returning a result. The application can call the datastore asynchronously, such that the app code can continue executing while the datastore is preparing a result. But the update itself does not return until it has confirmed the change.

If a user tries to update an entity while another user's update of the entity is in progress, the datastore returns immediately with a contention failure exception. Imagine the two users "contending" for a single piece of data: the first user to commit an update wins. The other user must try her operation again, possibly rereading values and calculating the update from fresh data. Contention is expected, so retries are common. In database terms, Cloud Datastore uses *optimistic concurrency control*: each user is "optimistic" that her commit will succeed, so she does so without placing a lock on the data.

Reading the entity never fails due to contention. The application just sees the entity in its most recent stable state. You can also read multiple entities from the same entity group by using a transaction to ensure that all the data in the group is current and consistent with itself.

In most cases, retrying a transaction on a contested entity will succeed. But if an application is designed such that many users might update a single entity, the more popular the application gets, the more likely users will get contention failures. It is important to design entity groups to avoid a high rate of contention failures even with a large number of users.

It is often important to read and write data in the same transaction. For example, the application can start a transaction, read an entity, update a property value based on the last read value, save the entity, and then commit the transaction. In this case, the save action does not occur unless the entire transaction succeeds without conflict with another transaction. If there is a conflict and the app wants to try again, the app should retry the entire transaction: read the (possibly updated) entity again, use the new value for the calculation, and attempt the update again. By including the read operation in the transaction, the datastore can assume that related writes and reads from multiple simultaneous requests do not interleave and produce inconsistent results.

With indexes and optimistic concurrency control, Cloud Datastore is designed for applications that need to read data quickly, ensure that the data it sees is in a consistent form, and scale the number of users and the size of the data automatically. While these goals are somewhat different from those of a relational database, they are especially well suited to web applications.

The Services

The datastore's relationship with the runtime environment is that of a service: the application uses an API to access a separate system that manages all its own scaling needs separately from application instances. Google Cloud Platform and App Engine include several other self-scaling services useful for web applications.

The memory cache (or *memcache*) service is a short-term key-value storage service. Its main advantage over the datastore is that it is fast—much faster than the datastore for simple storage and retrieval. The memcache stores values in memory instead of on disk for faster access. It is distributed like the datastore, so every request sees the same set of keys and values. However, it is not persistent like the datastore: if a server goes down, such as during a power failure, memory is erased. It also has a more limited sense of atomicity and transactionality than the datastore. As the name implies, the memcache service is best used as a cache for the results of frequently performed queries or calculations. The application checks for a cached value, and if the value isn't there, it performs the query or calculation and stores the value in the cache for future use.

Google Cloud Platform provides another storage service specifically for very large values, called Google Cloud Storage.[2] Your app can use Cloud Storage to store, manage, and serve large files, such as images, videos, or file downloads. Cloud Storage can also accept large files uploaded by users and offline processes. This service is distinct from Cloud Datastore to work around infrastructure limits on request and response sizes between users, application servers, and services. Application code can read values from Cloud Storage in chunks that fit within these limits. Code can also query for metadata about Cloud Storage values.

For when you really need a relational database, Google Cloud SQL provides full-featured MySQL database hosting. Unlike Cloud Datastore or Cloud Storage, Cloud SQL does not scale automatically. Instead, you create *SQL instances*, virtual machines running managed MySQL software. Instances are large, and you only pay for the storage you use and the amount of time an instance is running. You can even configure instances to turn themselves off when idle, and reactivate when a client attempts to connect. Cloud SQL can be the basis for an always-on web app, or a part of a larger data processing solution.

Yet another storage service is dedicated to providing full-text search infrastructure, known simply as the Search service.[3] As Cloud Datastore stores entities with properties, the Search service stores *documents* with *fields*. Your app adds documents to *indexes*. Unlike the datastore, you can use the Search service to perform faceted text searches over the fields of the documents in an index, including partial string matches, range queries, and Boolean search expressions. The service also supports stemming and tokenization.

App Engine applications can access other web resources using the URL Fetch service. The service makes HTTP requests to other servers on the Internet, such as to retrieve pages or interact with web services. Because remote servers can be slow to respond, the URL Fetch API supports fetching URLs in the background while a request handler does other things, but in all cases the fetch must start and finish within the request handler's lifetime. The application can also set a deadline, after which the call is canceled if the remote host hasn't responded.

App Engine applications can send email messages using the Mail service. The app can send email on behalf of the application itself or on behalf of the user who made the request that is sending the email (if the message is from the user). Many web applications use email to notify users, confirm user actions, and validate contact information.

---

2 An earlier version of this service was known as App Engine's "Blobstore" service. Both Blobstore and Cloud Storage are still available, with similar features. For new projects, prefer Cloud Storage. See the book's website (*http://www.dansanderson.com/appengine*) for a free bonus chapter about the Blobstore service.

3 The Search service is currently exclusive to App Engine.

An application can also receive email messages. If an app is configured to receive email, a message sent to the app's address is routed to the Mail service, which delivers the message to the app in the form of an HTTP request to a request handler.

App Engine applications can send and receive instant messages to and from chat services that support the XMPP protocol. An app sends an XMPP chat message by calling the XMPP service. As with incoming email, when someone sends a message to the app's address, the XMPP service delivers it to the app by calling a request handler.

You can accomplish real-time two-way communication directly with a web browser using the Channel service, a clever implementation of the Comet model of browser app communication. Channels allow browsers to keep a network connection open with a remote host to receive real-time messages long after a web page has finished loading. App Engine fits this into its request-based processing model by using a service: browsers do not connect directly to application servers, but instead connect to "channels" via a service. When an application decides to send a message to a client (or set of clients) during its normal processing, it calls the Channel service with the message. The service handles broadcasting the message to clients, and manages open connections. Paired with web requests for messages from clients to apps, the Channel service provides real-time browser messaging without expensive polling. App Engine includes a JavaScript client so your code in the browser can connect to channels.

Google Accounts, OpenID, and OAuth

App Engine integrates with Google Accounts, the user account system used by Google applications such as Google Mail, Google Docs, and Google Calendar. You can use Google Accounts as your app's user authentication system, so you don't have to build your own. And if your users already have Google accounts, they can sign in to your app using their existing accounts, with no need to create new accounts just for your app.

Google Accounts is especially useful for developing applications for your company or organization using Google Apps for Work (or Google Apps for Education). With Google Apps, your organization's members can use the same account to access your custom applications as well as their email, calendar, and documents. You can add your App Engine application to a subdomain of your Apps domain from your Google Apps dashboard, just like any other Google Apps feature.

Of course, there is no obligation to use Google Accounts. You can always build your own account system, or use an OpenID provider. App Engine includes special support for using OpenID providers in some of the same ways you can use Google Accounts. This is useful when building applications for the Google Apps Marketplace, which uses OpenID to integrate with enterprise single sign-on services.

App Engine includes built-in support for OAuth, a protocol that makes it possible for users to grant permission to third-party applications to access personal data in another service, without having to share their account credentials with the third party. For instance, a user might grant a mobile phone application access to her Google Calendar account, to read appointment data and create new appointments on her behalf. App Engine's OAuth support makes it straightforward to implement an OAuth service for other apps to use. Note that the built-in OAuth feature only works when using Google Accounts, not OpenID or a proprietary identity mechanism.

There is no special support for implementing an OAuth client in an App Engine app, but most OAuth client libraries work fine with App Engine. For Google services and APIs, the easiest way is to use the Google APIs Client Libraries, which are known to run from App Engine and are available for many languages.

Google Cloud Endpoints

APIs are an essential part of the modern Web. It is increasingly common for browser-based web applications to be implemented as rich JavaScript clients: the user's first visit downloads the client code to the browser, and all subsequent interactions with the server are performed by structured web requests issued by the JavaScript code (as XMLHttpRequests, or XHRs). Nonbrowser clients for web apps, especially native mobile apps running on smartphones and tablets, are also increasingly important. Both kinds of clients tend to use REST (Representational State Transfer) APIs provided by the web app, and tend to need advanced features such as OAuth for authenticating calls.

To address this important need, Google Cloud Platform provides a service and a suite of tools called Google Cloud Endpoints. Endpoints make it especially easy for a mobile or rich web client to call methods on the server. Endpoints includes libraries and tools for generating server functionality from a set of methods in Python and Java, and generating client code for Android, iOS, and browser-based JavaScript. The tools can also generate a "discovery document" that works with the Google APIs Client Libraries for many client languages. And OAuth support is built in, so you don't have to worry about authentication and can just focus on the application logic.

Task Queues and Cron Jobs

A web application must respond to web requests very quickly, usually in less than a second and preferably in just a few dozen milliseconds, to provide a smooth experience to the user sitting in front of the browser. This doesn't give the application much time to do work. Sometimes there is more work to do than there is time to do it. In such cases, it's usually OK if the work gets done within a few seconds, minutes, or hours, instead of right away, as the user is waiting for a response from the server. But the user needs a guarantee that the work will get done.

For this kind of work, an App Engine app uses *task queues*. Task queues let you describe work to be done at a later time, outside the scope of the web request. Queues ensure that every task gets done eventually. If a task fails, the queue retries the task until it succeeds.

There are two kinds of task queues: push queues and pull queues. With push queues, each task record represents an HTTP request to a request handler. App Engine issues these requests itself as it processes a push queue. You can configure the rate at which push queues are processed to spread the workload throughout the day. With pull queues, you provide the mechanism, such as a custom computational engine, that takes task records off the queue and does the work. App Engine manages the queuing aspect of pull queues.

A push queue performs a task by calling a request handler. It can include a data payload provided by the code that created the task, delivered to the task's handler as an HTTP request. The task's handler is subject to the same limits as other request handlers, with one important exception: a single task handler can take as long as 10 minutes to perform a task, instead of the 60-second limit applied to user requests. It's still useful to divide work into small tasks to take advantage of parallelization and queue throughput, but the higher time limit makes tasks easier to write in straightforward cases.

An especially powerful feature of task queues is the ability to enqueue a task within a Cloud Datastore transaction, when called via App Engine. This ensures that the task will be enqueued only if the rest of the datastore transaction succeeds. You can use transactional tasks to perform additional datastore operations that must be consistent with the transaction eventually, but that do not need the strong consistency guarantees of the datastore's local transactions. For example, when a user asks to delete a bunch of records, you can store a receipt of this request in the datastore and enqueue the corresponding task in a single transaction. If the transaction fails, you can report this to the user, and rest assured that neither the receipt nor the task are in the system.

App Engine has another service for executing tasks at specific times of the day: the scheduled tasks service. Scheduled tasks are also known as "cron jobs," a name borrowed from a similar feature of the Unix operating system. The scheduled tasks service can invoke a request handler at a specified time of the day, week, or month, based on a schedule you provide when you upload your application. Scheduled tasks are useful for doing regular maintenance or sending periodic notification messages.

We'll look at task queues, scheduled tasks, and some powerful uses for them in Chapter 16.

Namespaces

Cloud Datastore, Cloud Storage, memcache, Search, and task queues all store data for an app. It's often useful to partition an app's data across all services. For example, an app may be serving multiple companies, where each company sees its own isolated instance of the application, and no company should see any data that belongs to any other company. You could implement this partitioning in the application code, using a company ID as the prefix to every key. But this is prone to error: a bug in the code may expose or modify data from another partition.

To better serve this case, these storage services provide this partitioning feature at the infrastructure level. An app can declare it is acting in a *namespace* by calling an API. All subsequent uses of any of the data services will restrict themselves to the namespace automatically. The app does not need to keep track of which namespace it is in after the initial declaration.

The default namespace has a name equal to the empty string. This namespace is distinct from other namespaces. (There is no "global" namespace.) In the services that support it, all data belongs to a namespace.

Developer Tools

Google provides a rich set of tools and libraries for developing for Cloud Platform and App Engine. The main tool suite is the Cloud SDK, which, among other things, includes a package installer and updater for the other tools. You will use this installer to acquire the App Engine SDK for Java, and other components you might need.

One of the most useful parts of the SDK is the development web server. This tool runs your application on your local computer and simulates the runtime environment and services. The development server automatically detects changes in your Java class files and reloads them as needed, so you can keep the server running while you develop the application. This is well-suited to Java IDEs that automatically compile as you write, such as Eclipse.

If you're using Eclipse, Google provides a plugin that adds App Engine development features directly to the IDE. You can run the development server in the interactive debugger, and set breakpoints in your application code.

The development server's simulated datastore can automatically generate configuration for query indexes as the application performs queries, which App Engine will use to prebuild indexes for those queries. You can turn this feature off to test that queries have appropriate indexes in the configuration.

The development web server includes a built-in browser-based developer console for inspecting and prodding your app. You use this console to inspect and modify the contents of the simulated data storage services, manage task queue interactions, and simulate nonweb events such as incoming email messages.

You also use the toolkit to interact with App Engine directly, especially to deploy your application and run it on Cloud Platform. You can download log data from your live application, and manage the live application's datastore indexes and service configuration.

With a provided library, you can add a feature to your application that lets you access the running app's environment programmatically. This is useful for building administrative tools, uploading and downloading data, and even running a Python interactive prompt that can operate on live data.

But wait, there's more! The SDK also includes libraries for automated testing, and gathering reports on application performance. We'll cover one such tool, AppStats, in Chapter 17.

The Cloud Console

When your application is ready for its public debut, you create a *project*, then deploy your app's code to the project using a tool in the Cloud SDK. The project contains everything related to your app, including your App Engine code, data in all of Cloud Platform's data services, any Compute Engine VMs you might create with the app, and project-related settings and permissions. All of this is managed in a browser-based interface known as the Google Developers Console, or just "Cloud Console."

You sign in to the Cloud Console using your Google account. You can use your current Google account if you have one. You may also want to create a Google account just for your application, which you might use as the "from" address on email messages. Once you have created a project in Cloud Console, you can add additional Google accounts to the project. Each account has one of three possible roles: *owners* can change settings and manage permissions for other accounts, *editors* can change settings (but not permissions), and *viewers* can read (but not change) settings and project information.

The Console gives you access to real-time performance data about how your application is being used, as well as access to log data emitted by your application. You can query Cloud Datastore and other data services for the live application by using a web interface, and check on the status of datastore indexes and other features.

When you upload new code for your application, the uploaded version is assigned a version identifier, which you specify in the application's configuration file. The version used for the live application is whichever major version is selected as the "default." You control which version is the "default" by using the Cloud Console. You can access nondefault versions by using a special URL containing the version identifier. This allows you to test a new version of an app running on App Engine before making it official.

You use the Console to set up and manage the billing account for your application. When you're ready for your application to consume more resources beyond the free amounts, you set up a billing account using a credit card and Google Accounts. The owner of the billing account sets a *budget*, a maximum amount of money that can be charged per calendar day. Your application can consume resources until your budget is exhausted, and you are only charged for what the application actually uses beyond the free amounts.

Getting Started

You can start developing applications for Google App Engine without creating an account. All you need to get started is the Cloud SDK, which is a free download from the Cloud Platform website:

https://cloud.google.com/sdk/

For a brief guided tour of creating an App Engine app with some sample code, see this quick-start guide (sign-in required):

https://console.developers.google.com/start/appengine

And while you're at it, be sure to bookmark the official App Engine documentation, which includes tutorials, articles, and reference guides for all of App Engine's features:

https://cloud.google.com/appengine/docs

In the next chapter, we'll describe how to create a new project from start to finish, including how to create an account, upload the application, and run it on App Engine.

CHAPTER 2

Creating an Application

The App Engine development model is as simple as it gets:

1. Create the application.
2. Test the application on your own computer by using the web server software included with the App Engine development kit.
3. Deploy the finished application to App Engine.

In this chapter, we'll walk through the process of creating a new application, testing it with the development server, registering a new project ID with Google Cloud Platform, setting up a domain name, and uploading the app to App Engine. We'll look at some of the features of the Java software development kit (SDK) and the Cloud Console. We'll also discuss the workflow for developing and deploying an app.

We will take this opportunity to demonstrate a common pattern in web applications: managing user preferences data. This pattern uses several App Engine services and features.

Setting Up the Cloud SDK

To develop an App Engine app in Java, you need several things installed on your local computer:

- Java 7 SDK (JDK)
- Your favorite Java IDE, such as Eclipse
- The Google Cloud SDK
- Python 2.7 (used by the Cloud SDK)

If you want to use Eclipse as your IDE, you can download a version of Eclipse bundled with everything you need to do Java EE development for web apps. You can also get an Eclipse plugin from Google specifically for App Engine development.

The Google Cloud SDK is a collection of tools and libraries for developing, testing, and deploying software for the Cloud Platform, including App Engine. The centerpiece of the suite is the gcloud command, a multifunction tool which you use to install and update components, perform deployment and maintenance tasks, and otherwise interact with Cloud Platform as an administrator. The App Engine component provides tools for running your app locally on your computer for testing, and for deploying the app. These tools are implemented in Python, so you will need Python installed on your machine to use them.

The development server and app maintenance features are all available through command-line tools. You can use these tools from a command prompt or otherwise integrate them into your development environment as you see fit. For example, it's common to automate the deployment process with scripts that run the deployment tool and manage application versions and testing. There are also plugins for Java automation tools such as Apache Maven and Apache Ivy (Ant).

For Eclipse users, the Cloud SDK tools are optional: the Google plugin can install its own copy of the App Engine SDK and update it alongside other Eclipse plugins, and you can debug and deploy apps directly from Eclipse. The plugin does not install the tools for using other parts of Cloud Platform. I recommend the Cloud SDK, even if you intend to use the plugin to manage the App Engine SDK installation.

In the next few sections, we'll discuss installing the components related to Java app development, including the Eclipse plugin and the Cloud SDK.

Installing Java

The App Engine Java runtime environment uses Java 7. If you do not already have the Java 7 JDK, you can download it from Oracle's website (*http://www.oracle.com/technet work/java/javase/downloads/index.html*).

You can test whether the Java development kit is installed on your system and check which version it is by running the following command at a command prompt (in Windows, Command Prompt; in Mac OS X, Terminal):

```
javac -version
```

If you have the Java 7 JDK installed, the command will print a version number similar to javac 1.7.0_51. The actual output varies depending on which specific version you have.

App Engine Java apps use interfaces and features from Java Platform, Enterprise Edition (Java EE). The App Engine SDK includes implementations for the relevant Java EE features. You do not need to install a separate Java EE implementation.

Installing Python

The Cloud SDK tools require that Python 2.7 be installed on your system, so let's take care of that first. If you are using Mac OS X or Linux, or if you have used Python previously, you may already have Python on your system. You can test whether Python is installed on your system and check which version is installed by running the following command at a command prompt (in Windows, Command Prompt; in Mac OS X, Terminal):

```
python -V
```

(That's a capital "V.") If Python is installed, it prints its version number, like so:

```
Python 2.7.5
```

You can download and install Python 2.7 for your platform from the Python website:

http://www.python.org/

Be sure to get Python version 2.7 (such as 2.7.8) from the Downloads section of the site. As of this writing, the latest major version of Python is 3.4, and the latest 2.x-compatible release is 2.7.

Installing the Cloud SDK

There are several easy ways to install the Cloud SDK, depending on your operating system and personal preferences.

For Windows, visit the Cloud SDK website, select the Windows installation instructions, then click the "Download" button:

https://cloud.google.com/sdk/

Run *GoogleCloudSDKInstaller.exe* and follow the instructions. By default, the installer puts the SDK in *C:\Program Files\Google\Cloud SDK*, and offers to create appropriate shortcuts on the desktop. One of these shortcuts, the Google Cloud SDK Shell, opens a command prompt with its command lookup path amended to include the Cloud SDK commands.

The Windows installer prompts you to select which components to install. The App Engine SDK for Python and PHP is selected by default. To install the App Engine SDK for Java as part of this process, expand the "Google App Engine" menu and check "App Engine SDK for Java," then click Install. (You can also install the App Engine SDK for Java later, or skip this step and use the Eclipse plugin to install it.)

For Mac OS X or Linux, open a command prompt and run the following command:

```
curl https://sdk.cloud.google.com | bash
```

This downloads the Cloud SDK archive, unpacks it, and runs an interactive installation routine. If you'd rather invoke these steps manually, you can download the archive from the Cloud SDK website. The installation routine is this shell script: *./google-cloud-sdk/install.sh*

Either way you do it, the result is a *google-cloud-sdk* directory, which you can put in a convenient place. The installation script attempts to add the Cloud SDK commands to your command prompt's search path by amending your environment. If you're using a shell other than `bash`, you may need to finish this step manually. You can always invoke the Cloud SDK commands using their full path in the *google-cloud-sdk* directory.

Close and reopen your command prompt to pick up the changes to the command search path.

On all platforms, confirm that the SDK was installed successfully by running the `gcloud` command like so:

```
gcloud -h
```

The command will print some help text describing its various features. If instead the command prompt reports that the command is not found, double-check that the SDK is on the command path. In Windows, this is set up by the "SDK Shell," or the *cloud_env.bat* script in the main SDK folder. In Mac OS X and Linux, make sure you have restarted your command prompt to pick up the environment changes to your shell startup scripts, and that the *google-cloud-sdk/bin* directory is on your search path.

The Cloud SDK politely keeps all of its stuff in the *google-cloud-sdk* directory. To uninstall it, simply delete the directory, and undo the command search path modifications.

Authenticating with the Cloud SDK

Before doing anything else, run this command:

```
gcloud auth login
```

This opens a browser window for the Google authentication sequence. Sign in using your Google account (or register for a free account if you don't have one yet), then authorize the Google Cloud SDK to access Cloud services on your behalf.

The gcloud command remembers the authentication credentials it receives and uses them with subsequent commands that you run from your computer. To revoke these credentials (to "sign out" of gcloud), run this command:

```
gcloud auth revoke
```

You can use gcloud auth login to sign in with multiple accounts. Credentials for all accounts are remembered until revoked, and you can switch between them without signing in again. To add an account, simply gcloud auth login again with the new account. To list all accounts with stored credentials and see which account is currently active:

```
gcloud auth list
```

To switch the active account to another one with stored credentials:

```
gcloud config set account your.email@gmail.com
```

Installing the App Engine SDK

The Cloud SDK installation process already asked you if you wanted to install an App Engine SDK. If you answered in the affirmative and requested the App Engine SDK for Java, or if you'd rather install it via the Eclipse plugin, then you can skip this step.

If you have not yet installed the App Engine SDK for Java, you can do so with this command:

```
gcloud components update gae-java
```

You can test that the App Engine SDK is installed by running the following command, for Mac OS X or Linux:

```
dev_appserver --help
```

In Mac OS X or Linux, this command is called dev_appserver.sh.

The dev_appserver command can be used to start a local development server running a test version of your app. With the --help argument, the command simply prints help text and exits.

You use the gcloud components command to install, update, and manage the various components of the Cloud SDK. To see a list of all available components and which ones are installed, run this command:

```
gcloud components list
```

To update all components that need updating:

```
gcloud components update
```

It is possible to install the App Engine SDK without the Cloud SDK. If that interests you, see this page:

https://cloud.google.com/appengine/downloads

Here you can download Windows and Mac installers that put just the App Engine SDK and Launcher apps in the right places, as well as a general-purpose Zip archive with just the App Engine libraries and command-line tools.

I recommend using `gcloud` because it makes it easy to install other components as you start using more features of Cloud Platform. It won't be long before you'll want the Cloud SQL and Cloud Storage tools, which are not included in the direct download of the App Engine SDK.

Installing the Java SDK with the Google Plugin for Eclipse

One of the easiest ways to develop App Engine applications in Java is to use the Eclipse IDE and the Google Plugin for Eclipse. The plugin works with all versions of Eclipse from Eclipse 3.3 (Europa) to Eclipse 4.4 (Luna). You can get Eclipse for your platform for free at the Eclipse website:

http://www.eclipse.org/

If you're getting Eclipse specifically for App Engine development, get the "Eclipse IDE for Java EE Developers" bundle. This bundle includes several useful components for developing web applications, including the Eclipse Web Tools Platform (WTP) package.

You can tell Eclipse to use the JDK you have installed in the Preferences window. In Eclipse 4.4, select Preferences (Windows and Linux, in the Window menu; Mac OS X, in the Eclipse menu). In the Java category, select "Installed JREs." If necessary, add the location of the SDK to the list, and make sure the checkbox is checked.

To install the App Engine Java SDK and the Google Plugin, use the software installation feature of Eclipse. In Eclipse 4.4, select Install New Software from the Help menu, then type the following URL in the "Work with" field and click the Add button:

```
http://dl.google.com/eclipse/plugin/4.4
```

(This URL does not work in a browser; it only works with the Eclipse software installer.)

In the dialog box that opens, enter "Google" for the name, then click OK. Several items are added to the list. For a minimal App Engine development environment, select Google Plugin for Eclipse, then expand the SDKs category and select Google App Engine Java SDK. Figure 2-1 shows the Install Software window with these items selected.

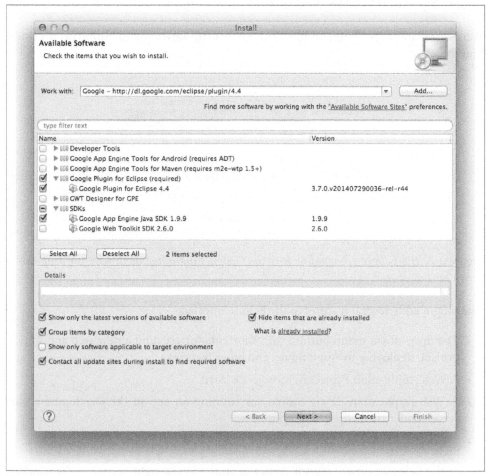

Figure 2-1. The Eclipse 4.4 (Luna) Install Software window, with the Google Plugin selected

There's other good stuff in here, all free of charge. Google Web Toolkit (GWT) is a development suite for making rich web user interfaces using Java, without having to write a single line of JavaScript. The Eclipse plugin makes it easy to create GWT apps that run on App Engine. There's also a set of tools for making apps for Android devices that use App Engine as a networked backend.

Check the boxes for the desired items, then click the Next button and follow the prompts.

For more information on installing the Google Plugin for Eclipse, including instructions for earlier versions of Eclipse, see the website for the plugin:

https://developers.google.com/eclipse/

After installation, the Eclipse toolbar has a new drop-down menu button, as shown in Figure 2-2.

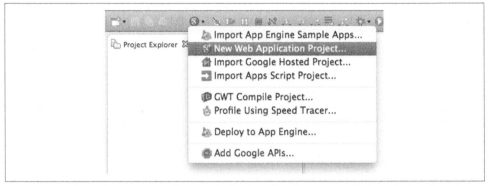

Figure 2-2. The Eclipse 4.4 window with the Google Plugin installed, with the drop-down menu button open

The plugin adds several features to the Eclipse interface:

- The drop-down menu button, with shortcuts for creating a new web application project, deploying to App Engine, and other features
- A Web Application Project new project wizard
- A Web Application debug profile, for running an app in the development web server under the Eclipse debugger
- A Google account sign-in indicator

Locate the Google account sign-in indicator in the lower-right corner of the window, then click it. Sign in with your Google account, then authorize the Eclipse plugin to interact with App Engine on your behalf.

You can use Eclipse to develop your application, and to deploy it to App Engine. To use other features of the SDK, like downloading log data, you must use the command-line tools from the App Engine SDK. Eclipse installs its own copy of the SDK in your Eclipse application directory, under *eclipse/plugins/*. The actual directory name depends on the specific version of the SDK installed, but it looks something like this:

```
com.google.appengine.eclipse.sdkbundle_1.9.18/appengine-java-sdk-1.9.18/
```

If you installed the Cloud SDK as described here, you don't need to worry about this directory, but it's good to know that it's there.

Developing the Application

It's time to write our first App Engine application!

So what is an App Engine app? An App Engine app is software that responds to web requests. It does so by calling *request handlers*, routines that accept request parameters and return responses. App Engine determines which request handler to use for a given request from the request's URL, using a configuration file included with the app that maps URLs to handlers.

An app can also include static files, such as images, CSS stylesheets, and browser Java-Script. App Engine serves these files directly to clients in response to requests for corresponding URLs without invoking any code. The app's configuration specifies which of its files are static, and which URLs to use for those files.

The application configuration includes metadata about the app, such as its project ID and version number. When you deploy the app to App Engine, all of the app's files, including the code, configuration files, and static files, are uploaded and associated with the project ID and version number mentioned in the configuration. An app can also have configuration files specific to the services, such as for datastore indexes, task queues, and scheduled tasks. These files are associated with the app in general, not a specific version of the app.

In the next few sections, we create the files needed for a simple application, and look at how to use the tools and libraries included with the SDK.

The User Preferences Pattern

The application we create in this section is a simple clock. When a user visits the site, the app displays the current time of day according to the server's system clock. By default, the app shows the current time in the Coordinated Universal Time (UTC) time zone. The user can customize the time zone by signing in using Google Accounts and setting a preference.

This app demonstrates three App Engine features:

- The datastore, primary storage for data that is persistent, reliable, and scalable
- The memory cache (or *memcache*), secondary storage that is faster than the datastore, but is not necessarily persistent in the long term
- Google Accounts, the ability to use Google's user account system for authenticating and identifying users

Google Accounts works similarly to most user account systems. If the user is not signed in to the clock application, she sees a generic view with default settings (the UTC time zone) and a link to sign in or create a new account. If the user chooses to sign in or register, the application directs her to a sign-in form managed by Google Accounts. Signing in or creating an account redirects the user back to the application.

Of course, you can implement your own account mechanism instead of using Google Accounts. Using Google Accounts has advantages and disadvantages—the chief advantage being that you don't have to implement your own account mechanism. If a user of your app already has a Google account, the user can sign in with that account without creating a new account for your app.

If the user accesses the application while signed in, the app loads the user's preferences data and uses it to render the page. The app retrieves the preferences data in two steps. First, it attempts to get the data from the fast secondary storage, the memory cache. If the data is not present in the memory cache, the app attempts to retrieve it from the primary storage (the datastore), and if successful, it puts it into the memory cache to be found by future requests.

This means that for most requests, the application can get the user's preferences from memcache without accessing the datastore. While reading from the datastore is reasonably fast, reading from the memcache is much faster and avoids the cost of a datastore call. The difference is substantial when the same data must be accessed every time the user visits a page.

Our clock application has two request handlers. One handler displays the current time of day, along with links for signing in and out. It also displays a web form for adjusting the time zone when the user is signed in. The second request handler processes the time zone form when it is submitted. When the user submits the preferences form, the app saves the changes and redirects the browser back to the main page.

The application gets the current time from the application server's system clock. It's worth noting that App Engine makes no guarantees that the system clocks of all its web servers are synchronized. Because two requests for this app may be handled by different servers, different requests may see different clocks. The server clock is not consistent enough as a source of time data for a real-world application, but it's good enough for this example.

A Simple App

Java web applications for App Engine use the Java Servlet standard interface for interacting with the application server. An application consists of one or more servlet classes, each extending a servlet base class. Servlets are mapped to URLs using a standard configuration file called a "deployment descriptor," also known as *web.xml*. When App Engine receives a request for a Java application, it determines which servlet class to use based on the URL and the deployment descriptor, instantiates the class, and then calls an appropriate method on the servlet object.

All the files for a Java application, including the compiled Java classes, configuration files, and static files, are organized in a standard directory structure called a Web Application Archive, or "WAR." Everything in the WAR directory gets deployed to App Engine. It's common to have your development workflow build the contents of the WAR from a set of source files, either using an automated build process or WAR-aware development tools.

If you are using the Eclipse IDE with the Google Plugin, you can create a new project by using the Web Application wizard. Click the Google drop-down menu button, then select New Web Application Project. (Alternatively, from the File menu, select New, then Other…, then locate Google, Web Application Project.) In the window that opens, enter a project name (such as Clock) and package name (such as clock).

Uncheck the "Use Google Web Toolkit" checkbox, and make sure the "Use Google App Engine" checkbox is checked. (If you leave the GWT checkbox checked, the new project will be created with GWT starter files. This is cool, but it's outside the scope of this chapter.) Figure 2-3 shows the completed dialog box for the Clock application. Click Finish to create the project.

If you are not using the Google Plugin for Eclipse, you will need to create the directories and files another way. If you are already familiar with Java web development, you can use your existing tools and processes to produce the final WAR. For the rest of this section, we assume you are using the directory structure that is created by the Eclipse plugin.

Figure 2-4 shows the project file structure, as depicted in the Eclipse Package Explorer.

The project root directory (*Clock*) contains two major subdirectories: *src* and *war*. The *src/* directory contains all the project's class files in the usual Java package structure. With a package path of clock, Eclipse created source code for a servlet class named ClockServlet in the file *clock/ClockServlet.java*.

The *war/* directory contains the complete final contents of the application. Eclipse compiles source code from *src/* automatically and puts the compiled class files in *war/WEB-INF/classes/*, which is hidden from Eclipse's Package Explorer by default. Eclipse copies the contents of *src/META-INF/* to *war/WEB-INF/classes/META-INF/* automatically, as well. Everything else, such as CSS or browser JavaScript files, must be created in the *war/* directory in its intended location.

Figure 2-3. The Google Plugin for Eclipse New Web Application Project dialog, with values for the Clock application

Let's start our clock application with a simple servlet that displays the current time. Open the file *src/clock/ClockServlet.java* for editing (creating it if necessary), and give it contents similar to Example 2-1.

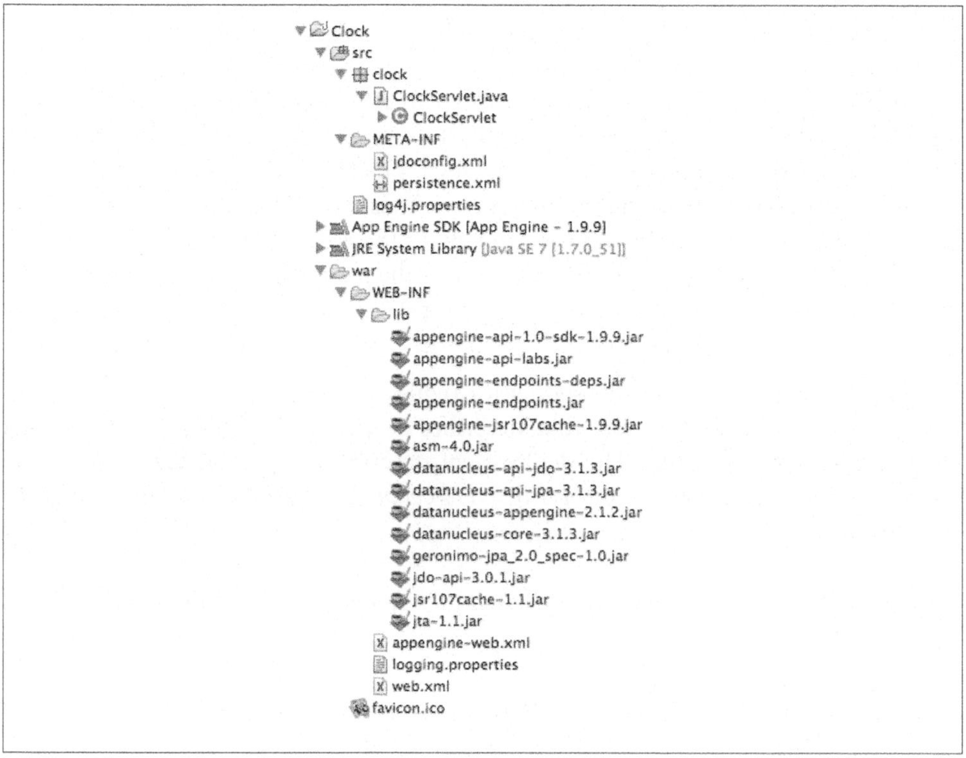

```
▼ ⬁ Clock
    ▼ ⬔ src
        ▼ ⊞ clock
            ▼ ⒥ ClockServlet.java
                ▶ ⊙ ClockServlet
            ▼ ⬂ META-INF
                ⊠ jdoconfig.xml
                ⬙ persistence.xml
            ⬚ log4j.properties
    ▶ ▨ App Engine SDK [App Engine - 1.9.9]
    ▶ ▨ JRE System Library [Java SE 7 [1.7.0_51]]
    ▼ ⬂ war
        ▼ ⬂ WEB-INF
            ▼ ⬂ lib
                ⬤ appengine-api-1.0-sdk-1.9.9.jar
                ⬤ appengine-api-labs.jar
                ⬤ appengine-endpoints-deps.jar
                ⬤ appengine-endpoints.jar
                ⬤ appengine-jsr107cache-1.9.9.jar
                ⬤ asm-4.0.jar
                ⬤ datanucleus-api-jdo-3.1.3.jar
                ⬤ datanucleus-api-jpa-3.1.3.jar
                ⬤ datanucleus-appengine-2.1.2.jar
                ⬤ datanucleus-core-3.1.3.jar
                ⬤ geronimo-jpa_2.0_spec-1.0.jar
                ⬤ jdo-api-3.0.1.jar
                ⬤ jsr107cache-1.1.jar
                ⬤ jta-1.1.jar
            ⊠ appengine-web.xml
            ⬚ logging.properties
            ⊠ web.xml
        ⬖ favicon.ico
```

Figure 2-4. A new Java project structure, as shown in the Eclipse Package Explorer

Example 2-1. A simple Java servlet

```java
package clock;

import java.io.IOException;
import java.io.PrintWriter;
import java.text.SimpleDateFormat;
import java.util.Date;
import java.util.SimpleTimeZone;
import javax.servlet.http.*;

@SuppressWarnings("serial")
public class ClockServlet extends HttpServlet {
    public void doGet(HttpServletRequest req,
                      HttpServletResponse resp)
        throws IOException {
        SimpleDateFormat fmt = new SimpleDateFormat("yyyy-MM-dd hh:mm:ss.SSSSSS");
        fmt.setTimeZone(new SimpleTimeZone(0, ""));

        resp.setContentType("text/html");
        PrintWriter out = resp.getWriter();
        out.println("<p>The time is: " + fmt.format(new Date()) + "</p>");
```

```
    }
}
```

The servlet class extends `javax.servlet.http.HttpServlet`, and overrides methods for each of the HTTP methods it intends to support. This servlet overrides the `doGet()` method to handle HTTP GET requests. The server calls the method with an `HttpServletRequest` object and an `HttpServletResponse` object as parameters. The `HttpServletRequest` contains information about the request, such as the URL, form parameters, and cookies. The method prepares the response, using methods on the `HttpServletResponse`, such as `setContentType()` and `getWriter()`. App Engine sends the response when the servlet method exits.

To tell App Engine to invoke this servlet for requests, we need a deployment descriptor: an XML configuration file that describes which URLs invoke which servlet classes, among other things. The deployment descriptor is part of the servlet standard. Open or create the file *war/WEB-INF/web.xml*, and give it contents similar to Example 2-2.

Example 2-2. The web.xml file, also known as the deployment descriptor, mapping all URLs to ClockServlet

```xml
<?xml version="1.0" encoding="utf-8"?>
<web-app xmlns:xsi="http://www.w3.org/2001/XMLSchema-instance"
  xmlns="http://java.sun.com/xml/ns/javaee"
  xmlns:web="http://java.sun.com/xml/ns/javaee/web-app_2_5.xsd"
  xsi:schemaLocation="http://java.sun.com/xml/ns/javaee
    http://java.sun.com/xml/ns/javaee/web-app_2_5.xsd" version="2.5">
  <servlet>
    <servlet-name>clock</servlet-name>
    <servlet-class>clock.ClockServlet</servlet-class>
  </servlet>
  <servlet-mapping>
    <servlet-name>clock</servlet-name>
    <url-pattern>/</url-pattern>
  </servlet-mapping>
</web-app>
```

Eclipse may open this file in its XML Design view, a table-like view of the elements and values. Select the Source tab at the bottom of the editor pane to edit the XML source.

web.xml is an XML file with a root element of `<web-app>`. To map URL patterns to servlets, you declare each servlet with a `<servlet>` element, then declare the mapping with a `<servlet-mapping>` element. The `<url-pattern>` of a servlet mapping can be a full URL path, or a URL path with a * at the beginning or end to represent a part of a path. In this case, the URL pattern / matches just the root URL path.

Be sure that each of your `<url-pattern>` values starts with a forward slash (/). Omitting the starting slash may have the intended behavior on the development web server but unintended behavior on App Engine.

App Engine needs one additional configuration file that isn't part of the servlet standard. Open or create the file *war/WEB-INF/appengine-web.xml*, and give it contents similar to Example 2-3.

Example 2-3. The appengine-web.xml file, with App Engine–specific configuration for the Java app

```
<?xml version="1.0" encoding="utf-8"?>
<appengine-web-app xmlns="http://appengine.google.com/ns/1.0">
  <application>clock</application>
  <version>1</version>
  <threadsafe>true</threadsafe>
</appengine-web-app>
```

In this example, the configuration file tells App Engine that this is version 1 of an application called `clock`. We also declare the app to be threadsafe, authorizing App Engine to reuse an application instance to serve multiple requests simultaneously. (Of course, we must also make sure our code is threadsafe when we do this.) You can also use this configuration file to control other behaviors, such as static files and sessions. For more information, see Chapter 3.

The WAR for the application must include several JARs from the App Engine SDK: the Java EE implementation JARs, and the App Engine API JAR. The Eclipse plugin installs these JARs in the WAR automatically. If you are not using the Eclipse plugin, you must copy these JARs manually. Look in the SDK directory in the *lib/user/* and *lib/shared/* subdirectories. Copy every *.jar* file from these directories to the *war/WEB-INF/lib/* directory in your project.

Finally, the servlet class must be compiled. Eclipse compiles all your classes automatically, as needed. If you are not using Eclipse, you probably want to use a build tool such as Apache Ant to compile source code and perform other build tasks. See the official App Engine documentation for information on using Apache Ant to build App Engine projects.

I suppose it's traditional to explain how to compile a Java project from the command line using the `javac` command. You can do so by putting each of the JARs from *war/WEB-INF/lib/* and the *war/WEB-INF/classes/* directory in the classpath, and making sure the compiled classes end up in the *classes/* directory. But in the real world, you want your IDE or an Ant script to take care of this for you.

One more thing for Eclipse users: the Eclipse new-project wizard created a static file named *war/index.html*. Delete it by right-clicking on it in the Project Explorer, selecting Delete, then clicking OK. If you don't delete it, this static file will take precedence over the servlet mapping we just created.

It's time to test this application with the development web server. The Eclipse plugin can run the application and the development server inside the Eclipse debugger. To start it, make sure the *ClockServlet.java* file is selected in the Project Explorer, then select the Run menu, Debug As, and Web Application. The server starts, and prints the following message (among others) to the Console panel:

```
Module instance default is running at http://localhost:8888/
```

If you are not using Eclipse, you can start the development server, using the `dev_app` `server` command (`dev_appserver.sh` for Mac OS X or Linux). The command takes the path to the WAR directory as an argument, like so:

```
dev_appserver war
```

The command-line tool uses a different default port than the Eclipse plugin uses (8080 instead of 8888). You can change the port used by the command-line tool with the `--port` argument, such as `--port=8888`.

Test your application by visiting the server's URL in a web browser:

http://localhost:8888

The browser displays a page similar to Figure 2-5.

Introducing JSPs, JSTL, and EL

Right now, our clock displays the time in the UTC time zone. We'd like for our application to let the user customize the time zone, and to remember the user's preference for future visits. To do that, we use Google Accounts to identify which user is using the application.

Before we go any further, we should introduce a way to keep our HTML separate from our servlet code. This allows us to maintain the "business logic"—the code that implements the main purpose of our app—separately from the appearance of the app, making our logic easier to test and our appearance easier to change. Typically, you would use a templating system to define the appearance of the app in files that contain the HTML, CSS, and JavaScript, and leave blanks where the dynamic data should go. There are many fine templating systems to choose from in Java, such as Apache Velocity.

Figure 2-5. The first version of the clock application viewed in a browser

For this example, we use Java Servlet Pages, or JSPs. JSPs are a standard part of Java EE, which means you do not have to install anything else to use them. A JSP contains a mix of text (HTML) and Java code that defines the logic of the page. The JSP compiles to a servlet, just like the ClockServlet we already defined, that's equivalent to writing out the HTML portions, and evaluating the Java portions. In a sense, JSPs are just another way of writing servlet code.

JSPs are often criticized for being too powerful. Because the full Java language is available from within a JSP, there is a risk that business logic may creep into the templates, and you no longer have a useful separation. To mitigate this, later versions of the JSP specification included new ways of describing template logic that are intentionally less powerful than full Java code: the Java Servlet Templating Language (JSTL) and the JSP Expression Language (EL). We use these features for this example, and other places in the book where templated output is required.

Edit *ClockServlet.java* to resemble Example 2-4.

Example 2-4. Code for ClockServlet.java that displays Google Accounts information and links

```
package clock;

import java.io.IOException;
import java.text.SimpleDateFormat;
import java.util.Date;
```

```
import java.util.SimpleTimeZone;
import javax.servlet.RequestDispatcher;
import javax.servlet.ServletException;
import javax.servlet.http.*;

import com.google.appengine.api.users.User;
import com.google.appengine.api.users.UserService;
import com.google.appengine.api.users.UserServiceFactory;

@SuppressWarnings("serial")
public class ClockServlet extends HttpServlet {
    public void doGet(HttpServletRequest req,
                      HttpServletResponse resp)
        throws IOException, ServletException {
        SimpleDateFormat fmt = new SimpleDateFormat("yyyy-MM-dd hh:mm:ss.SSSSSS");
        fmt.setTimeZone(new SimpleTimeZone(0, ""));

        UserService userService = UserServiceFactory.getUserService();
        User user = userService.getCurrentUser();
        String loginUrl = userService.createLoginURL("/");
        String logoutUrl = userService.createLogoutURL("/");

        req.setAttribute("user", user);
        req.setAttribute("loginUrl", loginUrl);
        req.setAttribute("logoutUrl", logoutUrl);
        req.setAttribute("currentTime", fmt.format(new Date()));

        resp.setContentType("text/html");

        RequestDispatcher jsp = req.getRequestDispatcher("/WEB-INF/home.jsp");
        jsp.forward(req, resp);
    }
}
```

Next, create a new file named *home.jsp* in the *war/WEB-INF/* directory of your project, and give it contents similar to Example 2-5.

Example 2-5. Code for ClockServlet.java that displays Google Accounts information and links

```
<%@ taglib uri="http://java.sun.com/jsp/jstl/core" prefix="c" %>
<html>
  <head>
    <title>The Time Is...</title>
  </head>
  <body>
    <c:choose>
      <c:when test="${user != null}">
        <p>
          Welcome, ${user.email}!
          You can <a href="${logoutUrl}">sign out</a>.
```

```
      </p>
    </c:when>
    <c:otherwise>
      <p>
        Welcome!
        <a href="${loginUrl}">Sign in or register</a> to customize.
      </p>
    </c:otherwise>
  </c:choose>
  <p>The time is: ${currentTime}</p>
 </body>
</html>
```

Using Eclipse, you can leave the development web server running while you edit code. When you save changes to code, Eclipse compiles the class, and if it compiles successfully, Eclipse injects the new class into the already-running server. In most cases, you can simply reload the page in your browser, and it will use the new code. If this doesn't work, stop the server and then start it again.

If you are not using Eclipse, shut down the development server by hitting Ctrl-C. Recompile your project, then start the server again.

Reload the new version of the clock app in your browser. The new page resembles Figure 2-6.

Figure 2-6. The clock app with a link to Google Accounts when the user is not signed in

Here's everything we're going to say about JSPs, JSTL, and EL in this book:

- Remember that *home.jsp* represents a servlet. In this case, it's one that expects certain attributes to be set in its context. `ClockServlet` invokes *home.jsp* by setting attributes on the `HttpServletRequest` object via its `setAttribute()` method, then forwarding the request and response to the *home.jsp* servlet.

- The forwarding takes place via a `RequestDispatcher` set up for the *home.jsp* servlet. In this case, we keep *home.jsp* inside the */WEB-INF/* directory, so that the servlet container doesn't map it to a URL. If the JSP resided outside of */WEB-INF/*, a URL to that path (from the WAR root) would map to the JSP servlet, and the servlet container would invoke it directly (assuming no explicit URL pattern matched the URL).

- The `getRequestDispatcher()` method of the request instance takes a path to a JSP and returns its `RequestDispatcher`. Make sure the path starts with a forward slash (/).

- In order to invoke the JSP, `ClockServlet` calls the `forward()` method of the `RequestDispatcher`, passing the `HttpServletRequest` and `HttpServletResponse` objects as arguments. The `forward()` method may throw the `ServletException`; in this example, we just add a `throws` clause to `doGet()`.

- A JSP contains text (HTML) and specially formatted directives. This example contains one directive, `<%@ taglib … %>`, which loads a JSTL tag library. You might also see `<% … %>`, which contains Java code that becomes part of the servlet, and `<%= … %>`, which contains a Java expression whose string form is printed to the page.

- `<c:choose>…</c:choose>`, `<c:when>…</c:when>`, and `<c:otherwise>…</c:otherwise>` are examples of JSTL tags. These come from the `/jsp/jstl/core` tag library imported by the `taglib` import directive in the first line. The `c:` is the prefix associated with the library in the import directive. Here, the `<c:choose>` structure renders the `<c:when>` block when the user is signed in, and the `<c:otherwise>` block otherwise.

- `${user != null}` is an example of an EL expression. An EL expression can appear in the text of the document, where its value is rendered into the text, or in a JSTL tag attribute, where its value is used by the tag. The expression `logoutUrl` renders the `String` value of the `logoutUrl` attribute set by `ClockServlet`. `${user.email}` is an example of accessing a JavaBean property of a value: the result is equivalent to calling the `getEmail()` method of the `User` object value. `${user != null}` shows how an EL expression can use simple operators, in this case producing a `boolean` value used by the `<c:when test="…">`.

For this book, we'll stick to simple features of JSPs, JSTL, and EL, and not provide additional explanation. For more information about these J2EE features, see *Head First Servlets and JSP* by Brian Basham et al. (O'Reilly).

 Be careful when mapping the URL pattern /* to a servlet in your deployment descriptor when using request dispatchers in this way. Explicit URL mappings override the default JSP path mapping, and the request dispatcher will honor it when determining the servlet for the path. If you have a /* URL mapping that might match a JSP path, you must have an explicit JSP URL mapping in the deployment descriptor that overrides it:

```
<servlet>
  <servlet-name>home-jsp</servlet-name>
  <jsp-file>/WEB-INF/home.jsp</jsp-file>
</servlet>
<servlet-mapping>
  <servlet-name>home-jsp</servlet-name>
  <url-pattern>/WEB-INF/home.jsp</url-pattern>
</servlet-mapping>

<servlet>
  <servlet-name>clock</servlet-name>
  <servlet-class>clock.ClockServlet</servlet-class>
</servlet>
<servlet-mapping>
  <servlet-name>clock</servlet-name>
  <url-pattern>/*</url-pattern>
</servlet-mapping>
```

Note that a mapping in /WEB-INF/ is still hidden from clients. A request for /WEB-INF/home.jsp will return a 404 Not Found error, and will not invoke the JSP servlet.

Users and Google Accounts

The ClockServlet in Example 2-4 calls the Users API to get information about the user who may or may not be signed in with a Google Account. This interface is provided by the com.google.appengine.api.users package. The app gets a UserService instance by calling the getUserService() method of the UserServiceFactory class. Then it calls the getCurrentUser() method of the User Service, which returns a User object, or null if the current user is not signed in. The getEmail() method of the User object returns the email address for the user.

The createLoginURL() and createLogoutURL() methods of the UserService generate URLs that go to Google Accounts. Each of these methods takes a URL path for the app where the user should be redirected after performing the desired task. The login URL goes to the Google Accounts page where the user can sign in or register for a new account. The logout URL visits Google Accounts to sign out the current user, and then immediately redirects back to the given application URL without displaying anything.

If you click on the "Sign in or register" link with the app running in the development server, the link goes to the development server's simulated version of the Google Accounts sign-in screen, similar to Figure 2-7. At this screen, you can enter any email address, and the development server will proceed as if you are signed in with an account that has that address.

Figure 2-7. The development server's simulated Google Accounts sign-in screen

If this app were running on App Engine, the login and logout URLs would go to the actual Google Accounts locations. Once signed in or out, Google Accounts redirects back to the given URL path for the live application.

Click on "Sign in or register," then enter an email address (such as test@example.com) and click on the Login button on the simulated Google Accounts screen. The clock app now looks like Figure 2-8. To sign out again, click the "sign out" link.

Figure 2-8. The clock app, with the user signed in

In addition to the UserService API, an app can also get information about the current user with the servlet "user principal" interface. The app can call the getUserPrincipal() method on the HttpServletRequest object to get a java.security.Principal object, or null if the user is not signed in. This object has a getName() method, which in App Engine is equivalent to calling the getEmail() method of a User object.

The main advantage to getting user information from the servlet interface is that the servlet interface is a standard. Coding an app to use standard interfaces makes the app easier to port to alternative implementations, such as other servlet-based web application environments or private servers. As much as possible, App Engine implements standard interfaces for its services and features.

The disadvantage to the standard interfaces is that not all standard interfaces represent all of App Engine's features, and in some cases the App Engine services don't implement every feature of an interface. All services include a nonstandard "low-level" API, which you can use directly or use to implement adapters to other interfaces.

Web Forms and the Datastore

Now that we can identify the user, we can prompt for the user's preferences and remember them for future requests. We can store preferences data in the Google Cloud Datastore.

There are several ways to use the datastore from Java. The simplest way is to call the datastore API directly. This API lets you create and manipulate entities (records) in the datastore by using instances of an Entity class. Entities have named properties, which you can get and set using getProperty() and setProperty() methods. The API is easy to understand, and has a direct correspondence with the concepts of the datastore. We'll use the datastore API for this tutorial and in the next few chapters.

 The datastore API is sufficient for many uses, but it's not particularly Java-like to represent to data objects as instances of a generic Entity class. It'd be better if data objects could be represented by real Java objects, with classes, fields, and accessor methods that describe the role of the data in your code.

The App Engine SDK includes support for two major standard interfaces for manipulating data in this way: Java Data Objects (JDO) and the Java Persistence API (JPA). With JDO and JPA, you use regular Java classes to describe the structure of data, and include annotations that tell the interface how to save the data to the datastore and re-create the objects when the data is fetched. We discuss JPA in detail in Chapter 10.

You may also want to consider Objectify (*https://code.google.com/p/objectify-appengine/*), a third-party open source library with many of these benefits. Objectify is easier to use than JDO and JPA, although it is specific to App Engine.

First, let's set up a way for a signed-in user to set a time zone preference. Edit *home.jsp* and add the following, just above the closing </body> tag:

```
<c:if test="${user != null}">
  <form action="/prefs" method="post">
    <label for="tz_offset">
      Timezone offset from UTC (can be negative):
    </label>
    <input name="tz_offset" id="tz_offset" type="text"
      size="4" value="${tzOffset}" />
    <input type="submit" value="Set" />
  </form>
</c:if>
```

(We will populate the tzOffset attribute in a moment. If you'd like to test the form now, remove the ${tzOffset} reference temporarily.)

This web form includes a text field for the user's time zone preference, and a button that submits the form. When the user submits the form, the browser issues an HTTP POST request (specified by the method attribute) to the URL /prefs (the action attribute), with a request body containing the form field data.

Naturally, we need a new servlet to handle these requests. Create a new servlet class PrefsServlet (*PrefsServlet.java*) with the code shown in Example 2-6.

Example 2-6. The PrefsServlet class, a servlet that handles the user preferences form

```java
package clock;

import java.io.IOException;

import javax.servlet.http.HttpServlet;
import javax.servlet.http.HttpServletRequest;
import javax.servlet.http.HttpServletResponse;

import com.google.appengine.api.datastore.DatastoreService;
import com.google.appengine.api.datastore.DatastoreServiceFactory;
import com.google.appengine.api.datastore.Entity;
import com.google.appengine.api.datastore.Key;
import com.google.appengine.api.datastore.KeyFactory;
import com.google.appengine.api.users.User;
import com.google.appengine.api.users.UserService;
import com.google.appengine.api.users.UserServiceFactory;

@SuppressWarnings("serial")
public class PrefsServlet extends HttpServlet {
    public void doPost(HttpServletRequest req,
            HttpServletResponse resp)
        throws IOException {

        UserService userService = UserServiceFactory.getUserService();
        User user = userService.getCurrentUser();

        DatastoreService ds = DatastoreServiceFactory.getDatastoreService();
        Key userKey = KeyFactory.createKey("UserPrefs", user.getUserId());
        Entity userPrefs = new Entity(userKey);

        try {
            double tzOffset = new Double(req.getParameter("tz_offset"))
                .doubleValue();

            userPrefs.setProperty("tz_offset", tzOffset);
            userPrefs.setProperty("user", user);
            ds.put(userPrefs);

        } catch (NumberFormatException nfe) {
            // User entered a value that wasn't a double.  Ignore for now.
        }

        resp.sendRedirect("/");
    }
}
```

A datastore entity has a *kind*, which groups related entities together for the purpose of queries. Here, the user's time zone preference is stored in an entity of the kind "User Prefs". This entity has two properties. The first is named "tzOffset", and its value is the user's time zone offset, a floating-point value (double) as a number of hours. The second is "user", which contains a representation of the User value that represents the currently signed-in user.

Each datastore entity has a key that is unique across all entities. A simple key contains the kind, and either an app-assigned string (the *key name*) or a system-assigned number (referred to in the API as an *ID*). In this case, we provide a key name equal to the user ID from the User value.

The entity is saved to the datastore by the call to the ds.put() method. If an entity with the given key does not exist, the put() method creates a new one. If the entity does exist, put() replaces it. In a more typical case involving more properties, you would fetch the entity by key or with a query, update properties, then save it back to the datastore. But for PrefsServlet, it is sufficient to replace the entity without reading the old data.

When we are done updating the datastore, we respond with a redirect back to the main page (/). It is a best practice to reply to the posting of a web form with a redirect, to prevent the user from accidentally resubmitting the form by using the "back" button of the browser. It'd be better to offer more visual feedback for this action, but this will do for now.

Edit *web.xml* to map the new servlet to the /prefs URL used by the form. Add these lines just before the closing </web-app> tag:

```
<servlet>
  <servlet-name>Prefs</servlet-name>
  <servlet-class>clock.PrefsServlet</servlet-class>
</servlet>
<servlet-mapping>
  <servlet-name>Prefs</servlet-name>
  <url-pattern>/prefs</url-pattern>
</servlet-mapping>

<security-constraint>
  <web-resource-collection>
    <web-resource-name>prefs</web-resource-name>
    <url-pattern>/prefs</url-pattern>
  </web-resource-collection>
  <auth-constraint>
    <role-name>*</role-name>
  </auth-constraint>
</security-constraint>
```

The order in which the URL mappings appear in the file does not matter. Longer patterns (not counting wildcards) match before shorter ones.

The <security-constraint> block tells App Engine that only users signed in with a Google account can access the URL /prefs. If a user who is not signed in attempts to access this URL, App Engine redirects the user to Google Accounts to sign in. When the user signs in, she is directed back to the URL she attempted to access. A security constraint is a convenient way to implement Google Accounts authentication for a set of URLs. In this case, it means that PrefsServlet does not need to handle the case where someone tries to submit data to the URL without being signed in.

Finally, edit the doGet() method in the ClockServlet class to fetch the UserPrefs entity and use its value, if one exists. Add this code prior to where the "currentTime" attribute is set, with the imports in the appropriate place:

```java
import com.google.appengine.api.datastore.DatastoreService;
import com.google.appengine.api.datastore.DatastoreServiceFactory;
import com.google.appengine.api.datastore.Entity;
import com.google.appengine.api.datastore.EntityNotFoundException;
import com.google.appengine.api.datastore.Key;
import com.google.appengine.api.datastore.KeyFactory;

// ...
        Entity userPrefs = null;
        if (user != null) {
            DatastoreService ds = DatastoreServiceFactory.getDatastoreService();
            Key userKey = KeyFactory.createKey("UserPrefs", user.getUserId());
            try {
                userPrefs = ds.get(userKey);
            } catch (EntityNotFoundException e) {
                // No user preferences stored.
            }
        }
        if (userPrefs != null) {
            double tzOffset = ((Double) userPrefs.getProperty("tz_offset"))
                .doubleValue();
            fmt.setTimeZone(
                new SimpleTimeZone((int) (tzOffset * 60 * 60 * 1000), ""));
            req.setAttribute("tzOffset", tzOffset);
        } else {
            req.setAttribute("tzOffset", 0);
        }
```

This code retrieves the UserPrefs entity by reconstructing its key, then calling the get() method of the DatastoreService. This either returns the Entity, or throws EntityNotFoundException. In this case, if it's not found, we fall back on the default setting of 0 for the time zone offset. If it is found, we update the SimpleDateFormat to use the setting. In either case, we populate the "tzOffset" attribute with a value, which is displayed in the form.

Notice the casting of the property value in this example. When we set the property in the PrefsServlet class, we used a double value. When we retrieve the property with getProperty(), it comes out as an Object. (This value is null if the entity has no property of that name.) We must cast the value to a Double, then call its double Value() method to get our double.

This is where a data framework like JPA or Objectify comes in handy. Such a framework handles the marshaling of values and casting of types automatically, and can provide a degree of protection for type consistency. The datastore itself is "schemaless," which is important to understand as you modify your data model over the lifetime of your application.

Restart your development server, then reload the page to see the customizable clock in action. Try changing the time zone by submitting the form. Also try signing out, then signing in again using the same email address, and again with a different email address. The app remembers the time zone preference for each user.

Caching with Memcache

So far, our application fetches the object from the datastore every time a signed-in user visits the site. Because user preferences data doesn't change very often, we can speed up the per-request data access using the memory cache service (*memcache*) as secondary storage.

We need to make two changes to our app to achieve this. The first is to update Clock Servlet to check the cache. If the value is found in the cache, ClockServlet uses it. If it is not found, it falls back on reading from the datastore as before. If the value is found in the datastore but not in the cache, it stores the value in the cache for use by future requests.

The second change we need is to PrefsServlet. When the user updates her preference, we must invalidate (delete) the value in the cache. The next attempt to read the value—likely the redirect to ClockServlet that immediately follows the form submission—will see the cache does not have the value, get it from the datastore, and update the cache.

We could have `PrefsServlet` update the cache itself, but we *must* have `ClockServlet` populate the cache as needed. Memcache is not durable storage, and could delete any value at any time. That's what makes it fast. If `ClockServlet` did not update the cache, the value could go missing, and performance would degrade until the next time the user updates her preference. To keep things simple, we make `ClockServlet` responsible for all cache updates, and simply delete the value from the cache when it changes in the datastore in `PrefsServlet`.

Edit the lines we just added to `ClockServlet` to use the cache, putting the new imports in the appropriate place:

```java
import com.google.appengine.api.memcache.MemcacheService;
import com.google.appengine.api.memcache.MemcacheServiceFactory;

// ...
        Entity userPrefs = null;
        if (user != null) {
            DatastoreService ds =
                DatastoreServiceFactory.getDatastoreService();
            MemcacheService memcache =
                MemcacheServiceFactory.getMemcacheService();

            String cacheKey = "UserPrefs:" + user.getUserId();
            userPrefs = (Entity) memcache.get(cacheKey);
            if (userPrefs == null) {
                Key userKey = KeyFactory.createKey("UserPrefs", user.getUserId());
                try {
                    userPrefs = ds.get(userKey);
                    memcache.put(cacheKey, userPrefs);
                } catch (EntityNotFoundException e) {
                    // No user preferences stored.
                }
            }
        }

        if (userPrefs != null) {
            double tzOffset = ((Double) userPrefs.getProperty("tz_offset"))
                .doubleValue();
            fmt.setTimeZone(
                new SimpleTimeZone((int) (tzOffset * 60 * 60 * 1000), ""));
            req.setAttribute("tzOffset", tzOffset);
        } else {
            req.setAttribute("tzOffset", 0);
        }
```

Similarly, edit the doPost() method of PrefsServlet to delete the cached value (if any) when performing an update:

```
import com.google.appengine.api.memcache.MemcacheService;
import com.google.appengine.api.memcache.MemcacheServiceFactory;

// ...
        MemcacheService memcache = MemcacheServiceFactory.getMemcacheService();
        String cacheKey = "UserPrefs:" + user.getUserId();

        try {
            double tzOffset = new Double(req.getParameter("tz_offset"))
                .doubleValue();

            userPrefs.setProperty("tz_offset", tzOffset);
            userPrefs.setProperty("user", user);
            ds.put(userPrefs);
            memcache.delete(cacheKey);

        } catch (NumberFormatException nfe) {
            // User entered a value that wasn't a double.  Ignore for now.
        }
```

Any object you store in the memcache must be serializable. That is, it must implement the Serializable interface from the java.io package. The Entity class is serializable. You can also use any serializable object as the key for a cache value; in this case, we just use a String.

Reload the page to see the new version work. To make the caching behavior more visible, you can add logging statements to ClockServlet, like so:

```
import java.util.logging.*;

// ...
public class ClockServlet extends HttpServlet {
    private static final Logger log =
        Logger.getLogger(ClockServlet.class.getName());

    public void doGet(HttpServletRequest req,
                      HttpServletResponse resp)
        throws IOException, ServletException {

        // ...
            userPrefs = (Entity) memcache.get(cacheKey);
            if (userPrefs == null) {
                log.warning("CACHE MISS");
            } else {
                log.warning("CACHE HIT");
            }

        // ...
```

```
        }
    }
```

The development server prints logging output to the console. If you are using Eclipse, these messages appear in the Console pane.

The Development Console

The development server has a handy feature for inspecting and debugging your application while testing on your local machine: a web-based development console. With your development server running, visit the following URL in a browser to access the console (replacing 8080 with 8888 if you're using Eclipse):

http://localhost:8080/_ah/admin

Figure 2-9 shows the Datastore Viewer in the console.

Figure 2-9. The Development Console's Datastore Viewer

The Development Console's Datastore Viewer gives you a read-only view of the data in the simulated datastore of the development server. You can also flush the memcache, which is useful when testing cache-related behaviors.

The Development Console includes features for managing other aspects of the simulated environment, such as task queues and messaging. We'll look at these when we discuss the corresponding services.

Registering the Application

Before you can upload your application to App Engine and share it with the world, you must first register a project ID. It's time to introduce the Cloud Console.

To access the Cloud Console, visit the following URL in your browser, signing in with your Google account if necessary:

https://console.developers.google.com/

Bookmark or memorize this URL, as you'll be back here frequently once your app is live. The Cloud Console is home base for all of your cloud projects.

The home screen lists all of your current projects (if any), and gives you access to your Cloud-related account settings and billing information.[1]

It costs nothing to create a project. You can have up to 25 free projects per Google account, and you can delete projects later. You can have an unlimited number of paid applications. Note that you will be reserving a unique ID when you create a project, and IDs for deleted projects cannot be reclaimed.

In the Projects section, click the Create Project button. When prompted, enter a project name. The Console generates a unique project ID for you, but you can change it to something more memorable if you like. As we're about to see, the ID is used in test URLs and a few other places. If you intend to register a domain name for your web application, you will not need to show your project ID to your users.[2] You cannot change the ID after the project has been created (but you can delete the project and create a new one). Click Create to create the project.

Uploading the Application

In a traditional web application environment, releasing an application to the world can be a laborious process. Getting the latest software and configuration to multiple web servers and backend services in the right order and at the right time to minimize downtime and prevent breakage is often a difficult and delicate process. With App Engine, deployment is as simple as uploading the files with a single click or com-

---

[1] The descriptions and screenshots of the Google Developers Console in this book are current as of the time this material was produced. Google improves the Console continuously, and some descriptions may be out of date by the time you read this. Such is life.

[2] As of this writing, there is one obscure feature that does not yet support custom domains: incoming XMPP messages. I'm not aware of another case where end users must interact with a project ID when the app has a custom domain.

---

mand. You can upload and test multiple versions of your application, and set any uploaded version to be the current public version.

Edit your *appengine-web.xml* configuration file, and replace the `<application>` value with the project ID you registered in the previous step:

```
<?xml version="1.0" encoding="utf-8"?>
<appengine-web-app xmlns="http://appengine.google.com/ns/1.0">
  <application>saucy-boomerang-123</application>
  <!-- ... -->
</appengine-web-app>
```

You can upload from Eclipse using the Google plugin, or from a command prompt. In Eclipse, open the Google toolbar menu, then select Deploy to App Engine…. Click the "App Engine project settings…" link, then update the "Application ID" field with your new project ID. Click OK. (You only need to set the project ID once.) When you're ready, click Deploy.

Or from a command prompt, run the `appcfg` (or `appcfg.sh`) command from the SDK's *bin/* directory as follows, using the path to your application's WAR directory for `war`:

```
appcfg update war
```

The `appcfg` tool uses your Google credentials to communicate with Google. These are the credentials you set up earlier with the `gcloud auth login` command.

 If you intend to use the `gcloud` command to access other Cloud Platform services, you can tell it to use your new project by default using this command:

```
gcloud config set project saucy-boomerang-123
```

To see all of the `gcloud` configuration fields that you can set in this way:

```
gcloud config list
```

The upload process determines the project ID and version number from the tool configuration or the app's *appengine-web.xml* configuration file, depending on what is set. Eclipse favors the project settings, `gcloud` favors the configuration file. It uploads and installs the files and configuration as the given version of the app. The app starts running on App Engine immediately.

Testing the App

Every App Engine project gets a free domain name consisting of the project ID followed by `.appspot.com`. For example, if your project ID is `saucy-boomerang-123`, you can access the app at this URL:

```
http://saucy-boomerang-123.appspot.com/
```

Visit your app's URL in a browser, and confirm that it works as expected.

Next, go back to the Cloud Console (*https://console.developers.google.com/*) and select your project. The Overview section now displays graphs representing your test traffic. Figure 2-10 shows an example.

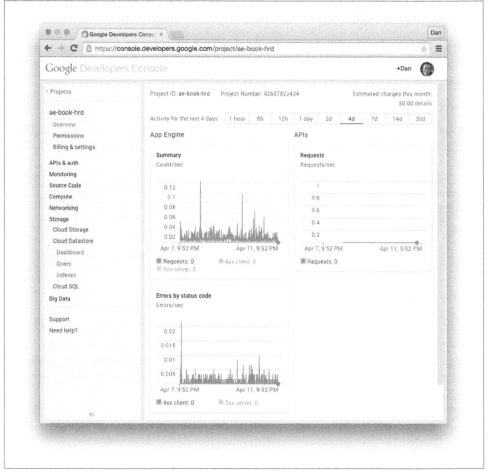

Figure 2-10. The Cloud Console overview screen for a small app (this book's website)

Navigate to Compute, then App Engine, and finally Dashboard. This dashboard shows more detailed graphs than the project overview and is specific to the App Engine part of Cloud Platform. You should see a small spike in the requests-per-second chart, referring to your test traffic. The scale of the chart goes up to the highest point in the chart, so the spike reaches the top of the graph, even though you have only accessed the application a few times.

Next, open Monitoring in the sidebar, then select the Logs panel. All requests served by App Engine are logged with details about the request and the app's response. These records also include all messages logged by the application code during the request. Click a record to expand it for more information. You can scroll up and down to attempt to load more records in either direction on the timeline. You can also filter records by log level (such as to only show requests during which your app logged errors), time, label, or a regular expression match.

Take a moment to browse the Console. Throughout this book, we discuss how an application consumes system resources, and how you can optimize an app for speed and cost effectiveness. You will use the Cloud Console to track resource consumption and diagnose problems.

 Google improves the Cloud Console continuously, and menus and buttons may have changed since the time this book was written. In particular, as features graduate from App Engine to Cloud Platform as a whole, their Console panels may relocate in the navigation bar.

Enabling Billing

When you created the project in Cloud Console, you were prompted to set up a billing account, or associate an existing billing account with the project. Google uses this account's payment information when the project accrues charges.

Google App Engine costs nothing to get started. Simply by creating a project, Google grants you a limited amount of application resources so you can create an app, try the features of the platform, and get your app working and serving live traffic. When you're ready, you can set a spending limit to make more resources available. This limit applies to all resources managed by App Engine. Other Cloud Platform services, such as Compute Engine, are billed separately.

The default budget is zero dollars, and you will not be billed for App Engine resources until you increase it. You can use the Cloud Console to set the budget. To do so, expand Compute in the sidebar nav, then App Engine, then Settings. Adjust the daily budget, then save your preferences.

CHAPTER 3

Configuring an Application

Many of App Engine's features can be tailored and controlled using configuration files that you deploy alongside your code. A few of these features apply to the entire project's use of a service, such as datastore index configuration (which we'll cover in Chapter 7). The most important set of configuration controls how App Engine manages incoming requests, how App Engine runs your code on its scalable servers, and how App Engine routes requests to your code on those servers.

To build an App Engine application, you write code for one or more *request handlers*, and provide configuration describing to App Engine which requests go to which handlers. The life of a request handler begins when a single request arrives, and ends when the handler has done the necessary work and computed the response. App Engine does all the heavy lifting of accepting incoming TCP/IP connections, reading HTTP request data, ensuring that an instance of your app is running on an application server, routing the request to an available instance, calling the appropriate request handler code in your app, and collecting the response from the handler and sending it back over the connection to the client.

The system that manages and routes requests is known generally as the App Engine *frontend*. You can configure the frontend to handle different requests in different ways. For instance, you can tell the frontend to route requests for some URLs to App Engine's static file servers instead of the application servers, for efficient delivery of your app's images, CSS, or JavaScript code. If your app takes advantage of Google Accounts for its users, you can tell the frontend to route requests from signed-in users to your application's request handlers, and to redirect all other requests to the Google Accounts sign-in screen. The frontend is also responsible for handling requests over secure connections, using HTTP over SSL/TLS (sometimes called "HTTPS," the URL scheme for such requests). Your app code only sees the request after it has been decoded, and the frontend takes care of encoding the response.

In this chapter, we take a look at App Engine's request handling architecture, and follow the path of a web request through the system. We discuss how to configure the system to handle different kinds of requests, including requests for static content, requests for the application to perform work, and requests over secure connections. We also cover other frontend features such as custom error pages, and application features you can activate called "built-ins."

We'll also take this opportunity to discuss related features that you manage from the Cloud Console, including setting up custom domain names and SSL/TLS certificates.

The App Engine Architecture

The architecture of App Engine—and therefore an App Engine application—can be summarized as shown in Figure 3-1. (There are some lines missing from this simplified diagram. For instance, frontends have direct access to Cloud Storage for serving large data objects from app URLs. We'll take a closer look at these in later chapters.)

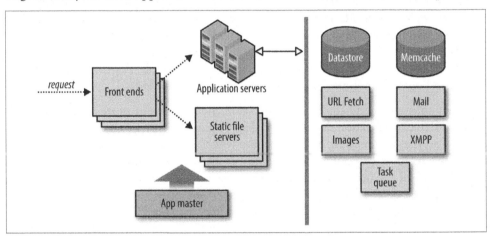

Figure 3-1. The App Engine request handling architecture

The first stop for an incoming request is the App Engine frontend. A load balancer, a dedicated system for distributing requests optimally across multiple machines, routes the request to one of many frontend servers. The frontend determines the app for which the request is intended from the request's domain name, either the associated custom domain or subdomain, or the *appspot.com* subdomain. It then consults the app's configuration to determine the next step.

The app's configuration describes how the frontends should treat requests based on their URL paths. A URL path may map to a static file that should be served to the client directly, such as an image or a file of JavaScript code. Or, a URL path may map to a request handler, application code that is invoked to determine the response for the request. You upload this configuration data along with the rest of your application.

If the URL path for a request does not match anything in the app's configuration, the frontends return an HTTP 404 Not Found error response to the client. By default, the frontends return a generic error response. If you want clients to receive a custom response when accessing your app, such as a friendly HTML message along with the error code, you can configure the frontend to serve a static HTML file. (In the case of Not Found errors, you can also just map all unmatched URL paths to an application handler, and respond any way you like.)

If the URL path of the request matches the path of one of the app's static files, the frontend routes the request to the static file servers. These servers are dedicated to the task of serving static files, with network topology and caching behavior optimized for fast delivery of resources that do not change often. You tell App Engine about your app's static files in the app's configuration. When you upload the app, these files are pushed to the static file servers.

If the URL path of the request matches a pattern mapped to one of the application's request handlers, the frontend sends the request to the app servers. The app server pool starts up an *instance* of the application on a server, or reuses an existing instance if there is one already running. The server invokes the app by calling the request handler that corresponds with the URL path of the request, according to the app configuration.

An instance is a copy of your application in the memory of an application server. The instance is isolated from whatever else is running on the machine, set up to perform equivalently to a dedicated machine with certain hardware characteristics. The code itself executes in a *runtime environment* prepared with everything the request handler needs to inspect the request data, call services, and evaluate the app's code. There's enough to say about instances and the runtime environment that an entire chapter is dedicated to the subject (Chapter 4).

You can configure the frontend to authenticate the user with Google Accounts. The frontend can restrict access to URL paths with several levels of authorization: all users, users who have signed in, and users who are application administrators. The frontend checks whether the user is signed in, and redirects the user to the Google Accounts sign-in screen if needed.

The frontend takes the opportunity to tailor the response to the client. Most notably, the frontend compresses the response data, using the gzip format, if the client gives some indication that it supports compressed responses. This applies to both app responses and static file responses, and is done automatically. The frontend uses several techniques to determine when it is appropriate to compress responses, based on web standards and known browser behaviors. If you are using a custom client that does not support compressed content, simply omit the "Accept-Encoding" request header to disable the automatic gzip behavior. Similarly, for clients that support the SPDY protocol, App Engine will use SPDY instead of HTTP 1.1, automatically and invisibly.

The frontends, app servers, and static file servers are governed by an "app master." Among other things, the app master is responsible for deploying new versions of application software and configuration, and updating the "default" version served on an app's user-facing domain. Updates to an app propagate quickly, but are not atomic in the sense that only code from one version of an app is running at any one time. If you switch the default version to new software, all requests that started before the switch are allowed to complete using their version of the software. If you have an app that makes an HTTP request to itself, you might run into a situation where an older version is calling a newer version or vice versa, but you can manage this in code if needed.

Configuring a Java App

A Java application consists of files bundled in a standard format called WAR (short for "web application archive"). The WAR standard specifies the layout of a directory structure for a Java web application, including the locations of several standard configuration files, compiled Java classes, JAR files, static files, and other auxiliary files. Some tools that manipulate WARs support compressing the directory structure into a single file similar to a JAR. App Engine's tools generally expect the WAR to be a directory on your computer's filesystem.

Java servlet applications use a file called a "deployment descriptor" to specify how the server invokes the application. This file uses an XML format, and is part of the servlet standard specification. In a WAR, the deployment descriptor is a file named *web.xml* that resides in a directory named *WEB-INF/*, which itself is in the WAR's root directory. Example 3-1 shows a very simple deployment descriptor.

Example 3-1. An example of a web.xml deployment descriptor file

```
<?xml version="1.0" encoding="utf-8"?>
<web-app xmlns="http://java.sun.com/xml/ns/javaee" version="2.5">
  <servlet>
    <servlet-name>ae-book</servlet-name>
    <servlet-class>aebook.MainServlet</servlet-class>
  </servlet>
  <servlet-mapping>
    <servlet-name>ae-book</servlet-name>
    <url-pattern>/*</url-pattern>
  </servlet-mapping>
</web-app>
```

The deployment descriptor tells the App Engine frontend most of what it needs to know, but not all. For the rest, App Engine uses a file named *appengine-web.xml*, also in the *WEB-INF/* directory and also using XML syntax. If your code editor supports XML validation, you can find the schema definition for this file in the App Engine Java SDK. Example 3-2 shows a brief example.

Example 3-2. An example of an appengine-web.xml configuration file

```xml
<?xml version="1.0" encoding="utf-8"?>
<appengine-web-app xmlns="http://appengine.google.com/ns/1.0">
  <application>ae-book</application>
  <version>1</version>
  <threadsafe>true</threadsafe>
</appengine-web-app>
```

The development server may add elements to this file with some default values the first time it is run.

When Google releases major new features for the Java API, the release includes a new version of the SDK with an updated *appengine-api-... .jar* file. App Engine knows which version of the API the app is expecting by examining the API JAR included in the app's WAR. The server may replace the JAR with a different but compatible implementation when the app is run.

Configuring a Java App with YAML Files

Deployment descriptors are part of the Java servlet standard, and together with App Engine's XML configuration files, they're a good choice for a typical servlet-based application, especially if you may need to port your app to another servlet container in the future. The App Engine Java SDK also supports configuring a Java app by using the YAML syntax, similar to that used by other runtime environments. You might use YAML files instead of XML files if your app is written in a language other than Java that uses the JVM (such as JRuby), or to take advantage of the more convenient syntax for features like access control.

To use YAML configuration files with the Java runtime environment, create a file named *app.yaml* in your *WEB-INF/* directory. If the App Engine SDK finds this file, the development server will rewrite it as *web.xml* and *appengine-web.xml* files, overwriting any already present. The *app.yaml* file must contain values for `application` (the application ID), `version` (the application version), and `runtime` (java instead of python), and one or more `handlers`. For example:

```yaml
application: clock
version: 1
runtime: java

handlers:
```

```
- url: /prefs
  servlet: clock.PrefsServlet
  login: required

- url: /*
  servlet: clock.ClockServlet
```

Java YAML configuration files bear only a partial resemblance to those used by the other runtime environments. Some important differences:

- You do not specify a version number for the runtime environment for Java. As when using a deployment descriptor, the runtime version is determined by the App Engine JARs in the app's WAR.

- URL patterns are not full regular expressions. Instead, they are similar to URL patterns in deployment descriptors. You can use a * wildcard at the beginning or end of a URL pattern to represent zero or more characters, and you can only use one wildcard in a pattern.

- Static file configuration does not use the same syntax. Instead, you configure static files and resources in a manner similar to *appengine-web.xml*, using top-level `static_files:` and `resource_files:` elements in the YAML file.

YAML configuration for Java supports the same access control (`login:`) and secure connection (`secure:`) attributes for servlet configuration as other runtime environments do for script handlers. Features such as inbound services, warmup requests, Cloud Console pages, and custom error pages also have app configuration. The separate configuration files for services, such as datastore indexes and task queues, can also be specified using YAML files (e.g., *index.yaml* and *queue.yaml*); these files reside in your *WEB-INF/* directory.

Java YAML configuration also supports features specific to deployment descriptors, including servlet parameters, servlet filters, context listeners, JSPs, system properties, and environment variables, using YAML syntax. You can even include a set of deployment descriptor XML in the *app.yaml* file by using the `web_xml` element. Features specific to *appengine-web.xml* (such as sessions) also have YAML equivalents (e.g., `sessions_enabled: true`).

We describe all of these features throughout this book, but we will not make additional asides to describe Java YAML configuration. See the official App Engine documentation for a complete description of using YAML configuration with Java.

App IDs and Versions

Every App Engine application has an application ID that uniquely distinguishes the app from all other applications. As described in Chapter 2, you can register an ID for a new application using the Cloud Console. Once you have an ID, you add it to the app's configuration so the developer tools know that the files in the app root directory belong to the app with that ID. This ID appears in the `appspot.com` domain name:

`app-id.appspot.com`

The app's configuration also includes a version identifier. Like the app ID, the version identifier is associated with the app's files when the app is uploaded. App Engine retains one set of files and frontend configuration for each distinct version identifier used during an upload. If you do not change the app version in the configuration before you upload files, the upload replaces the existing files for that version.

Each distinct version of the app is accessible at its own domain name, of the following form:

`version-id.app-id.appspot.com`

When you have multiple versions of an app uploaded to App Engine, you can use the Cloud Console to select which version is the one you want the public to access. The Console calls this the "default" version. When a user visits your custom domain or the `appspot.com` domain without the version ID, she sees the default version.

The `appspot.com` domain containing the version ID supports an additional domain part, just like the default `appspot.com` domain:

`anything.version-id.app-id.appspot.com`

Unless you explicitly prevent it, anyone who knows your application ID and version identifiers can access any uploaded version of your application using the `appspot.com` URLs. You can restrict access to nondefault versions of the application by using code that checks the domain of the request and only allows authorized users to access the versioned domains. You can't restrict access to static files this way.

Another way to restrict access to nondefault versions is to use Google Accounts authorization, described later in this chapter. You can restrict access to app administrators while a version is in development, then replace the configuration to remove the restriction just before making that version the default version.

All versions of an app access the same datastore, memcache, and other services, and all versions share the same set of resources. Later on, we'll discuss other configuration files that control these backend services. These files are separate from the configuration files that control the frontend because they are not specific to each app version.

There are several ways to use app versions. For instance, you can have just one version, and always update it in place. Or you can have a "dev" version for testing and a "live" version that is always the public version, and do separate uploads for each.

Some developers generate a new app version identifier for each upload based on the version numbers used by a source code revision control system.

You can have up to 60 active versions, if billing is enabled for the app. You can delete previous versions, using the Cloud Console.

Application IDs and version identifiers can contain numbers, lowercase letters, and hyphens.

The application ID and version identifier appear in the *appengine-web.xml* file. The app ID is specified with the XML element `<application>`, and the version identifier is specified with `<version>`. For example:

```
<?xml version="1.0" encoding="utf-8"?>
<appengine-web-app xmlns="http://appengine.google.com/ns/1.0">
  <application>ae-book</application>
  <version>dev</version>
</appengine-web-app>
```

This would be accessible using this domain name:

```
http://dev.ae-book.appspot.com
```

Multithreading

The Java runtime environment supports handling multiple requests concurrently within each instance. This is a significant way to make the most of your instances, and is recommended. However, your code must be written with the knowledge that it will be run concurrently, and take the appropriate precautions with shared data. You must declare whether your code is "threadsafe" in your application configuration.

To set this preference, specify the `<threadsafe>` element in *appengine-web.xml*:

```
<threadsafe>true</threadsafe>
```

Request Handlers

The app configuration tells the frontend what to do with each request, routing it to either the application servers or the static file servers. The destination is determined by the URL path of the request. For instance, an app might send all requests whose URL paths start with `/images/` to the static file server, and all requests for the site's home page (the path `/`) to the app servers. The configuration specifies a list of patterns that match URL paths, with instructions for each pattern.

For requests intended for the app servers, the configuration also specifies the request handler responsible for specific URL paths. A request handler is an entry point into the application code. As with all Java servlet containers, a request handler is a servlet class, instantiated and invoked to produce the response.

The URL /form is reserved by App Engine and cannot be used by the app. The explanation for this is historical and internal to App Engine, and unfortunately this is easy to stumble upon by accident. This URL will always return a 404 Not Found error.

All URL paths under /_ah/ are reserved for use by App Engine libraries and tools.

A Java web application maps URL patterns to servlets in the deployment descriptor (*web.xml*). You set up a servlet in two steps: the servlet declaration, and the servlet mapping.

The <servlet> element declares a servlet. It includes a <servlet-name>, a name for the purposes of referring to the servlet elsewhere in the file, and the <servlet-class>, the name of the class that implements the servlet. Here's a simple example:

```
<servlet>
  <servlet-name>ae-book</servlet-name>
  <servlet-class>aebook.MainServlet</servlet-class>
</servlet>
```

The servlet declaration can also define initialization parameters for the servlet. This is useful if you want to use the same servlet class in multiple servlet declarations, with different parameters for each one. For example:

```
<servlet>
  <servlet-name>ae-book</servlet-name>
  <servlet-class>aebook.MainServlet</servlet-class>
  <init-param>
    <param-name>colorscheme</param-name>
    <param-value>monochrome</param-value>
  </init-param>
  <init-param>
    <param-name>background</param-name>
    <param-value>dark</param-value>
  </init-param>
</servlet>
```

To map a servlet to a URL path pattern, you use the <servlet-mapping> element. A mapping includes the <servlet-name> that matches a servlet declaration, and a <url-pattern>:

```
<servlet-mapping>
  <servlet-name>ae-book</servlet-name>
  <url-pattern>/home/*</url-pattern>
</servlet-mapping>
```

The URL pattern matches the URL path. It can use a * character at the beginning or end of the pattern to represent zero or more of any character. Note that this wildcard can only appear at the beginning or end of the pattern, and you can only use one wildcard per pattern.

The order in which URL mappings appear is not significant. The "most specific" matching pattern wins, determined by the number of nonwildcard characters in the pattern. The pattern /* matches all URLs, but will only match if none of the other patterns in the deployment descriptor match the URL.

JSPs are supported, as servlets invoked from other servlets, as servlets named explicitly in the descriptor, and as standalone servlets mapped to URL paths that resemble their file paths. If a request path does not match an explicit URL pattern in the deployment descriptor but does match the path to a *.jsp* file from the root of the WAR (and the *.jsp* file is not under *WEB-INF/*), the JSP servlet will be compiled and invoked.

Static Files and Resource Files

Most web applications have a set of files that are served verbatim to all users, and do not change as the application is used. These can be media assets like images used for site decoration, CSS stylesheets that describe how the site should be drawn to the screen, JavaScript code to be downloaded and executed by a web browser, or HTML for full pages with no dynamic content. To speed up the delivery of these files and improve page rendering time, App Engine uses dedicated servers for static files. Using dedicated servers also means the app servers don't have to spend resources on requests for static files.

Static files are uploaded with your code when you deploy the application. This makes them well suited for web support files like images of icons, but not so well suited for content files like photos to accompany a magazine article. In most cases, content served by your web application belongs in a content management system built into your app that separates the content publishing workflow from the application deployment workflow.

Locally, static files sit with your app code in the app's root directory. You tell the deployment process and the frontend which of the application's files are static files using app configuration. The deployment process reads the configuration and delivers the static files to the dedicated static file servers. The frontend remembers which URL paths refer to static files, so it can route requests for those paths to the appropriate servers.

The static file configuration can also include a recommendation for a cache expiration interval. App Engine returns the cache instructions to the client in the HTTP header along with the file. If the client chooses to heed the recommendation (and most web browsers do), it will retain the file for up to that amount of time, and use its local copy instead of asking for it again. This reduces the amount of bandwidth used, but at the expense of clients retaining old copies of files that may have changed.

To save space and reduce the amount of data involved when setting up new app instances, static files are not pushed to the application servers. This means application code cannot access the contents of static files by using the filesystem.

The files that do get pushed to the application servers are known as "resource files." These can include app-specific configuration files, web page templates, or other static data that is read by the app but not served directly to clients. Application code can access these files by reading them from the filesystem. The code itself is also accessible this way.

As we saw earlier, the WAR directory structure for a Java web application keeps all application code, JARs, and configuration in a subdirectory named *WEB-INF/*. Typically, files outside of *WEB-INF/* represent resources that the user can access directly, including static files and JSPs. The URL paths to these resources are equivalent to the paths to these files within the WAR.

Say an app's WAR has the following files:

```
main.jsp
forum/home.jsp
images/logo.png
images/cancelbutton.png
images/okbutton.png
terms.html
WEB-INF/classes/com/example/Forum.class
WEB-INF/classes/com/example/MainServlet.class
WEB-INF/classes/com/example/Message.class
WEB-INF/classes/com/example/UserPrefs.class
WEB-INF/lib/appengine-api.jar
```

This app has four static files: three PNG images and an HTML file named *terms.html*. When the app is uploaded, these four files are pushed to the static file servers. The frontends know to route requests for URL paths equivalent to these file paths (such as `/images/logo.png`) to the static file servers.

The two *.jsp* files are assumed to be JSPs, and are compiled to servlet classes and mapped to the URL paths equivalent to their file paths. Because these are application code, they are handled by the application servers. The JSP source files themselves are not pushed to the static file servers.

By default, *all* files in the WAR are pushed to the application servers, and are accessible by the application code via the filesystem. This includes the files that are identified as static files and also copied to the static file servers. In other words, all files are considered resource files, and all files except for JSPs and files in the *WEB-INF/* directory are considered static files.

You can change which files are considered resource files and which are considered static files by using the *appengine-web.xml* file, with the `<resource-files>` and `<static-files>` elements, respectively. These elements can contain `<include>` and `<exclude>` elements that modify the default behavior of including all files. For example:

```
<resource-files>
  <exclude path="/images/**" />
</resource-files>
```

This example excludes the contents of the *images/* directory and all subdirectories from the set of resource files. This reduces the amount of data that is pushed to the application servers when starting up a new application instance, at the expense of not being able to access those files from within the application (probably fine for site images). The ** pattern matches any number of characters in file and directory names, including subdirectories.

Another example:

```
<static-files>
  <exclude path="/**.xml" />
  <include path="/sitemap.xml" />
</static-files>
```

This excludes all files with names ending in *.xml* from the set of static files, except for *sitemap.xml*. Perhaps the XML files are intended for the application's eyes only, but we want to make sure search engines can see the site map.

Files in the *WEB-INF/* directory are always considered resource files. They cannot be included as static files or excluded from the set of resource files.

Browsers rely on the web server to tell them the type of the file being served. The static file server determines the MIME content type of a file from the extension on the filename. For instance, a file whose name ends in *.jpeg* is served with a MIME type of `image/jpeg`. The server has a built-in set of mappings from filename extensions to MIME types. You can specify additional mappings using `<mime-mapping>` elements in the deployment descriptor (*web.xml*). See a *web.xml* reference or the App Engine documentation for more information.

Browsers also need to know if a file is safe to cache, and for how long. The static file server can suggest a cache expiration duration when it serves a file (although a browser is not obligated to honor it). You can specify that a set of static files should be cached for a particular duration by including an `expiration` attribute on the `<include>` element in *appengine-web.xml*:

```
<static-files>
  <include path="images/**" expiration="30d" />
</static-files>
```

The value of `expiration` is a duration specified as numbers and units, where `d` is days, `h` is hours, `m` is minutes, and `s` is seconds. You can add values of multiple units by specifying them separated with spaces: `3d 12h`.

Domain Names

Every app gets a free domain name on *appspot.com*, based on the application ID. Requests for URLs that use your domain name are routed to your app by the frontend:

```
http://app-id.appspot.com/path...
```

But chances are, you want to use a custom domain name with your app. You can register your custom domain name with any Internet domain registrar. With your domain name, you will also need Domain Name Service (DNS) hosting, a service that advertises the destination associated with your name (in this case, App Engine). Name registrars such as Hover (*http://www.hover.com/*) include DNS hosting with the cost of the registration. Alternatively, you can use Google Cloud DNS (*https://cloud.google.com/dns/docs*), a high-performance DNS solution with powerful features.

You can configure your domain name so that all requests for the name (`example.com`) go to App Engine, or so only requests for a subdomain (such as `www.example.com`) go to App Engine. You might use a subdomain if the root domain or other subdomains are pointing to other services, such as a company website hosted on a different service.

> If you intend to support secure web traffic over secure connections (SSL/TLS, aka "HTTPS"), skip ahead to the next section, "Google Apps" on page 67. You must use Google Apps to set up your custom domain to use SSL/TLS with the domain.
>
> The `appspot.com` domain supports SSL/TLS. See "Configuring Secure Connections" on page 70 for more information.

To set up a custom domain, go to the Cloud Console, select the project, then select Compute, App Engine, Settings. From the tabs along the top, select "Custom domains." This panel is shown in Figure 3-2.

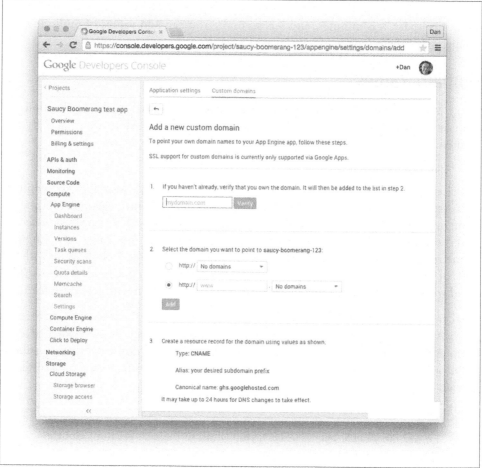

Figure 3-2. The "Custom domains" settings panel

The setup procedure involves three main steps:

1. Verify that you own the domain. You can verify the domain by adding a verification code to the DNS record, or if the domain is already pointing to a web host, by adding a verification code to a file on the web host.

2. Add the domain or subdomain to the project.

3. Configure the DNS record to point to App Engine.

Cloud Console will walk you through these steps with specific instructions.

The `appspot.com` domain has a couple of useful features. One such feature is the ability to accept an additional domain name part:

anything.app-id.appspot.com

Requests for domain names of this form, where *anything* is any valid single domain name part (that cannot contain a dot, .), are routed to the application. This is useful for accepting different kinds of traffic on different domain names, such as for allowing your users to serve content from their own subdomains.

You can determine which domain name was used for the request in your application code by checking the `Host` header on the request. Here's how you check this header in Java:

```
@SuppressWarnings("serial")
public class ClockServlet extends HttpServlet {
    public void doGet(HttpServletRequest req, HttpServletResponse resp)
        throws IOException {
        resp.setContentType("text/plain");

        String host = req.getHeader("Host");
        resp.getWriter().println("Host: " + host);
    }
}
```

Google Apps

Google Apps is a service that gives your organization its own suite of Google's productivity applications, such as Gmail, Docs, Drive, and Hangouts. These apps live on subdomains of your organization's Internet domain name (such as Google Drive on `drive.example.com`), and your organization's employees all get Google accounts using the domain name (`juliet@example.com`). Access to all of the apps and accounts can be managed by the domain administrator, making the suite suitable for businesses, schools, and government institutions. Google Apps for Work is available for a per user per month fee. If your organization is a school, be sure to look for Google Apps for Education, which is free of charge.

A compelling feature of Google Apps is the ability to add an App Engine application on a subdomain (`yourapp.example.com`, or even `www.example.com`). You can configure App Engine's Google accounts features to support domain accounts specifically, making it easy to built intranet apps that only your organization's members can see. You can also make the app on your domain accessible to the public—with no per-user fee for doing so. (The per-user fee only applies to accounts on the domain. You will still need one administrator account.) You can configure a public app on a domain to accept regular Google accounts, or you can implement your own account mechanism.

Google Apps is currently the only way to use secure connections (SSL/TLS, aka "HTTPS") with custom domains on App Engine. This has the advantage of using the Google Apps SSL/TLS infrastructure. In exchange, you lose the ability to serve the App Engine app from the "naked" domain (`http://example.com/`): all Google Apps applications must be associated with a subdomain (such as `www.example.com`). We'll discuss that next, in "Secure Connections with Custom Domains" on page 72.

Google Apps can perform a redirect from the naked domain to any desired subdomain. For example, you can set the naked domain to redirect to `www`, and put the app on that subdomain.

To get started, go to the Google Apps for Work website (*https://www.google.com/work/apps/business/*), or if you're part of an educational institution, use the Google Apps for Education website (*https://www.google.com/work/apps/education/*).

Follow the instructions to create a Google Apps account. You must already have registered your domain name to set up Google Apps. This process will include the opportunity to create an "administrator" account for the domain, which is a new Google account with an email address on the domain (`your.name@example.com`).

Next, add the App Engine app to the domain, as follows:

1. From the Google Admin console (*https://admin.google.com/*) (the Google Apps console), sign in using the Apps domain's administrator account.

2. Expand the "More controls" panel at the bottom, then locate App Engine Apps and click it. You may need to click the right arrow to find it.

3. Click "Add services to your domain," or click the plus symbol (+).

4. Under Other Services, in the Enter App ID field, enter the project ID for your App Engine app. Click "Add it now." Follow the prompts to accept the terms of service.

5. When prompted, under "Web address," click "Add new URL," and enter the subdomain you wish to use. If you try to use the `www` subdomain and it complains "Already used, please remove previous mapping first," this is likely because Google Sites is configured to use `www`. Navigate to Google Apps, click Sites, then click Web Address Mapping. Check the `www` mapping in this list, then click Delete Mapping(s). Navigate back to App Engine Apps, select the app, then try again.

6. As instructed, in another browser window, go to your domain's DNS service, and create a CNAME record for the subdomain. Set the destination to `ghs.googlehosted.com`. Return to the Google Admin panel window, then click "I've comple-

ted these steps." Google verifies your CNAME record. It may take a few minutes for your DNS service to update its records.

Your app can now be accessed using the custom domain, with the subdomain you configured.

While you're here, you should make the Apps domain's administrator account an owner of the app. This is required for setting up secure connections. There are three parts to this: adding the Cloud Console as an "app" that the domain admin can use, inviting the domain admin to be an owner of the app, and finally accepting the invitation as the domain admin. (You must add the Cloud Console as a service before the domain admin can accept the invitation.)

To enable the Cloud Console as a service for the domain:

1. While signed in as the domain administrator, return to the Google Admin console's dashboard.
2. Locate and click on Apps, then select Additional Google services.
3. In the list, locate Google Developers Console, then click the pop-up menu icon on the right. Select the "On for everyone" option from the menu. Confirm that you want domain users to be able to access the Google Developers Console.

To make the domain administrator an owner of the app:

1. Sign out of Google, then sign in with the account you used to create the App Engine app.
2. From the Cloud Console (*https://console.developers.google.com/*), select the app, then click Permissions.
3. Add the Apps domain's administrator account as a member, and set its permission to "Is owner."
4. Sign out of Google again, then sign in again using the Apps domain's administrator account.
5. Go to the account's Gmail inbox (*https://mail.google.com/*), find the invitation email, then click the link to accept the invitation to join the project.

App Engine developer invitations do not work well with Google's multiple sign-in feature. If you click an invitation link, it will attempt to accept the invitation on behalf of the first ("primary") account you're using, then fail because the signed-in account is not the intended recipient of the invitation. To perform this self-invitation maneuver, you must sign out of Google completely then sign in again with the invited account. Alternatively, you can use a Chrome Incognito window to sign in with the invited account and visit the invitation link.

If you intend to use the Google accounts features of App Engine with accounts on your organization's domain, go to Cloud Console, then select Compute, App Engine, Settings. Change the Google Authentication option to "Google Apps domain," then click Save. This ensures that only your domain accounts can be authorized with the app via these features. See "Authorization with Google Accounts" on page 75 for more information.

As you can see, Google Apps is a sophisticated service and requires many steps to set up. With Apps on your domain, not only can you run your App Engine app on a sub-domain, but you get a customized instance of Google's application suite for your company or organization. Take a deep breath and congratulate yourself on getting this far. Then proceed to the next section.

Configuring Secure Connections

When a client requests and retrieves a web page over an HTTP connection, every aspect of the interaction is transmitted over the network in its final intended form, including the URL path, request parameters, uploaded data, and the complete content of the server's response. For web pages, this usually means human-readable text is flying across the wire, or through the air if the user is using a wireless connection. Anyone else privy to the network traffic can capture and analyze this data, and possibly glean sensitive information about the user and the service.

Websites that deal in sensitive information, such as banks and online retailers, can use a secure alternative for web traffic. With servers that support it, the client can make an HTTPS connection (HTTP over the Secure Socket Layer, or SSL/TLS). All data sent in either direction over the connection is encrypted by the sender and decrypted by the recipient, so only the participants can understand what is being transmitted even if the encrypted messages are intercepted. Web browsers usually have an indicator that tells the user when a connection is secure.

App Engine supports secure connections for incoming web requests. By default, App Engine accepts HTTPS connections for all URLs, and otherwise treats them like HTTP requests. You can configure the frontend to reject or redirect HTTP or HTTPS requests for some or all URL paths, such as to ensure that all requests not using a secure connection are redirected to their HTTPS equivalents. The application code itself doesn't need to know the difference between a secure connection and a standard connection: it just consumes the decrypted request and provides a response that is encrypted by App Engine.

All URL paths can be configured to use secure connections, including those mapped to application code and those mapped to static files. The frontend takes care of the secure connection on behalf of the app servers and static file servers.

App Engine only supports secure connections over TCP port 443, the standard port used by browsers for `https://` URLs. Similarly, App Engine only supports standard connections over port 80. The App Engine frontend returns an error for URLs that specify a port other than the standard port for the given connection method.

The development server does not support secure connections, and ignores the security settings in the configuration. You can test these URLs during development by using the nonsecure equivalent URLs.

You can use the deployment descriptor to require secure connections for certain URL paths. In the *web.xml* file, you declare a security constraint for a URL path or set of URL paths as follows:

```
<security-constraint>
  <web-resource-collection>
    <web-resource-name>home</web-resource-name>
    <url-pattern>/home/*</url-pattern>
  </web-resource-collection>
  <user-data-constraint>
    <transport-guarantee>CONFIDENTIAL</transport-guarantee>
  </user-data-constraint>
</security-constraint>
```

A security constraint, indicated by the `<security-constraint>` element, describes the minimum security requirements a request must meet to access a resource. You identify the resource by using a URL pattern in a `<web-resource-collection>` element containing a `<url-pattern>` element. (According to the spec, `<web-resource-collection>` must have a `<web-resource-name>`, although this name is not used for anything.) As with URL patterns in servlet mappings, the URL pattern can be a single URL path, or a partial URL path with a * wildcard at the beginning or at the end.

You specify a security constraint requiring a secure connection with a `<user-data-constraint>` element containing a `<transport-guarantee>` element, itself containing the value `CONFIDENTIAL`. (The transport guarantee `INTEGRAL` is also supported as a synonym for `CONFIDENTIAL`.) App Engine does not support other transport guarantee constraints.

If you do not want users accessing your app with HTTPS, you can disable secure connections by adding this to your *appengine-web.xml* configuration file:

```
<ssl-enabled>false</ssl-enabled>
```

When configured to allow (or require) SSL, you can access the default version of your app using the HTTPS version of the `appspot.com` URL:

```
https://ae-book.appspot.com/
```

Because HTTPS uses the domain name to validate the secure connection, requests to versioned `appspot.com` URLs, such as `https://3.ae-book.appspot.com/`, will display a security warning in the browser saying that the domain does not match the security certificate, which only applies to the immediate subdomains (`*.app spot.com`). To prevent this, App Engine has a trick up its sleeve: replace the dots (`.`) between the version and app IDs with `-dot-` (that's hyphen, the word "dot," and another hyphen), like this:

```
https://3-dot-ae-book.appspot.com/
```

A request to this domain uses the certificate for `*.appspot.com`, and avoids the security warning.

Using the deployment descriptor and *appengine-web.xml*, you can only enable or disable SSL for the entire application. The deployment descriptor standard does not have a concept of accepting secure connections for some URL paths and not others. You can configure SSL for specific URL paths using YAML configuration files with the Java runtime environment. See "Configuring a Java App with YAML Files" on page 57.

Secure Connections with Custom Domains

To enable secure connections over a custom domain for your app, you need to set up Google Apps for the domain, with the app added on a subdomain and the domain administrator account set up as an owner of the app. If you haven't done this yet, see "Google Apps" on page 67.[1]

The protocol for secure connections depends on an *SSL/TLS certificate*,[2] a document that says who you are and that you are responsible for traffic served from the domain.

---

1 The procedure for setting up secure connections via Google Apps is a bit convoluted. If your only interest is to use SSL with a custom domain, check the Cloud Console and the official documentation for an easier way in case one was added since this book was published.

2 TLS, or Transport Layer Security, refers to the latest standard, and is a successor to SSL, or Secure Socket Layer. SSL is still sometimes used as an umbrella term for secure connections.

You acquire a certificate from a *certificate authority* (CA). The CA may also be certified, and this certification can be traced back to a list of known CAs built in to your user's web browser. Browsers will only make secure connections with websites whose certificates can be traced back to known authorities, thereby assuring the user that the connection to your app is genuine, and not being intercepted by a third party.

You can purchase a certificate valid for a limited time from any of a number of CAs, much like registering a domain name from a registrar. CAs offer certificates at different levels of assurance, and some CAs, such as StartSSL (*https://www.startssl.com/*), offer free certificates at the lowest level. Some browsers attempt to communicate the assurance level to the user in various ways. Be sure to follow your CA's procedures for verifying your domain name and adding it to the certificate, and for creating a TLS/SSL certificate for a web server.

For example, StartSSL initially grants you an "S/MIME and Authentication" certificate to authenticate with its website. After you have used the StartSSL website to validate your email address and domain name, you can generate a "Web Server TLS/SSL certificate," with a private key protected by a password. StartSSL then prompts you to copy and paste the encrypted private key into a text file (*ssl.key*), then run the following command to encode it using the RSA method:

```
openssl rsa -in ssl.key -out ssl.key
```

Enter the password you used to encrypt the private key when prompted. The key is decrypted, then encoded using RSA, suitable for uploading to Google.

 The openssl command is installed on most Mac OS X and Linux systems. Windows users can get it from the OpenSSL website (*https://www.openssl.org/*).

Whatever process your CA uses, the end result should be a TLS/SSL certificate associated with your root domain name and your app's subdomain, as well as the unencrypted RSA-encoded private key. You will upload both of these files to Google in the next step.

Before you can complete this process, you must decide which method App Engine should use to serve your secure traffic. There are two choices: Server Name Indication (SNI) or Virtual IP (VIP). SNI associates one or more certificates with your app's domain name. SNI is a relatively new standard, and only modern web clients (most browsers) support it. If you need broader support for SSL-capable clients, Google also offers a virtual IP (VIP) solution, which ties your certificate and application to an IP address. This expensive resource comes with a monthly fee.

You are now ready to activate SSL for your domain, using the Google Apps Admin console:

1. Open the Google Admin console (*https://admin.google.com/*). Expand "More controls" (located at the bottom of the page), then locate and select Security. Select SSL for Custom Domains, clicking "Show more" if necessary to reveal it.

2. In the panel that opens, enter the project ID for the app. This confirms that the app will be responsible for SSL-related computation.

3. On the following screen,[3] click Enable SSL. You are returned to the Google Apps Admin console to complete the process. Now that SSL is enabled, you can get to this screen at any point in the future by navigating to Security, SSL for Custom Domains.

4. If you wish to use SNI for the certificate, click the "Increase SNI certificate slots by 5" button. If you need the VIP solution, look for the Add a VIP button. If it is disabled with a message prompting you to increase the budget for the app, do so in the Cloud Console, under Compute, App Engine, Settings. The VIP option needs a nonzero budget for its resources.

5. Still in the SSL for Custom Domains screen, click Configure SSL Certificates. In the subsequent screen, click "Upload a new certificate." For the "PEM encoded X.509 certificate," select the certificate file. For the "Unencrypted PEM encoded RSA private key," select the *ssl.key* file. Click Upload. The certificate information appears in the window.

6. In the box that has appeared, under "Current state," change "Serving mode" to the method you have chosen, either SNI or VIP. An Assigned URLs section appears. Use it to assign your subdomain to the certificate. For VIP, use your domain's DNS hosting to add a CNAME record with the value shown. (No DNS change is needed for SNI only.)

7. Click "Save changes."

That's it! It was a long haul, but you now have full HTTPS support for your app on a custom domain. Give it a try: visit your subdomain using the `https://` method in your browser. The browser indicates that a secure connection is successful, usually with an icon in the address bar. In Chrome and other browsers, you can click on the icon to get more information about the certificate.

---

3 As of August 2014, this screen appears on *appengine.google.com,* a website we haven't mentioned yet. This is the old App Engine console, the one App Engine launched with in 2008. It is in the process of being replaced by the Cloud Console. Once the last few features (such as this screen) have been moved to Cloud Console, this old site will be decommissioned. For now, you can use either console to access any of these features.

Authorization with Google Accounts

Back in Chapter 2, we discussed how an App Engine application can integrate with Google Accounts to identify and authenticate users. We saw how an app can use library calls to check whether the user making a request is signed in, access the user's email address, and calculate the sign-in and sign-out URLs of the Google Accounts system. With this API, application code can perform fine-grained access control and customize displays.

Another way to do access control is to leave it to the frontend. With just a little configuration, you can instruct the frontend to protect access to specific URL handlers such that only signed-in users can request them. If a user who is not signed in requests such a URL, the frontend redirects the user to the Google Accounts sign-in and registration screen. Upon successfully signing in or registering a new account, the user is redirected back to the URL.

You can also tell the frontend that only the registered developers of the application can access certain URL handlers. This makes it easy to build administrator-only sections of your website, with no need for code that confirms the user is an administrator. You can manage which accounts have developer status in the Cloud Console, in the Developers section. If you revoke an account's developer status, that user is no longer able to access administrator-only resources, effective immediately.

Later on, we will discuss App Engine services that call your application in response to events. For example, the scheduled tasks service (the "cron" service) can be configured to trigger a request to a URL at certain times of the day. Typically, you want to restrict access to these URLs so not just anybody can call them. For the purposes of access control enforced by the frontend, these services act as app administrators, so restricting these URLs to administrators effectively locks out meddling outsiders while allowing the services to call the app.

This coarse-grained access control is easy to set up in the frontend configuration. And unlike access control in the application code, frontend authentication can restrict access to static files as well as application request handlers.

To establish a frontend access control policy, you use a security constraint in the deployment descriptor. We introduced security constraints earlier when we discussed secure connections. Authentication constraints are similar: they specify the minimum level of a condition required to access a resource.

Here's what an authentication constraint looks like in *web.xml*:

```
<security-constraint>
  <web-resource-collection>
    <web-resource-name>myaccount</web-resource-name>
    <url-pattern>/myaccount/*</url-pattern>
  </web-resource-collection>
```

```
      <auth-constraint>
        <role-name>*</role-name>
      </auth-constraint>
    </security-constraint>
```

As before, the security constraint identifies a resource with a URL pattern, then specifies the constraint to apply. An `<auth-constraint>` element contains a `<role-name>` element that specifies the minimum level of authentication.

`<role-name>` can be one of two values: * (a single asterisk) or `admin`. If the role name is *, then any user that has signed in can access the resource. If the user is not signed in, the frontend sends an HTTP redirect code with the Google Accounts sign-in and registration page as the destination. If the role name is `admin`, then only a user who is both signed in and a registered developer for the application can access the resource.

If a URL does not have an authentication constraint, then anyone can access the URL, regardless of whether the client represents a signed-in user, and regardless of whether the app is set to use a members-only access policy.

Environment Variables

You can use app configuration to specify a list of environment variables to be set prior to calling any request handlers. This is useful to control components that depend on environment variables, without having to resort to hacks in your code to set them.

In Java, you can set both environment variables and system properties in *appengine-web.xml*. You set environment variables with an `<env-variables>` element containing one or more `<env-var>` elements, each with a `name` and a `value`. You set system properties with a `<system-properties>` element containing one or more `<property>` elements. Like so:

```
<system-properties>
  <property name="com.gnero.new-player-strength" value="1000" />
  <property name="com.gnero.beta-shield" value="true" />
</system-properties>

<env-variables>
  <env-var name="ZOMBIE_APOCALYPSE" value="false" />
</env-variables>
```

Inbound Services

Some App Engine services call an application's request handlers in response to external events. For example, the Mail service can call a request handler at a fixed URL when it receives an email message at an email address associated with the app. This is a common design theme in App Engine: all application code is in the form of request handlers, and services that need the app to respond to an event invoke request handlers to do it.

Each service capable of creating inbound traffic must be enabled in app configuration, to confirm that the app is expecting traffic from those services on the corresponding URL paths. To enable these services, provide the `<inbound-services>` element in *appengine-web.xml* with a list of service names:

```
<inbound-services>
  <service>mail</service>
  <service>warmup</service>
</inbound-services>
```

Table 3-1 lists the services that can be enabled this way, and where to find more information about each service.

Table 3-1. Services that create inbound traffic for an app, which must be enabled in service configuration

Service	Description	Name	Handler URLs
Channel Presence	Receive channel connection notifications	`chan nel_presence`	`/_ah/channel/.*`
Mail	Receive email at a set of addresses; see Chapter 14	`mail`	`/_ah/mail/.*`
XMPP Messages	Receive XMPP chat messages; for all XMPP services, see Chapter 15	`xmpp_message`	`/_ah/xmpp/ message/chat/`
XMPP Presence	Receive XMPP presence notifications	`xmpp_presence`	`/_ah/xmpp/presence"/.*`
XMPP Subscribe	Receive XMPP subscription notifications	`xmpp_subscribe`	`/_ah/xmpp/ subscription/.*`
XMPP Error	Receive XMPP error messages	`xmpp_error`	`/_ah/xmpp/error/`
Warmup Requests	Initialize an instance, with warmup requests enabled; see "Warmup Requests" on page 97	`warmup`	`/_ah/warmup`

Custom Error Responses

When your application serves a status code that represents an error (such as 403 Forbidden or 500 Internal Server Error) in a response to a browser, it can also include an HTML page in the body of the response. The browser typically shows this HTML to the user if the browser expected to render a full page for the request. Serving an error page can help prevent the user from being disoriented by a generic error message—or no message at all.

There are cases when an error condition occurs before App Engine can invoke your application code, and must return an error response. For example, if none of the request handler mappings in the app's configuration match the request URL, App Engine has no request handler to call and must return a 404 Not Found message. By default, App Engine adds its own generic HTML page to its error responses.

You can configure custom error content to be used instead of App Engine's error page. You provide the response body in a file included with your app, and mention the file in your application configuration.

To set error pages, add a `<static-error-handler>` element to your *appengine-web.xml*. The element contains a `<handler>` element for each error file:

```
<static-error-handlers>
  <handler file="error.html" />
  <handler error-code="over_quota" file="busy_error.html" />
  <handler error-code="dos_api_denial" file="dos_denial.txt"
          mime-type="text/plain" />
</static-error-handlers>
```

The `file` value specifies the path from the application root directory to the error file. The optional `mime-type` specifies the MIME content type for the file, which defaults to `text/html`.

The `error-code` value associates the error file with a specific error condition. If omitted, the file is associated with every error condition that doesn't have a specific error file of its own. Error codes include the following:

over_quota
: The request cannot be fulfilled because the app has temporarily exceeded a resource quota or limit.

dos_api_denial
: The origin of the request is blocked by the app's denial-of-service protection configuration. (See the App Engine documentation for more information about this feature.)

timeout
: The request handler did not return a response before the request deadline.

 Custom error files must be stored on application servers. They must not be static files. Be careful not to configure static file handlers that match these files.

Java Servlet Sessions

The Java runtime environment includes an implementation of the J2EE HTTP session interface. With sessions enabled, a new visitor to your application is issued a session ID, which is stored in a cookie in the visitor's browser and recalled on all subsequent requests. You can set attributes on the user's session, and these attributes are available during subsequent requests from the same user. The App Engine implementation uses the datastore and memcache to provide this functionality.

To use sessions, you must first enable this functionality in application configuration. In your *appengine-web.xml*, add the `<sessions-enabled>` element:

```
<sessions-enabled>true</sessions-enabled>
```

Session data is written to both the memcache and the datastore, and read from the memcache whenever possible. By default, if session attributes are modified during a request, the request handler updates both the memcache and the datastore before returning the response. You can configure this behavior so the (slower) datastore update is deferred out of the request handler using a task queue. This improves the response time of your request handlers in exchange for a modest risk of temporary session data inconsistency. (We'll discuss the datastore, memcache, and task queues in great detail later in this book, so you may want to refer to those chapters, then reread this paragraph.) In general, it's a good idea to enable this feature.

To enable asynchronous writing of session data to durable storage, add the following element to *appengine-web.xml*:

```
<async-session-persistence enabled="true" />
```

By default, the asynchronous write feature uses the default queue. To use a specific named queue (for example, to configure a more aggressive queue-processing rate), add the `queue-name="…"` attribute to `<async-session-persistence>`.

You access the `HttpSession` object by calling the `getSession()` method on the `HttpServletRequest`. This object has `getAttribute()` and `setAttribute()` methods for manipulating session attributes. With App Engine's implementation, all attribute values must be serializable, so they can be stored in the memcache and datastore.

Here's a simple example of using a session attribute. It prints the value of a session attribute on every request, along with a form that updates the value. When you update the value, it changes. When you reload the page, the previous value persists:

```
import java.io.IOException;
import javax.servlet.http.*;

@SuppressWarnings("serial")
public class TestServlet extends HttpServlet {
    public void doGet(HttpServletRequest req, HttpServletResponse resp)
            throws IOException {
```

```
        resp.setContentType("text/html");

        String v = (String) req.getSession().getAttribute("v");
        if (v != null) {
            // Normally you would HTML-escape this.
            resp.getWriter().println(
                    "<p>v is: " + v + "</p>");
        } else {
            resp.getWriter().println(
                    "<p>v is not set.</p>");
        }

        resp.getWriter().println(
                "<form action=\"/\" method=\"post\">" +
                "<input type=\"text\" name=\"v\" />" +
                "<input type=\"submit\" />" +
                "</form>");
    }

    public void doPost(HttpServletRequest req, HttpServletResponse resp)
            throws IOException {
        String newV = req.getParameter("v");
        if (newV != null) {
            req.getSession().setAttribute("v", newV);
        }
        resp.sendRedirect("/");
    }
}
```

(This assumes TestServlet is mapped to the URL path /.)

CHAPTER 4

Request Handlers and Instances

When a request arrives intended for your application code, the App Engine frontend routes it to the application servers. If an instance of your app is running and available to receive a user request, App Engine sends the request to the instance, and the instance invokes the request handler that corresponds with the URL of the request. If none of the running instances of the app are available, App Engine starts up a new one automatically. App Engine will also shut down instances it no longer needs.

The *instance* is your app's unit of computing power. It provides memory and a processor, isolated from other instances for both data security and performance. Your application's code and data stay in the instance's memory until the instance is shut down, providing an opportunity for local storage that persists between requests.

Within the instance, your application code runs in a *runtime environment*. The environment includes the language interpreter, libraries, and other environment features you selected in your app's configuration. Your app can also access a read-only filesystem containing its files (those that you did not send exclusively to the static file servers). The environment manages all the inputs and outputs for the request handler, setting up the request at the beginning, recording log messages during, and collecting the response at the end.

If you have multithreading enabled, an instance can handle multiple requests concurrently, with all request handlers sharing the same environment. With multithreading disabled, each instance handles one request at a time. Multithreading is one of the best ways to utilize the resources of your instances and keep your costs low. But it's up to you to make sure your request handler code runs correctly when handling multiple requests concurrently.

The runtime environment and the instance are abstractions. They rest above, and take the place of, the operating system and the hardware. It is these abstractions that allow your app to scale seamlessly and automatically on App Engine's infrastructure. At no point must you write code to start or stop instances, load balance requests, or monitor resource utilization. This is provided for you.

In fact, you could almost ignore instances entirely and just focus on request handlers: a request comes in, a request handler comes to life, a response goes out. During its brief lifetime, the request handler makes a few decisions and calls a few services, and leaves no mark behind. The instance only comes into play to give you more control over efficiency: local memory caching, multithreading, and warmup initialization. You can also configure the hardware profile and parameters of instance allocation, which involve trade-offs of performance and cost.

In this chapter, we discuss the features of the runtime environments and instances. We introduce a way of thinking about request handlers, and how they fit into the larger notion of instances and the App Engine architecture. We also cover how to tune your instances for performance and resource utilization.

We'll focus this discussion on App Engine's automatic scaling features for the user-facing parts of an application. In the next chapter, we'll branch out into modules and other scaling patterns, and see how to use instances in various ways to build more complex application architecture.

The Runtime Environment

All code execution occurs in the runtime environment you have selected for your app. There are four major runtime environments: Java, Python 2.7, PHP, and Go. For this version of the book, we're focusing on the Java environment.

The runtime environment manages all the interaction between the application code and the rest of App Engine. To invoke an application to handle a request, App Engine prepares the runtime environment with the request data, calls the appropriate request handler code within the environment, then collects and returns the response. The application code uses features of the environment to read inputs, call services, and calculate the response data.

The environment isolates and protects your app to guarantee consistent performance. Regardless of what else is happening on the physical hardware that's running the instance, your app sees consistent performance as if it is running on a server all by itself. To do this, the environment must restrict the capabilities normally provided by a traditional server operating system, such as the ability to write to the local filesystem.

An environment like this is called a "sandbox": what's yours is yours, and no other app can intrude. This sandbox effect also applies to your code and your data. If a piece of physical hardware happens to be running instances for two different applications, the applications cannot read each other's code, files, or network traffic.

App Engine's services are similarly partitioned on an app-by-app basis, so each app sees an isolated view of the service and its data. The runtime environment includes APIs for calling these services in the form of language-specific libraries. In a few cases, portions of standard libraries have been replaced with implementations that make service calls.

The Sandbox

The runtime environment does not expose the complete operating system to the application. Some functions, such as the ability to create arbitrary network connections, are restricted. This "sandbox" is necessary to prevent other applications running on the same server from interfering with your application (and vice versa). Instead, an app can perform some of these functions using App Engine's scalable services, such as the URL Fetch service.

The most notable sandbox restrictions include the following:

- An app cannot spawn additional processes. All processing for a request must be performed by the request handler's process. Multiple threads within the process are allowed, but when the main thread has returned a response, all remaining threads are terminated. There is a way to create long-lived background threads using modules and manual scaling, but this is an exception. You'll most likely use automatic scaling for handling user traffic, and this is the default.

- An app cannot make arbitrary network connections. Networking features are provided by the App Engine services, such as URL Fetch and Mail.

- The app does not manipulate the socket connection with the client directly. Instead, the app prepares the response data, then exits. App Engine takes care of returning the response. This isolates apps from the network infrastructre, at the expense of preventing some niceties like streaming partial results data.

- An app can only read from the filesystem, and can only read its own code and resource files. It cannot create or modify files. Instead of files, an app can use the datastore to save data.

- An app cannot see or otherwise know about other applications or processes that may be running on the server. This includes other request handlers from the same application that may be running simultaneously.

- An app cannot read another app's data from any service that stores data. More generally, an app cannot pretend to be another app when calling a service, and all services partition data between apps.

These restrictions are implemented on multiple levels, both to ensure that the restrictions are enforced and to make it easier to troubleshoot problems that may be related to the sandbox. For example, some standard library calls have been replaced with behaviors more appropriate to the sandbox.

Quotas and Limits

The sandboxed runtime environment monitors the system resources used by the application and limits how much the app can consume. For the resources you pay for, such as running time and storage, you can lift these limits by allocating a daily resource budget in the Cloud Console. App Engine also enforces several system-wide limits that protect the integrity of the servers and their ability to serve multiple apps.

In App Engine parlance, "quotas" are resource limits that refresh at the beginning of each calendar day (at midnight, Pacific Time). You can monitor your application's daily consumption of quotas using the Cloud Console, in the Quota Details section.

Because Google may change how the limits are set as the system is tuned for performance, we won't state some of the specific values of these limits in this book. You can find the actual values of these limits in the official App Engine documentation. Google has said it will give 90 days' notice before changing limits in a way that would affect existing apps.

Request limits

Several system-wide limits specify how requests can behave. These include the size and number of requests over a period of time, and the bandwidth consumed by inbound and outbound network traffic.

One important request limit is the request timer. An application has 60 seconds to respond to a user request.

Near the end of the 60-second limit, the server raises an exception that the application can catch for the purposes of exiting cleanly or returning a user-friendly error message. In Java, the request timer throws a `com.google.apphosting.api.DeadlineExceededException`.

If the request handler has not returned a response or otherwise exited after 60 seconds, the server terminates the process and returns a generic system error (HTTP code 500) to the client.

The 60-second limit applies to user web requests, as well as requests for web hooks such as incoming XMPP and email requests. A request handler invoked by a task queue or scheduled task can run for up to 10 minutes in duration. Tasks are a convenient and powerful tool for performing large amounts of work in the background. We'll discuss tasks in Chapter 16.

The size of a request is limited to 32 megabytes, as is the size of the request handler's response.

Service limits

Each App Engine service has its own set of quotas and limits. As with system-wide limits, some can be raised using a billing account and a budget, such as the number of recipients the application has sent emails to. Other limits are there to protect the integrity of the service, such as the maximum size of a response to the URL Fetch service.

In Java, the service call throws a `com.google.apphosting.api.ApiProxy.OverQuo taException` when a service limit is exceeded. (Note the `apphosting` package name here, not `appengine`.)

With a few notable exceptions, the size of a service call and the size of the service response are each limited to 1 megabyte. This imposes an inherent limit on the size of datastore entities and memcache values. Although an incoming user request can contain up to 32 megabytes, only 1 megabyte of that data can be stored using a single datastore entity or memcache value.

The datastore has a "batch" API that allows you to store or fetch multiple data objects in a single service call. The total size of a batch request to the datastore is unlimited: you can attempt to store or fetch as many entities as can be processed within an internal timing limit for datastore service calls. Each entity is still limited to 1 megabyte in size.

The memcache also has a batch API. The total size of the request of a batch call to the memcache, or its response, can be up to 32 megabytes. As with the datastore, each memcache value cannot exceed 1 megabyte in size.

The URL Fetch service, which your app can use to connect to remote hosts using HTTP, can issue requests up to 10 megabytes, and receive responses up to 32 megabytes.

We won't list all the service limits here. Google raises limits as improvements are made to the infrastructure, and numbers printed here may be outdated. See the official documentation for a complete list, including the latest values.

Deployment limits

Two limits affect the size and structure of your application's files. A single application file cannot be larger than 32 megabytes. This applies to resource files (code, configuration) as well as static files. Also, the total number of files for an application cannot be larger than 10,000, including resource files and static files. The total size of all files must not exceed 150 megabytes.

These limits aren't likely to cause problems in most cases, but some common tasks can approach these numbers. Some third-party libraries or frameworks can be many hundreds of files. Sites consisting of many pages of text or images (not otherwise stored in the datastore) can reach the file count limit. A site offering video or software for download might have difficulty with the 32-megabyte limit.

Java applications have a common solution for reducing the file count for application code: JARs. If your app has too many *.class* files, simply put them in a JAR file by using the `jar` utility included with the Java development kit. App caching reduces the overhead of unpacking JARs.

Also make sure to use `<static-files>` and `<resource-files>` directives in your *appengine-web.xml* file to exclude the appropriate files. By default, all files outside of *WEB-INF/* belong to both groups, and so are counted *twice*, once for each group. The file count limit is the total count for both groups.

Projects

Each Google account can own or be a member of up to 25 Cloud projects. A Cloud project has exactly one App Engine "app," so you can think of this as being a developer of up to 25 apps. A project includes all of the Cloud resources for a major application, and there isn't much reason to use more than one project toward a single purpose. Features such as App Engine modules (discussed in Chapter 5) and Compute Engine give each project a tremendous amount of flexibility in its architecture and scope. Most services and features that can be used for multiple purposes within a single app have ways of segmenting their data within the app and within the Cloud Console. (For example, you can look at logs for each module and version individually.)

That said, having multiple projects for different purposes is often useful just to keep things organized. Each project has its own billing configuration and list of contributors. A single company that produces multiple web products might have one project per product.

If 25 projects per account is a burden in your case, Google offers more apps with their paid support programs (*https://cloud.google.com/support/*).

Versions

When you deploy your app, it is uploaded as a *version* of your app. The version ID is set either in your *appengine-web.xml* file or as a command-line argument when you deploy. If you deploy an app using the same version ID as a previous deployment, the version is replaced. Otherwise, a new version is created.

All traffic to your live app (on your custom domain or your primary `appspot.com` domain) goes to the *default version*. You can change which version is the default version using the Cloud Console, or with another command-line invocation. Nondefault versions are accessible on separate appspot.com domains. This makes versions a valuable part of your deployment workflow: you can deploy a release candidate to a nondefault version ID, test it, then switch the default version to make the upgrade. See Chapter 19 for more details.

With billing enabled, each app can have up to 60 versions at one time. (The limit is 15 if billing is not enabled.) You can delete unused versions from the Cloud Console.

Billable quotas

Every application gets a limited amount of computing resources for free, so you can start developing and testing your application right away. You can purchase additional computing resources at competitive rates. You only pay for what you actually use, and you specify the maximum amount of money you want to spend.

You can create an app by using the free limits without setting up a billing account. Free apps never incur charges, but are constrained by the free quotas.

When you are ready for your app to accept live traffic or otherwise exceed the free quotas, you enable billing for the app, and set a resource budget. Apps with billing enabled get higher free quotas automatically, and you can keep the resource budget at zero dollars to prevent the app from incurring charges. If you're in a position to associate a credit card with your account, you can claim these extra free resources just by enabling billing.

To enable billing, sign in to the Cloud Console with the developer account that is to be the billing account. Select Billing Settings from the sidebar. Click the Enable Billing button, and follow the prompts to enter your payment information. This billing account applies to all Cloud services you use with the project, including App Engine.

When you are ready to grow beyond the free resource limits, you set a maximum daily resource budget for the app. This limit applies to App Engine resources specifically, such as App Engine–managed computation. For now, it also applies to the Cloud Datastore.[1] The budget specifies the amount of money App Engine can "spend" on resources, at the posted rates, over the course of a day. This budget is in addition to the free quotas: the budget is not consumed until after a resource has exceeded its free quota. After the budget for the calendar day is exhausted, service calls that would require more resources raise an exception. If there are not enough resources remaining to invoke a request handler, App Engine will respond to requests

---

1 Cloud Datastore was originally a feature exclusive to App Engine, and is now a standalone service with a REST API as well as its original App Engine integration. As of September 2014, Datastore billing is still managed by App Engine's quota system, but this may change in the future.

with a generic error message. The budget resets at the beginning of each calendar day (Pacific Time).

To set the budget, visit the Console while signed in with the billing account. Select Compute from the sidebar, then App Engine, then Settings. Adjust the "Daily budget" setting, then click Save. A change to your budget takes about 10 minutes to complete, and you will not be able to change the setting again during those 10 minutes. Figure 4-1 shows the Settings panel with a daily budget being set.

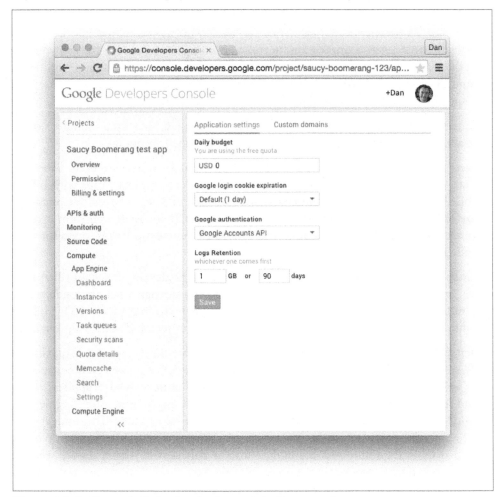

Figure 4-1. Setting a daily budget in the app's Settings panel

It's worth repeating: you are only charged for the resources your app uses. If you set a high daily resource budget and App Engine only uses a portion of it, you are only charged for that portion. Typically, you would test your app to estimate resource consumption, then set the budget generously so every day comes in under the budget. The budget maximum is there to prevent unexpected surges in resource usage from draining your bank account—a monetary surge protector, if you will. If you're expecting a spike in traffic (such as for a product launch), you may want to raise your budget in advance of the event.

The official documentation includes a complete list of the free quota limits, the increased free quota limits with billing enabled, the maximum allocation amounts, and the latest billing rates. You can view the app's current quota consumption by navigating to Compute, App Engine, "Quota details" in the Console.

The Java Runtime Environment

The Java runtime environment behaves like a J2EE servlet container. When the app instance receives a request, it determines the servlet class to call by comparing the URL path to the servlet mappings in the deployment descriptor. The server uses the standard servlet interface to invoke the servlet, passing it a populated request object and an empty response object. The application's servlet code populates the response object and exits, and App Engine returns the response to the client.

The Java runtime environment uses the Java 7 virtual machine (JVM). The JVM runs Java bytecode, which is what you get from passing Java code to a Java compiler. It's also what you get from compilers for other languages that produce Java bytecode, such as Scala, and from interpreters for other languages implemented in Java bytecode, such as JRuby (Ruby), Rhino (JavaScript), Groovy, and even Jython (a Python interpreter implemented in Java). You can use any language that compiles to or has an interpreter for the JVM to write applications for App Engine, as long as the result implements a servlet interface.

Having a complete JVM also means you can use many third-party libraries with your application. Some restrictions apply—we'll look at a few in a moment—but in most cases, using a library is a simple matter of including the JAR or class files in the application's WAR.

An app can ask for information about the current environment by using the System Property API, in the `com.google.appengine.api.utils` package. App Engine sets static fields of this class to the application ID (`applicationId`), the application version (`applicationVersion`), the version of the runtime environment (`version`), and whether the app is running in the development environment or on App Engine (`environment`):

```
import com.google.appengine.api.utils.SystemProperty;

// ...
        String applicationId = SystemProperty.applicationId.get();

        if (SystemProperty.environment.value() ==
            SystemProperty.Environment.Value.Development) {
            // ... only executed in the development server ...
        }
```

In the Java runtime environment, sandbox restrictions are enforced within the JVM. These restrictions are implemented using a combination of JVM permissions, a Java Runtime Environment (JRE) class whitelist, and alternative implementations for specific functions. This fine-grained approach allows more third-party libraries to work and makes other code easier to port than relying on JVM permissions alone.

The Java runtime environment includes a subset of the JRE classes. You can find a complete list of supported JRE classes in the official documentation. The development server enforces this list, so if your code (or some library code) crosses a line, the development server throws an exception.

Reflection is supported for all the app's own classes. Custom class loaders are supported, but with all classes granted the same permissions. Native JNI code is not supported.

The Request Handler Abstraction

Let's review what we know so far about request handlers. A request handler is an entry point into the application code, mapped to a URL pattern in the application configuration. In Java, the entry point is defined as a servlet, and is configured using the Java Enterprise Edition standard *WEB-INF/web.xml* file, like so:

```
<?xml version="1.0" encoding="utf-8"?>
<web-app xmlns:xsi="http://www.w3.org/2001/XMLSchema-instance"
         xmlns="http://java.sun.com/xml/ns/javaee"
         xmlns:web="http://java.sun.com/xml/ns/javaee/web-app_2_5.xsd"
         xsi:schemaLocation="http://java.sun.com/xml/ns/javaee
                             http://java.sun.com/xml/ns/javaee/web-app_2_5.xsd"
         version="2.5">
  <servlet>
    <servlet-name>Profile</servlet-name>
    <servlet-class>myapp.ProfileServlet</servlet-class>
  </servlet>
  <servlet-mapping>
    <servlet-name>Profile</servlet-name>
    <url-pattern>/profile/*</url-pattern>
  </servlet-mapping>
</web-app>
```

The servlet is a class we define that describes how to respond to a request. App Engine invokes the servlet by calling a method that corresponds to the HTTP verb of the request, passing the request data and an empty response object as arguments. The method populates the response object, then returns:

```
package myapp;

import java.io.IOException;

import javax.servlet.RequestDispatcher;
import javax.servlet.ServletException;
import javax.servlet.http.*;

import com.google.appengine.api.datastore.DatastoreService;
import com.google.appengine.api.datastore.DatastoreServiceFactory;
import com.google.appengine.api.datastore.Entity;
import com.google.appengine.api.datastore.Query;
import com.google.appengine.api.datastore.Query.FilterOperator;
import com.google.appengine.api.users.User;
import com.google.appengine.api.users.UserService;
import com.google.appengine.api.users.UserServiceFactory;

@SuppressWarnings("serial")
public class ProfileServlet extends HttpServlet {
    public void doGet(HttpServletRequest req, HttpServletResponse resp)
        throws IOException, ServletException {

        // Call the Users service to identify the user making the request,
        // if the user is signed in.
        UserService userService = UserServiceFactory.getUserService();
        User user = userService.getCurrentUser();

        // Call the Datastore service to retrieve the user's profile data.
        DatastoreService datastore =
            DatastoreServiceFactory.getDatastoreService();
        Entity profile = null;
        if (user != null) {
            Query q = new Query("Profile").setFilter(
                new Query.FilterPredicate(
                    "user",
                    FilterOperator.EQUAL,
                    user));
            profile = datastore.prepare(q).asSingleEntity();
        }

        // Render a response page using a JSP template.
        req.setAttribute("user", user);
        req.setAttribute("profile", profile);
        RequestDispatcher jsp =
            req.getRequestDispatcher("/WEB-INF/profile.jsp");
        jsp.forward(req, resp);
```

        }
    }

When a user visits the URL path /profile/ on this application's domain, App Engine matches the request to ProfileServlet via the application configuration, instantiates the class, then calls its doGet() method to produce the response. The method code makes use of two App Engine services, the Users service and the Datastore service, to access resources outside of the app code. It uses that data to make a web page, then exits.

In theory, the application process only needs to exist long enough to handle the request. When the request arrives, App Engine figures out which request handler it needs, makes room for it in its computation infrastructure, and creates it in a runtime environment. Once the request handler has created the response, the show is over, and App Engine is free to purge the request handler from memory. If the application needs data to live on between requests, it stores it by using a service like the datastore. The application itself does not live long enough to remember anything on its own.

Figure 4-2 illustrates this abstract life cycle of a request handler.

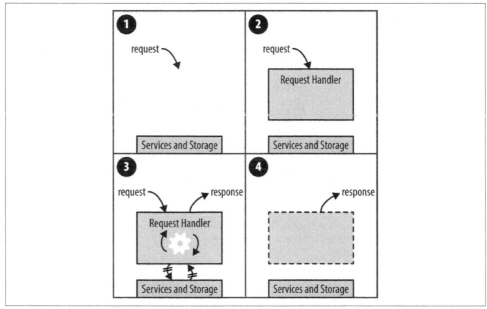

Figure 4-2. Request handlers in the abstract: (1) a request arrives; (2) a request handler is created; (3) the request handler calls services and computes the response; (4) the request handler terminates, the response is returned

On App Engine, a web application can handle many requests simultaneously. There could be many request handlers active at any given moment, in any stage of its life cycle. As shown in Figure 4-3, all these request handlers access the same services.

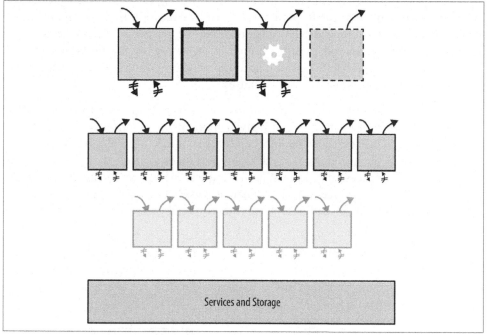

Figure 4-3. A web application handles many requests simultaneously; all request handlers access the same services

Each service has its own specification for managing concurrent access from multiple request handlers, and for the most part, a request handler doesn't have to think about the fact that other request handlers are in play. The big exception here is datastore transactions, which we'll discuss in detail in Chapter 8.

The request handler abstraction is useful for thinking about how to design your app, and how the service-oriented architecture is justified. App Engine can create an arbitrary number of request handlers to handle an arbitrary number of requests simultaneously, and your code barely has to know anything about it. This is how your app scales with traffic automatically.

Introducing Instances

The idea of a web application being a big pot of bubbling request handlers is satisfying, but in practice, this abstraction fails to capture an important aspect of real-world system software. Starting a program for the first time on a fresh system can be expensive: code is read into RAM from disk, memory is allocated, data structures are set up with starting values, and configuration files are read and parsed. App Engine initializes new runtime environments prior to using them to execute request handlers, so the environment initialization cost is not incurred during the handler execution. But application code often needs to perform its own initialization that App Engine can't do on its own ahead of time. The JVM is designed to exploit local memory, and many web application frameworks perform initialization, expecting the investment to pay off over multiple requests. It's wasteful and impractical to do this at the beginning of every request handler, while the user is waiting.

App Engine solves this problem with *instances*, long-lived containers for request handlers that retain local memory. At any given moment, an application has a pool of zero or more instances allocated for handling requests. App Engine routes new requests to available instances. It creates new instances as needed, and shuts down instances that are excessively idle. When a request arrives at an instance that has already handled previous requests, the instance is likely to have already done the necessary preparatory work, and can serve the response more quickly than a fresh instance.

The picture now looks something like Figure 4-4. The request handler still only lives as long as it takes to return the response, but its actions can now affect instance memory. This instance memory remains available to the next request handler that executes inside the instance.

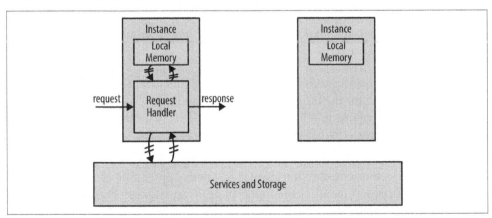

Figure 4-4. An instance handles a request, while another instance sits idle

Keep in mind that instances are created and destroyed dynamically, and requests are routed to instances based purely on availability. While instances are meant to live longer than request handlers, they are as ephemeral as request handlers, and any given request may be handled by a new instance. There is no guarantee that requests of a particular sort will always be handled by the same instance, nor is it assured that an instance will still be around after a given request is handled. Outside of a request handler, the application is not given the opportunity to rescue data from local memory prior to an instance being shut down. If you need to store user-specific information (such as session data), you must use a storage service. Instance memory is only suitable for local caching.

Instances can provide another crucial performance benefit: multithreading. With multithreading enabled in your application configuration, an instance will start additional request handlers in separate threads as local resources allow, and execute them concurrently. All threads share the same instance memory just like any other multithreaded application—which means your code must take care to protect shared memory during critical sections of code. You can use Java's language and library features for synchronizing access to shared memory.

Figure 4-5 illustrates an instance with multithreading enabled. Refer to "Multithreading" on page 60 for information on how to enable or disable multithreading in application configuration.

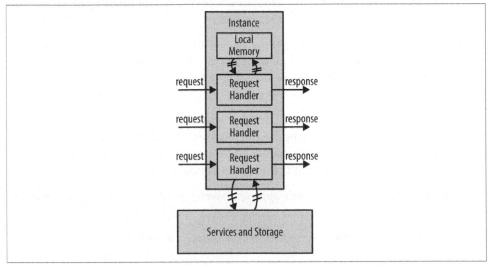

Figure 4-5. A multithreaded instance handles multiple requests concurrently

Instance uptime is App Engine's billable unit for computation, measured in fractions of an *instance hour*. This makes multithreading an important technique for maximizing throughput and minimizing costs. Most request handlers will spend a significant amount of time waiting for service calls, and a multithreaded instance can use the CPU for other handlers during that time.

Request Scheduling and Pending Latency

App Engine routes each request to an available instance. If all instances are busy, App Engine starts a new instance. This is App Engine's *automatic scaling* feature, and is what makes it especially useful for handling real-time user traffic for web and mobile clients.

App Engine considers an instance to be "available" for a request if it believes the instance can handle the request in a reasonable amount of time. With multithreading disabled, this definition is simple: an instance is available if it is not presently busy handling a request.

With multithreading enabled, App Engine decides whether an instance is available based on several factors. It considers the current load on the instance (CPU and memory) from its active request handlers, and its capacity. It also considers historical knowledge of the load caused by previous requests to the given URL path. If it seems likely that the new request can be handled effectively in the capacity of an existing instance, the request is scheduled to that instance.

Incoming requests are put on a *pending queue* in preparation for scheduling. App Engine will leave requests on the queue for a bit of time while it waits for existing instances to become available, before deciding it needs to create new instances. This waiting time is called the *pending latency*.

You can control how App Engine decides when to start and stop instances in response to variances in traffic. App Engine uses sensible defaults for typical applications, but you can tune several variables to your app based on how your app uses computational resources and what traffic patterns you're expecting.

To set these variables, you edit your *appengine-web.xml* file, and add an <automatic-scaling> section, like so:

```
<appengine-web-app xmlns="http://appengine.google.com/ns/1.0">
  <!-- ... -->

  <automatic-scaling>
    <min-pending-latency>automatic</min-pending-latency>
    <max-pending-latency>30ms</max-pending-latency>
  </automatic-scaling>

</appengine-web-app>
```

The *maximum pending latency* (<max-pending-latency>) is the most amount of time a request will wait on the pending queue before App Engine decides more instances are needed to handle the current level of traffic. Lowering the maximum pending latency potentially reduces the average wait time, at the expense of activating more instances. Conversely, raising the maximum favors reusing existing instances, at the expense of potentially making the user wait a bit longer for a response. The setting is a number of milliseconds, with `ms` as the unit.

The *minimum pending latency* (`<min-pending-latency>`) specifies a minimum amount of time a request must be on the pending queue before App Engine can conclude a new instance needs to be started. Raising the minimum encourages App Engine to be more conservative about creating new instances. This minimum only refers to creating new instances. Naturally, if an existing instance is available for a pending request, the request is scheduled immediately. The setting is a number of milliseconds (with the unit: `5ms`), or `automatic` to let App Engine adjust this value on the fly as needed (the default).

Warmup Requests

There is a period of time between the moment App Engine decides it needs a new instance and the moment the instance is available to handle the next request off the request queue. During this time, App Engine initializes the instance on the server hardware, sets up the runtime environment, and makes the app files available to the instance. App Engine takes this preparation period into account when scheduling request handlers and instance creation.

The goal is to make the instance as ready as possible prior to handling the first request, so when the request handler begins, the user only waits on the request handler logic, not the initialization. But App Engine can only do so much on its own. Many initialization tasks are specific to your application code.

App-specific initialization potentially puts undue burden on the first request handler to execute on a fresh instance. A "loading request" typically takes longer to execute than subsequent requests handled by the same instance. This is common enough that App Engine will add a log message automatically when a request is the first request for an instance, so you can detect a correlation between performance issues and app initialization.

You can mitigate the impact of app initialization with a feature called *warmup requests*. With warmup requests enabled, App Engine will attempt to issue a request to a specific warmup URL immediately following the creation of a new instance. You can associate a warmup request handler with this URL to perform initialization tasks that are better performed outside of a user-facing request handler.

To enable warmup requests, activate the `warmup` inbound service in your app configuration. (Refer to "Inbound Services" on page 76.) Set this in your *appengine-web.xml* file:

```
<inbound-services>
  <service>warmup</service>
</inbound-services>
```

Warmup requests are issued to this URL path:

```
/_ah/warmup
```

You bind your warmup request handler to this URL path in the usual way.

 There are a few rare cases where an instance will not receive a warmup request prior to the first user request even with warmup requests enabled. Make sure your user request handler code does not depend on the warmup request handler having already been called on the instance.

Resident Instances

Instances stick around for a while after finishing their work, in case they can be reused to handle more requests. If App Engine decides it's no longer useful to keep an instance around, it shuts down the instance. An instance that is allocated but is not handling any requests is considered an *idle instance*.

Instances that App Engine creates and destroys as needed by traffic demands are known as *dynamic instances*. App Engine uses historical knowledge about your app's traffic to tune its algorithm for dynamic instance allocation to find a balance between instance availability and efficient use of resources.

You can adjust how App Engine allocates instances by using two settings: minimum idle instances and maximum idle instances. To adjust these settings, edit your *appengine-web.xml* file, and set the appropriate values in the `<automatic-scaling>` section, like so:

```
<automatic-scaling>
  <min-idle-instances>0</min_idle_instances>
  <max-idle-instances>automatic</max-idle-instances>
</automatic-scaling>
```

The *minimum idle instances* (`<min-idle-instances>`) setting ensures that a number of instances are always available to absorb sudden increases in traffic. They are started once and continue to run even if they are not being used. App Engine will try to keep resident instances in reserve, starting new instances dynamically (*dynamic instances*) in response to load. When traffic increases and the pending queue heats up, App Engine uses the resident instances to take on the extra load while it starts new dynamic instances.

Setting a nonzero minimum for idle instances also ensures that at least this many instances are never terminated due to low traffic. Because App Engine does not start and stop these instances due to traffic fluctuations, these instances are not dynamic; instead, they are known as *resident instances*.

You *must* enable warmup instances to set the minimum idle instances to a nonzero value.

Reserving resident instances can help your app handle sharp increases in traffic. For example, you may want to increase the resident instances prior to launching your product or announcing a new feature. You can reduce them again as traffic fluctuations return to normal.

App Engine only maintains resident instances for the default version of your app. While you can make requests to nondefault versions, only dynamic instances will be created to handle those requests. When you change the default version (in the Versions panel of the Cloud Console), the previous resident instances are allowed to finish their current request handlers, then they are shut down and new resident instances running the new default version are created.

 Resident instances are billed at the same rate as dynamic instances. Be sure you want to pay for 24 instance hours per day per resident instance before changing this setting. It can be annoying to see these expensive instances get little traffic compared to dynamic instances. But when an app gets high traffic at variable times, the added performance benefit may be worth the investment.

The *maximum idle instances* (`<max-idle-instances>`) setting adjusts how aggressively App Engine terminates idle instances above the minimum. Increasing the maximum causes idle dynamic instances to live longer; decreasing the maximum causes them to die more quickly. A larger maximum is useful for keeping more dynamic instances available for rapid fluctuations in traffic, at the expense of greater unused (dynamic) capacity. The name "maximum idle instances" is not entirely intuitive, but it opposes "minimum idle instances" in an obvious way: the maximum can't be lower than the minimum. A setting of `automatic` lets App Engine decide how quickly to terminate instances based on traffic patterns.

Instance Classes and Utilization

App Engine uses several factors to decide when to assign a request to a given instance. If the request handlers currently running on an instance are consuming most of the instance's CPU or memory, App Engine considers the instance fully utilized, and either looks for another available instance, leaves the request on the pending queue, or schedules a new instance to be started.

For safety's sake, App Engine also assumes a maximum number of concurrent requests per instance. The default maximum is 10 concurrent request handlers. If you know in advance that your request handlers consume few computational resources on an instance, you can increase this limit to as much as 100. To do so, in the *appengine-web.xml* file, edit the `<automatic-scaling>` section to include the `<max-concurrent-requests>` setting:

```
<automatic-scaling>
  <!-- ... -->
  <max-concurrent-requests>20</max-concurrent-requests>
</automatic-scaling>
```

Naturally, App Engine may consider an instance utilized when fewer request handlers than the maximum are running. The maximum just gives App Engine some guidance as to what's typical, so it can start more instances before the existing instances get too hot.

Another way to fit more concurrent requests onto an instance is to just use instances with more memory and faster CPUs. The *instance class* determines the computational resources available to each instance. By default, App Engine uses the smallest instance class. Larger instance classes provide more resources at a proportionally higher cost per instance hour.

You set the instance class for the app using the `<instance-class>` setting in *appengine-web.xml*:

```
<appengine-web-app xmlns="http://appengine.google.com/ns/1.0">
  <!-- ... -->

  <instance-class>F4</instance-class>

</appengine-web-app>
```

With automatic scaling, you can choose from the following instance classes:

F1
: 128 MB of memory, 600 MHz CPU (this is the default)

F2
: 256 MB of memory, 1.2 GHz CPU

F4
: 512 MB of memory, 2.4 GHz CPU

F4_1G
: 1024 MB (1 GB) of memory, 2.4 GHz CPU

Instance Hours and Billing

Instance use is a resource measured in instance hours. An instance hour corresponds to an hour of clock time that an instance is alive. An instance is on the clock regardless of whether it is actively serving traffic or is idle, or whether it is resident or dynamic.

Each instance incurs a mandatory charge of 15 minutes, added to the end of the instance's lifespan. This accounts for the computational cost of instance creation and other related resources. This is one reason why you might adjust the minimum pending latency and maximum idle instances settings to avoid excess instance creation.

The free quotas include a set of instance hours for dynamic instances. The free quota for dynamic instances is enough to power one instance of the most basic class ("F1") continuously, plus a few extra hours per day.

Computation is billed by the instance hour. Larger instance classes have proportionally larger costs per instance hour. See the official documentation for the current rates. (This industry is competitive, and prices change more frequently than books do.)

The Instances Console Panel

The Cloud Console includes a panel for inspecting your app's currently active instances. A portion of such a panel is shown in Figure 4-6. In the sidebar navigation, this is the Instances panel under Compute, App Engine.

You can use this panel to inspect the general behavior of your application code running in an instance. This includes summary information about the number of instances, and averages for QPS, latency, and memory usage per instance over the last minute of activity. Each active instance is also itemized, with its own QPS and latency averages, total request and error counts over the lifetime of the instance, the age of the instance, current memory usage, and whether the instance is resident or dynamic. You can query the logs for requests handled by the individual instance.

You can also shut down an instance manually from this panel. If you shut down a resident instance, a new resident instance will be started in its place, effectively like restarting the instance. If you shut down a dynamic instance, a new instance may or may not be created as per App Engine's algorithm and the app's idle instance settings.

As with several other Console panels, the Instances panel is specific to the selected version of your app. If you want to inspect instances handling requests for a specific app version, be sure to select it from the Console's app version drop-down at the top of the screen.

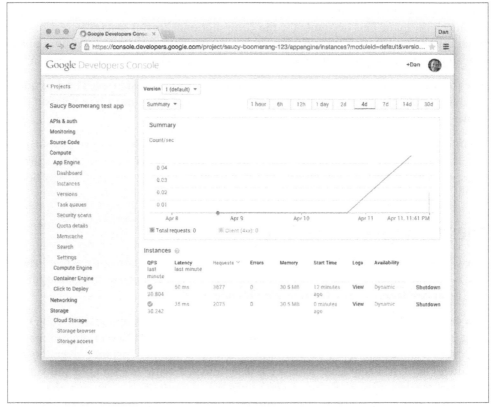

Figure 4-6. The Instances panel of the Cloud Console

Traffic Splitting

The most important use of versions is to test new software candidates before launching them to all of your users. You can test a nondefault version yourself by addressing its version URL, while all of your live traffic goes to the default version. But what if you want to test a new candidate with a percentage of your actual users? For that, you use traffic splitting.

With traffic splitting enabled, App Engine identifies the users of your app, partitions them according to percentages that you specify, and routes their requests to the versions that correspond to their partitions. You can then analyze the logs of each version separately to evaluate the candidate for issues and other data.

To enable traffic splitting, go to the Versions panel. If you have more than one module, select the module whose traffic you want to split. (We'll look at modules in more depth in Chapter 5.) Click the "Enable traffic splitting" button, and set the parameters for the traffic split in the dialog that opens.

The dialog asks you to decide whether users should be identified by IP address or by a cookie. Splitting by cookie is likely to be more accurate for users with browser clients, and accommodates cases where a single user might appear to be sending requests from multiple IP addresses. If the user is not using a client that supports cookies, or you otherwise don't want to use them, you can split traffic by IP address. The goal is for each user to always be assigned the same partition throughout a session with multiple requests, so clients don't get confused talking to multiple versions, and your experiment gets consistent results.

Traffic splitting occurs with requests sent to the main URL for the app or module. Requests for the version-specific URLs bypass traffic splitting.

CHAPTER 5

Using Modules

You can build large web applications using just App Engine's automatically scaling instances, and many have. Automatic scaling is well suited to large scale user traffic and can accommodate real-world traffic spikes with ease. But it isn't long before you want to do more computational tasks with App Engine besides serving user traffic and residual tasks. Other parts of a mature app's architecture, such as batch jobs, long-running computing tasks, and special purpose always-on backend services, don't quite fit the same mold. Performance tuning that's suited to one kind of computation doesn't suit another. Your web traffic may work well with small instance classes and aggressive pending queues, while your nightly data crawl needs more memory on a single instance. And you probably don't want your user traffic instance pool saturated by a batch job.

App Engine lets you define sets of instances for different purposes, called *modules*. Each module can be configured and tuned separately using all of the options we've discussed so far, such as instance classes and automatic scaling parameters. Each module gets its own URL, so it can be addressed individually. You can make a module's URL publicly accessible or just call it internally from other modules. Each module can scale its own instances according to its purpose-specific traffic patterns.

For even greater flexibility, App Engine offers two additional scaling patterns beyond automatic scaling: *manual scaling* and *basic scaling*. With manual scaling, you start and stop instances directly using the Cloud SDK or within the app by calling an API. Basic scaling has the same features as manual scaling, with the addition of a simple configurable scheduler that can start new instances in response to requests and stop idle instances after a period of time. Each module can be configured to use any of the three available scaling strategies.

Modules can also be deployed separately from each other, at separate times and with separate versions. It's easiest to use the same code base for all modules, but this gives you more options as to when software versions are deployed or rolled back.

With modules, you can design an architecture that meets your application's needs, and develop and tune each component separately.

An Example Layout

Let's consider a simple modular architecture for our hypothetical multiplayer game. Refer to Figure 5-1.

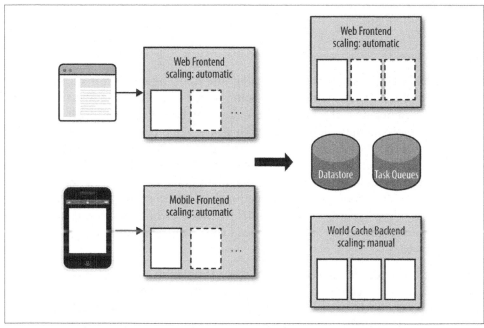

Figure 5-1. An example of an application architecture using modules

In this example, a "web frontend" module handles all of the user traffic coming from browsers, using the automatic scaling strategy. This is the default module for the website for the game, and serves all traffic for the main domain name. All apps have at least one module, and typically the default module uses automatic scaling. The example apps we've discussed so far have one module using this default configuration.

This multiplayer game has a mobile app. The mobile app communicates with the App Engine app via an API hosted in the "mobile frontend" module, with its own URL. Just like the web frontend, this API traffic comes from users, so we use automatic scaling for this module as well. Making it a separate module from the web traffic isolates it for the purposes of performance tuning and makes it easier to deploy changes to the web and mobile experiences separately. We may want to coordinate API support with mobile app store releases, or provision additional resident instances in anticipation of a scheduled mobile launch.

Both user-facing frontend modules use small instance classes and run code tailored to produce fast responses to user client requests. They communicate with the built-in App Engine services as usual, such as the datastore, memcache, and task queue services. We use two additional modules to provide custom services of our own.

The "battle simulation backend" service performs heavy-duty computation for updating the game world in response to major events. We configure this module to use a large instance class to take advantage of the faster CPU. We use the basic scaling strategy for this so we can provision more instances automatically, up to a fixed maximum number of instances. If we eventually discover that we need more battle simulation instances, we can evaluate the costs and benefits, and adjust the configuration accordingly. We might use the "pull queue" feature of the task queue service to send work to this backend, or we can call it directly from the frontends using an API of our own design. (For more information on task queues, see Chapter 16.)

The "world cache backend" maintains a copy of the data that describes the game world. This module is configured to use an instance class with a large amount of RAM and a fixed number of always-on resident instances. Of course, we must persist the game world to the datastore on a regular basis or risk losing data. So (in this hypothetical example) we use a *write-behind cache* that updates RAM first then periodically flushes to the datastore with minimal risk of loss. We use manual scaling because we want this special cache to stay resident as long as possible, and the amount of memory we need is proportional to the size of the world, not to the number of active users.

This example is simplified for illustration purposes; a real multiplayer game architecture might be more sophisticated. This provides a basic idea of how separate modules with distinct configurations allow you to optimize costs and performance.

Configuring Modules

The simple examples of apps we've seen so far have used only one module, the default module configured with automatic scaling. Your Java project builds a standard Java Web Application Archive (WAR), including compiled code, static files, and configuration kept in a *WEB-INF/* subdirectory. The code and configuration of the WAR represents the contents of the default module. More specifically, it is the contents of a version of the default module, the version whose ID appears as the <version> in the *appengine-web.xml* file.

When you deploy a WAR to App Engine, App Engine checks the *appengine-web.xml* file for the application ID and the version ID, then sets up the WAR as the given version of the default module in the given application. It knows to use the default module because no module ID is specified in the file. To declare that the WAR is intended for a module other than the default, you add the desired module name as the `<module>` element in *appengine-web.xml*.

Continuing the previous example, we can configure the mobile frontend module (`mobile-fe`) like so:

```xml
<?xml version="1.0" encoding="utf-8"?>
<appengine-web-app xmlns="http://appengine.google.com/ns/1.0">
  <application>saucy-boomerang-123</application>
  <module>mobile-fe</module>
  <version>1</version>
  <threadsafe>true</threadsafe>

  <instance-class>F2</instance-class>
  <automatic-scaling>
    <min-idle-instances>3</min-idle-instances>
  </automatic-scaling>

</appengine-web-app>
```

One way to create an app with multiple modules is to create separate WARs, then configure them with matching app IDs and distinct module IDs, omitting `<module>` for the default module. But this is far from the best way. In most cases, you need the ability to test multiple modules together in a single development server, and to deploy all of an application's modules with one action.

Java EE's solution is the Enterprise Archive (EAR), a standard structure for bundling multiple module WARs and application-wide configuration. You can deploy an EAR to App Engine just as you can a single WAR, and App Engine will install all of the modules it finds. As with the WAR, an EAR is just a Java archive or directory in a standard structure.

First, we'll look at the structure of the final EAR that gets deployed to App Engine. Then we'll see how to set up a development environment to build the EAR using Eclipse Web Tools.

The Enterprise Archive Layout

The root of an Enterprise Archive contains one directory for each module, including one for the default module. It's typical to name the directory after the module, but this is not required: App Engine gets the module name from the inner *appengine-web.xml* file. Each module directory is the root for the module's WAR, and has the same structure we've already seen with single-module apps, with built JARs, data files, and a *WEB-INF/* directory for module-specific configuration.

The root also contains a *META-INF/* directory. Inside this directory are two files: *application.xml* and *appengine-application.xml*.

application.xml is a Java EE standard file that lists the modules in the application. For our example App Engine app, it looks like this:

```
<?xml version="1.0" encoding="utf-8"?>
<application xmlns="http://java.sun.com/xml/ns/javaee"
  xmlns="http://java.sun.com/xml/ns/javaee"
  xmlns:xsi="http://www.w3.org/2001/XMLSchema-instance"
  xsi:schemaLocation="http://java.sun.com/xml/ns/javaee
                      http://java.sun.com/xml/ns/javaee/application_5.xsd"
  version="5">

  <description>Saucy Boomerang: The Game</description>
  <display-name>Saucy Boomerang</display-name>

  <module>
    <web>
      <web-uri>default</web-uri>
      <context-root>default</context-root>
    </web>
  </module>
  <module>
    <web>
      <web-uri>mobile-fe</web-uri>
      <context-root>mobile-fe</context-root>
    </web>
  </module>
  <module>
    <web>
      <web-uri>battle-sim</web-uri>
      <context-root>battle-sim</context-root>
    </web>
  </module>
  <module>
    <web>
      <web-uri>world-cache</web-uri>
      <context-root>world-cache</context-root>
    </web>
  </module>
</application>
```

All of these elements are required to meet the Java EE schema. Only the `<web-uri>` elements are actually useful: they must match the `<module>` IDs in each module's *appengine-web.xml* file. The `<context-root>` element is required but ignored. The `default` module is required and must be listed first.

appengine-application.xml is specific to App Engine. It declares the application ID to use with all modules in the EAR:

```
<?xml version="1.0" encoding="utf-8"?>
<appengine-application xmlns="http://appengine.google.com/ns/1.0">
  <application>saucy-boomerang-123</application>
</appengine-application>
```

In summary, here is the general layout of an EAR with these modules, where `main` is the default module:

```
META-INF/
  application.xml
  appengine-application.xml

battle-sim/
  WEB-INF/
    appengine-web.xml
    web.xml

main/
  WEB-INF/
    appengine-web.xml
    web.xml

mobile-fe/
  WEB-INF/
    appengine-web.xml
    web.xml

world-cache/
  WEB-INF/
    appengine-web.xml
    web.xml
```

Making Modules with Eclipse

You can develop and deploy apps with multiple modules from Eclipse using a combination of the Google Plugin for Eclipse and Eclipse Web Tools Platform. We covered how to get the Google Plugin in Chapter 2. The Eclipse Web Tools Platform (WTP) is included with the Eclipse Java EE bundle. If you did not acquire the Java EE bundle when you installed Eclipse, you must install WTP (*http://wiki.eclipse.org/WTP_FAQ#How_do_I_install_WTP.3F*) before proceeding.

The general strategy for developing one app with multiple modules is to create a separate "Dynamic Web Project" for each module, and associate them with a central "EAR project." WTP knows how to interact with the Google Plugin and the App Engine Java SDK to run all of the modules in a single development server, and deploy them as a single application.

Create your first module by navigating to File, New, Other.... In the new object wizard, expand the Web category, then select the Dynamic Web Project type. Click the Next button to run the wizard, shown in Figure 5-2.

Figure 5-2. The Dynamic Web Project wizard in Eclipse, with values for a new module

If this is the first time you've created a Dynamic Web Project for App Engine, you may need to update the target runtime. The "Google App Engine" runtime is probably selected by default, but the wizard will complain that it isn't valid. Under "Target runtime," click the New Runtime... button. Make sure the Google App Engine type is selected, then click Finish. The new runtime appears with the version number, such as "Google App Engine (1.9.18)."

Under "Configuration," ensure that the "Default Configuration for Google App Engine" is selected.

Under "EAR membership," check the box for "Add project to an EAR." Enter a name for the EAR project. This project will be created automatically by the wizard if it doesn't exist.

Click the Next button for an additional screen of options. Enter your application ID, and this module's version and module IDs. These values will appear in the generated configuration files. If you omit these values or skip this screen, you can always edit the configuration files later.

Finally, click Finish. The wizard creates the module project and the EAR project.

For subsequent modules for the same application, the process is the same, except you select the existing EAR project for the EAR membership field.

The EAR project has an *EarContent* folder with the app's *META-INF* folder in it with prepared files. Eclipse adds each new module to the *application.xml* file automatically. The *appengine-application.xml* file has boilerplate, and if you entered the application ID on the second screen of the wizard, it appears in this file.

The module projects are all created with appropriate starter files. The layout used by the Dynamic Web Project wizard differs slightly from the one used by the Google Plugin's Web Application Project wizard we covered earlier, but the main pieces are there, including the *appengine-web.xml* file. Figure 5-3 shows the project layout created by the Dynamic Web Project wizard for four modules and one EAR project.

WTP needs a "server" configured before it will run the app in a local development server. If it isn't already selected, switch to the Java EE perspective (such as via the Window menu, Open Perspective...). Select the Servers panel, then click the helpful link to create a new server. In the dialog that opens, make sure the Google App Engine server type is selected, and change the "Server runtime environment" to match the one used by the modules ("Google App Engine (1.9.18)").

Click Next. You can adjust the options on this screen (such as the server port) if you like, but the defaults are usually fine. Click Next again. Add the EAR project and all of its modules to the "Configured" column, either by selecting the EAR project and clicking Add, or by clicking Add All.

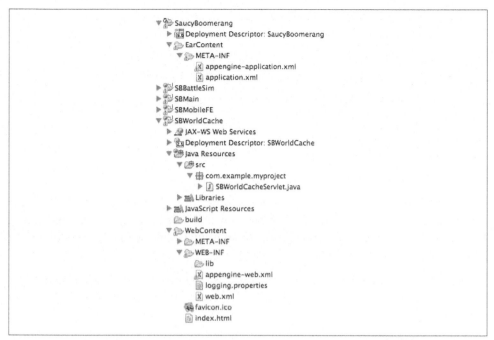

Figure 5-3. The file layout created by the Dynamic Web Project wizard for four modules and one EAR project

Finally, click Finish. The new server appears in the Servers panel.

To start the development server, select the EAR project in the Project Explorer. Go to the Run menu, select Run As, then Run on Server. Confirm that you want to use the server you just created with this project, optionally checking the "Always use this server" checkbox. Click Finish. The development server starts.

Similarly, to run the development server in the debugger, go to the Run menu, select Debug As, then Debug on Server.

Manual and Basic Scaling

By default, modules use the automatic scaling strategy. As we saw in Chapter 4, you can configure elements of this strategy using an `<automatic-scaling>` element in the module's *appengine-web.xml* file. Automatic scaling is selected for the module if this element is present, or if this element is absent and no other scaling strategy is configured.

To declare that the module uses a manual scaling strategy, include a `<manual-scaling>` element in the configuration (and do not include an `<automatic-scaling>`

element). Our game's world data cache is scaled manually with five instances to start, so it can be configured like so:

```
<appengine-web-app xmlns="http://appengine.google.com/ns/1.0">
  <!-- ... -->

  <instance-class>B4_1G</instance-class>

  <manual-scaling>
    <instances>5</instances>
  </manual-scaling>

</appengine-web-app>
```

The `<instances>` element sets the number of instances started when the configuration is deployed for the first time. You can start and stop instances after deployment by hand with the Cloud Console or programmatically with the modules API (described in "The Modules API" on page 127).

To declare that the module uses basic scaling, use the `<basic-scaling>` element. We can use this for our game's battle simulation infrastructure, which is only needed on demand:

```
<appengine-web-app xmlns="http://appengine.google.com/ns/1.0">
  <!-- ... -->

  <instance-class>B8</instance-class>

  <manual-scaling>
    <max-instances>10</max-instances>
    <idle-timeout>5m</idle-timeout>
  </manual-scaling>

</appengine-web-app>
```

With basic scaling, `<max-instances>` is the maximum number of instances to start in response to requests to the module. If a request arrives when all instances are busy and the number of active instances is less than the maximum, a new instance is started. `<idle-timeout>` is the amount of time an instance must be idle before it is shut down automatically, specified as a number and a unit (m for minutes).

Modules with manual or basic scaling use a different set of instance classes than modules with automatic scaling: B1, B2, B4, B4_1G, and B8. These are similar to the corresponding F* classes, with the addition of B8, which has 1 GB of memory and a 4.8 GHz CPU. If not specified, the default instance class for manual or basic scaling is B2.

Manual Scaling and Versions

You can create multiple versions of a module by changing the `<version>` element in its configuration file, then deploying the module. Exactly one version is the default version for the module, and you can change the default version using the Cloud Console or the `appcfg` command. You can delete unused versions from the Cloud Console or the `appcfg.sh` command as well.

With manual scaling, App Engine starts the requested number of instances when the module is deployed. If you have multiple versions of a manually scaled module, App Engine may be running the requested number of instances for *each* version of the module. Be sure to delete unused versions or shut down their instances to avoid burning through your quota or your budget.

This is different from automatic scaling and resident (minimum idle) instances: resident instances are only started and maintained for the default version. Manual scaling instances are started for all versions when they are deployed, and stay running until they are shut down via the Cloud Console, the `appcfg` command, or an API call.

Startup Requests

An instance does not run any code until it receives a request. This is reasonable for modules that respond to requests, such as a service that waits for an API call before doing any work. In many cases, you probably want the instance to start doing some work right away, either to kick off a long-running process or to prepare the instance for responding to future events.

When App Engine starts an instance in a module with manual or basic scaling, it issues a "start" request at the following URL path:

```
/_ah/start
```

You can map a request handler to this path in the deployment descriptor (the *web.xml* file). This handler is called on each instance that is started.

If the start handler returns, it must return an HTTP status code indicating success (200–299). A 404 status code is also considered "success," in case there is no handler mapped to the URL path. If the handler returns a server error, App Engine considers the instance startup to have failed and terminates the instance. It then starts a new instance, if needed.

An instance will not respond to other requests until the start handler has returned. If the module does not need to respond to requests, then you can put all of the module's work in the start handler. The start handler can even be a continuously running process: modules with manual scaling do not have a request deadline. If the module must do both background work and respond to requests, a better option is for the start handler to create a background thread, then exit immediately. We'll look at background threads in a moment.

Startup requests for modules with manual and basic scaling are similar to warmup requests for automatic scaling, but you set them up in different ways and use them for different purposes. (Refer back to "Warmup Requests" on page 97.)

Shutdown Hooks

There are two ways that application code can know when an instance is being shut down. One is to call a method periodically. The `getInstance()` static method of the `LifecycleManager` class (from the `com.google.appengine.api` package) returns an object of the class that represents the App Engine instance. Its `isShuttingDown()` method returns `true` if the instance is about to be shut down:

```
import com.google.appengine.api.LifecycleManager;
// ...

@SuppressWarnings("serial")
public class StartServlet extends HttpServlet {
    public void doGet(HttpServletRequest req, HttpServletResponse resp)
            throws IOException {

        // Initialization.
        // ...

        while (!LifecycleManager.getInstance().isShuttingDown()) {
            // Do a bit of work...
        }

        // Clean up.
        // ...
    }
}
```

Alternatively, the app can register a *shutdown hook* with the runtime environment. To implement a hook, create a class that implements the `LifecycleManager.Shutdown Hook` interface with a `shutdown()` method. Register the hook by providing an object of this class to the `LifecycleManager`'s `setShutdownHook()` method. App Engine calls the `shutdown()` method when it is about to shut down the instance.

The `LifecycleManager` returned by `LifecycleManager.getInstance()` includes a method named `interruptAllRequests()`. You can call this method from the shutdown hook to cancel all threads on the instance. This makes it easy for the shutdown hook to interrupt all work in progress and coordinate cleanup efforts.

Here's an example using an anonymous class for the shutdown hook:

```
import com.google.appengine.api.LifecycleManager;
import com.google.appengine.api.LifecycleManager.ShutdownHook;

// ...
        LifecycleManager.getInstance().setShutdownHook(
            new ShutdownHook() {
                public void shutdown() {
                    LifecycleManager.getInstance().interruptAllRequests();

                    // Clean up.
                    // ...
                }
            });

    // Initialization.
    // ...

    while (true) {
        // Do work...
    }
```

Once App Engine has decided to shut down an instance, the app has 30 seconds after the shutdown hook is called to finish what it is doing. At the end of the 30 seconds, the instance goes away.

Neither the shutdown hook nor the 30-second runway are guaranteed. Under rare circumstances, App Engine may need to kill an instance before the shutdown hook can be called or completed. Long-running processes should persist their state periodically and be able to recover from a sudden interruption.

App Engine logs a request to the URL path /_ah/stop when it initiates shutdown on an instance. You can't map a request handler to this URL: it uses a built-in handler that invokes the shutdown hook. You can look for this request in the logs when you're troubleshooting issues with shutdown logic.

Background Threads

During a request handler, an app can invoke regular Java threads to perform concurrent work. Once the handler returns a response, App Engine assumes that any unfinished threads are no longer needed and terminates them. Regular threads cannot outlast the request handler. This isn't a problem for modules that do request handling with automatic scaling, as the request handler exits once it has a response and can use other means (such as task queues) to defer work. Nor is this a problem for a simple always-on instance with manual scaling, which can perform a large or continuously running job in its start handler and manage threads inside that process without terminating.

We need another solution for the case where a module with manual scaling needs to perform work in the background and also accept requests. Putting the background job in the start handler is insufficient because the instance can't accept requests until the start handler finishes. Instead, we need a way to initiate work from the start handler, then exit from the handler while the work continues in the background.

For this purpose, App Engine provides *background threads,* a special kind of thread that detaches from the request handler and continues running after the handler returns. Only instances with manual or basic scaling can use background threads.

The ThreadManager class of the com.google.appengine.api package provides utilities for creating background threads. The static method createBackgroundThread() takes a java.lang.Runnable as an argument and starts the thread running the given code. You can also create regular (request-bound) threads with this class, and get thread factories of both types:

```
import com.google.appengine.api.ThreadManager;

// ...
    Thread thread = ThreadManager.createBackgroundThread(
        new Runnable() {
            public void run() {
                while (true) {
                    // Do work...
                }
            }
        });

    thread.start();
```

Log messages for background tasks appear in your logs under a virtual request for the URL /_ah/background. The virtual request information includes the ID of the instance on which it is running, and how much time has elapsed since it was started.

Modules and the Development Server

The development server can run multiple modules simultaneously on your local machine. Each module gets its own port number on localhost, chosen automatically from the available ports. The development server prints the selected port numbers for each module to the console as it starts up:

```
... com.google.appengine.tools.development.AbstractModule startup
INFO: Module instance world-cache is running at http://localhost:55500/
... com.google.appengine.tools.development.AbstractModule startup
INFO: The admin console is running at http://localhost:55500/_ah/admin
```

You can use these ports to send test traffic to modules directly. Traffic to the module ports is distributed to instances according to the scaling policy for the module.

Notice that the development server reports that each module has its own development console (/_ah/admin). These consoles all do the same thing, and have no module-specific features.

The development server simulates automatic scaling and manual scaling. For modules configured with basic scaling, the development server initializes the maximum number of instances, then issues the /_ah/start request for each instance when the instance receives its first request.

Unfortunately, there is no way to shut down a simulated instance in the development server. To test your shutdown hook, you must deploy the app to App Engine. When running on App Engine, you can shut down instances manually from the command line or the Cloud Console.

 When calling one module from another, you do not need to hard-code the localhost URLs into your app for testing. Instead, you can determine the URL for a module by calling a function. See "Addressing Modules with URLs" on page 120.

Deploying Modules

In Chapter 2, we saw two ways to deploy a single-module app: via a menu option provided by the Google Plugin for Eclipse, or with the appcfg update command.

To deploy an EAR project from Eclipse, you do not use the Google Plugin's menu option directly. Instead, you use a WTP menu option provided by the Google Plugin. In the Java EE perspective, locate the Servers panel. Right-click on the Google App Engine server you created earlier. In the pop-up menu, locate Google App Engine WTP, then select Deploy to Remote Server. You may be prompted to sign in or enter an application ID if you hadn't done that earlier. The app and all of its modules are deployed.

Deploying a module with manual or basic scaling causes all of its active instances to be stopped and started. If you know a module hasn't changed and you do not want its instances to be restarted when you deploy, be sure to exclude that module's configuration file from the appcfg update command.

The appcfg update command we saw earlier accepted a WAR as its argument, either in the form of an archive file or a directory with the appropriate contents. You can also use the appcfg update command with an EAR file or directory, if you have your own way of building it. Deploying the EAR this way uploads all modules in the archive:

```
appcfg update ear
```
You can also deploy each module WAR individually this way.

 So if the runtime environment is selected by a field in the module's configuration file, and each module can be deployed separately with different code, does that mean one app can use different runtime environments for different modules? Can you have one module implemented in Java and another module implemented in Python?

The answer is yes (!), with a proviso. You can write a module in Python and deploy it to an app that already has another module (possibly the default module) in Java, using the same application ID, different module IDs, and different runtime configurations. The proviso is that you can't easily test interactions between the two modules in a development server. The Java app and the Python app must run in separate development servers from their corresponding SDKs, and these development servers know nothing about each other. They can't share a simulated datastore or other data services, and they don't know each other's development URLs automatically. At the very least, you'd have to implement a layer that detects whether the app is in a development server (via `System Property.environment.value()` in Java) and stub out the service calls.

This is still a useful scenario if you're willing to develop and test the modules separately, which is a reasonable thing to do anyway. And you can always deploy nondefault versions to App Engine for integration testing.

Also notice that if you're using an EAR, the EAR must own the default module. You can create a single-module app and configure it as a module to avoid this requirement.

Addressing Modules with URLs

We've already seen how you can access a deployed application using its `appspot.com` URL, with the application ID as the leftmost subdomain:

```
http://app-id.appspot.com/
```

We now know that this URL accesses the *default version* of the *default module*. The default version is the version selected as the default in the Versions panel of the Cloud Console. The default module is the module whose configuration file omits the `mod ule:` parameter or sets it to `default`, typically *app.yaml*.

If the app has multiple modules, each module gets its own domain name. This domain is formed by taking the `appspot.com` URL for the app and prefixing the module ID:

```
http://module-id.app-id.appspot.com/
```

This URL accesses the default version of the specified module. If the module has multiple instances, App Engine routes a web request for this URL to an instance selected by its load-balancing algorithm. With automatic scaling, and with basic scaling where the number of active instances is below the configured maximum, App Engine may start a new instance if all active instances are busy, though this doesn't have an immediate impact on where the current request is routed.

You may recall that it's possible to access a specific version of an app, with a URL like this:

```
http://version-id.app-id.appspot.com/
```

More specifically, this accesses a specific version of the default module. You've probably already guessed that this means there's a potential for version IDs on the default module and module IDs to conflict, and you're right. You can't use the same ID for a module and one of the versions of the default module.

You've also probably guessed that it's possible to access a specific version of a specific module, and you're right again:

```
http://version-id.module-id.app-id.appspot.com/
```

If a module with manual or basic scaling has multiple instances, you can address the instance directly with one more piece of the domain:

```
http://instance-id.module-id.app-id.appspot.com/
```

In this case, the instance ID must be a running instance of the default version for the module. You can also access an instance of a nondefault version of a module using the longest possible URL, containing all of the IDs:

```
http://instance-id.version-id.module-id.app-id.appspot.com/
```

Instance IDs are determined at runtime, so you need to call an API to figure out what they are. We'll see how in "The Modules API" on page 127.

Calling Modules from Other Modules

One of the most common uses of modules is to build backend services for other modules to access via endpoints. You can send a request from one module to another using the URL Fetch service, an App Engine service that manages outgoing HTTP requests. (See Chapter 13 for a complete introduction to this service.) The request can go to the module's URL, like any other:

```
import java.net.URL;
import java.net.MalformedURLException;
import java.io.IOException;
import java.io.InputStream;

// ...
        try {
            URL moduleUrl = new URL("http://module-id.app-id.appspot.com/api/list");

            InputStream inStream = moduleUrl.openStream();
            // ...

        } catch (MalformedURLException e) {
            // ...
        } catch (IOException e) {
            // ...
        }
```

Adding the module URL directly to the code like this is not a good practice. Better would be to calculate the module URL from environmental factors, including whether the app is running in the development server and what the current app's ID is. Helpfully, App Engine has an API for this:

```
import com.google.appengine.api.modules.ModulesService;
import com.google.appengine.api.modules.ModulesServiceFactory;

// ...
        ModulesService modules = ModulesServiceFactory.getModulesService();
        try {
            URL moduleUrl = new URL(
                "http://" +
                modules.getVersionHostname("module-id", null) +
                "/api/list");

            InputStream inStream = moduleUrl.openStream();
            // ...

        } catch (MalformedURLException e) {
            // ...
        } catch (IOException e) {
            // ...
        }
```

The getVersionHostname() method of the ModulesService (returned by the getModulesService() static method of the ModulesServiceFactory from the com.google.appengine.api.modules package) returns the appropriate module-specific domain name for the environment. In a development server, this is the local host hostname with the appropriate port number added. On App Engine, this is calculated from the module ID and the current app ID.

`getVersionHostname()` takes two parameters: a module ID and a version ID. If the module ID is `null`, the module running the code is assumed. If the version ID is `null`, the assumed version is either the version running the code if the module is the current module, or the default version of the requested module.

Module endpoints that are called by the app itself usually should not be called by outsiders that happen to know the URL. App Engine makes it easy to secure these endpoints so only calls from within the app and authenticated requests from the app's developers can access it. To set this up, configure the handler for the endpoint in the deployment descriptor (*web.xml*) to use an `<auth-constraint>` and `<role-name>` of admin:

```
<security-constraint>
  <web-resource-collection>
    <web-resource-name>api</web-resource-name>
    <url-pattern>/api/*</url-pattern>
  </web-resource-collection>
  <auth-constraint>
    <role-name>admin</role-name>
  </auth-constraint>
</security-constraint>
```

We saw this administrator-only configuration in "Authorization with Google Accounts" on page 75. `<role-name>admin</role-name>` lets through URL Fetch requests coming from the app itself. We'll see this again later for other kinds of self-calling, such as in Chapter 16.

Module URLs and Secure Connections

Back in "Configuring Secure Connections" on page 70, we mentioned that app spot.com URLs with multiple parts need special treatment when using HTTPS. The same applies to all module-specific appspot.com URLs as well.

As a reminder, to access a module-specific URL with HTTPS, replace all of the dots (`.`) to the left of the app ID with `-dot-` (hyphen, the word "dot," hyphen), like so:

```
https://module-id-dot-app-id.appspot.com/
https://version-id-dot-module-id-dot-app-id.appspot.com/
```

Module URLs and Custom Domains

The `appspot.com` URLs are sufficient for internal calls. If you want to accept external requests directly to a specific module and you don't mind sharing your app ID with the world, you can advertise the `appspot.com` URL. There's nothing inherently wrong with exposing an app ID, but you might prefer to avoid it for aesthetic reasons.

If you set up a custom domain using the procedure discussed in "Domain Names" on page 65, you can use subdomains of your custom domain to access modules. For this to work, you must update the DNS record with your DNS hosting service so that the appropriate subdomains go to Google. You can make this a "wildcard subdomain," so all subdomains for your custom domain will work, and you don't have to update DNS records as you make changes to module names. Wildcard subdomains are required if you want to address individual instances directly, because instance IDs are determined dynamically.

With the appropriate DNS configuration in place, you can access a module using the module ID as a subdomain, like so:

```
http://module-id.example.com/
```

Similarly, you can access instances like so:

```
http://instance-id.module-id.example.com/
```

Subdomains of custom domains always use the default version for the module.

You cannot access modules via subdomains of a custom domain set up as a Google Apps domain. Unfortunately, at this time, this means that you cannot access modules with custom domains via HTTPS. If you need HTTPS, the only option is the appspot.com domain, using the -dot- notation.

Dispatching Requests to Modules

Sometimes you want requests to reach nondefault modules, but you don't want to expose URLs on subdomains. Instead, you want to map URL paths on the main domain to modules. For example, instead of using http://mobile-fe.example.com/ for your mobile REST API, you'd prefer to use http://www.example.com/api/

App Engine lets you do this using yet another configuration file, called *dispatch.xml*. You put this file in the *WEB-INF/* directory of the default module. It looks like this:

```xml
<?xml version="1.0" encoding="utf-8"?>
<dispatch-entries>
  <dispatch>
    <url>*/static/*</url>
    <module>default</module>
  </dispatch>

  <dispatch>
    <url>*/api/*</url>
    <module>module-fe</module>
  </dispatch>

  <dispatch>
    <url>saucy-boomerang-123.appspot.com/test/*</url>
    <module>test</module>
```

```
    </dispatch>
  </dispatch-entries>
```

By necessity, this file is very simple: each dispatch rule is a directive for Google's high-performance frontends to override its own decision about how to route a request. The file can contain up to 10 rules. Each rule consists of a `<url>` pattern, and the name of the module that should handle the request, where `default` is the name of the default module.

The URL pattern matches both the domain of the request and the URL path. The first slash (/) in the pattern always matches the boundary between the domain and the path, and so must be included. You can use a wildcard (*) character at the beginning, at the end, or both, to match zero or more characters. Fancier pattern matching is not supported.

Consider this `<url>` value:

```
<dispatch>
  <url>*/api/*</url>
  <module>module-fe</module>
</dispatch>
```

The beginning wildcard appears before the first slash, and so this rule applies to all domains, including the custom domain, the `appspot.com` domain, and all subdomains. The pattern after the first slash matches all URL paths that begin with `/api/`, followed by zero or more characters. All requests whose domain and path match this pattern are routed to the `mobile-fe` module.

If none of the rules in the *dispatch.xml* file match the request, then the usual dispatch logic takes over.

As with other app-wide configuration files, the *dispatch.xml* file is deployed with the rest of the application. You can also deploy just this file to the app by running the `appcfg update_dispatch` command with the default module.

Starting and Stopping Modules

When you deploy a module with manual scaling, App Engine ensures that the number of instances requested in the configuration file's `instances` parameter have started, starting new ones if necessary. From that point on, the number of instances in the module can be adjusted via the Cloud Console in the Instances panel, via the `appcfg` command, or programmatically by calling the modules API from the app.

Instances in a module with basic scaling can also be started and stopped in these ways. The main difference with basic scaling is that instances are also started and stopped in response to incoming requests and idle timeouts, respectively. Basic instances are stopped during a deployment so they can be restarted to pick up the new software.

To shut down instances from the Cloud Console, go to the Instances panel under Compute, App Engine, then select the appropriate module and version from the drop-down menus at the top. (The module drop-down only appears if multiple modules are deployed.) The panel includes performance graphs specific to the module and version, as well as a list of active instances. Click the Shutdown button to stop an instance.

There is no way to increase the number of instances in a module from the Cloud Console. The expectation with manual scaling is that the app will start instances as it needs them via the API. Or you can use the command-line tool.

From the command line, you can stop a module, and start a module. Stopping a module shuts down all of its instances, and starting a stopped module activates all of the instances configured for the module. The command takes the path to the module's WAR directory as an argument, or you can specify the application ID, module ID, and version ID as the -A, -M, and -V arguments, respectively:

```
appcfg stop_module_version world-cache
appcfg start_module_version world-cache

appcfg stop_module_version -A saucy-boomerang-123 \
  -M world-cache -V alpha
```

Finally, you can use the modules API to stop and start modules, and also adjust the number of instances for a module with manual scaling without deploying a configuration change. We'll see how to do that in "The Modules API" on page 127.

Managing and Deleting Modules and Versions

When you deploy a module, App Engine checks the `<version>` parameter in the configuration file and either creates a new version of the module with that ID if it does not exist, or replaces the version with that ID if it does.

When you deploy a module for the first time, the first version created becomes the default version. Otherwise, the default version doesn't change unless you use the Cloud Console or the `appcfg` command to change it. To change the default version from the Cloud Console, go to the Versions panel under Compute, App Engine. Click the checkbox next to the version you want to make the default, then click the "Make default" button.

Changing the default version for a module with manual or basic scaling changes the destination of requests to the module URL, and otherwise has no immediate effect on the module's instances. Each version's instances continue to run according to their scaling policies.

When you're working with automatic scaling, nondefault versions are mostly inconsequential, because versions that don't receive traffic don't consume resources. They either serve their purpose (as testing versions, for example), or they sit around waiting to be cleaned up when a developer notices that the app has hit its version count limit. With manual scaling, cleaning up old versions is much more important. Versions of modules with manual scaling keep their instances running until they are explicitly shut down or the version is deleted. It's worth keeping careful track of which versions have active instances that are not being used, and either shutting them down or deleting them as part of your deployment process.

To delete a version from the Cloud Console, go to the Versions panel as before. Click the checkboxes next to the versions to delete, then click the Delete button.

Notice that the default module does not have a checkbox next to it. This is a safety catch to prevent you from deleting the version that is serving the main traffic for the module. To delete the default version, you must first either make another version the default, or you must delete all of the other versions. Deleting all versions (by deleting all nondefault versions, then deleting the default version) deletes the module.

To delete a version from the command line, use the `appcfg delete_version` command, passing the app ID, module ID, and version ID as the `-A`, `-M`, and `-V` arguments, respectively. The `-M` argument can be omitted to delete a version from the default module, or you can specify `-M default`:

```
appcfg delete_version -A saucy-boomerang-123 -M world-cache -V alpha
```

This command will fail if you attempt to delete the default version and other versions exist. It won't try to pick a new default version automatically. You can delete the default version if it is the last version in a module.

The Modules API

App Engine gives you programmatic access to information about the modules and versions of the running app, as well as the identifiers of the module, version, and instance running the code. You can also adjust the number of instances for a module with manual scaling, and start and stop module versions just as you can from the command line. All of these functions are provided by the `ModulesService` interface.

```
import com.google.appengine.api.modules.ModulesService;
import com.google.appengine.api.modules.ModulesServiceFactory;

// ...
        ModulesService modules = ModulesServiceFactory.getModulesService();
```

We already looked at `getVersionHostname()`. This is essential for calculating the URL the app should use when calling one of its own modules via the URL Fetch service. This is the only method that will return `localhost` URLs when running in the development server.

You can get the IDs for the module, version, and instance running the current code using the `getCurrentModule()`, `getCurrentVersion()`, and `getCurrentInstanceId()` functions. They take no arguments.

The `getModules()` function returns a complete list of the app's module names, including `default` if it exists. (It is technically possible to deploy only named modules to an app, and therefore have no default module.)

The `getVersions(String module)` function returns a list of version IDs. When passed `null` as its argument, it returns the versions of the current module. When given a module name as its argument, it returns the versions for that module, or raises an exception if the given module does not exist.

The related function `getDefaultVersion(String module)` returns the version ID of the default version. It too takes an optional module name argument, and uses the current module if this is `null`.

There are four methods you can use to manipulate the instances of modules with manual or basic scaling. You can use `getNumInstances(String module, String version)` and `setNumInstances(String module, String version, long instances)` to manipulate the number of instances for the module. As with the other methods, `null` values for the module or version use the module or version of the instance running the code. Deploying a module resets the number of instances to the number specified in the configuration file.

Finally, you can start and stop module versions with `startVersion(String module, String version)` and `stopVersion(String module, String version)`. Calling `stopVersion()` with `null` arguments is a good way for a module to stop itself.

Remember that stopping an instance will invoke its shutdown hook, if any, and wait 30 seconds for it to complete.

An Always-On Example

The following simple example illustrates how the start handler and background threads work together on an always-on instance. The start handler kicks off the background thread, then returns. The background thread increments a counter in the instance's global memory once per second. You can inspect the current value of the counter in a browser with a web request for the "/" URL path.

Here is the Java code for the start handler's servlet, *StartServlet.java*:

```java
package com.example.myproject;

import java.io.IOException;

import javax.servlet.http.HttpServlet;
import javax.servlet.http.HttpServletRequest;
import javax.servlet.http.HttpServletResponse;

import com.google.appengine.api.ThreadManager;

@SuppressWarnings("serial")
public class StartServlet extends HttpServlet {
    public void doGet(HttpServletRequest req, HttpServletResponse resp)
                throws IOException {
        Thread thread = ThreadManager.createBackgroundThread(
                        new Runnable() {
                    public void run() {
                        try {
                            while (Counter.getValue() < 600) {
                                Counter.increment();
                                Thread.sleep(1000);
                            }
                        } catch (InterruptedException e) {
                            // Sleep interrupted
                        }
                    }
                });

        thread.start();
    }
}
```

Here's the interactive display, *MainServlet.java*:

```java
package com.example.myproject;

import java.io.IOException;

import javax.servlet.http.HttpServlet;
import javax.servlet.http.HttpServletRequest;
import javax.servlet.http.HttpServletResponse;

@SuppressWarnings("serial")
public class MainServlet extends HttpServlet {
    public void doGet(HttpServletRequest req, HttpServletResponse resp)
                throws IOException {
        resp.setContentType("text/html");
        resp.getWriter().println(
                        "Global counter: " +
                        Counter.getValue());
```

```
        }
    }
```

We keep our in-memory global counter in its own static class, *Counter.java*:

```java
package com.example.myproject;

public class Counter {
    private static long value = 0L;

    public static long getValue() {
            return value;
    }

    public static void increment() {
            value++;
    }
}
```

The *appengine-web.xml* configuration file for this module specifies manual scaling and one instance:

```xml
<?xml version="1.0" encoding="utf-8"?>
<appengine-web-app xmlns="http://appengine.google.com/ns/1.0">
  <application>saucy-boomerang-123</application>
  <version>1</version>
  <module>world-cache</module>
  <threadsafe>true</threadsafe>

  <instance-class>B1</instance-class>
  <manual-scaling>
       <instances>1</instances>
  </manual-scaling>
</appengine-web-app>
```

The *web.xml* file maps the /_ah/start and / URL paths to the appropriate servlets:

```xml
<?xml version="1.0" encoding="UTF-8"?>
<web-app
   xmlns:xsi="http://www.w3.org/2001/XMLSchema-instance"
   xmlns="http://java.sun.com/xml/ns/javaee"
   xsi:schemaLocation="http://java.sun.com/xml/ns/javaee
                       http://java.sun.com/xml/ns/javaee/web-app_2_5.xsd"
   id="WebApp_ID" version="2.5">
  <display-name>SBWorldCache</display-name>

  <servlet>
    <servlet-name>StartServlet</servlet-name>
    <servlet-class>com.example.myproject.StartServlet</servlet-class>
  </servlet>
  <servlet-mapping>
    <servlet-name>StartServlet</servlet-name>
    <url-pattern>/_ah/start</url-pattern>
  </servlet-mapping>
```

```
<servlet>
  <servlet-name>MainServlet</servlet-name>
  <servlet-class>com.example.myproject.MainServlet</servlet-class>
</servlet>
<servlet-mapping>
  <servlet-name>MainServlet</servlet-name>
  <url-pattern>/</url-pattern>
</servlet-mapping>

</web-app>
```

Once deployed, we can access the interactive display with this URL (given the application and module IDs shown):

```
http://counter.module-demo.appspot.com/
```

If you want to try deploying this example, remember that with manual scaling, all of the requested instances are started as soon as you deploy. Instance running time consumes the "backend instance hours" quota, and apps without a budget set only get so many free hours a day. You'll want to keep close tabs on the running instance, and shut it down (or delete the module) when you're done experimenting.

You can reduce the risk of this example burning through your backend instance hours quota by changing it to use basic scaling. With basic scaling, the instance won't start until you load the interactive display. While the instance is running, the background thread will increment the counter once per second, up to 600 (the condition on the `while` loop). After 600 seconds, the instance will go idle, then shut down after the idle timeout you set in the configuration.

CHAPTER 6

Datastore Entities

Most scalable web applications use separate systems for handling web requests and for storing data. The request handling system routes each request to one of many servers, and the server handles the request without knowledge of other requests going to other servers. Each request handler behaves as if it is *stateless,* acting solely on the content of the request to produce the response. But most web applications need to maintain state, whether it's remembering that a customer ordered a product, or just remembering that the user who made the current request is the same user who made an earlier request handled by another server. For this, request handlers must interact with a central database to fetch and update the latest information about the state of the application.

Just as the request handling system distributes web requests across many machines for scaling and robustness, so does the database. But unlike the request handlers, databases are by definition *stateful,* and this poses a variety of questions. Which server remembers which piece of data? How does the system route a data query to the server or servers that can answer the query? When a client updates data, how long does it take for all servers that know that data to get the latest version, and what does the system return for queries about that data in the meantime? What happens when two clients try to update the same data at the same time? What happens when a server goes down?

Google Cloud Platform offers several data storage services, and each service answers these questions differently. The most important service for scalable applications is Google Cloud Datastore, or as it is known to App Engine veterans, simply "the datastore." When App Engine was first launched in 2008, it included the datastore as its primary means of scalable data storage. The datastore has since gone through major revisions, and is now a prominent service in the Cloud Platform suite, accessible from

App Engine via the original API or from Compute Engine or elsewhere via a REST API.

As with App Engine's request handling, Cloud Datastore manages the scaling and maintenance of data storage automatically. Your application interacts with an abstract model that hides the details of managing and growing a pool of data servers. This model and the service behind it provide answers to the questions of scalable data storage specifically designed for web applications.

Cloud Datastore's abstraction for data is easy to understand, but it is not obvious how to best take advantage of its features. In particular, it is surprisingly different from the kind of database with which most of us are most familiar, the relational database (such as the one provided by Google Cloud SQL). It's different enough that we call it a "datastore" instead of a "database." (We're mincing words, but the distinction is important.)

Cloud Datastore is a robust, scalable data storage solution. Your app's data is stored in several locations by using a best-of-breed consensus protocol (similar to the "Paxos" protocol), making your app's access to this data resilient to most service failures and all planned downtime. When we discuss queries and transactions, we'll see how this affects how data is updated. For now, just know that it's a good thing.

We dedicate the next several chapters to this important subject.[1]

Entities, Keys, and Properties

Cloud Datastore is best understood as an object database. An object in the datastore is known as an *entity*.

An entity has a *key* that uniquely identifies the object across the entire system. If you have a key, you can fetch the entity for the key quickly. Keys can be stored as data in entities, such as to create a reference from one entity to another. A key has several parts, some of which we'll discuss here and some of which we'll cover later.

---

[1] In 2011–2012, App Engine transitioned from an older datastore infrastructure, known as the "master/slave" (M/S) datastore, to the current one, known as the "high replication" datastore (HR datastore, or HRD). The two architectures differ in how data is updated, but the biggest difference is that the M/S datastore requires scheduled maintenance periods during which data cannot be updated, and is prone to unexpected failures. The HR datastore stays available during scheduled maintenance, and is far more resistant to system failure. All new App Engine applications use the HR datastore, and the M/S datastore is no longer an option. I only mention it because you'll read about it in older articles, and may see occasional announcements about maintenance of the M/S datastore. You may also see mentions of a datastore migration tool, which old apps still using the M/S datastore can use to switch to the new HR datastore. In this book, "the datastore" always refers to the HR datastore.

One part of the key is the project ID, which ensures that nothing else about the key can collide with the entities of any other project. It also ensures that no other app can access your app's data, and that your app cannot access data for other apps. This feature of keys is automatic, and doesn't appear in the API (or in any examples shown here).

An important part of the key is the *kind*. An entity's kind categorizes the entity for the purposes of queries, and for ensuring the uniqueness of the rest of the key. For example, a shopping cart application might represent each customer order with an entity of the kind "Order." The application specifies the kind when it creates the entity.

The key also contains an *entity ID*. This can be an arbitrary string specified by the app, or it can be an integer generated automatically by the datastore.[2] An entity has either a string ID or a numeric ID, but not both.

System-assigned numeric IDs are generally increasing, although they are not guaranteed to be monotonically increasing. If you want a strictly increasing ID, you must maintain this yourself in a transaction. (For more information on transactions, see Chapter 8.) If you purposefully do not want an increasing ID, such as to avoid exposing data sizes to users, you can either generate your own string ID, or allow the system to generate a numeric ID, then encrypt it before exposing it to users.

Consider a simple example where we store information about books in an online book catalog. We might represent each book with an entity in the datastore. The key for such an entity might use a kind of Book, and a system-assigned numeric ID, like so:

```
Book, 13579
```

Alternatively, we could use an externally defined identifier for each book, such as the ISBN, stored as a string ID on the key:

```
Book, "978-0-24680-321-0"
```

Once an entity has been created, its key cannot be changed. This applies to all parts of its key, including the kind and the ID.

The data for the entity is stored in one or more *properties*. Each property has a name and at least one value. Each value is of one of several supported data types, such as a string, an integer, a date-time, or a null value. We'll look at property value types in detail later in this chapter.

---

2 An entity ID specified by the app is sometimes known as the "key name" in older documentation, to distinguish it from the numeric ID. The newer terminology is simpler: every entity has an ID, and it's either a string provided by the app or a number provided by the datastore.

A property can have multiple values, and each value can be of a different type. As you will see in "Multivalued Properties" on page 142, multivalued properties have unusual behavior, but are quite useful for modeling some kinds of data, and surprisingly efficient.

 It's tempting to compare these concepts with similar concepts in relational databases: kinds are tables, entities are rows, and properties are fields or columns. That's a useful comparison, but watch out for differences.

Unlike a table in a relational database, there is no relationship between an entity's kind and its properties. Two entities of the same kind can have different properties set or not set, and can each have a property of the same name but with values of different types. You can (and often will) enforce a data schema in your own code, and App Engine includes libraries to make this easy, but this is not required by the datastore.

Also, unlike relational databases, keys are not properties. You can perform queries on IDs just like properties, but you cannot change a string ID after the entity has been created.

A relational database cannot store multiple values in a single cell, while an App Engine property can have multiple values.

Introducing the Java Datastore API

App Engine for Java includes support for two major standard interfaces for databases: Java Data Objects (JDO) and the Java Persistence API (JPA). Like the other standards-based interfaces in the App Engine Java API, using one of these interfaces makes it easier to move your application from and to another platform. JDO and JPA support different kinds of databases, including object databases and relational databases. They provide an object-oriented interface to your data, even if the underlying database is not an object store.

Many of the concepts of these interfaces translate directly to App Engine datastore concepts: classes are kinds, objects are entities, and fields are properties. App Engine's implementation also supports several advanced features of these interfaces, such as object relationships. Inevitably, some concepts do not translate directly and have behaviors that are specific to App Engine.

We'll discuss one of these interfaces, JPA, in Chapter 10. For now, here is a simple example of a data class using JPA:

```
import java.util.Date;
import javax.persistence.Entity;
import javax.persistence.GeneratedValue;
import javax.persistence.GenerationType;
```

```java
import javax.persistence.Id;

@Entity
public class Book {
    @Id
    @GeneratedValue(strategy = GenerationType.IDENTITY)
    private Long id;

    private String title;
    private String author;
    private int copyrightYear;
    private Date authorBirthdate;

    public Long getId() {
        return id;
    }

    public String getTitle() {
        return title;
    }
    public void setTitle(String title) {
        this.title = title;
    }

    public String getAuthor() {
        return author;
    }
    public void setAuthor(String author) {
        this.author = author;
    }

    public int getCopyrightYear() {
        return copyrightYear;
    }
    public void setCopyrightYear(int copyrightYear) {
        this.copyrightYear = copyrightYear;
    }

    public Date getAuthorBirthdate() {
        return authorBirthdate;
    }
    public void setAuthorBirthdate(Date authorBirthdate) {
        this.authorBirthdate = authorBirthdate;
    }
}
```

The JDO and JPA implementations are built on top of a low-level API for the App Engine datastore. The low-level API exposes all of the datastore's features, and corresponds directly to datastore concepts. For instance, you must use the low-level API to manipulate entities with properties of unknown names or value types. You can also use the low-level API directly in your applications, or use it to implement your own data management layer.

The following code creates a Book entity by using the low-level API:

```
import java.io.IOException;
import java.util.Calendar;
import java.util.Date;
import java.util.GregorianCalendar;

import javax.servlet.http.HttpServlet;
import javax.servlet.http.HttpServletRequest;
import javax.servlet.http.HttpServletResponse;

import com.google.appengine.api.datastore.DatastoreService;
import com.google.appengine.api.datastore.DatastoreServiceFactory;
import com.google.appengine.api.datastore.Entity;

// ...
        DatastoreService ds = DatastoreServiceFactory.getDatastoreService();

        Entity book = new Entity("Book");

        book.setProperty("title", "The Grapes of Wrath");
        book.setProperty("author", "John Steinbeck");
        book.setProperty("copyrightYear", 1939);
        Date authorBirthdate =
            new GregorianCalendar(1902, Calendar.FEBRUARY, 27).getTime();
        book.setProperty("authorBirthdate", authorBirthdate);

        ds.put(book);

    // ...
```

Notice that the application code, not the datastore, is responsible for managing the structure of the data. JDO and JPA impose this structure by using classes whose fields are persisted to the datastore behind the scenes. This can be both a benefit and a burden when you need to change the structure of existing data.

To illustrate the datastore concepts, we will use the low-level API for Java examples in the next few chapters. In Chapter 10, we reintroduce JPA, and discuss how JPA concepts correspond with App Engine concepts. For more information on the Java Data Objects interface, see the official App Engine documentation.

If you'd prefer object-oriented management of datastore entities but do not need to use JPA for portability purposes, consider Objectify, a third-party open source project. Objectify is specific to App Engine, and supports most of the features of the low-level API. See the Objectify website for more information:

https://code.google.com/p/objectify-appengine/

Property Values

Each value data type supported by the datastore is represented by a primitive type in the language for the runtime or a class provided by the API. The data types and their language-specific equivalents are listed in Table 6-1. In this table, `datastore` is the Java package `com.google.appengine.api.datastore`.

Table 6-1. Datastore property value types and equivalent Java types

Data type	Java type
Unicode text string (up to 500 bytes, indexed)	`java.lang.String`
Long Unicode text string (not indexed)	`datastore.Text`
Short byte string (up to 500 bytes, indexed)	`datastore.ShortBlob`
Long byte string (not indexed)	`datastore.Blob`
Boolean	`boolean`
Integer (64-bit)	`byte`, `short`, `int`, or `long` (converted to `long`)
Float (double precision)	`float` or `double` (converted to `double`)
Date-time	`java.util.Date`
Null value	`null`
Entity key	`datastore.Key`
A Google account	`...api.users.User`
A geographical point (GD)	`datastore.GeoPt`

Example 6-1 demonstrates the use of several of these data types.

Example 6-1. Java code to set property values of various types

```java
import com.google.appengine.api.datastore.DatastoreService;
import com.google.appengine.api.datastore.DatastoreServiceFactory;
import com.google.appengine.api.datastore.Entity;
import com.google.appengine.api.users.User;
import com.google.appengine.api.users.UserService;
import com.google.appengine.api.users.UserServiceFactory;

import java.util.Date;

@SuppressWarnings("serial")
public class NewMessageServlet extends HttpServlet {
    public void doPost(HttpServletRequest req, HttpServletResponse resp)
        throws IOException {
        UserService userService = UserServiceFactory.getUserService();
        User user = userService.getCurrentUser();

        DatastoreService datastore =
            DatastoreServiceFactory.getDatastoreService();
        Entity comment = new Entity("Comment");
        comment.setProperty("commenter", user);
        comment.setProperty("message", req.getParameter("message"));
        comment.setProperty("date", new Date());
        datastore.put(comment);

        // Redirect to a result page...
    }
}
```

When you use the low-level datastore API, types that are widened to other types when stored come back as the wider datastore types when you retrieve the entity. For instance, a Java Integer comes back as a Long. If you use these APIs in your app, it's best to use the native datastore types, so the value types stay consistent.

The data modeling interfaces offer a way to store values in these alternative types and convert them back automatically when retrieving the entity. (For information on data modeling with the JPA API, see Chapter 10.)

Strings, Text, and Bytes

The datastore has two distinct data types for storing strings of text: short strings and long strings. Short strings are indexed; that is, they can be the subject of queries, such as a search for every Person entity with a given value for a last_name property. Short string values must be less than 500 bytes in length. Long strings can be longer than 500 bytes, but are not indexed.

Text strings, short and long, are strings of characters from the Unicode character set. Internally, the datastore stores Unicode strings by using the UTF-8 encoding, which represents some characters using multiple bytes. This means that the 500-byte limit for short strings is not necessarily the same as 500 Unicode characters. The actual limit on the number of characters depends on which characters are in the string.

In the Java API, this distinction is described with separate types. Short text strings are simply `String` values. If you attempt to add a string that exceeds the length limit for short strings, an `IllegalArgumentException` is raised. For long strings, you wrap the value in a `datastore.Text` object. This and other custom datastore value type classes are provided in the `com.google.appengine.api.datastore` package:

```
import com.google.appengine.api.datastore.Entity;
import com.google.appengine.api.datastore.Text;

// ...
        Entity entity = new Entity("MyKind");

        String shortStringVal = "This is a short string value.";
        entity.setProperty("shortString", shortStringVal);

        Text longStringVal = new Text(
            "This is a long string.  It can be longer than 500 characters. " +
            "It is not indexed, and so cannot be the subject of a query " +
            "filter or sort order.");
        entity.setProperty("longString", longStringVal);
```

The datastore also supports two additional classes for sequences of bytes, or "blobs." Blobs are not assumed to be of any particular format, and their bytes are preserved. This makes them good for nontext data, such as images, movies, or other media. As with text strings, the blob types come in indexed and nonindexed varieties. In Java, the blob types are `datastore.ShortBlob` and `datastore.Blob`:

```
import com.google.appengine.api.datastore.Entity;
import com.google.appengine.api.datastore.ShortBlob;
import com.google.appengine.api.datastore.Blob;

// ...
        // byte[] data = ...

        Entity entity = new Entity("MyKind");

        // Short blobs must be no larger than 500 bytes.
        ShortBlob shortBlobVal = new ShortBlob(data);
        entity.setProperty("shortBlob", shortBlobVal);

        // Blobs can exceed 500 bytes in size, but are not indexed.
        Blob blobVal = new Blob(data);
        entity.setProperty("blob", blobVal);
```

Unset Versus the Null Value

One possible value of a property is the null value. In code, this value is `null`.

A property with the null value is not the same as an unset property. Consider the following:

```
DatastoreService datastore =
    DatastoreServiceFactory.getDatastoreService();

Entity entityA = new Entity("MyKind");
entityA.setProperty("prop1", "abc");
entityA.setProperty("prop2", null);
datastore.put(entityA);

Entity entityB = new Entity("MyKind");
entityB.setProperty("prop1", "def");
datastore.put(entityB);
```

This creates two entities of the kind `MyKind`. Both entities have a property named `prop1`. The first entity has a property named `prop2`; the second does not.

Of course, an unset property can be set later:

```
entityB.setProperty("prop2", 123);
datastore.put(entityB);

# entityB now has a property named "prop2."
```

Similarly, a set property can be made unset. You remove a set property with the `removeProperty()` method:

```
entityB.removeProperty("prop2");
datastore.put(entityB);

# entityB no longer has a property named "prop2."
```

Multivalued Properties

As we mentioned earlier, a property can have multiple values. We'll discuss the more substantial aspects of multivalued properties when we talk about queries and data modeling. But for now, it's worth a brief mention.

A property can have one or more values. A property cannot have zero values: a property without a value is simply unset. Each value for a property can be of a different type, and can be the null value.

In Java, you provide multiple values for a property as a `Collection` type. When you pass a `Collection` to `setProperty()`, it iterates over the values, and stores them in the order returned during iteration. When you access the multivalued property with getProperty(), it returns the values as a java.util.List, not the original Collection type:

```java
import java.util.SortedSet;
import java.util.TreeSet;

// ...
        Entity entity = new Entity("MyKind");

        // Prepare an MVP value list using a sorted data structure:
        SortedSet<Long> values = new TreeSet<Long>();
        values.add(24680L);
        values.add(123456789L);
        values.add(13579L);
        entity.setProperty("mvp", values);

        @SuppressWarnings("unchecked")
        List<Long> mvp = (List<Long>) entity.getProperty("mvp");

// mvp contains [13579L, 24680L, 123456789L],
// originally sorted by TreeSet.
```

The datastore remembers which properties were last set as multivalued properties. This helps the API handle empty collections sensibly. While storing an empty Collection is equivalent to removing the property (or leaving it unset) with respect to queries, the datastore will remember that it's a multivalued property so that get Property() returns an empty List instead of null.

This example parameterized the List type as a List<Long>. To store values of multiple types in a single multivalued property, you'd use a List<Object>.

Keys and Key Objects

The key for an entity is a value that can be retrieved, passed around, and stored like any other value. If you have the key for an entity, you can retrieve the entity from the datastore quickly, much more quickly than with a datastore query. Keys can be stored as property values, as an easy way for one entity to refer to another.

The getKey() method of the Entity returns the entity's Key. The Key has methods to access its various parts. getKind() returns the kind of the entity (a String). If the entity has a system-assigned numeric ID, getId() returns it (a long). If the app assigned a string ID, then getName() returns its value:[3]

---

[3] This is one of few places in the API where a Cloud Datastore entity's string ID is known as a "name." You might see this nomenclature in a few other places as well.

```
import com.google.appengine.api.datastore.Key;
```

// ...
```
        // Entity entity;

        Key k = entity.getKey();
        String kind = k.getKind();
        long id = k.getId();
```

You can also create a `Key` directly, such as to fetch an entity by its key, or to create a new entity with a specific key via the `Entity(key)` constructor. You can do this from scratch using the `KeyFactory.createKey()` static method:

```
import com.google.appengine.api.datastore.KeyFactory;
```

// ...
```
        Key k = KeyFactory.createKey("MyKind", "custom-id");
```

Keys have a feature we haven't discussed yet called *ancestor paths*. Ancestor paths are related to how the datastore does transactions. (We'll get to them in Chapter 8.) For the entities we have created so far, the "path" is just the kind followed by the ID.

When you construct a new entity object and do not provide a string ID, the entity object has a key, but the key does not yet have an ID. The ID is populated when the entity object is saved to the datastore for the first time. You can get the key object prior to saving the object, but it will be incomplete:

```
        Entity entity = new Entity("MyKind");

        Key k = entity.getKey();

        // k.isComplete() == false
```

If the entity object was constructed with a string ID, the key is complete before the object is saved—although, if the entity has not been saved, the string ID is not guaranteed to be unique.

Once you have a complete key, you can assign it as a property value on another entity to create a reference:

```
import com.google.appengine.api.datastore.DatastoreService;
import com.google.appengine.api.datastore.DatastoreServiceFactory;
```

// ...
```
        DatastoreService datastore =
            DatastoreServiceFactory.getDatastoreService();

        Entity entityA = new Entity("MyKind");
        Entity entityB = new Entity("MyKind");

        datastore.put(entityA);
        // entityA.getKey().isComplete() == true
```

```
entityB.setProperty("reference", entityA.getKey());
datastore.put(entityB);
```

Keys can be converted to string representations for the purposes of passing around as textual data, such as in a web form or cookie. The string representation avoids characters considered special in HTML or URLs, so it is safe to use without escaping characters. The encoding of the value to a string is simple and easily reversed, so if you expose the string value to users, be sure to encrypt it, or make sure all key parts (such as kind names) are not secret. When accepting an encoded key string from a client, always validate the key before using it.

To convert between a key object and an encoded key string:

```
String k_str = KeyFactory.keyToString(k);

// ...

Key k = KeyFactory.stringToKey(k_str);
```

The Key class's toString() method does not return the key's string encoding. You must use KeyFactory.keyToString() to get the string encoding of a key.

Using Entities

Let's look briefly at how to retrieve entities from the datastore by using keys, how to inspect the contents of entities, and how to update and delete entities. The API methods for these features are straightforward.

Getting Entities Using Keys

Given a complete key for an entity, you can retrieve the entity from the datastore.

To get an entity by its key, you determine the Key for the entity, then call the get() method of the DatastoreService. As we've already seen in a few examples, you get an implementation of DatastoreService using the static method getDatastoreService() of the DatastoreServiceFactory class:

```
import com.google.appengine.api.datastore.DatastoreService;
import com.google.appengine.api.datastore.DatastoreServiceFactory;
import com.google.appengine.api.datastore.KeyFactory;

// ...

        DatastoreService datastore =
            DatastoreServiceFactory.getDatastoreService();

        Key k = KeyFactory.createKey("MyKind", "custom-id");
        Entity entity = datastore.get(k);
```

The `get()` method throws `EntityNotFoundException` if no entity with that key exists.

If you want to fetch multiple entities from the datastore by their keys, you can do so in a single batch call. A batch call saves on the overhead of calling the datastore multiple times in sequence. To make a batched get, simply pass an `Iterable<Key>` to `get()`. The method returns a `Map` of `Key`s to `Entity`s:

```
import java.util.Arrays;
import java.util.Map;

// ...
        Key k1 = KeyFactory.createKey("MyKind", 1);
        Key k2 = KeyFactory.createKey("MyKind", 2);
        Key k3 = KeyFactory.createKey("MyKind", 3);

        Map<Key, Entity> results = datastore.get(Arrays.asList(k1, k2, k3));

        Entity e2 = results.get(k2);
```

If a key in the batch call does not have a corresponding entity, the key is omitted from the map. (It does not throw `EntityNotFoundException`.)

Of course, you won't always have the keys for the entities you want to fetch from the datastore. To retrieve entities that meet other criteria, you use datastore queries. (We'll discuss queries in Chapter 7.)

Saving Entities

You save entities to the datastore using the `put()` method of a `DatastoreService` instance. As with `get()`, the method takes a single `Entity` for a single put, or an `Iterable<Entity>` for a batch put:

```
import com.google.appengine.api.datastore.DatastoreService;
import com.google.appengine.api.datastore.DatastoreServiceFactory;
import com.google.appengine.api.datastore.Entity;

import java.util.Date;

// ...
        DatastoreService datastore =
            DatastoreServiceFactory.getDatastoreService();

        Entity entity = new Entity("MyKind");
        entity.setProperty("prop1", "value");
        entity.setProperty("prop2", 123);
        entity.setProperty("prop3", new Date());

        datastore.put(entity);
```

When you update an entity, the app sends the complete contents of the entity to the datastore. The update is all or nothing: there is no way to send just the properties that have changed to the datastore. There is also no way to update a property on an entity without retrieving the complete entity, making the change, and then sending the new entity back.

You use the same API to create an entity as you do to update an entity. The datastore does not make a distinction between creates and updates. If you save an entity with a complete key (such as a key with a kind and a string ID) and an entity already exists with that key, the datastore replaces the existing entity with the new one:

```
Key k = KeyFactory.createKey("MyKind", "custom-id");
Entity entity = datastore.get(k);

entity.setProperty("prop2", 987);
datastore.put(entity);
```

If you want to test that an entity with a given key does not exist before you create it, you can do so using a transaction. You must use a transaction to ensure that another process doesn't create an entity with that key after you test for it and before you create it. For more information on transactions, see Chapter 8.

When the call to `put()` returns, the datastore entity records are up-to-date, and all future fetches of these entities in the current request handler and other handlers will see the new data. The specifics of how the datastore gets updated are discussed in detail in Chapter 8.

Deleting Entities

To delete an entity, you acquire or construct its `Key`, then call the `delete()` method of `DatastoreService`:

```
DatastoreService datastore =
    DatastoreServiceFactory.getDatastoreService();

Key k = KeyFactory.createKey("MyKind", "custom-id");
datastore.delete(k);
```

As with `get()` and `put()`, the `delete()` method can also take an `Iterable<Key>` to make a batch call. Unlike those methods, the `delete()` method also accepts multiple keys as a variable-length argument list:

```
datastore.delete(k1, k2, k3);
```

Allocating System IDs

When you create a new entity without specifying an explicit string ID, the datastore assigns a numeric system ID to the entity. Your code can read this system ID from the entity's key after the entity has been created.

Sometimes you want the system to assign the ID, but you need to know what ID will be assigned before the entity is created. For example, say you are creating two entities, and the property of one entity must be set to the key of the other entity. One option is to save the first entity to the datastore, then read the key of the entity, set the property on the second entity, and then save the second entity:

```
Entity entityA = new Entity("MyKind");
datastore.put(entityA);

Entity entityB = new Entity("MyKind");
entityB.setProperty("reference", entityA.getKey());
datastore.put(entityB);
```

This requires two separate calls to the datastore in sequence, which takes valuable clock time. It also requires a period of time where the first entity is in the datastore but the second entity isn't.

We can't read the key of the first entity before we save it, because it is incomplete: reading `entityA.getKey()` before calling `datastore.put(entityA)` would return an unusable value. We could use a string ID instead of a system ID, giving us a complete key, but it's often the case that we can't easily calculate a unique string ID, which is why we'd rather have a system-assigned ID.

To solve this problem, the datastore provides a method to allocate system IDs ahead of creating entities. You call the datastore to allocate an ID (or a range of IDs for multiple entities), then create the entity with an explicit ID. Notice that this is not the same as using a string ID: you give the entity the allocated numeric ID, and it knows the ID came from the system.

To do this, you call the `allocateIds()` service method. It takes a kind (as a `String`) and the number of IDs to allocate. If the new key will have an ancestor in its path, the parent `Key` must be the first argument. The method returns a `KeyRange`, an iterable object that generates `Key` objects in the allocated ID range. `KeyRange` also has a `get Start()` method, which returns the first `Key`. To create an entity with a given `Key`, you provide the `Key` as the sole argument to the `Entity` constructor:

```
import java.util.ArrayList;
import java.util.Arrays;
import com.google.appengine.api.datastore.DatastoreService;
import com.google.appengine.api.datastore.Entity;
import com.google.appengine.api.datastore.Key;
import com.google.appengine.api.datastore.KeyRange;

// ...
        // DatastoreService ds = ...;
        KeyRange range = ds.allocateIds("Entity", 1);
        Key e1Key = range.getStart();
        Entity e1 = new Entity(e1Key);
        Entity e2 = new Entity("Entity");
        e2.setProperty("reference", e1Key);

        ds.put(new ArrayList<Entity>(Arrays.asList(e1, e2)));
```

A batch put of two entities does not guarantee that both entities are saved together. If your app logic requires that either both entities are saved or neither are saved, you must use a transaction. For more information, see Chapter 8. (As you can probably tell by now, that's an important chapter.)

The Development Server and the Datastore

The development server simulates the datastore service on your local machine while you're testing your app. All datastore entities are saved to a local file. This file is associated with your app, and persists between runs of the development server, so your test data remains available until you delete it.

The datastore data file is named *local_db.bin*, and is stored in your application's *war/WEB-INF/appengine-generated/* directory. To reset your development datastore, stop your server, delete this file, and then start the server again.

Despite living under *war/...*, the generated *local_db.bin* file is not deployed with your application. As long as the development server is doing what you need it to, you can ignore this file.

CHAPTER 7

Datastore Queries

Inevitably, an application that manages data must do more than store and retrieve that data one record at a time. It must also answer questions about that data: which records meet certain criteria, how records compare to one another, what a set of records represents in aggregate. Web applications in particular are expected not only to know the answers to questions about large amounts of data, but to provide them quickly in response to web requests.

Most database systems provide a mechanism for executing queries, and Cloud Datastore is no exception. But the datastore's technique differs significantly from that of traditional database systems. When the application asks a question, instead of rifling through the original records and performing calculations to determine the answer, Cloud Datastore simply finds the answer in a list of possible answers prepared in advance. The datastore can do this because it knows which questions are going to be asked.

This kind of list, or *index*, is common to many database technologies, and relational databases can be told to maintain a limited set of indexes to speed up some kinds of queries. But Cloud Datastore is different: it maintains an index for *every* query the application is going to perform. Because the datastore only needs to do a simple scan of an index for every query, the application gets results back quickly. And for large amounts of data, Cloud Datastore can spread the data and the indexes across many machines, and get results back from all of them without an expensive aggregate operation.

This indexing strategy has significant drawbacks. The datastore's built-in query engine is downright weak compared to some relational databases, and is not suited to sophisticated data processing applications that would prefer slow but powerful run-time queries to fast simple ones. But most web applications need fast results, and the dirty secret about those powerful query engines is that they can't perform at web speeds with large amounts of data distributed across many machines. Cloud Datastore uses a model suited to scalable web applications: calculate the answers to known questions when the data is written, so reading is fast.

In this chapter, we explain how queries and indexes work, how the developer tools help you configure indexes automatically, and how to manage indexes as your application evolves. We also discuss several powerful features of the query engine, including cursors and projection queries. By understanding indexes, you will have an intuition for how to design your application and your data to make the most of the scalable datastore.

Queries and Kinds

You've seen how to retrieve an entity from the datastore given its key. But in most cases, the application does not know the keys of the entities it needs; it has only a general idea that it needs entities that meet certain criteria. For example, a leaderboard for the game app would need to retrieve the 10 Player entities with the highest score property values.

To retrieve entities this way, the app performs a *query*. A query includes:

- The kind of the entities to query
- Zero or more *filters*, criteria that property values must meet for an entity to be returned by the query
- Zero or more *sort orders* that determine the order in which results are returned based on property values

A query based on property values can only return entities of a single kind. This is the primary purpose of kinds: to determine which entities are considered together as possible results for a query. In practice, kinds correspond to the intuitive notion that each entity of the same nominal kind represents the same kind of data. But unlike other database systems, it's up to the app to enforce this consistency if it is desired, and the app can diverge from it if it's useful.

It is also possible to perform a limited set of queries on entities regardless of kind. Kindless queries can use a filter on the ID or key name, or on ancestors. We'll discuss ancestors and kindless queries in Chapter 8.

Query Results and Keys

When retrieving results for an entity query, the datastore returns the full entity for each result to the application.

For large entities, this may mean more data is transmitted between the datastore and the app than is needed. It's possible to fetch only a subset of properties under certain circumstances (we'll see this in "Projection Queries" on page 190), but these are not full entities. Another option is to store frequently accessed properties on one entity, and less popular properties on a separate related entity. The first entity stores the key of the second entity as a property, so when the app needs the less popular data, it queries for the first entity, then follows the reference to the second entity.

The datastore can return just the keys for the entities that match your query instead of fetching the full entities. A keys-only query is useful for determining the entities that match query criteria separately from when the entities are used. Keys can be remembered in the memcache or in a datastore property, and vivified as full entities when needed. We'll look at the API for keys-only queries a bit later.

The Query API

If you are using the JPA interface or the JDO interface, you will use the query facilities of those interfaces to perform datastore queries: JPQL or JDOQL, respectively. The concepts of those interfaces map nicely to the concepts of datastore queries: a query has a kind (a class), filters, and sort orders. We'll look at the calling conventions for JPQL when we look at JPA in Chapter 10.

Naturally, the low-level Java datastore API includes a query interface as well, and it has more features. Here is a brief example:

```
import com.google.appengine.api.datastore.DatastoreService;
import com.google.appengine.api.datastore.DatastoreServiceFactory;
import com.google.appengine.api.datastore.Entity;
import com.google.appengine.api.datastore.PreparedQuery;
import com.google.appengine.api.datastore.Query;

// ...
        DatastoreService ds = DatastoreServiceFactory.getDatastoreService();

        Query q = new Query("Book");
        q.setFilter(
            new Query.FilterPredicate(
                "copyrightYear",
                Query.FilterOperator.LESS_THAN_OR_EQUAL,
                1950));
        q.addSort("title");
```

```
PreparedQuery pq = ds.prepare(q);
for (Entity result : pq.asIterable()) {
    String title = (String) result.getProperty("title");

    // ...
}
```

To perform a query, you instantiate the `Query` class (from the `com.goo`
`gle.appengine.api.datastore` package), providing the name of the kind of the entities to query as an argument to the constructor. You call methods on the query object
to add filters and sort orders. To perform the query, you pass the query object to a
method of the `DatastoreService` instance. This method returns a `PreparedQuery`
object, which you can manipulate to retrieve the results.

If this were SQL, this query would look something like this:

```
SELECT * FROM Book WHERE copyrightYear <= 1950 ORDER BY title
```

Of course, Cloud Datastore doesn't support every feature of the SQL language. (That's
what Cloud SQL is for.) For concision, we'll use SQL-like syntax when describing
queries a bit later in this chapter, but the features of the datastore query engine are
available in the Java API.

 In fact, the SQL-like syntax we are using in this chapter is a SQL
subset called *GQL*.[1] You can use GQL to perform queries from the
Cloud Console. In the sidebar, navigate to Storage, Cloud Datastore, Query. Locate the drop-down menu that reads "Query by
kind," then change it to "Query using GQL." Enter the GQL statement, then click the Run button to run it.

Note that to perform a query in the Console, the app must already
have an index that corresponds to the query. We'll discuss indexes
throughout this chapter.

---

1 GQL was originally developed for the Python version of the Cloud Datastore library. There is no official Java
  implementation of GQL, but there is an unofficial GQL library for Java called gql4j (*https://code.google.com/p/*
  gql4j/) if you'd like to try it.

When you create or update an entity with new data, the indexes that support queries about that data are also updated. For the type of queries discussed in this chapter, the call to put() may return before the indexes have been updated. If you perform such a query immediately after an update, the results may not reflect the change. The development server simulates this possibility with a delay:

```
Entity book = new Entity("Book");
book.setProperty("copyrightYear", 1939);
ds.put(book);

// put() returns while the Book.copyrightYear
// index update is still in progress.

Query q = new Query("Book");
q.setFilter(
    new Query.FilterPredicate(
        "copyrightYear",
        Query.FilterOperator.LESS_THAN_OR_EQUAL,
        1950));
PreparedQuery pq = ds.prepare(q);
for (Entity result : pq.asIterable()) {
    // Results may not contain the new Book.
    // ...
}
```

We'll discuss consistency guarantees and how to formulate queries transactionally in Chapter 8.

Let's take a closer look at building queries, and then fetching results.

Building the Query

You start a query by constructing a Query instance. To query entities of a kind, you provide the kind name as a constructor argument, as a string:

```
Query q = new Query("Book");
```

Without calling any additional methods, this represents a query for all entities of the kind "Book".

You can tell the query to filter the results by calling the setFilter() method. A query has one filter, which can have one or more predicates. A predicate is a single property name, a comparison operator, and a value. If your query filter only has one predicate, you can construct a Query.FilterPredicate, and pass it directly to setFilter():

```
q.setFilter(
    new Query.FilterPredicate(
        "copyrightYear",
        Query.FilterOperator.LESS_THAN_OR_EQUAL,
        1950));
```

Filter predicate operators include `LESS_THAN`, `LESS_THAN_OR_EQUAL`, `EQUAL`, `NOT_EQUAL`, `GREATER_THAN_OR_EQUAL`, `GREATER_THAN`, and `IN`.

To build a filter with more than one predicate, you use a `Query.CompositeFilter`. A composite filter is a collection of filters united by a logical operator, either "and" or "or." Each filter in the collection can be a filter predicate or another composite filter, allowing you to build complex filters.

The first argument to the `Query.CompositeFilter` constructor is the composite operator, either `Query.CompositeFilterOperator.AND` or `Query.CompositeFilter Operator.OR`. The second argument is a `Collection` of filters, each of which can be either a `Query.FilterPredicate` or a `Query.CompositeFilter` instance. The verbose object-oriented syntax looks like this:

```
q.setFilter(
    new Query.CompositeFilter(
        Query.CompositeFilterOperator.AND,
        new ArrayList<Query.Filter>(Arrays.asList(
            new Query.FilterPredicate(
                "copyrightYear",
                Query.FilterOperator.LESS_THAN_OR_EQUAL,
                1950),
            new Query.FilterPredicate(
                "category",
                Query.FilterOperator.EQUAL,
                "Science Fiction")))));
```

That can get a little unwieldy, so there's also a shortcut API using methods on the composite and predicate operator classes. `Query.CompositeFilterOperator.and()` and `Query.CompositeFilterOperator.or()` are static methods that take one or more filters and return a composite filter with the appropriate operator. Each filter predicate operator constant has an `of()` method that takes a property name and a value. The preceding example shortens to this:

```
q.setFilter(
    Query.CompositeFilterOperator.and(
        Query.FilterOperator.LESS_THAN_OR_EQUAL.of(
            "copyrightYear", 1950),
        Query.FilterOperator.EQUAL.of(
            "category", "Science Fiction")));
```

 The filter predicate operators `IN` or `NOT_EQUAL` and the composite operator `OR` are not supported by the datastore natively. They are implemented by performing multiple datastore queries and processing the results. While it's possible to build arbitrarily complex query filters with the Java Query API, it's best to limit the use of these operators. See "Not-Equal and IN Filters" on page 175.

You can specify that the results of a query be sorted by calling the `addSort()` method for each sort order. The method takes a property name, and an optional `Query.SortDirection`, either `Query.SortDirection.ASCENDING` or `Query.SortDirection.DESCENDING`. The default is `ASCENDING`:

```
q.addSort("title");
```

Fetching Results with PreparedQuery

The query is not actually performed until you attempt to access results, using the `PreparedQuery` object. If you access the results by using an iterator via the `asIterable()` or `asIterator()` methods, the act of iterating causes the API to fetch the results in batches. When these methods are called without arguments, the resulting iterator keeps going until all results for the query have been returned. If a query has a large number of results, this may take longer than the time allowed for the request.

The `asIterable()` and `asIterator()` methods accept an optional argument, a `Fetch Options` object, that controls which results are returned. Options can include an *offset*, a number of results to skip prior to returning any, and a *limit*, a maximum number of results to return. `FetchOptions` uses a builder-style interface, as follows:

```
import com.google.appengine.api.datastore.Entity;
import com.google.appengine.api.datastore.FetchOptions;
import com.google.appengine.api.datastore.PreparedQuery;
import com.google.appengine.api.datastore.Query;

// ...
        // Query q = ...
        PreparedQuery pq = ds.prepare(q);

        Iterable<Entity> results =
            pq.asIterable(FetchOptions.Builder.withLimit(10).offset(20));

        for (Entity result : results) {
            String title = (String) result.getProperty("title");

            // ...
        }
```

This tells the datastore to skip the first 20 results, and return up to the next 10 results (if any).

In order to perform a fetch with an offset, the datastore must find the first result for the query and then scan down the index to the offset. The amount of time this takes is proportional to the size of the offset, and may not be suitable for large offsets.

If you just want to retrieve results in batches, such as for a paginated display, there's a better way: query cursors. For information on cursors, see "Query Cursors" on page 186.

Instead of fetching results in batches, you can get all results in a list by calling the asList() method of the PreparedQuery class. The method returns a List<Entity>. Unlike the iterator interface, which gets results in batches, this method retrieves all results with a single service call. The method requires that a limit be specified using FetchOptions.

If a query is expected to have only one result, you can call the asSingleEntity() method. This retrieves the result and returns an Entity object, or null if there is no result. It throws a TooManyResultsException if the query returns more than one result unexpectedly.

If you just want a count of the results and not the entities themselves, you can call the countEntities() method of the PreparedQuery. Because the datastore has to perform the query to get the count, the speed of this call is proportional to the count, although faster than actually fetching the results.

To test whether a query would return a result without retrieving the result, call countEntities() with a limit of 1:

```
if (pq.countEntities(FetchOptions.Builder.withLimit(1)) == 1) {
    // The query has at least one result.
}
```

This is the fastest possible such test: it finds the first place in the index where there might be a result for the query, then attempts to count one result, and reports whether that count was successful.

Keys-Only Queries

You can fetch just the keys for the entities that match a query instead of the full entities by using the low-level Java datastore API. To declare that a query should return just the keys, call the setKeysOnly() method on the Query object:

```
Query q = new Query("Book");

q.setKeysOnly();
```

When a query is set to return only keys, the results of the query are `Entity` objects without any properties set. You can get the key from these objects by using the `get Key()` method:

```
PreparedQuery pq = ds.prepare(q);
for (Entity result : pq.asIterable()) {
    Key k = result.getKey();

    // ...
}
```

You can also perform keys-only queries using the JDO and JPA interfaces. See Chapter 10.

Introducing Indexes

For every query an application performs, Cloud Datastore maintains an index, a single table of possible answers for the query. Specifically, it maintains an index for a set of queries that use the same filters and sort orders, possibly with different values for the filters. Consider the following simple query:

```
SELECT * FROM Player WHERE name = 'druidjane'
```

To perform this query, Cloud Datastore uses an index containing the keys of every `Player` entity and the value of each entity's `name` property, sorted by the `name` property values in ascending order. Such an index is illustrated in Figure 7-1.

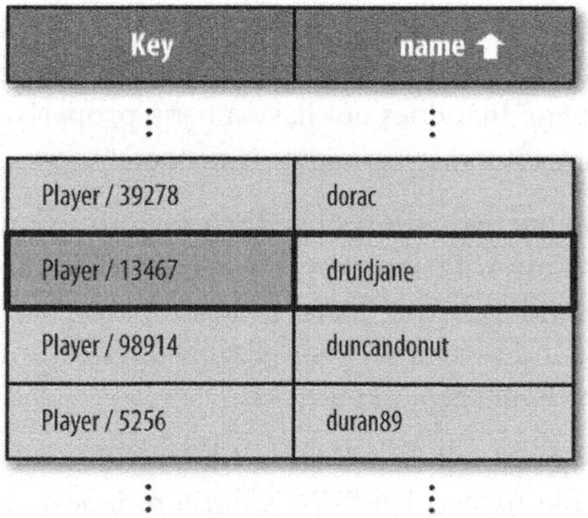

Key	name ⬆
⋮	⋮
Player / 39278	dorac
Player / 13467	druidjane
Player / 98914	duncandonut
Player / 5256	duran89
⋮	⋮

Figure 7-1. An index of Player entity keys and "name" property values, sorted by name in ascending order, with the result for WHERE name = druidjane

To find all entities that meet the conditions of the query, Cloud Datastore finds the first row in the index that matches, then it scans down to the first row that doesn't match. It returns the entities mentioned on all rows in this range (not counting the nonmatching row), in the order they appear in the index. Because the index is sorted, all results for the query are guaranteed to be on consecutive rows in the table.

Cloud Datastore would use this same index to perform other queries with a similar structure but different values, such as the following query:

```
SELECT * FROM Player WHERE name = 'duran89'
```

This query mechanism is fast, even with a very large number of entities. Entities and indexes are distributed across multiple machines, and each machine scans its own index in parallel with the others. Each machine returns results to Cloud Datastore as it scans its own index, and Cloud Datastore delivers the final result set to the app, in order, as if all results were in one large index.

Another reason queries are fast has to do with how the datastore finds the first matching row. Because indexes are sorted, the datastore can use an efficient algorithm to find the first matching row. In the common case, finding the first row takes approximately the same amount of time regardless of the size of the index. In other words, the speed of a query is not affected by the size of the data being queried.

Cloud Datastore updates all relevant indexes when property values change. In this example, if an application retrieves a Player entity, changes the name, and then saves the entity with a call to the put() method, Cloud Datastore updates the appropriate row in the previous index. It also moves the row if necessary so the ordering of the index is preserved.

Similarly, if the application creates a new Player entity with a name property, or deletes a Player entity with a name property, Cloud Datastore updates the index. In contrast, if the application updates a Player but does not change the name property, or creates or deletes a Player that does not have a name property, Cloud Datastore does not update the name index because no update is needed.

Cloud Datastore maintains two indexes like the previous example for every property name and entity kind, one with the property values sorted in ascending order and one with values in descending order. Cloud Datastore also maintains an index of entities of each kind. These indexes satisfy some simple queries, and Cloud Datastore also uses them internally for bookkeeping purposes.

For other queries, you must tell App Engine which indexes to prepare. You do this using a configuration file named *WEB-INF/datastore-indexes.xml*, which gets uploaded along with your application's code.

It'd be a pain to write this file by hand, but thankfully you don't have to. While you're testing your application in the development web server from the SDK, when the app performs a datastore query, the server checks that the configuration file has an appropriate entry for the needed index. If it doesn't find one, it adds one. As long as the app performs each of its queries at least once during testing, the resulting configuration file will be complete.

The index configuration file must be complete, because when the app is running on App Engine, if the application performs a query for which there is no index, the query returns an error. You can tell the development web server to behave similarly if you want to test for these error conditions. (How to do this depends on which SDK you are using; see "Configuring Indexes" on page 193.)

Indexes require a bit of discipline to maintain. Although the development tools can help add index configuration, they cannot know when an index is unused and can be deleted from the file. Extra indexes consume storage space and slow down updates of properties mentioned in the index. And while the version of the app you're developing may not need a given index, the version of the app still running on App Engine may still need it. The App Engine SDK and the Cloud Console include tools for inspecting and maintaining indexes. We'll look at these tools in Chapter 19.

Before we discuss index configuration, let's look more closely at how indexes support queries. We just saw an example where the results for a simple query appear on consecutive rows in a simple index. In fact, this is how most queries work: the results for every query that would use an index appear on consecutive rows in the index. This is both surprisingly powerful in some ways and surprisingly limited in others, and it's worth understanding why.

Automatic Indexes and Simple Queries

As we mentioned, Cloud Datastore maintains two indexes for every single property of every entity kind, one with values in ascending order and one with values in descending order. Cloud Datastore builds these indexes automatically, regardless of whether they are mentioned in the index configuration file. These automatic indexes satisfy the following kinds of queries using consecutive rows:

- A simple query for all entities of a given kind, no filters or sort orders
- One filter on a property using the equality operator (=)
- Filters using greater-than, greater-than or equal to, less-than, or less-than or equal to operators (>, >=, <, <=) on a single property
- One sort order, ascending or descending, and no filters, or with filters only on the same property used with the sort order
- Filters or a sort order on the entity key
- Kindless queries with or without key filters

Let's look at each of these in action.

All Entities of a Kind

The simplest datastore query asks for every entity of a given kind, in any order. Stated in SQL, a query for all entities of the kind Player looks like this:

```
SELECT * FROM Player
```

Cloud Datastore maintains an index mapping kinds to entity keys. This index is sorted using a deterministic ordering for entity keys, so this query returns results in "key order." The kind of an entity cannot be changed after it is created, so this index is updated only when entities are created and deleted.

Because a query can only refer to one kind at a time, you can imagine this index as simply a list of entity keys for each kind. Figure 7-2 illustrates an example of this index.

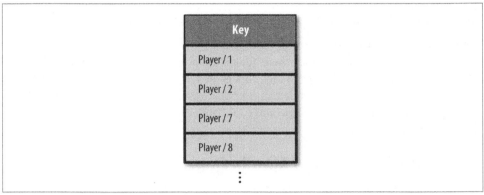

*Figure 7-2. An index of all Player entity keys, with results for SELECT * FROM Player*

When the query results are fetched, Cloud Datastore uses the entity keys in the index to find the corresponding entities, and returns the full entities to the application.

One Equality Filter

Consider the following query, which asks for every Player entity with a level property with a value of the integer 10:

```
SELECT * FROM Player WHERE level = 10
```

This query uses an index of Player entities with the level property, ascending—one of the automatic indexes. It uses an efficient algorithm to find the first row with a level equal to 10. Then it scans down the index until it finds the first row with a level not equal to 10. The consecutive rows from the first matching to the last matching represent all the Player entities with a level property equal to the integer 10. This is illustrated in Figure 7-3.

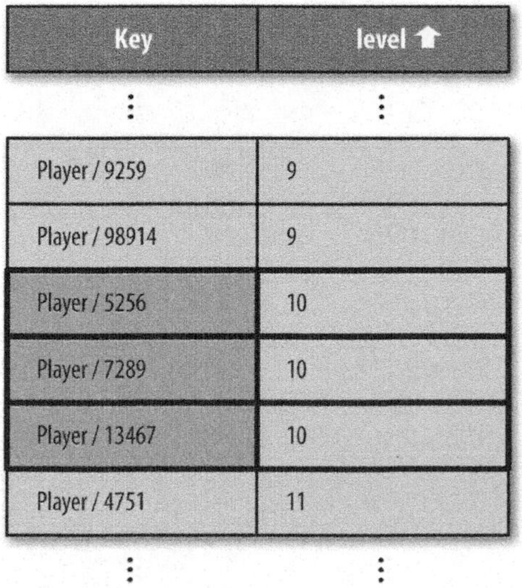

Key	level ⬆
⋮	⋮
Player / 9259	9
Player / 98914	9
Player / 5256	10
Player / 7289	10
Player / 13467	10
Player / 4751	11
⋮	⋮

Figure 7-3. An index of the Player entity "level" properties, sorted by level then by key, with results for WHERE level = 10

Greater-Than and Less-Than Filters

The following query asks for every `Player` entity with a `score` property whose value is greater than the integer 500:

```
SELECT * FROM Player WHERE score > 500
```

This uses an index of `Player` entities with the `score` property, ascending, also an automatic index. As with the equality filter, it finds the first row in the index whose `score` is greater than 500. In the case of greater-than, because the table is sorted by `score` in ascending order, every row from this point to the bottom of the table is a result for the query. See Figure 7-4.

Similarly, consider a query that asks for every `Player` with a `score` less than 1,000:

```
SELECT * FROM Player WHERE score < 1000
```

Cloud Datastore uses the same index (`score`, ascending), and the same strategy: it finds the first row that matches the query, in this case the first row. Then it scans to the next row that doesn't match the query, the first row whose `score` is greater than or equal to `1000`. The results are represented by everything above that row.

Finally, consider a query for `score` values between 500 and 1,000:

```
SELECT * FROM Player WHERE score > 500 AND score < 1000
```

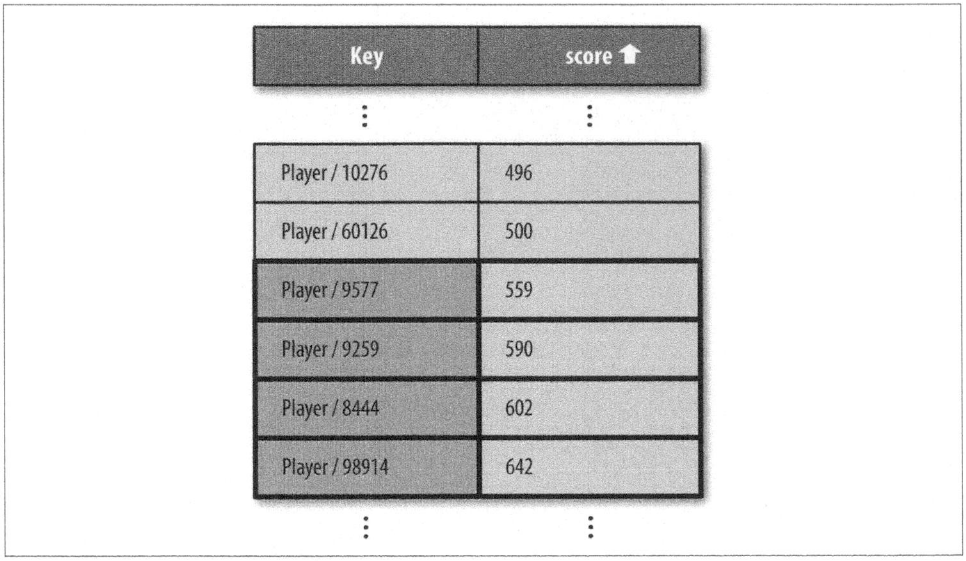

Figure 7-4. An index of the Player entity "score" properties, sorted by "score" then by key, with results for WHERE score > 500

Once again, the same index and strategy prevail: Cloud Datastore scans from the top down, finding the first matching and next nonmatching rows, returning the entities represented by everything in between. This is shown in Figure 7-5.

If the values used with the filters do not represent a valid range, such as score < 500 AND score > 1000, the query planner notices this and doesn't bother performing a query, as it knows the query has no results.

One Sort Order

The following query asks for every Player entity, arranged in order by level, from lowest to highest:

```
SELECT * FROM Player ORDER BY level
```

As before, this uses an index of Player entities with level properties in ascending order. If both this query and the previous equality query were performed by the application, both queries would use the same index. This query uses the index to determine the order in which to return Player entities, starting at the top of the table and moving down until the application stops fetching results, or until the bottom of the table. Recall that every Player entity with a level property is mentioned in this table. See Figure 7-6.

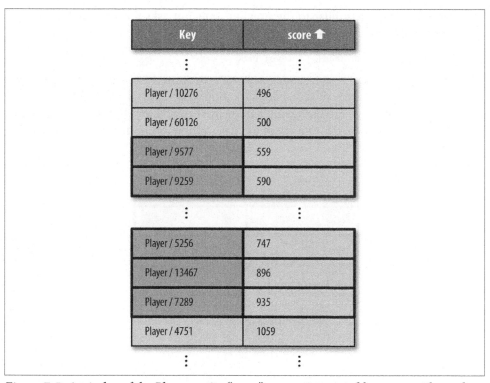

Figure 7-5. An index of the Player entity "score" properties, sorted by score, with results for WHERE score > 500 AND score < 1000

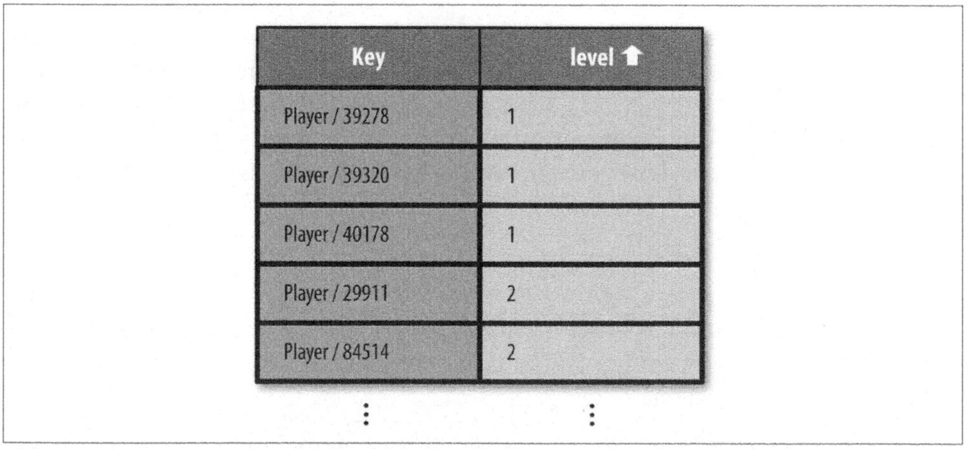

Key	level ⬆
Player / 39278	1
Player / 39320	1
Player / 40178	1
Player / 29911	2
Player / 84514	2

Figure 7-6. An index of the Player entity "level" properties sorted by level in ascending order, with results for ORDER BY level

The following query is similar to the previous one, but asks for the entities arranged by level from highest to lowest:

```
SELECT * FROM Player ORDER BY level DESC
```

This query cannot use the same index as before, because the results are in the wrong order. For this query, the results should start at the entity with the highest level, so the query needs an index where this result is in the first row. Cloud Datastore provides an automatic index for single properties in descending order for this purpose. See Figure 7-7.

Key	level ⬇
Player / 3359	12
Player / 4751	11
Player / 7243	11
Player / 5256	10
Player / 7289	10
⋮	⋮

Figure 7-7. An index of the Player entity "level" properties sorted by level in descending order, with results for ORDER BY level DESC

If a query with a sort order on a single property also includes filters on that property, and no other filters, Cloud Datastore still needs only the one automatic index to fulfill the query. In fact, you may have noticed that for these simple queries, the results are returned sorted by the property in ascending order, regardless of whether the query specifies the sort order explicitly. In these cases, the ascending sort order is redundant.

Queries on Keys

In addition to filters and sort orders on properties, you can also perform queries with filters and sort orders on entity keys. You can refer to an entity's key in a filter or sort order using the special name __key__.

An equality filter on the key isn't much use. Only one entity can have a given key, and if the key is known, it's faster to perform a get() than a query. But an inequality filter on the key can be useful for fetching ranges of keys. (If you're fetching entities in batches, consider using query cursors. See "Query Cursors" on page 186.)

Cloud Datastore provides automatic indexes of kinds and keys, sorted by key in ascending order. The query returns the results sorted in key order. This order isn't useful for display purposes, but it's deterministic. A query that sorts keys in descending order requires a custom index.

Cloud Datastore uses indexes for filters on keys in the same way as filters on properties, with a minor twist: a query using a key filter in addition to other filters can use an automatic index if a similar query without the key filter could use an automatic index. Automatic indexes for properties already include the keys, so such queries can just use the same indexes. And of course, if the query has no other filters beyond the key filter, it can use the automatic key index.

Kindless Queries

In addition to performing queries on entities of a given kind, the datastore lets you perform a limited set of queries on entities of all kinds. Kindless queries cannot use filters or sort orders on properties. They can, however, use equality and inequality filters on keys (IDs or names).

Kindless queries are mostly useful in combination with ancestors, which we'll discuss in Chapter 8. They can also be used to get every entity in the datastore. (If you're querying a large number of entities, you'll probably want to fetch the results in batches. See "Query Cursors" on page 186.)

In the Java API, you perform a kindless query by calling the `Query` constructor without a kind argument:

```
Query q = new Query();

q.setFilter(new Query.FilterPredicate(
    "__key__",
    Query.FilterOperator.GREATER_THAN,
    last_key));
```

The results of a kindless query are returned in key order, ascending. Kindless queries use an automatic index.

The datastore maintains statistics about the apps data in a set of datastore entities. When the app performs a kindless query, these statistics entities are included in the results. The kind names for these entities all begin with the characters __Stat_ (two underscores, the word "Stat," and another underscore). Your app will need to filter these out if they are not desired.

For more information about datastore statistics, see "Accessing Metadata from the App" on page 223.

Custom Indexes and Complex Queries

All queries not covered by the automatic indexes must have corresponding indexes defined in the app's index configuration file. We'll refer to these as "custom indexes," in contrast with "automatic indexes." App Engine needs these hints because building every possible index for every combination of property and sort order would take a gargantuan amount of space and time, and an app isn't likely to need more than a fraction of those possibilities.

In particular, the following queries require custom indexes:

- A query with multiple sort orders
- A query with an inequality filter on a property and filters on other properties
- Projection queries

A query that uses just equality filters on properties does not need a custom index in most cases thanks to a specialized query algorithm for this case, which we'll look at in a moment. Also, filters on keys do not require custom indexes; they can operate on whatever indexes are used to fulfill the rest of the query.

Let's examine these queries and the indexes they require. We'll cover projection queries in "Projection Queries" on page 190.

Multiple Sort Orders

The automatic single-property indexes provide enough information for one sort order. When two entities have the same value for the sorted property, the entities appear in the index in adjacent rows, ordered by their entity keys. If you want to order these entities with other criteria, you need an index with more information.

The following query asks for all `Player` entities, sorted first by the `level` property in descending order, then, in the case of ties, sorted by the `score` property in descending order:

```
SELECT * FROM Player ORDER BY level DESC, score DESC
```

The index this query needs is straightforward: a table of `Player` entity keys, `level` values, and `score` values, sorted according to the query. This is not one of the indexes provided by the datastore automatically, so it is a custom index, and must be mentioned in the index configuration file. If you performed this query in the Java development web server, the server would add the following lines to the *war/WEB-INF/appengine-generated/datastore-indexes-auto.xml* file:

```
<datastore-indexes autoGenerate="true">
  <datastore-index kind="Player" ancestor="false">
    <property name="level" direction="desc" />
```

```
        <property name="score" direction="desc" />
    </datastore-index>
</datastore-indexes>
```

To configure this index manually, you would place this in *war/WEB-INF/datastore-indexes.xml*. Be sure to include the `autoGenerate="true"` attribute to say that you want the custom configuration merged with the generated configuration.

The order the properties appear in the configuration file matters. This is the order in which the rows are sorted: first by `level` descending, then by `score` descending.

This configuration creates the index shown in Figure 7-8. The results appear in the table, and are returned for the query in the desired order.

Key	level ⬇	score ⬇
Player / 3359	12	1366
Player / 7243	11	1280
Player / 4751	11	1059
Player / 7289	10	935
Player / 13467	10	896
⋮	⋮	⋮

Figure 7-8. An index of the Player entity "level" and "score" properties, sorted by level descending, then score descending, then by key ascending

Filters on Multiple Properties

Consider the following query, which asks for every `Player` with a `level` greater than the integer `10` and a `charclass` of the string `'mage'`:

```
SELECT * FROM Player WHERE charclass = 'mage' AND level > 10
```

To be able to scan to a contiguous set of results meeting both filter criteria, the index must contain columns of values for these properties. The entities must be sorted first by `charclass`, then by `level`.

The index configuration for this query would appear as follows in the *datastore-indexes.xml* file:

```
<datastore-indexes autoGenerate="true">
    <datastore-index kind="Player" ancestor="false">
        <property name="charclass" direction="asc" />
        <property name="level" direction="asc" />
```

```
    </datastore-index>
  </datastore-indexes>
```

This index is illustrated in Figure 7-9.

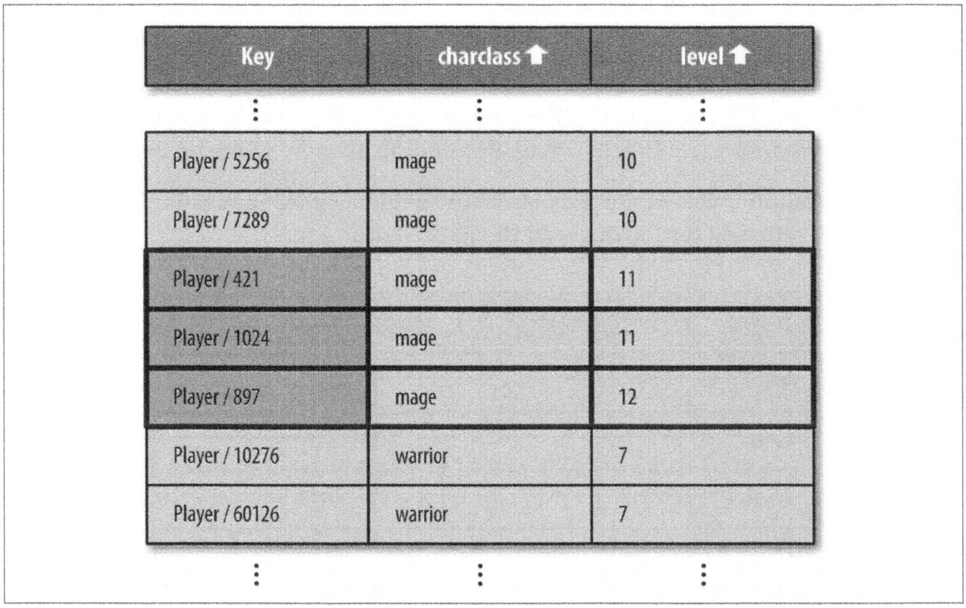

Key	charclass ⬆	level ⬆
⋮	⋮	⋮
Player / 5256	mage	10
Player / 7289	mage	10
Player / 421	mage	11
Player / 1024	mage	11
Player / 897	mage	12
Player / 10276	warrior	7
Player / 60126	warrior	7
⋮	⋮	⋮

Figure 7-9. An index of the Player entity "charclass" and "level" properties, sorted by charclass, then level, then key, with results for WHERE charclass = "mage" AND level > 10

The ordering sequence of these properties is important! Remember: the results for the query must all appear on adjacent rows in the index. If the index for this query were sorted first by level then by charclass, it would be possible for valid results to appear on nonadjacent rows. Figure 7-10 demonstrates this problem.

The index ordering requirement for combining inequality and equality filters has several implications that may seem unusual when compared to the query engines of other databases. Heck, they're downright weird. The first implication, illustrated previously, can be stated generally:

> **The First Rule of Inequality Filters:** If a query uses inequality filters on one property and equality filters on one or more other properties, the index must be ordered first by the properties used in equality filters, then by the property used in the inequality filters.

This rule has a corollary regarding queries with both an inequality filter and sort orders. Consider the following possible query:

```
SELECT * FROM Player WHERE level > 10 ORDER BY score DESC
```

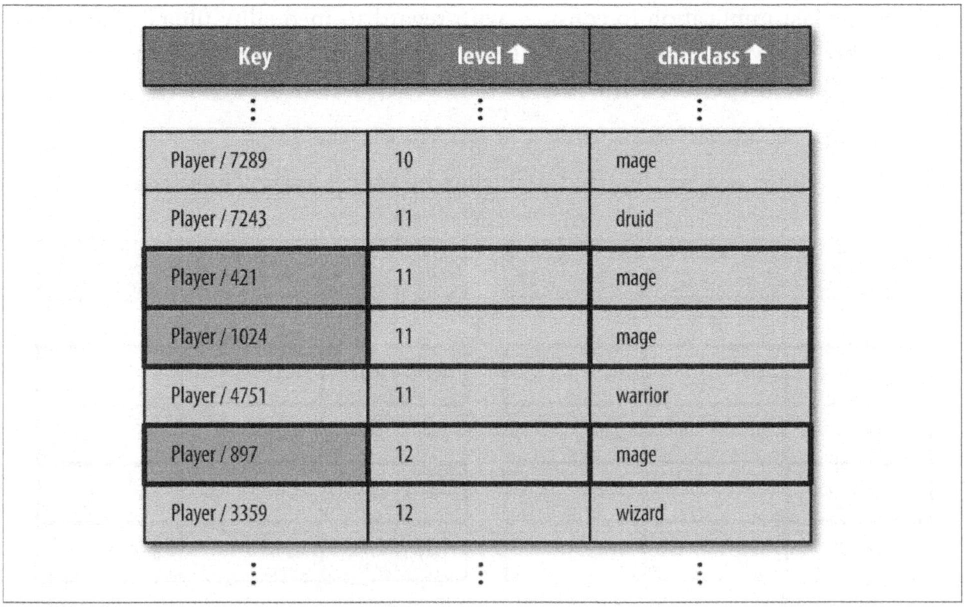

Figure 7-10. An index of the Player entity "charclass" and "level" properties, sorted first by level then by charclass, which cannot satisfy WHERE charclass = "mage" AND level > 10 with consecutive rows

What would the index for this query look like? For starters, it would have a column for the level, so it can select the rows that match the filter. It would also have a column for the score, to determine the order of the results. But which column is ordered first?

The First Rule implies that level must be ordered first. But the query requested that the results be returned sorted by score, descending. If the index were sorted by score, then by level, the rows may not be adjacent.

To avoid confusion, App Engine requires that the correct sort order be stated explicitly in the query:

```
SELECT * FROM Player WHERE level > 10 ORDER BY level, score DESC
```

In general:

> **The Second Rule of Inequality Filters:** If a query uses inequality filters on one property and sort orders of one or more other properties, the index must be ordered first by the property used in the inequality filters (in either direction), then by the other desired sort orders. To avoid confusion, the query must state all sort orders explicitly.

There's one last implication to consider with regard to inequality filters. The following possible query attempts to get all `Player` entities with a `level` less than 10 and a `score` less than 500:

```
SELECT * FROM Player WHERE level < 10 AND score < 500
```

Consider an index ordered first by `level`, then by `score`, as shown in Figure 7-11.

Key	level ⬆	score ⬆	Key	score ⬆	level ⬆
⋮	⋮	⋮	⋮	⋮	⋮
Player / 5052	8	498	Player / 5052	498	8
Player / 5176	8	500	Player / 8311	498	10
Player / 5844	9	499	Player / 5844	499	9
Player / 8311	10	498	Player / 5178	500	8
⋮	⋮	⋮	⋮	⋮	⋮

Figure 7-11. Neither possible index of the Player entity "level" and "score" properties can satisfy WHERE level < 10 AND score < 500 with consecutive rows

In fact, there is no possible index that could satisfy this query completely using consecutive rows. This is not a valid App Engine datastore query.

> **The Third Rule of Inequality Filters:** A query cannot use inequality filters on more than one property.

A query *can* use multiple inequality filters on the same property, such as to test for a range of values.

Multiple Equality Filters

For queries using just equality filters, it's easy to imagine custom indexes that satisfy them. For instance:

```
SELECT * FROM Player WHERE charclass = 'mage' AND level = 10
```

A custom index containing these properties, ordered in any sequence and direction, would meet the query's requirements. But App Engine has another trick up its sleeve for this kind of query. For queries using just equality filters and no sort orders, instead of scanning a single table of all values, App Engine can scan the automatic single-property indexes for each property, and return the results as it finds them. App Engine can perform a "merge join" of the single-property indexes to satisfy this kind of query.

In other words, the datastore doesn't need a custom index to perform queries using just equality filters and no sort orders. If you add a suitable custom index to your configuration file, the datastore will use it. But a custom index is not required, and the development server's automatic index configuration feature will not add one if it doesn't exist.

Let's consider how the algorithm would perform the following query, using single-property indexes:

```
SELECT * FROM Kind WHERE a=1 AND b=2 AND c=3
```

Recall that each of these tables contains a row for each entity with the property set, with fields for the entity's key and the property's value. The table is sorted first by the value, then by the key. The algorithm takes advantage of the fact that rows with the same value are consecutive, and within that consecutive block, rows are sorted by key.

To perform the query, the datastore uses the following steps:

1. The datastore checks the a index for the first row with a value of 1. The entity whose key is on this row is a candidate, but not yet a confirmed result.

2. It then checks the b index for the first row whose value is 2 *and* whose key is greater than or equal to the candidate's key. Other rows with a value of 2 may appear above this row in the b index, but the datastore knows those are not candidates because the first a scan determined the candidate with the smallest key.

3. If the datastore finds the candidate's key in the matching region of b, that key is still a candidate, and the datastore proceeds with a similar check in the index for c. If the datastore does not find the candidate in the b index but does find another larger key with a matching value, that key becomes the new candidate, and it proceeds to check for the new candidate in the c index. (It'll eventually go back to check a with the new candidate before deciding it is a result.) If it finds neither the candidate nor a matching row with a larger key, the query is complete.

4. If a candidate is found to match all criteria in all indexes, the candidate is returned as a result. The datastore starts the search for a new candidate, using the previous candidate's key as the minimum key.

Figure 7-12 illustrates this zigzag search across the single-property indexes, first with a failed candidate, then two successful candidates.

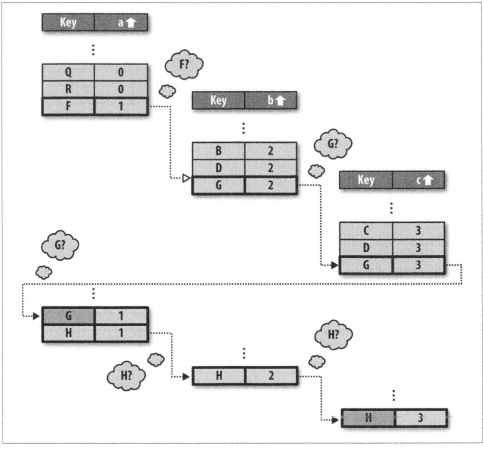

Figure 7-12. The merge join algorithm finding two entities WHERE a = 1 AND b = 2 AND c = 3

A key feature of this algorithm is that it finds results in the order in which they are to be returned: key order. The datastore does not need to compile a complete list of possible results for the query—possibly millions of entities—and sort them to determine which results ought to be first. Also, the datastore can stop scanning as soon as it has enough results to fulfill the query, which is always a limited number of entities.

Of course, this query could also use a custom index with all the filter properties in it. If you provide configuration for such an index, the query will use the custom index instead of doing the zigzag join. This can result in a query faster than the zigzag join, at the expense of added time to update the indexed entities.

A zigzag-capable query using equality filters on properties can also use inequality filters on keys without needing a custom index. This is useful for fetching a large number of results in key ranges. (But if you're fetching batches, cursors might be more effective. See "Query Cursors" on page 186.)

Not-Equal and IN Filters

The query API supports two operators we haven't discussed yet: != (not-equal) and IN. These operators are not actually supported by the datastore itself. Instead, they are implemented by the datastore API as multiple queries in terms of the other operators.

The filter prop != value matches every entity whose property does not equal the value. The datastore API determines the result set by performing two queries: one using prop < value in place of the not-equal filter, and one using prop > value in place of the filter. It returns both sets of results as one result set, which it can do reasonably quickly because the results are already in order.

Because not-equal is actually implemented in terms of the inequality operators, it is subject to the three rules of inequality operators:

- The query's index must be ordered by the property used with the not-equal filter before other sort orders.
- If the query uses other explicit sort orders, the not-equal filter's property must be explicitly ordered first.
- And finally, any query using a not-equal filter cannot also use inequality or not-equal filters on other properties.

A not-equal filter will never return an entity that doesn't have the filtered property. This is true for all filters, but can be especially counterintuitive in the case of not-equal.

The filter prop IN (value1, value2, value3) matches every entity whose property equals any of the values. The datastore API implements this as a series of equality queries, one for each value to test. The more values that appear in the list, the longer the full set of queries will take to execute.

If a single query includes multiple IN filters on multiple properties, the datastore API must perform equality queries for every combination of values in all filters. prop1 IN (value1, value2, value3, value4) AND prop2 IN (value5, value6, value7) is equivalent to 12 queries using equality filters.

The != and IN operators are useful shortcuts. But because they actually perform multiple queries, they take longer to execute than the other operators. It's worth understanding their performance implications before using them.

Unset and Nonindexed Properties

As you've seen, an index contains columns of property values. Typically, an app creates entities of the same kind with the same set of properties: every Player in our game has a name, a character class, a level, and a score. If every entity of a kind has a given property, then an index for that kind and property has a row corresponding to each entity of the kind.

But the datastore neither requires nor enforces a common layout of properties across entities of a kind. It's quite possible for an entity to not have a property that other entities of the same kind have. For instance, a Player entity might be created without a character class, and go without until the user chooses one.

It is possible to set a property with a null value, but a property set to the null value is distinct from the property not being set at all. This is different from a tabular database, which requires a value (possibly null) for every cell in a row.

If an entity does not have a property used in an index, the entity does not appear in the index. Stated conversely, an entity must have *every* property mentioned in an index to appear in the index. If a Player does not have a charclass property, it does not appear in any index with a charclass column.

If an entity is not mentioned in an index, it cannot be returned as a result for a query that uses the index. Remember that queries use indexes for both filters and sort orders. A query that uses a property for any kind of filter or any sort order can never return an entity that doesn't have that property. The charclass-less Player can never be a result for a Player query that sorts results by charclass.

In "Strings, Text, and Bytes" on page 140, we mentioned that text and blob values are not indexed. Another way of saying this is that, for the purposes of indexes, a property with a text or blob value is treated as if it is unset. If an app performs a query by using a filter or sort order on a property that is always set to a text or blob value, that query will always return no results.

It is sometimes useful to store property values of other types, and exempt them from indexes. This saves space in index tables, and reduces the amount of time it takes to save the entity.

In the Java API, you can set a property as unindexed by using the setUnindexedProperty() method of the Entity object, instead of the setProperty() method. An entity can only have one property of a given name, so an unindexed property overwrites an indexed one, and vice versa. You can also declare properties as unindexed in the JDO and JPA interfaces; see Chapter 10.

If you need an entity to qualify as a result for a query, but it doesn't make sense in your data model to give the entity every property used in the query, use the null value to represent the "no value" case, and always set it. The JDO and JPA interfaces make it easy to ensure that properties always have values.

Sort Orders and Value Types

App Engine keeps the rows of an index sorted in an order that supports the corresponding query. Each type of property value has its own rules for comparing two values of the same type, and these rules are mostly intuitive: integers are sorted in numeric order, strings in Unicode order, and so forth.

Two entities can have values of different types for the same property, so App Engine also has rules for comparing such values, although these rules are not so intuitive. Values are ordered first by type, then within their type. For instance, all integers are sorted above all strings.

One effect of this that might be surprising is that all floats are sorted below all integers. The datastore treats floats and integers as separate value types, and so sorts them separately. If your app relies on the correct ordering of numbers, make sure all numbers are stored using the same type of value.

The datastore stores eight distinct types of values, not counting the nonindexed types (text and blob). The datastore supports several additional types by storing them as one of the eight types, then marshaling them between the internal representation and the value your app sees automatically. These additional types are sorted by their internal representation. For instance, a date-time value is actually stored as an integer, and will be sorted among other integer values in an index. (When comparing date-time values, this results in chronological order, which is what you would expect.)

Table 7-1 describes the eight indexable types supported by the datastore. The types are listed in their relative order, from first to last.

Table 7-1. How the datastore value types are sorted

Data type	Java type	Ordering
The null value	`null`	-
Integer and date-time	`long` (other integer types are widened), `java.util.Date`, `datastore.Rating`	Numeric (date-time is chronological)
Boolean	`boolean` (`true` or `false`)	False, then true
Byte string	`datastore.ShortBlob`	Byte order

Data type	Java type	Ordering
Unicode string	`java.lang.String`, `datastore.Category`, `datastore.Email`, `datastore.IMHandle`, `datastore.Link`, `datastore.PhoneNumber`, `datastore.PostalAddress`	Unicode character order
Floating-point number	`double`	Numeric
Geographical point	`datastore.GeoPt`	By latitude, then longitude (floating-point numbers)
A Google account	`users.User`	By email address, Unicode order
Entity key	`datastore.Key`	Kind (byte string), then ID (numeric) or name (byte string)

Queries and Multivalued Properties

In a typical database, a field in a record stores a single value. A record represents a data object, and each field represents a single, simple aspect of the object. If a data object can have more than one of a particular thing, each of those things is typically represented by a separate record of an appropriate kind, associated with the data object by using the object's key as a field value. Cloud Datastore supports both of these uses of fields: a property can contain a simple value or the key of another entity.

But Cloud Datastore can do something most other databases can't: it can store more than one value for a single property. With multivalued properties (MVPs), you can represent a data object with more than one of something without resorting to creating a separate entity for each of those things, if each thing could be represented by a simple value.

One of the most useful features of multivalued properties is how they match an equality filter in a query. The datastore query engine considers a multivalued property equal to a filter value if any of the property's values is equal to the filter value. This ability to test for membership means MVPs are useful for representing sets.

Multivalued properties maintain the order of values, and can have repeated items. The values can be of any datastore type, and a single property can have values of different types.

MVPs in Code

Consider the following example. The players of our online game can earn trophies for particular accomplishments. The app needs to display a list of all the trophies a player has won, and the app needs to display a list of all the players who have won a particular trophy. The app doesn't need to maintain any data about the trophies themselves; it's sufficient to just store the name of the trophy. (This could also be a list of keys for trophy entities.)

One option is to store the list of trophy names as a single delimited string value for each Player entity. This makes it easy to get the list of trophies for a particular player, but impossible to get the list of players for a particular trophy. (A query filter can't match patterns within string values.)

Another option is to record each trophy win in a separate property named after the trophy. To get the list of players with a trophy, you just query for the existence of the corresponding property. However, getting the list of trophies for a given player would require either coding the names of all the trophies in the display logic, or iterating over all the Player entity's properties looking for trophy names.

With multivalued properties, we can store each trophy name as a separate value for the trophies property. To access a list of all trophies for a player, we simply access the property of the entity. To get a list of all players with a trophy, we use a query with an equality filter on the property.

Here's what this example looks like in code:

```
Key k = KeyFactory.createKey("Player", userId);
Entity player = datastore.get(k);
// (catch EntityNotFoundException)

// Entity player = ...
List<String> trophies = new ArrayList<String>();
trophies.add("Lava Polo Champion");
trophies.add("World Building 2008, Bronze");
trophies.add("Glarcon Fighter, 2nd class");
player.setProperty("trophies", trophies);
datastore.put(player);

// List all trophies for a player.
trophies = (List<String>) player.getProperty("trophies");
for (String trophy : trophies) {
    // ...
}

// Query all players that have a trophy.
Query q = new Query("Player");
q.setFilter(
        new Query.FilterPredicate(
            "trophies",
            FilterOperator.EQUAL,
            "Lava Polo Champion"));
PreparedQuery pq = datastore.prepare(q);
for (Entity result : pq.asIterable()) {
```

```
        // ...
    }
```

The Java low-level datastore API represents multivalued properties as `java.util.List` objects, parameterized with a native datastore type. When you call `setProperty()` on an `Entity`, the value can be any `Collection` of a native type. The values are stored in iterator order. When you retrieve the property value with `get Property()`, the values are returned in a `List`:

```
Entity trophyCase = new Entity("TrophyCase");

List<String> trophyNames = new ArrayList<String>();
trophyNames.add("Goblin Rush Bronze");
trophyNames.add("10-Hut! (built 10 huts)");
trophyNames.add("Moon Landing");
trophyCase.setProperty("trophyNames", trophyNames);

ds.put(trophyCase);

// ...

// Key tcKey = ...
Entity newTrophyCase = ds.get(tcKey);
@SuppressWarnings("unchecked")
List<String> newTrophyNames =
    (List<String>) trophyCase.getProperty("trophyNames");
```

To represent a multivalued property with diverse value types, use `List<Object>`. Storing an unsupported type in such a `List` is a runtime error.

A property must have at least one value, otherwise the property does not exist. To enforce this, the Java API throws a runtime error if you assign an empty collection to a property. When using the low-level datastore API, your code must handle this as a special case, and represent "no values" by not setting (or by deleting) the property.

Remember that `List` (or `Collection`) is not a datastore type. It can only contain native types, and not another `Collection`.

MVPs and Equality Filters

As you've seen, when a multivalued property is the subject of an equality filter in a query, the entity matches if any of the property's values are equal to the filter value:

```
Entity e1 = new Entity("MyKind");
e1.setProperty("prop", Arrays.asList(3.14, "a", "b"));
datastore.put(e1);

Entity e2 = new Entity("MyKind");
e2.setProperty("prop", Arrays.asList("a", 1, 6));
datastore.put(e2);
```

```
// Returns e1 but not e2:
Query q1 = new Query("MyKind");
q1.setFilter(
    new Query.FilterPredicate(
        "prop",
        FilterOperator.EQUAL,
        3.14));
// ...

// Returns e2 but not e1:
Query q2 = new Query("MyKind");
q2.setFilter(
    new Query.FilterPredicate(
        "prop",
        FilterOperator.EQUAL,
        6));
// ...

// Returns both e1 and e2:
Query q3 = new Query("MyKind");
q3.setFilter(
    new Query.FilterPredicate(
        "prop",
        FilterOperator.EQUAL,
        "a"));
// ...
```

Recall that a query with a single equality filter uses an index that contains the keys of every entity of the given kind with the given property and the property values. If an entity has a single value for the property, the index contains one row that represents the entity and the value. If an entity has multiple values for the property, the index contains one row for each value. The index for this example is shown in Figure 7-13.

This brings us to the first of several odd-looking queries that nonetheless make sense for multivalued properties. Because an equality filter is a membership test, it is possible for multiple equality filters to use the same property with different values and still return a result. An example in SQL:

```
SELECT * FROM Entity WHERE prop = 'a' AND prop = 'b'
```

Cloud Datastore uses the "merge join" algorithm, described in "Multiple Equality Filters" on page 172 for multiple equality filters, to satisfy this query, using the prop single-property index. This query returns the e1 entity because the entity key appears in two places in the index, once for each value requested by the filters.

The way multivalued properties appear in an index gives us another way of thinking about multivalued properties: an entity has one or more properties, each with a name and a single value, and an entity can have multiple properties with the same name. The API represents the values of multiple properties with the same name as a list of values associated with that name.

Key	prop ⬆
e2	1
e2	6
e1	a
e2	a
e1	b
e1	3.14

Figure 7-13. An index of two entities with multiple values for the "prop" property, with results for WHERE prop = 'a'

The datastore does not have a way to query for the exact set of values in a multivalued property. You can use multiple equality filters to test that each of several values belongs to the list, but there is no filter that ensures that those are the only values that belong to the list, or that each value appears only once.

MVPs and Inequality Filters

Just as an equality filter tests that any value of the property is equal to the filter value, an inequality filter tests that any value of the property meets the filter criterion:

```
Entity e1 = new Entity("MyKind");
e1.setProperty("prop", Arrays.asList(1, 3, 5));
datastore.put(e1);

Entity e2 = new Entity("MyKind");
e2.setProperty("prop", Arrays.asList(4, 6, 8));
datastore.put(e2);

// Returns e1 but not e2:
Query q1 = new Query("MyKind");
q1.setFilter(
    new Query.FilterPredicate(
        "prop",
        FilterOperator.LESS_THAN,
        2));
// ...

// Returns e2 but not e1:
Query q2 = new Query("MyKind");
q2.setFilter(
```

```
        new Query.FilterPredicate(
            "prop",
            FilterOperator.GREATER_THAN,
            7));
// ...

// Returns both e1 and e2:
Query q3 = new Query("MyKind");
q3.setFilter(
    new Query.FilterPredicate(
        "prop",
        FilterOperator.GREATER_THAN,
        3));
// ...
```

Figure 7-14 shows the index for this example, with the results of prop > 3 highlighted.

In the case of an inequality filter, it's possible for the index scan to match rows for a single entity multiple times. When this happens, the first occurrence of each key in the index determines the order of the results. If the index used for the query sorts the property in ascending order, the first occurrence is the smallest matching value. For descending, it's the largest. In this example, prop > 3 returns e2 before e1 because 4 appears before 5 in the index.

Key	prop ⬆
e1	1
e1	3
e2	4
e1	5
e2	6
e2	8

Figure 7-14. An index of two entities with multiple values for the "prop" property, with results for WHERE prop > 3

MVPs and Sort Orders

To summarize things we know about how multivalued properties are indexed:

- A multivalued property appears in an index with one row per value.
- All rows in an index are sorted by the values, possibly distributing property values for a single entity across the index.
- The first occurrence of an entity in an index scan determines its place in the result set for a query.

Together, these facts explain what happens when a query orders its results by a multivalued property. When results are sorted by a multivalued property in ascending order, the smallest value for the property determines its location in the results. When results are sorted in descending order, the largest value for the property determines its location.

This has a counterintuitive—but consistent—consequence:

```
Entity e1 = new Entity("MyKind");
e1.setProperty("prop", Arrays.asList(1, 3, 5));
datastore.put(e1);

Entity e2 = new Entity("MyKind");
e2.setProperty("prop", Arrays.asList(2, 3, 4));
datastore.put(e2);

// Returns e1, e2:
Query q1 = new Query("MyKind");
q1.addSort("prop", Query.SortDirection.ASCENDING);
// ...

// Also returns e1, e2:
Query q2 = new Query("MyKind");
q1.addSort("prop", QUery.SortDirection.DESCENDING);
// ...
```

Because e1 has both the smallest value and the largest value, it appears first in the result set in ascending order *and* in descending order. See Figure 7-15.

Key	prop ⬆	Key	prop ⬇
e1	1	e1	5
e2	2	e2	4
e1	3	e1	3
e2	3	e2	3
e2	4	e2	2
e1	5	e1	1

Figure 7-15. Indexes of two entities with multiple values for the "prop" property, one ascending and one descending

MVPs and the Query Planner

The query planner tries to be smart by ignoring aspects of the query that are redundant or contradictory. For instance, `a = 3 AND a = 4` would normally return no results, so the query planner catches those cases and doesn't bother doing work it doesn't need to do. However, most of these normalization techniques don't apply to multivalued properties. In this case, the query could be asking, "Does this MVP have a value that is equal to 3 and another value equal to 4?" The datastore remembers which properties are MVPs (even those that end up with one or zero values), and never takes a shortcut that would produce incorrect results.

But there is one exception. A query that has both an equality filter and a sort order on the same property will drop the sort order. If a query asks for `a = 3 ORDER BY a DESC` and `a` is a single-value property, the sort order has no effect because all values in the result are identical. For an MVP, however, `a = 3` tests for membership, and two MVPs that meet that condition are not necessarily identical.

The datastore drops the sort order in this case anyway. To do otherwise would require too much index data and result in exploding indexes in cases that could otherwise survive. As always, the actual sort order is deterministic, but it won't be the requested order.

Exploding Indexes

There's one more thing to know about indexes when considering multivalued properties for your data model.

When an entity has multiple values for a property, each index that includes a column for the property must use multiple rows to represent the entity, one for each possible combination of values. In a single property index on the multivalued property, this is simply one row for each value, two columns each (the entity key and the property value).

In an index of multiple properties where the entity has multiple values for one of the indexed properties and a single value for each of the others, the index includes one row for each value of the multivalued property. Each row has a column for each indexed property, plus the key. The values for the single-value properties are repeated in each row.

Here's the kicker: if an entity has more than one property with multiple values, and more than one multivalued property appears in an index, the index must contain one row for each combination of values to represent the entity completely.

If you're not careful, the number of index rows that need to be updated when the entity changes could grow very large. It may be so large that the datastore cannot complete an update of the entity before it reaches its safety limits, and returns an error.

To help prevent "exploding indexes" from causing problems, Cloud Datastore limits the number of property values—that is, the number of rows times the number of columns—a single entity can occupy in an index. The limit is 5,000 property values, high enough for normal use, but low enough to prevent unusual index sizes from inhibiting updates.

If you do include a multivalued property in a custom index, be careful about the possibility of exploding indexes.

Query Cursors

A query often has more results than you want to process in a single action. A message board may have thousands of messages, but it isn't useful to show a user thousands of messages on one screen. It would be better to show the user a dozen messages at a time, and let the user decide when to look at more, such as by clicking a Next link, or scrolling to the bottom of the display.

A *query cursor* is like a bookmark in a list of query results. After fetching some results, you can ask the query API for the cursor that represents the spot immediately after the last result you fetched. When you perform the query again at a later time, you can include the cursor value, and the next result fetched will be the one at the spot where the cursor was generated.

Cursors are fast. Unlike with the "offset" fetch parameter, the datastore does not have to scan from the beginning of the results to find the cursor location. The time to fetch results starting from a cursor is proportional to the number of results fetched. This makes cursors ideal for paginated displays of items.

The following is code for a simple paginated display:

```java
package messages;

import java.io.IOException;
import java.util.Date;

import javax.servlet.RequestDispatcher;
import javax.servlet.ServletException;
import javax.servlet.http.*;

import com.google.appengine.api.datastore.Cursor;
import com.google.appengine.api.datastore.DatastoreService;
import com.google.appengine.api.datastore.DatastoreServiceFactory;
import com.google.appengine.api.datastore.Entity;
import com.google.appengine.api.datastore.FetchOptions;
import com.google.appengine.api.datastore.PreparedQuery;
import com.google.appengine.api.datastore.Query;
import com.google.appengine.api.datastore.QueryResultList;

@SuppressWarnings("serial")
public class MessagesServlet extends HttpServlet {
    private static int PAGE_SIZE = 10;

    public void doGet(HttpServletRequest req, HttpServletResponse resp)
            throws IOException, ServletException {
        DatastoreService datastore =
            DatastoreServiceFactory.getDatastoreService();

        Query q = new Query("Message");
        q.addSort("createDate", Query.SortDirection.DESCENDING);

        String cursorStr = req.getParameter("c");
        FetchOptions options = FetchOptions.Builder.withLimit(PAGE_SIZE);
        if (cursorStr != null) {
            Cursor cursor = Cursor.fromWebSafeString(cursorStr);
            options = options.startCursor(cursor);
        }

        PreparedQuery pq = datastore.prepare(q);
        QueryResultList<Entity> results = pq.asQueryResultList(options);

        Cursor newCursor = results.getCursor();
```

```
        String newCursorStr = null;
        if (results.size() == PAGE_SIZE) {
            newCursorStr = newCursor.toWebSafeString();
        }

        req.setAttribute("results", results);
        req.setAttribute("cursor", newCursorStr);
        RequestDispatcher jsp =
            req.getRequestDispatcher("/WEB-INF/messages.jsp");
        jsp.forward(req, resp);
    }
}
```

The */WEB-INF/messages.jsp* template is as follows (note the Next link in particular):

```
<%@ taglib uri="http://java.sun.com/jsp/jstl/core" prefix="c"%>
<html>
<head>
  <title>Messages</title>
</head>
<body>
  <c:choose>
      <c:when test="${not empty results}">
    <p>Messages:</p>
      <ul>
        <c:forEach var="result" items="${results}">
          <li>${result.key.id}</li>
        </c:forEach>
      </ul>
      <c:if test="${cursor != null}">
        <p>
          <a href="/messages?c=${cursor}">Next</a>
        </p>
      </c:if>
    </c:when>
    <c:otherwise>
      <p>There are no messages.</p>
    </c:otherwise>
  </c:choose>
</body>
</html>
```

This example displays the IDs all of the Message entities in the datastore, in reverse chronological order, in pages of 10 messages per page. If there are more results after the last result displayed, the app shows a Next link back to the request handler with the c parameter set to the cursor pointing to the spot after the last-fetched result. This causes the next set of results fetched to start where the previous page left off.

A cursor is a base64-encoded string. It is safe to use as a query parameter this way: it cannot be corrupted by the user to fetch results outside of the expected query range. Note that, like the string form of datastore keys, the base64-encoded value can be decoded to reveal the names of kinds and properties, so you may wish to further encrypt or hide the value if these are sensitive.

The Cursor value is available from the QueryResultList<Entity> or QueryResultIterator<Entity> object representing the results, which you get when you execute the PreparedQuery via the asQueryResultList() or asQueryResultIterator() methods, respectively. (Similarly, you can call asQueryResultIterable() for the QueryResultIterable<Entity>, then get the QueryResultIterator with its iterator() method.) On these objects, the getCursor() method returns the Cursor that represents the cursor position after the last result returned.

Notice that you'll get a cursor even if no more results are available after the cursor. If you need to know definitively that there are more results, you must perform another brief query for one more result based on the cursor.

You get the string form of a Cursor with its toWebSafeString() method. To get a Cursor from a string, you use the static method Cursor.fromWebSafeString().

To use a Cursor with a query, you set it in the FetchOptions used when fetching results from the PreparedQuery. You can set a *start cursor*, which indicates the position in the results to start returning results. In the preceding example, the cursor is the position just after the last result returned, so the first result returned by the query using the cursor as the start cursor will be the next unreturned result, or no results if none are available after the cursor.

You can also set an *end cursor*, which indicates the position at which to stop returning results. Because the cursor you get from query results represents the position after the last result returned by the fetch, using the cursor as the end cursor will stop returning results after that result.

This example shows how to use cursors to set up a Next link in a paginated display. Setting up a Previous link is left as an exercise for the reader. Hint: the cursor used to display the current page, if any, is the one the next page needs for the link.

A cursor is only valid for the query used to generate the cursor value. All query parameters, including kinds, filters, sort orders, and whether or not the query is keys-only, must be identical to the query used to generate the cursor.

A cursor remains valid over time, even if results are added or removed above or below the cursor in the index. A structural change to the indexes used to satisfy the query invalidates cursors for that query. This includes adding or removing fields of a custom index, or switching between built-in indexes and custom indexes for a query. These only occur as a result of you updating your index configuration. Rare internal changes to datastore indexes may also invalidate cursors. Using a cursor that is invalid for a given query (for whatever reason) will raise an exception.

Because a cursor stays valid even after the data changes, you can use cursors to watch for changes in some circumstances. For example, consider a query for entities with creation timestamps, ordered by timestamp. A process traverses the results to the end, and then stores the cursor for the end of the list (with no results after it). When new entities are created with later timestamps, those entities are added to the index after the cursor. Running the query with the cursor pick ups the new results.

Conceptually, a cursor is a position in a list of results. Actually, a cursor is a position in the index (or path through multiple indexes) that represents the results for the query. This has a couple of implications.

You can't use a cursor on a query that uses not-equal (!=) or set membership (IN) queries. These queries are performed by multiple primitive queries behind the scenes, and therefore do not have all results in a single index (or index path).

A query with a cursor may result in a duplicate result if the query operates on a property with multiple values. Recall that an entity with multiple values for a property appears once for each value in the corresponding indexes. When a query gathers results, it ignores repeated results (which are consecutive in the index). Because a cursor represents a point in an index, it is possible for the same entity to appear both before and after the cursor. In this case, the query up to the cursor and the query after the cursor will both contain the entity in their results. It's a rare edge case—the entity would have to change after the cursor is created—but it's one to be aware of if you're using multivalued properties with queries and cursors.

Projection Queries

We've described the datastore as an object store. You create an entity with all of its properties. When you fetch an entity by key, the entire entity and all its properties come back. When you want to update a property of an entity, you must fetch the complete entity, make the change to the object locally, then save the entire object back to the datastore.

The types of queries we've seen so far reflect this reality as well. You can either fetch entire entities that match query criteria:

```
SELECT * FROM Kind WHERE ...
```

Or you can fetch just the keys:

```
SELECT __key__ FROM Kind WHERE ...
```

And really, an entity query is just a key query that fetches the entities for those keys. The query criteria drive a scan of an index (or indexes) containing property values and keys, and the keys are returned by the scan.

But sometimes you only need to know one or two properties of an entity, and it's wasteful to retrieve an entire entity just to get at those properties. For times like these, Cloud Datastore has another trick up its sleeve: *projection queries*. Projection queries let you request specific properties of entities, instead of full entities, under certain conditions:

```
SELECT prop1, prop2 FROM Kind WHERE ...
```

The entity objects that come back have only the requested properties (known as the "projected properties") and their keys set. Only the requested data is returned by the datastore service to the app.

The idea of projection queries is based on how indexes are used to resolve queries. While a normal query uses indexes of keys and property values to look up keys then fetch the corresponding entities, projection queries take the requested values directly from the indexes themselves.

Every projection query requires a custom index of the properties involved in the query. As with other complex queries, the development server adds index configuration for each combination of projected properties, kind, and other query criteria.

Projection queries tend to be faster than full queries, for several reasons. Result entities are not fetched in a separate step, as with normal queries. Instead, the result data comes directly from the index. And naturally, less data means less communication with the datastore service. The entire procedure is to find the first row of the custom index and scan to the last row, returning the columns for the projected properties.

Several restrictions fall out of this trick, and they're fairly intuitive. Only indexed properties can be in a projection. Another way of saying this is, only entities with all the projected properties set to an indexable value can be a result for a projection query. A projection query needs a custom index even if the equivalent full-entity query does not.

There's another weird behavior we need to note here, and yes, once again it involves multivalued properties. As we saw earlier, if an entity contains multiple values for a property, an index containing that property contains a row for each value (and a row for each combination of values if you're indexing more than one multivalued property), repeating each of the single-valued properties in the index. Unlike an entity or key query, a projection query makes no attempt to de-duplicate the result list in this case. Instead, a projection on a multivalued property returns a separate result for each row in the index. Each result contains just the values of the properties on that row. Such a query returns one result for each combination of matching property values.

Each projection requires its own custom index. If you have two queries with the same kind and filter structures, but different projected properties, the queries require two custom indexes:

```
SELECT prop1, prop2 FROM Kind ...
SELECT prop1, prop3 FROM Kind ...
```

In this case, you can save space and time-to-update by using the same projection in both cases, and ignoring the unused properties:

```
SELECT prop1, prop2, prop3 FROM Kind ...
```

You request a projection query by calling the addProjection() method on the Query object for each property in the projection. (If you never call this method, the query is an entity query, and full entities are returned.) The addProjection() method takes a PropertyProjection, whose constructor takes the name of the property and an optional (but recommended) value type class:

```
import com.google.appengine.api.datastore.PropertyProjection;

// ...
        Query query = new Query("Message");
        query.addProjection(new PropertyProjection("prop1", String.class));
```

Each query result is an Entity with only the projected properties set. As usual, calling getProperty() will return the value as an Object, which you can then cast to the expected value type.

If projected properties may be of different types, you can pass null as the second argument of the PropertyProjection constructor. If you do this, the getProperty() method on the result will return the raw value wrapped in a RawValue instance. This wrapper provides several accessor methods with varying amounts of type control. get Value() returns the raw value as an Object; you can use introspection on the result to determine its type. asType() takes a java.lang.Class and returns a castable Object, as if you provided the class to the PropertyProjection constructor. And finally, <T> asStrictType(java.lang.Class<T>) provides an additional level of type control at compile time.

As shown, a projection query will return one result for each row in the index it is scanning, which includes one or more rows for each entity that has all of the projected properties. For properties with common values, the results can be a bit repetitive:

```
        Query query = new Query("Player");
        query.addProjection(new PropertyProjection("charclass", String.class));
        query.addProjection(new PropertyProjection("level", String.class));
```

This might get results like this:

```
(charclass="mage", level=1)
(charclass="mage", level=1)
(charclass="mage", level=1)
(charclass="mage", level=2)
(charclass="mage", level=2)
(charclass="mage", level=3)
(charclass="warrior", level=1)
(charclass="warrior", level=1)
(charclass="warrior", level=1)
```

Projection queries have a special feature for when you only want to know which distinct combinations of projected properties exist in the data, eliminating the duplicates. To request this, call the setDistinct(true) method of the Query:

```
Query query = new Query("Player");
query.addProjection(new PropertyProjection("charclass", String.class));
query.addProjection(new PropertyProjection("level", String.class));
query.setDistinct(true);
```

In this example, this would reduce the result set to one entry for each distinct combination of the charclass and level values:

```
(charclass="mage", level=1)
(charclass="mage", level=2)
(charclass="mage", level=3)
(charclass="warrior", level=1)
```

Distinct projection queries use only a minor modification to the index scanning algorithm. The rows are scanned in order as before, but a result is only emitted if it differs from the previous row. Only the projected properties are considered: two results are considered equivalent if all of the projected properties are equal between them, even if the nonprojected properties on the corresponding entities are not.

 The Java Persistence API supports projection queries in its own query language, comparable to field selection in SQL. See Chapter 10 for more information on JPA.

Configuring Indexes

An application specifies the custom indexes it needs in a configuration file. Each index definition includes the kind, and the names and sort orders of the properties to include. A configuration file can contain zero or more index definitions.

Most of the time, you can leave the maintenance of this file to the development web server. The development server watches the queries the application makes, and if a query needs a custom index and that index is not defined in the configuration file, the server adds appropriate configuration automatically.

The development server will not remove index configuration. If you are sure your app no longer needs an index, you can edit the file manually and remove it. Note that removing index configuration does not automatically delete the index from App Engine. After you upload the new configuration and when you are sure no versions of the app are using the index, you must issue the `appcfg vacuum_indexes` command. (We'll cover this in more depth in Chapter 9.)

You can disable the automatic index configuration feature. Doing so causes the development server to behave like App Engine: if a query doesn't have an index and needs one, the query fails. How to do this is particular to the runtime environment, so we'll get to that in a moment.

Index configuration is global to all versions of your application. All versions of an app share the same datastore, including indexes. If you deploy a version of the app and the index configuration has changed, Cloud Datastore will use the new index configuration for all versions.

You add index configuration to a file named *datastore-indexes.xml*, in the directory *WEB-INF/* in the WAR. This is an XML file with a root element named `<datastore-indexes>`. This contains zero or more `<datastore-index>` elements, one for each index.

Each `<datastore-index>` specifies the kind by using the `kind` attribute. It also has an `ancestor` attribute, which is `true` if the index supports queries with ancestor filters, and `false` otherwise.

A `<datastore-index>` contains one or more `<property>` elements, one for each column in the index. Each `<property>` has a `name` attribute (the name of the property) and a `direction` attribute (`asc` for ascending, `desc` for descending). The order of the `<property>` elements is significant: the index is sorted by the first column first, then by the second column, and so on.

Here's an example:

```
<datastore-indexes autoGenerate="true">
  <datastore-index kind="Player" ancestor="false">
    <property name="charclass" direction="asc" />
    <property name="level" direction="desc" />
  </datastore-index>

  <datastore-index kind="Player" ancestor="false">
    <property name="level" direction="desc" />
    <property name="score" direction="desc" />
  </datastore-index>
</datastore-indexes>
```

The `<datastore-indexes>` root element has an attribute named `autoGenerate`. If it's `true`, or if the app does not have a *datastore-indexes.xml* file, the Java development server generates new index configuration when needed for a query. If it's `false`, the development server behaves like App Engine: if a query needs an index that is not defined, the query fails.

The development server does not modify *datastore-indexes.xml*. Instead, it generates a separate file named *datastore-indexes-auto.xml*, in the directory *WEB-INF/appengine-generated/*. The complete index configuration is the total of the two configuration files.

The Java server will never remove index configuration from the automatic file, so if you need to delete an index, you may need to remove it from the automatic file. You can move configuration from the automatic file to the manual file if that's easier to manage, such as to check it into a revision control repository.

CHAPTER 8

Datastore Transactions

With web applications, many users access and update data concurrently. Often, multiple users need to read or write to the same unit of data at the same time. This requires a data system that can give some assurances that simultaneous operations will not corrupt any user's view of the data. Most data systems guarantee that a single operation on a single unit of data maintains the integrity of that unit, typically by scheduling operations that act on the unit to be performed in a sequence, one at a time.

Many applications need similar data integrity guarantees when performing a set of multiple operations, possibly over multiple units of data. Such a set of operations is called a *transaction*. A data system that supports transactions guarantees that if a transaction succeeds, all the operations in the transaction are executed completely. If any step of the transaction fails, then none of its effects are applied to the data. The data remains in a consistent and predictable state before and after the transaction, even if other processes are attempting to modify the data concurrently.

For example, say you want to post a message to the bulletin board in the town square inviting other players to join your guild. The bulletin board maintains a count of how many messages have been posted to the board, so readers can see how many messages there are without reading every message object in the system. Posting a message requires three datastore operations:

1. Read the old message count

2. Update the message count with an incremented value

3. Create the new message object

Without transactions, these operations may succeed or fail independently. The count may be updated but the message object may not be created. Or, if you create the message object first, the object may be created, but the count not updated. In either case, the resulting count is inaccurate. By performing these operations in a single transaction, if any step fails, none of the effects are applied, and the application can try the entire transaction again.

Also consider what happens when two players attempt to post to the message board at the same time. To increment the message count, each player process must read the old value, and then update it with a new value calculated from the old one. Without transactions, these operations may be interleaved:

1. Process A reads the original count (say, 10).
2. Process B reads the count (also 10).
3. Process A adds 1 and updates the count with the new value (11).
4. Process B adds 1 to its value and updates the count (11).

Because Process B doesn't know that Process A updated the value, the final count is 1 less than it ought to be (12). With transactions, Process B knows right away that another process is updating the data and can do the right thing.

A scalable web application has several requirements that are at odds with transactions. For one, the application needs access to data to be fast, and to not be affected by how much data is in the system or how it is distributed across multiple servers. The longer it takes for a transaction to complete, the longer other processes have to wait to access the data reserved by the transaction. The combined effect on how many transactions can be completed in a period of time is called *throughput*. For web apps, high throughput is important.

A web app usually needs transactions to finish completely and consistently, so it knows that the effects of the transaction can be relied upon by other processes for further calculations. The transaction is complete when it is committed, replicated to multiple machines, and ready to be served to any process that asks for it. The promise that all processes can see the changes once a transaction is complete is known as *strong consistency*.

An alternative policy known as *eventual consistency* trades this promise for greater flexibility in how changes are applied. With strong consistency, if a process wants to read a value, but a change for that value has been committed to the datastore and is not yet ready, the process waits until the save is complete, then reads the value. But if the process doesn't need the latest value, it can read the older value directly without waiting. Consistency is eventual because the impatient processes are not guaranteed to see the latest value, but will see it after the value is ready.

Cloud Datastore provides transactions with strong consistency and low overhead. It does this by limiting the scope of transactions: a single transaction can only read or write to entities that belong to a single *entity group*. Every entity belongs to an entity group, by default a group of its own. The app assigns an entity to a group when the entity is created, and the assignment is permanent.

By having the app arrange entities into groups, Cloud Datastore can treat each group independently when applying concurrent transactions. Two transactions that use different groups can occur simultaneously without harm. With a bit of thought, an app can ensure that entities are arranged to minimize the likelihood that two processes will need to access the same group, and thereby maximize throughput.

Entity groups also come into play with queries and indexes. If a query only needs results from a single entity group, the query can return strongly consistent results, as the group's local index data is updated transactionally with the group's entities. The query requests this behavior by identifying the group as part of the query, using a part of the key path, or *ancestor*. (We're finally going to explain what key paths are: they form entity groups by arranging keys in a hierarchy.)

Whereas ancestor queries are strongly consistent, queries across all entity groups are eventually consistent: global kind-based indexes are not guaranteed to be up-to-date by the time changes to entities are ready. This makes ancestor queries—and good entity group design in general—a powerful weapon in your datastore arsenal.

An app can request more flexible behaviors, with their corresponding trade-offs. *Cross-group transactions* (sometimes called "XG transactions") can act on up to five entity groups, in exchange for added latency and a greater risk of contention with other processes. An app can specify a *read policy* when reading data, which can request a faster eventually consistent read instead of a strongly consistent read that may have to wait on pending updates.

In this chapter, we discuss what happens when you update an entity group, how to create entities in entity groups, how to perform ancestor queries, and how to perform multiple operations on an entity group, using a transaction. We also discuss batch operations, how query indexes are built, and the consistency guarantees of Cloud Datastore.

Entities and Entity Groups

When you create, update, or delete a single entity, the change occurs in a transaction: either all your changes to the entity succeed, or none of them do. If you change two properties of an entity and save it, every request handler process that fetches the entity will see both changes. At no point during the save will a process see the new value for one property and the old value for the other. And if the update fails, the entity stays as it was before the save. In database terms, the act of updating an entity is *atomic*.

It is often useful to update multiple entities atomically, such that any process's view of the data is consistent across the entities. In the bulletin board example, the message count and each of the messages may be stored as separate entities, but the combined act of creating a new message entity and updating the count ought to be atomic. We need a way to combine multiple actions into a single transaction, so they all succeed or all fail.

To do this in a scalable way, Cloud Datastore must know in advance which entities may be involved in a single transaction. These entities are stored and updated together, so the datastore can keep them consistent and still access them quickly. You tell Cloud Datastore which entities may be involved in the same transaction by using entity groups.

Every entity belongs to an entity group, possibly a group containing just itself. An entity can only belong to one group. You assign an entity to a group when the entity is created. Group membership is permanent; an entity cannot be moved to another group once it has been created.

The datastore uses entity groups to determine what happens when two processes attempt to update data in the entity group at the same time. When this happens, the first update that completes "wins," and the other update is canceled. App Engine notifies the process whose update is canceled by raising an exception. In most cases, the process can just try the update again and succeed. But the app must decide for itself how to go about retrying, as important data may have changed between attempts.

This style of managing concurrent access is known as *optimistic concurrency control*. It's "optimistic" in the sense that the database tries to perform the operations without checking whether another process is working with the same data (such as with a "locking" mechanism), and only checks for collisions at the end, optimistic that the operations will succeed. The update is not guaranteed to succeed, and the app must reattempt the operations or take some other course of action if the data changes during the update.

Multiple processes vying for the opportunity to write to an entity group at the same time is known as *contention*. Two processes are contending for the write; the first to commit wins. A high rate of contention slows down your app, because it means many processes are getting their writes canceled and have to retry, possibly multiple times. In egregious cases, contention for a group may exclude a process to the point of the failure of that process. You can avoid high rates of contention with careful design of your entity groups.

Optimistic concurrency control is a good choice for web applications because reading data is fast—a typical reader never waits for updates—and almost always succeeds. If an update fails due to contention, it's usually easy to try again, or return an error message to the user. Most web applications have only a small number of users updating the same piece of data, so contention failures are rare.

 Updating an entity in a group can potentially cancel updates to *any* other entity in the group by another process. You should design your data model so that entity groups do not need to be updated by many users simultaneously.

Be especially careful if the number of simultaneous updates to a single group grows as your application gets more users. In this case, you usually want to spread the load across multiple entity groups, and increase the number of entity groups automatically as the user base grows. Scalable division of a data resource like this is known as *sharding*.

Also be aware that some data modeling tasks may not be practical on a large scale. Incrementing a value in a single datastore entity every time any user visits the site's home page is not likely to work well with a distributed strong consistency data system.

Keys, Paths, and Ancestors

To create an entity in a group with other entities, you associate it with the key of another entity from that group. One way to do this is to make the existing entity's key the *parent* of the new entity. The key of the parent becomes part of the key of the child. These parent–child relationships form a path of ancestors down to a *root* entity that does not have a parent. Every entity whose key begins with the same root is in the same group, including the root entity itself.

When you create an entity and do not specify a parent, the entity is created in a new group by itself. The new entity is the root of the new group.

We alluded to paths earlier when we discussed keys, so let's complete the picture. An entity's key consists of the path of ancestors in the entity's group, starting from the group's root. Each entity in the path is represented by the entity's kind followed by either the system-assigned numeric ID or the app-assigned string ID. The full path is a sequence of kind and ID pairs.

The following keys represent entities in the same group, because they all have the same root ancestor:

```
MessageBoard, "The_Archonville_Times"

MessageBoard, "The_Archonville_Times" / Message, "first!"

MessageBoard, "The_Archonville_Times" / Message, "pk_fest_aug_21"

MessageBoard, "The_Archonville_Times" / Message, "first!" / Message, "keep_clean"
```

You create a new entity with a parent by specifying the parent key to the `Entity` constructor:

```
import com.google.appengine.api.datastore.Entity;
import com.google.appengine.api.datastore.Key;
import com.google.appengine.api.datastore.KeyFactory;

// ...
        Key parentKey = KeyFactory.createKey("MessageBoard",
                                             "The_Archonville_Times");
        Entity e = new Entity("Message", parentKey);
```

You can also build the complete key path by using the `KeyFactory.Builder`, then pass the entire key to the `Entity` constructor:

```
        Key entityKey = new KeyFactory.Builder("MessageBoard",
                                               "The_Archonville_Times")
            .addChild("Message", 127)
            .getKey();
        Entity e = new Entity(entityKey);
```

Notice that entities of different kinds can be in the same entity group. In the datastore, there is no relationship between kinds and entity groups. (You can enforce such a relationship in your app's code, if you like.)

Ancestors do not have to exist for a key to be valid. If you create an entity with a parent and then delete the parent, the key for the child is still valid and can still be assembled from its parts (such as with `KeyFactory.Builder`). This is true even for a group's root entity: the root can be deleted and other entities in the group remain in the group.

You can even use a made-up key for an entity that doesn't exist as the parent for a new entity. Neither the kind nor the ID of an ancestor needs to represent an actual entity. Group membership is defined by the first key part in the ancestor path, regardless of whether that part corresponds to an entity.

Ancestor Queries

The root ancestor in a key path determines group membership. Intermediate ancestors have no affect on group membership, which poses the question, what good are ancestor paths? One possible answer to that question: ancestor queries.

A datastore query can include a filter that limits the results to just those entities with a given ancestor. This can match any ancestor, not just the immediate parent. In other words, a query can match a sequence of key parts starting from the root.

Continuing the town square bulletin board example, where each `MessageBoard` is the root of an entity group containing things attached to the board, the following GQL query returns the 10 most recent `Message` entities attached to a specific board:

```
SELECT * FROM Message
        WHERE ANCESTOR IS KEY(MessageBoard,
                                'The_Archonville_Times')
        ORDER BY post_date DESC
        LIMIT 10
```

Most queries that use an ancestor filter need custom indexes. There is one unusual exception: a query does not need a custom index if the query also contains equality filters on properties (and no inequality filters or sort orders). In this exceptional case, the "merge join" algorithm can use a built-in index of keys along with the built-in property indexes. In cases where the query would need a custom index anyway, the query can match the ancestor to the keys in the custom index.

In Java, you create an ancestor query by passing the ancestor key to the `Query` constructor:

```
Key ancestorKey = KeyFactory.createKey("MessageBoard",
                                        "The_Archonville_Times");
Query query = Query("Message", ancestorKey);
query.addSort("post_date", Query.SortDirection.DESCENDING);
```

As we mentioned in Chapter 7, the datastore supports queries over entities of all kinds. Kindless queries are limited to key filters and ancestor filters. Because ancestors can have children of disparate kinds, kindless queries are useful for getting every child of a given ancestor, regardless of kind:

```
SELECT * WHERE ANCESTOR IS KEY('MessageBoard', 'The_Archonville_Times')
```

A kindless ancestor query in code looks like this:

```
Key ancestorKey = KeyFactory.createKey("MessageBoard",
                                        "The_Archonville_Times");
Query query = new Query(ancestorKey);
```

 Although ancestor queries can be useful, don't get carried away building large ancestor trees. Remember that every entity with the same root belongs to the same entity group, and more simultaneous users that need to write to a group mean a greater likelihood of concurrency failures.

If you want to model hierarchical relationships between entities without the consequences of entity groups, consider using multi-valued properties to store paths. For example, if there's an entity whose path in your hierarchy can be represented as /A/B/C/D, you can store this path as `e.parents = ['/A', '/A/B', '/A/B/C']`. Then you can perform a query similar to an ancestor query on this property: … `WHERE parents = '/A/B'`.

What Can Happen in a Transaction

Entity groups ensure that the operations performed within a transaction see a consistent view of the entities in a group. For this to work, a single transaction must limit its operations to entities in a single group. The entity group determines the scope of the transaction.

Within a transaction, you can fetch, update, or delete an entity by using the entity's key. You can create a new entity that either is a root entity of a new group that becomes the subject of the transaction, or that has a member of the transaction's entity group as its parent. You can also create other entities in the same group.

You can perform queries over the entities of a single entity group in a transaction. A query in a transaction must have an ancestor filter that matches the transaction's entity group. The results of the query, including both the indexes that provide the results as well as the entities themselves, are guaranteed to be consistent with the rest of the transaction.

You do not need to declare the entity group for a transaction explicitly. You simply perform datastore actions on entities of the same group. If you attempt to perform actions that involve different entity groups within a transaction, the API raises an exception. The API also raises an exception if you attempt to perform a query in a transaction that does not have an ancestor filter. (We'll see the specific exception that is raised in the next few sections.)

Transactions have a maximum size. A single transaction can write up to 10 megabytes of data.

Transactional Reads

Sometimes it is useful to fetch entities in a transaction even if the transaction does not update any data. Reading multiple entities in a transaction ensures that the entities are consistent with one another. As with updates, entities fetched in a transaction must be members of the same entity group.

A transaction that only reads entities never fails due to contention. As with reading a single entity, a read-only transaction sees the data as it appears at the beginning of the transaction, even if other processes make changes after the transaction starts and before it completes.

The same is true for ancestor-only queries within a transaction. If the transaction does not create, update, or delete data from the entity group, it will not fail due to contention.

The datastore can do this because it remembers previous versions of entities, using timestamps associated with the entity groups. The datastore notes the current time at the beginning of every operation and transaction, and this determines which version of the data the operation or transaction sees. This is known as *multiversion concurrency control*, a form of optimistic concurrency control. This mechanism is internal to the datastore; the application cannot access previous versions of data, nor can it see the timestamps.

This timestamp mechanism has a minor implication for reading data within transactions. When you read an entity in a transaction, the datastore returns the version of the entity most recent to the beginning of the transaction. If you update an entity and then refetch the same entity within the same transaction, the datastore returns the entity as it appeared *before* the update. In most cases, you can just reuse the in-memory object you modified (which has your changes) instead of refetching the entity.

Eventually Consistent Reads

As described in the previous section, transactional reads are strongly consistent. When the app fetches an entity by key, the datastore ensures that all changes committed prior to the beginning of the current transaction are complete—and are therefore returned by the read—before continuing. Occasionally, this can involve a slight delay as the datastore catches up with a backlog of committed changes. In a transaction, a strongly consistent read can only read entities within the transaction's entity group.

Similarly, when the app performs an ancestor query in a transaction, the query uses the group's local indexes in a strongly consistent fashion. The results of the index scans are guaranteed to be consistent with the contents of the entities returned by the query.

You can opt out of this protection by specifying a *read policy* that requests eventual consistency. With an eventually consistent read of an entity, your app gets the current known state of the entity being read, regardless of whether there are still committed changes to be applied. With an eventually consistent ancestor query, the indexes used for the query are consistent with the time the indexes are read.

In other words, an eventual consistency read policy causes gets and queries to behave as if they are not a part of the current transaction. This may be faster in some cases, as the operations do not have to wait for committed changes to be written before returning a result.

Perhaps more importantly: an eventually consistent get operation can get an entity outside of the current transaction's entity group.

We'll look at the APIs for read policies in the next two sections.

Transactions in Java

The JDO and JPA interfaces provide their own mechanisms for formulating transactions. Google's online documentation describes JDO, and we'll cover the JPA interface in Chapter 10.

To perform multiple operations within a single transaction, you call the `beginTransaction()` method of the `DatastoreService` instance. This method returns a `Transaction` object that represents the transaction. You perform the datastore operations as you usually do, calling the `put()`, `get()`, and `delete()` methods of the `DatastoreService`. Finally, you call the `commit()` method of the `Transaction` object to complete the transaction.

Updates (`put()` and `delete()`) do not take effect until you commit the transaction. Fetching an entity by using `get()` after it has been updated in the same transaction will return an `Entity` object that represents the state of the entity *before* the update.

If the transaction cannot be committed due to a concurrency failure, the commit throws a `java.util.ConcurrentModificationException`. For other datastore errors, it throws a `DatastoreFailureException`:

```java
import java.util.ConcurrentModificationException;

import com.google.appengine.api.datastore.DatastoreFailureException;
import com.google.appengine.api.datastore.EntityNotFoundException;
import com.google.appengine.api.datastore.Transaction;

// ...
        DatastoreService ds = DatastoreServiceFactory.getDatastoreService();

        Key boardKey;
        Entity messageBoard;

        try {
            Transaction txn = ds.beginTransaction();

            try {
                boardKey = KeyFactory.createKey("MessageBoard",
                                                "The_Archonville_Times");
                messageBoard = ds.get(boardKey);

            } catch (EntityNotFoundException e) {
                messageBoard = new Entity("MessageBoard",
                                          "The_Archonville_Times");
                messageBoard.setProperty("count", 0);
                boardKey = ds.put(messageBoard);
            }

            txn.commit();
```

```
        } catch (ConcurrentModificationException e) {
            // Datastore contention...
        } catch (DatastoreFailureException e) {
            // A different error...
        }
```

If you do not commit the transaction, the transaction is rolled back automatically after the servlet exits, and changes are not applied. You can roll back the transaction explicitly by calling the rollback() method of the Transaction object.

By default, each datastore operation is associated with the transaction started by the most recent call to beginTransaction(), known in the API as the "current" transaction. If you call beginTransaction() more than once, each Transaction is remembered in a stack. Calling commit() or rollback() removes the Transaction from the stack. If you commit or roll back the current transaction and there is another transaction on the stack, the next most recent transaction becomes the current transaction.

You can associate a datastore operation with a specific transaction explicitly by passing the Transaction object to the operation method:

```
Transaction txn = ds.beginTransaction();

ds.put(txn, messageBoard);

txn.commit();
```

If there is no current transaction on the stack, calling an operation method performs the operation without a transaction. Updates occur immediately. If there is a current transaction but you would like the operation performed immediately and outside of the transaction, provide null as the first argument to the operation:

```
Transaction txn = ds.beginTransaction();

// Add an update of entityOne to the transaction.
ds.put(txn, entityOne);

// Update entityTwo immediately, outside of the transaction.
ds.put(null, entityTwo);

// Commit the transaction, updating entityOne.
txn.commit();
```

Alternatively, you can disable the automatic behavior of these methods by setting the implicit transaction management policy when you create the DatastoreService instance:

```
import com.google.appengine.api.datastore.DatastoreServiceConfig;
import com.google.appengine.api.datastore.ImplicitTransactionManagementPolicy;

// ...
```

```
DatastoreService datastore =
    DatastoreServiceFactory.getDatastoreService(
        DatastoreServiceConfig.Builder
        .withImplicitTransactionManagementPolicy(
            ImplicitTransactionManagementPolicy.NONE));
```

The default policy is ImplicitTransactionManagementPolicy.AUTO: most operations
(put(), get(), delete()) will join the most recently started transaction if you don't
explicitly pass a Transaction to the method. If you set this policy to
ImplicitTransactionManagementPolicy.NONE, calling a method without an explicit
Transaction will cause it to start its own independent transaction for the operation.

Note that ds.prepare() never joins a transaction automatically. You must tell it
which transaction to join. If omitted, it will always start its own transaction.

With optimistic concurrency control, it is usually appropriate for the application to
try the transaction again in the event of a concurrency failure. The following example
retries the transaction up to three times before reporting an error to the user:

```java
import java.util.ConcurrentModificationException;
import com.google.appengine.api.datastore.DatastoreService;
import com.google.appengine.api.datastore.DatastoreServiceFactory;
import com.google.appengine.api.datastore.Entity;
import com.google.appengine.api.datastore.EntityNotFoundException;
import com.google.appengine.api.datastore.Key;
import com.google.appengine.api.datastore.KeyFactory;
import com.google.appengine.api.datastore.PreparedQuery;
import com.google.appengine.api.datastore.Query;
import com.google.appengine.api.datastore.Transaction;

// ...
    DatastoreService ds = DatastoreServiceFactory.getDatastoreService();

    int retries = 3;
    boolean success = false;
    while (!success && retries > 0) {
        --retries;
        try {
            Transaction txn = ds.beginTransaction();

            Key boardKey;
            Entity messageBoard;
            try {
                boardKey = KeyFactory.createKey("MessageBoard", boardName);
                messageBoard = ds.get(boardKey);

            } catch (EntityNotFoundException e) {
                messageBoard = new Entity("MessageBoard", boardName);
                messageBoard.setProperty("count", 0);
                boardKey = ds.put(messageBoard);
            }
```

```
        Entity message = new Entity("Message", boardKey);
        message.setProperty("message_title", messageTitle);
        message.setProperty("message_text", messageText);
        message.setProperty("post_date", postDate);
        ds.put(message);

        long count = (Long) messageBoard.getProperty("count");
        ++count;
        messageBoard.setProperty("count", count);
        ds.put(messageBoard);

        log.info("Posting msg, updating count to " + count);

        txn.commit();

        // Break out of retry loop.
        success = true;

    } catch (ConcurrentModificationException e) {
        // Allow retry to occur.
    }
}
if (!success) {
    // Tell the user it didn't work out...
    resp.getWriter().println
        ("<p>A new message could not be posted.  Try again later.</p>");
}

// ...

Key boardKey = KeyFactory.createKey("MessageBoard", boardName);
try {
    Entity messageBoard = ds.get(boardKey);
    long count = (Long) messageBoard.getProperty("count");
    resp.getWriter().println("<p>Latest messages posted to
            " + boardName + " (" + count + " total):</p>");

    Query q = new Query("Message", boardKey);
    PreparedQuery pq = ds.prepare(q);
    for (Entity result : pq.asIterable()) {
        resp.getWriter().println("<h3>"
                + result.getProperty("message_title")
                + "</h3><p>"
                + result.getProperty("message_text")
                + "</p>");
    }
} catch (EntityNotFoundException e) {
    resp.getWriter().println("<p>No message board found.</p>");
}
```

Within a transaction, reading entities and fetching results from an ancestor query uses a read policy of strong consistency. There's no reason (or ability) to use another read policy in this case: a transactional read either sees the latest committed state (as with strong consistency) or the transaction fails because the entity group has been updated since the transaction was started.

How Entities Are Updated

To fully understand how the datastore guarantees that your data stays consistent, it's worth discussing how transactions are performed behind the scenes. To do so, we must mention BigTable, Google's distributed data system that is the basis of the App Engine datastore. We won't go into the details of how entities, entity groups, and indexes are stored in BigTable, but we will refer to BigTable's own notion of atomic transactions in our explanation.

Figure 8-1 shows the phases of a successful transaction.

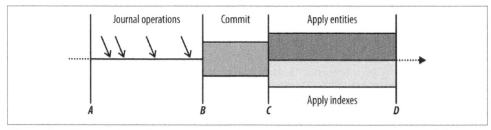

Figure 8-1. The timeline of a transaction: the operations, the commit phase, and the apply phase

The datastore uses a "journal" to keep track of changes that need to be applied to entities in an entity group. Each journal entry has a unique timestamp that indicates the order in which the changes were made. The datastore remembers the timestamp of the most recent change that has been committed, and guarantees that attempts to read the data will see all changes up to that point.

When an app begins a transaction for an entity group, the datastore makes a note of the current last-committed timestamp for the group (point A in Figure 8-1). As the app calls the datastore to update entities, the datastore writes the requested changes to the journal. Each change is marked as "uncommitted."

When the app finishes the transaction (point B), the datastore checks the group's last-committed timestamp again. If the timestamp hasn't changed since the transaction began, it marks all the transaction's changes as "committed" and then advances the group's timestamp. Otherwise, the timestamp was advanced by another request handler since the beginning of the transaction, so the datastore aborts the current transaction and reports a concurrency failure to the app.

Verifying the timestamp, committing the journal entries, and updating the timestamp all occur in an atomic BigTable operation. If another process attempts to commit a transaction to the same entity group while the first transaction's commit is in progress, the other process waits for the first commit to complete. This guarantees that if the first commit succeeds, the second process sees the updated timestamp and reports a concurrency failure. This is illustrated in Figure 8-2.

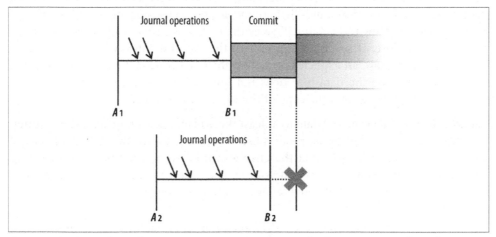

Figure 8-2. A timeline of two concurrent transactions; the first to commit "wins"

Once the journal entries have been committed (point C in Figure 8-1), the datastore applies each committed change to the appropriate entity and appropriate indexes, then marks the change as "applied." If there are multiple unapplied changes for an entity in the journal, they are applied in the order they were performed.

Here's the sneaky bit. If the apply phase fails for whatever reason (hard drive failure, power outage, meteorite), the committed transaction is still considered successful. If there are committed but unapplied changes the next time someone performs an operation on an entity in the entity group (within or without an explicit transaction), the datastore reruns the apply phase before performing the operation. This ensures that operations and transactions always see all changes that have been committed prior to the start of the operation or transaction. The datastore also uses background processes to roll forward unapplied operations, as well as purge old journal entries.

The roll-forward mechanism also ensures that subsequent operations can see all committed changes even if the apply phase is still in progress. At the beginning of an operation or transaction, the datastore notes the current time, then waits for all changes committed prior to that time to be applied before continuing.

Notice that the apply phase does not need to occur inside a BigTable transaction. Because of this, the datastore can spread multiple entities in the same group across multiple machines, and can allow an entity group to get arbitrarily large. Only the group's last-committed timestamp and journal need to be stored close enough together for a BigTable transaction. The datastore makes an effort to store entities of the same group "near" each other for performance reasons, but this does not limit the size or speed of entity groups.

When an app updates an entity outside of a transaction, the datastore performs the update with the same transactional mechanism, as if it were a transaction of just one operation. The datastore assumes that an update performed outside of a transaction is safe to perform at any time, and will retry the update automatically in the event of a concurrency failure. If several attempts fail, the datastore throws the concurrency exception. In contrast, an explicit transaction throws a concurrency exception on the first failure, because the datastore does not know if it is safe to commit the same changes. The app must retry the explicit transaction on its own.

Cloud Datastore replicates all data to at least three places in each of at least two different data centers. The replication process uses a consensus algorithm based on "Paxos" to ensure that all sites agree that the change will be committed before proceeding. This level of replication ensures that your app's datastore remains available for both reads and writes during all planned outages—and most unplanned outages.

 When an app calls the datastore to update data, the call does not return until the apply phase is complete. If an error occurs at any point in the process, the datastore call raises an exception in the application.

This is true even if the error occurs during the apply phase, after the commit phase is complete and the update is guaranteed to be applied before the next transaction. Because the application can't tell the difference between an error during the commit phase and an error during the apply phase, the application should react as if the update has not taken place.

In most cases, the app can simply retry the update. More care is needed if retrying the update relies on the previous attempt being unsuccessful, but these cases usually require testing the state of the data in a transaction, and the solution is simply to retry the entire transaction. If the transaction creates a new entity, one way to avoid creating a duplicate entity is to use a key name instead of a system-supplied numeric ID, precalculating and testing for the nonexistence of a global unique ID (GUID) if necessary.

Failures during the apply phase are very rare, and most errors represent a failure to commit. One of the most important principles in scalable app design is to be tolerant of the most rare kinds of faults.

How Entities Are Read

The timestamp mechanism explains what happens when two processes attempt to write to the same entity group at the same time. When one process commits, it updates the timestamp for the group. When the other process tries to commit, it notices the timestamp has changed, and aborts. The app can retry the transaction with fresh data, or give up.

The transaction is aborted only if the app attempted to update an entity during the transaction and another process has since committed changes. If the app only reads data in the transaction and does not make changes, the app simply sees the entities as they were at the beginning of the transaction. To support this, the datastore retains several old versions of each entity, marked with the timestamp of the most recently applied journal entry. Reading an entity in a transaction returns the version of the entity most recent to the timestamp at the beginning of the transaction.

Reading an entity outside of a transaction or with an eventual consistency read policy does not roll forward committed-but-unapplied changes. Instead, the read returns the entity as it appears as of the most recently applied changes. This is faster than waiting for pending changes to be applied, and usually not a concern for reads outside of transactions. But this means the entity may appear older or newer than other entities. If you need any consistency guarantees when reading multiple entities, use transactions and the strong consistency read policy.

Batch Updates

When you read, create, update, or delete an entity, the runtime environment makes a service call to the datastore. Each service call has some overhead, including serializing and deserializing parameters and transmitting them between machines in the data center. If you need to update multiple entities, you can save time by performing the updates together as a batch in one service call.

We introduced batch calls in Chapter 6. Here's a quick example:

```
// Creating multiple entities:
Entity e1 = new Entity("Message");
Entity e2 = new Entity("Message");
Entity e3 = new Entity("Message");
datastore.put(Arrays.asList(e1, e2, e3));

// Getting multiple entities using keys:
Key k1 = KeyFactory.createKey("Message", "first");
Key k2 = KeyFactory.createKey("Message", "second");
Key k3 = KeyFactory.createKey("Message", "third");
Map<Key, Entity> resultMap =
    datastore.get(Arrays.asList(k1, k2, k3));
```

```
// Deleting multiple entities:
datastore.delete(Arrays.asList(k1, k2, k3));
```

When the datastore receives a batch call, it bundles the keys or entities by their entity groups, which it can determine from the keys. Then it dispatches calls to the datastore machines responsible for each entity group. The datastore returns results to the app when it has received all results from all machines.

If the call includes changes for multiple entities in a single entity group, those changes are performed in a single transaction. There is no way to control this behavior, but there's no reason to do it any other way. It's faster to commit multiple changes to a group at once than to commit them individually, and no less likely to result in concurrency failures.

Outside of a transaction, a batch call can operate on multiple entity groups. Each entity group involved in a batch update may fail to commit due to a concurrency failure. If a concurrency failure occurs for any update, the API raises the concurrency failure exception—even if updates to other groups were committed successfully.

Batch updates in disparate entity groups are performed in separate threads, possibly by separate datastore machines, executed in parallel to one another. This can make batch updates especially fast compared to performing each update one at a time.

Remember that if you use the batch API during a transaction, every entity or key in the batch must use the same entity group as the rest of the transaction.

How Indexes Are Updated

As we saw in Chapter 7, datastore queries are powered by indexes. The datastore updates these indexes as entities change, so results for queries can be determined without examining the entity properties directly. This includes an index of keys, an index for each kind and property, and custom indexes described by your app's configuration files that fulfill complex queries. When an entity is created, updated, or deleted, each relevant index is updated and sorted so subsequent queries match the new state of the data.

The datastore updates indexes after changes have been committed, during the apply phase. Changes are applied to indexes and entities in parallel. Updates of indexes are themselves performed in parallel, so the number of indexes to update doesn't necessarily affect how fast the update occurs.

As with entities, the datastore retains multiple versions of index data, labeled with timestamps. When you perform a query, the datastore notes the current time, then uses the index data that is most current up to that time. However, unless the query has an ancestor filter, the datastore has no way to know which entity groups are involved in the result set and so cannot wait for changes in progress to be applied.

This means that, for a brief period during an update, a query that doesn't have an ancestor filter (a nonancestor query, or global query) may return results that do not match the query criteria. While another process is updating an entity, the query may see the old version of its index but return the new version of the entity. And because changes to entities and changes to indexes are applied in parallel, it is possible for a query to see the new version of its index but return the old version of the entity.

Figure 8-3 illustrates one possibility of what nontransactional reads and queries may see while changes are being applied.

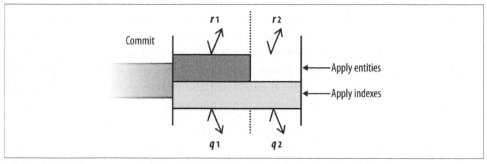

Figure 8-3. What nontransactional fetches and queries may see while changes are applied

Although fetches *r1* and *r2* both occur after the commit, because they do not occur within transactions, they see different data: *r1* fetches the entity as it is before the update, and *r2* fetches the entity as it is after the update has been applied. Queries *q1* and *q2* may use the same (preupdate) index data to produce a list of results, but they return different entity data depending on whether changes have been applied to the entities.

In rare cases, it's also possible for changes to indexes to be applied prior to changes to entities, and for the apply phase to fail and leave committed changes unapplied until the next transaction on the entity group. If you need stronger guarantees, fetch or query entities within transactions to ensure all committed changes are applied before the data is used.

A query with an ancestor filter knows its entity group, and can therefore offer the same strong consistency guarantees within transactions as fetches. But many useful queries span entity groups, and therefore cannot be performed in transactions. If it is important to your application that a result for a nontransactional query match the criteria exactly, verify the result in the application code before using it.

Cross-Group Transactions

Transactions and entity groups present a fundamental tension in designing data for the App Engine datastore. If all we cared about was data consistency, we'd put all our data in a single entity group, and every transaction would have a consistent and current view of the entire world—and would be battling with every other simultaneous transaction to commit a change. Conversely, if we wanted to avoid contention as much as possible, we'd keep every entity in its own group and never perform more than one operation in a transaction.

Entity groups are a middle ground. They allow us to define limited sets of data that demand strongly consistent transactional updates, and with some thought we can organize these boundaries so an increase in traffic does not result in an increase in simultaneous updates to a single group. For example, if a user only ever updates an entity group dedicated to that user, then an increase in users will never increase the number of users writing to a given group simultaneously.

But real-world data patterns are not always so clean. Most useful applications involve sharing data between users. At another extreme, it's possible all users can view and modify the same set of data. At that point, we need to make some sacrifices to operate at scale, using techniques like sharding and eventually consistent data structures updated by background tasks to spread the updates over time and space.

There are many common scenarios where it'd be convenient if we could just operate on a few entity groups in a transaction, when one group is too constraining but we don't need to update the world. Sometimes we need to operate on several disparate sets of data at once, but it'd make our data model too complex to try and manage them in groups. For these cases, App Engine has a feature: *cross-group transactions*.

A cross-group transaction (or an "XG transaction") is simply a transaction that's allowed to operate on up to five entity groups transactionally. The datastore uses a slightly different—and slightly slower—mechanism for this, so to use more than one group transactionally, you must declare that your transaction is of the cross-group variety. The cross-group mechanism is built on top of the existing single-group mechanism in BigTable. It manages the updates so all groups commit or fail completely.

The important idea here is that you do not need to say ahead of time which groups will be involved in a transaction. Any given cross-group transaction can pick any entity groups on which to operate, up to five.

As with a single group transaction, a cross-group transaction can read from, write to, and perform ancestor queries on any of the groups in the transaction. If any group in a given cross-group transaction is updated after the transaction is started but before it tries to commit, the entire transaction fails and must be retried. Whether failure due to contention is more likely with more groups depends entirely on the design of your app.

In Java, you declare a transaction to be a cross-group transaction by providing an appropriately configured `TransactionOptions` instance to the `beginTransaction()` method to make it a cross-group transaction:

```
import com.google.appengine.api.datastore.TransactionOptions;

// ...
        Transaction transaction = datastore.beginTransaction(
            TransactionOptions.Builder.withXG(true));
```

CHAPTER 9

Datastore Administration

Your data is the heart of your application, so you'll want to take good care of it. You'll want to watch it, and understand how it grows and how it affects your app's behavior. You'll want to help it evolve as your app's functionality changes. You may even want up-to-date information about data types and sizes. And you'll want to poke at it, and prod it into shape using tools not necessarily built into your app.

App Engine provides a variety of administrative tools for learning about, testing, protecting, and fixing your datastore data. In this chapter, we look at a few of these tools, and their associated best practices.

Inspecting the Datastore

The first thing you might want to do with your app's datastore is see what's in it. Your app provides a natural barrier between you and how your data is stored physically in the datastore, so many data troubleshooting sessions start with pulling back the covers and seeing what's there.

In the Storage section of the Cloud Console is a set of panels for Cloud Datastore (Figure 9-1). This is your main view of your project's datastore entities. The Dashboard summarizes how your storage space is used, including space for entities and their properties, as well as space for built-in and custom (composite) indexes. Select a kind from the drop-down menu to see a breakdown by named property.

In the Query panel, you can browse entities by kind. You can also apply query filters to this view by clicking the Filters button. The panel knows the names of all of the indexed properties of entities of the given kind, making it easy to compose queries on existing properties.

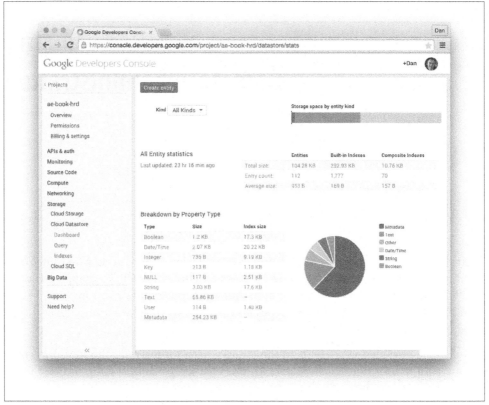

Figure 9-1. The Cloud Datastore Dashboard in the Cloud Console

From any of these panels, you can click the Create Entity button to create a new entity. You can pick from a list of existing kinds, and property names and types known to be used with existing entities will appear automatically. You can also create an entity of a new kind, and add and remove arbitrary properties. Currently, only simple keys (without ancestors) are supported for entities created via the Console.

When browsing entities in the Query panel, you can click on the key of an entity to view its properties in more detail. You can also edit the properties in this view, within the limitations of the Console's property editor.

The property value types supported by the Console for property editing and query filters include the following:

A date and time

You enter a date and time into the form field using the format YYYY-MM-DD HH:MM:SS, such as 2014-12-31 23:59:59. As with storing datetime values in general, there is no time zone component.

A string

> Note that string values in the form field have leading and trailing spaces truncated, and there is no way to specify a value with leading or trailing spaces.

A number

> The datastore treats integers and floating-point values as distinct types. In these panels, a number value containing a decimal point (5.0) is interpreted as a floating-point value. Without the point (5), it's an integer.

A Boolean value

> Here, the panel helps you out and displays a drop-down menu for the value (either true or false).

A Google user

> The value is the current email address of the corresponding account, whether an account for that address exists or not.

A datastore key

> A key value is a sequence of kind/ID pairs, with single quotes around kinds and string IDs, wrapped in a Key(...) specifier. For example: Key('MessageBoard', 'The_Archonville_Times', 'Message', 12345)

Currently, the Console does not support null values and geographical point values in the property editor and query composer. It also doesn't support multivalued properties. You also cannot create or edit blob values (unindexed binary values) with this interface.

The Datastore panels are useful for inspecting entities and troubleshooting data issues, and may be sufficient for administrative purposes with simple data structures. However, you will probably want to build a custom administrative panel for browsing app-specific data structures and performing common administrative tasks.

 Applying filters in the Query panel performs a datastore query just as your application does. These filters are subject to the same restrictions, and use the same indexes as the app. If a set of filters requires a custom index (such as inequality filters on two distinct properties), that index must already be in the app's deployed index configuration to support querying with those filters from the Console. See Chapter 7.

Managing Indexes

When you upload the datastore index configuration for an app, the datastore begins building indexes that appear in the configuration but do not yet exist. This process is *not* instantaneous, and may take many minutes for new indexes that contain many rows. The datastore needs time to crawl all the entities to build the new indexes.

You can check on the build status of new indexes using the Cloud Console, in the Indexes section. An index being built appears with a status of "Building." When it is ready, the status changes to "Serving." Figure 9-2 shows a simple example of the Indexes section.

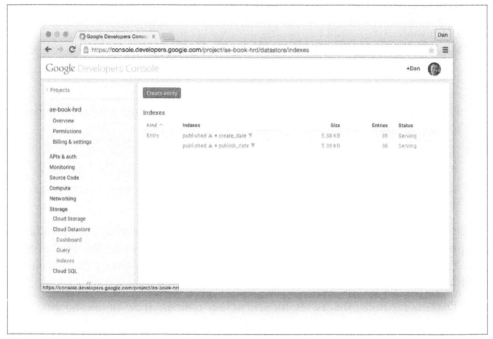

Figure 9-2. The Cloud Datastore Indexes panel in the Cloud Console

If an index's build status is "Error," the index build failed. It's possible that the failure was due to a transient error. To clear this condition, you must first remove the index from your configuration and then upload the new configuration. It is also possible for an index build to fail due to an entity reaching its index property value limit. In these cases, you can delete the entities that are causing the problem. Once that is done, you can add the index configuration back and upload it again.

If your application performs a query while the index for the query is building, the query will fail. You can avoid this by uploading the index configuration, waiting until the index is built, and then making the app that uses that query available. The most convenient way to do this depends on whether you upload the new application in a new version:

- If you are uploading the new application with the version identifier that is currently the "default" version, upload the index configuration alone using the `appcfg update_indexes` command. When the indexes are built, upload the app.

- If you are uploading the application as a new version, or as a version that isn't the default and that nobody is actively using, you can safely upload the application and index configuration together (`appcfg update`). Wait until the indexes are built before making the new version the default.

If you upload index configuration that does not mention an index that has already been built, the datastore does not delete the unused index, as it might still be in use by an older version of the app. You must tell App Engine to purge unused indexes. To do this, run the AppCfg command with the `vacuum_indexes` option. For instance:

```
appcfg vacuum_indexes app-dir
```

App Engine will purge all custom indexes not mentioned in the index configuration uploaded most recently. This reclaims the storage space used by those indexes.

 As we saw earlier, the development server tries to be helpful by creating new index configuration entries for queries that need them as you're testing your app. The development server will *never* delete an index configuration. As your app's queries change, this can result in unnecessary indexes being left in the file. You'll want to look through this file periodically, and confirm that each custom index is needed. Remove the unused index configuration, upload the file, and then vacuum indexes.

Accessing Metadata from the App

There are several ways to get information about the state of your datastore from within the application itself. The information visible in the Datastore Dashboard panel of the Cloud Console is also readable and queryable from entities in your app's datastore. Similarly, the facilities that allow the Query panel to determine the current kinds and property names are available to your app in the form of APIs and queryable metadata. You can also use APIs to get additional information about entity groups, index build status, and query planning.

We won't describe every metadata feature here. Instead, we'll look at a few representative examples. You can find the complete details in the official App Engine documentation.

Querying Statistics

App Engine gathers statistics about the contents of the datastore periodically, usually about once a day. It stores these statistics in datastore entities in your application. The Datastore Dashboard panel of the Cloud Console gets its information from these entities. Your app can also fetch and query these entities to access the statistics.

In Java, you query statistics entities by setting up queries on the statistics entity kind names, just like any other datastore query. The query returns entities with statistics as property values.

Here's an example that queries storage statistics for each entity kind:

```java
package clock;
import java.io.IOException;
import javax.servlet.http.*;

import com.google.appengine.api.datastore.DatastoreService;
import com.google.appengine.api.datastore.DatastoreServiceFactory;
import com.google.appengine.api.datastore.Entity;
import com.google.appengine.api.datastore.PreparedQuery;
import com.google.appengine.api.datastore.Query;
import java.util.logging.Logger;

@SuppressWarnings("serial")
public class ClockServlet extends HttpServlet {
    private static final Logger log =
        Logger.getLogger(ClockServlet.class.getName());

    public void doGet(HttpServletRequest req, HttpServletResponse resp)
        throws IOException {
        DatastoreService datastore =
            DatastoreServiceFactory.getDatastoreService();
        PreparedQuery pq = datastore.prepare(new Query("__Stat_Kind__"));

        for (Entity stat : pq.asIterable()) {
            String kind = (String) stat.getProperty("kind_name");
            long entities = (long) stat.getProperty("count");
            long total_bytes = (long) stat.getProperty("bytes");
            long entity_bytes = (long) stat.getProperty("entity_bytes");

            log.info(
                "Stats for kind " + kind + ":" +
                entities + " entities, " +
                "total " + total_bytes + " bytes " +
                "(" + entity_bytes + " entity bytes)");
        }
    }
}
```

Here's another example that reports the properties per kind taking up more than a terabyte of space:

```java
// ...
import com.google.appengine.api.datastore.Query.FilterOperator;
import com.google.appengine.api.datastore.Query.FilterPredicate;

@SuppressWarnings("serial")
public class ClockServlet extends HttpServlet {
    // ...
    public void doGet(HttpServletRequest req, HttpServletResponse resp)
        throws IOException {
        DatastoreService datastore =
            DatastoreServiceFactory.getDatastoreService();
        PreparedQuery pq = datastore.prepare(
                new Query("__Stat_PropertyType_Kind__")
                .setFilter(new FilterPredicate(
                        "bytes",
                        FilterOperator.GREATER_THAN,
                        1024 * 1024 * 1024 * 1024)));

        for (Entity stat : pq.asIterable()) {
            String kind = (String) stat.getProperty("kind_name");
            String property = (String) stat.getProperty("property_type");
            long total_bytes = (long) stat.getProperty("entity_bytes");

            log.info(
                "Large property detected: " + kind + ":" + property +
                "total size " + total_bytes);
        }
    }
}
```

Every statistic entity has a count property, a bytes property, and a timestamp property. count and bytes represent the total count and total size of the unit represented by the entity. The statistic for a kind has a bytes property equal to the total amount of storage used by entities of the kind for properties and indexes. The timestamp property is the last time the statistic entity was updated. Statistic entity kinds have additional properties specific to the kind.

The __Stat_Total__ kind represents the grand total for the entire app. The count and bytes properties represent the number of all entities, and the total size of all entities and indexes. These numbers are broken down further in several properties: entity_bytes is the storage for just the entities (not indexes), builtin_index_bytes and builtin_index_count are the total size and number of indexed properties in just the built-in indexes, and composite_index_bytes and composite_index_count are the same for just custom (composite) indexes. There is only one __Stat_Total__ entity for the app.

The __Stat_Kind__ kind represents statistics for each datastore kind individually, as existed at the time the statistics were last updated. There is one of these statistic entities for each kind. The kind_name property is set to the kind name, so you can query for a specific kind's statistics, or you can iterate over all kinds to determine which kinds there are. These entities have the same statistic properties as __Stat_Total__.

The __Stat_PropertyName_Kind__ kind represents each named property of each kind. The property_name and kind_name properties identify the property and kind for the statistic. The statistic properties are count, bytes, entity_bytes, builtin_index_bytes, and builtin_index_count.

For a complete list of the statistics entity kinds, see the official App Engine website.

Querying Metadata

The datastore always knows which namespaces, kinds, and property names are in use by an application. Unlike statistics, this metadata is available immediately. Querying this metadata can be slower than querying a normal entity, but the results reflect the current state of the data.

To access this metadata, you query the datastore for entities of specially named kinds, as before. But unlike datastore statistics, metadata values are calculated immediately when you perform the query.

Each namespace that contains datastore data has an entity of the kind __name space__. (This kind name is also available as the constant Entities.NAMESPACE_META DATA_KIND from the com.google.appengine.api.datastore.Entities class.) Each kind is a __kind__ (Entities.KIND_METADATA_KIND), and each property name (regardless of kind) is a __property__ (Entities.PROPERTY_METADATA_KIND). These entities have no properties: all information is stored in the key name. For example, a __kind__ entity uses the kind name as its key name: the full key is __kind__ / Kind Name. A __property__ entity has both the kind name and the property name encoded in its key name.

This information is derived entirely from the built-in indexes. As such, only indexed properties have corresponding __property__ entities.

Here's a simple example that lists all the kinds for which there is an entity:

```
import com.google.appengine.api.datastore.Entities;

// ...
        DatastoreService datastore =
            DatastoreServiceFactory.getDatastoreService();
        PreparedQuery pq = datastore.prepare(
            new Query(Entities.KIND_METADATA_KIND));
```

```
    for (Entity metadata : pq.asIterable()) {
        String kind = (String) metadata.getKind();
        log.info("Found a datastore kind: " + kind);
    }
```

Index Status and Queries

The Datastore Indexes panel of the Cloud Console reports on the indexes configured for the app, and the serving status of each. The app can get this same information by using the datastore API.

In Java, the datastore service method getIndexes() returns a Map<Index, Index.IndexState>. An Index has accessor methods getKind(), isAncestor(), and getProperties(). The getProperties() method returns a List<Index.Property>, where each Index.Property provides getName() and getDirection() (a Query.Sort Direction). The index state is one of Index.IndexState.BUILDING, Index.Index State.SERVING, Index.IndexState.DELETING, or Index.IndexState.ERROR:

```
import java.util.Map;
import java.util.logging.Logger;
import com.google.appengine.api.datastore.DatastoreService;
import com.google.appengine.api.datastore.DatastoreServiceFactory;
import com.google.appengine.api.datastore.Index;
import com.google.appengine.api.datastore.Query;

public class MyServlet extends HttpServlet {
    private static final Logger log =
        Logger.getLogger(MyServlet.class.getName());

    public void doGet(HttpServletRequest req, HttpServletResponse resp)
        throws IOException {

        // ...

        DatastoreService datastore =
            DatastoreServiceFactory.getDatastoreService();

        Map<Index, Index.IndexState> indexes = datastore.getIndexes();
        for (Index index : indexes.keySet()) {
            if (indexes.get(index) != Index.IndexState.SERVING) {
                StringBuffer indexPropertySpec = new StringBuffer();
                for (Index.Property prop : index.getProperties()) {
                    indexPropertySpec.append(prop.getName());
                    indexPropertySpec.append(
                        prop.getDirection() ==
                        Query.SortDirection.ASCENDING ?
                        " ASC " : " DESC ");
                }

                log.info(
```

```
                "Index is not serving: " +
                index.getKind() +
                (index.isAncestor() ? " (ancestor) " : " ") +
                indexPropertySpec.toString());
        }
      }
    }
  }
```

Entity Group Versions

In Chapter 8, we described the datastore as using multiversioned optimistic concurrency control, with the entity group as the unit of transactionality. Each time any entity in an entity group is updated, the datastore creates a new version of the entity group. If any process reads an entity in the entity group before the new version is fully stored, the process simply sees the earlier version.

Each of these versions gets an ID number, and this number increases strictly and monotonically. You can use the metadata API to get the entity group version number for an entity.

In Java, you get this information by fetching a fake entity with a specific key. You get the entity group key by calling the static method `Entities.createEntityGroup Key()`, passing it the `Key` of an entity in the group. The `Entity` that corresponds to the entity group key has a `__version__` property with an integer value:

```
import com.google.appengine.api.datastore.DatastoreService;
import com.google.appengine.api.datastore.DatastoreServiceFactory;
import com.google.appengine.api.datastore.Entities;
import com.google.appengine.api.datastore.Entity;

// ...
        DatastoreService datastore =
            DatastoreServiceFactory.getDatastoreService();

        // Write to an entity group, and get its version number.
        Entity parent = new Entity("MyKind");
        datastore.put(parent);
        Key groupKey = Entities.createEntityGroupKey(parent.getKey());
        Long version =
            (Long) datastore.get(groupKey).getProperty("__version__");

        // Update the entity group by creating a child entity.
        Entity child = new Entity("MyKind", parent.getKey());
        datastore.put(child);

        // The version number of the entire group has been incremented.
        Long version2 =
            (Long) datastore.get(groupKey).getProperty("__version__");
```

Remote Controls

One of the nice features of a relational database running in a typical hosting environment is the ability to connect directly to the database to perform queries and updates with administrative tools running on your local machine. App Engine has a facility for doing something similar, and it works for more than just the datastore: you can call any live service on behalf of your application using tools running on your computer. The tools do this using a remote proxy API.

The proxy API is a request handler that you install in your app. It is restricted to administrators. You run a client tool that authenticates as an administrator, connects to the request handler, and issues service calls over the connection. The proxy performs the calls and returns the results.

App Engine includes a version of the proxy handler for Java apps, as well as a Java client library that can call it.

 The remote API is clever and useful, but it's also slow: every service call is going over the network from your local computer to the app, then back. It is not suitable for running large jobs over arbitrary amounts of data. For large data transformation jobs, you're better off building something that runs within the app, using task queues or a backend module.

Let's take a look at how to set up the proxy for Java, and how to write a Java program that calls the API.

Setting Up the Remote API

To use the remote API tools with a Java application, you set up a URL path with a servlet provided by the SDK, namely com.google.apphosting.utilsremoteapi.RemoteApiServlet. You can choose any URL path; you will give this path to the remote API tools in a command-line argument. Be sure to restrict access to the URL path to administrators.

The following excerpt for your deployment descriptor (*web.xml*) associates the remote API servlet with the URL path /remote_api, and restricts it to administrator accounts:

```
<servlet>
  <servlet-name>remoteapi</servlet-name>
  <servlet-class>
    com.google.apphosting.utils.remoteapi.RemoteApiServlet
  </servlet-class>
</servlet>
<servlet-mapping>
```

```
      <servlet-name>remoteapi</servlet-name>
      <url-pattern>/remote_api</url-pattern>
    </servlet-mapping>

    <security-constraint>
      <web-resource-collection>
        <web-resource-name>remoteapi</web-resource-name>
        <url-pattern>/remote_api</url-pattern>
      </web-resource-collection>
      <auth-constraint>
        <role-name>admin</role-name>
      </auth-constraint>
    </security-constraint>
```

 The App Engine SDK for Python includes a client library that works with both the Java and Python versions of the remote proxy. The Python client library assumes a slightly different URL: /_ah/ remote_api. If you intend to use the Python client with a Java server app, be sure to map this additional path to RemoteApiServlet, and secure it with the admin role.

Using the Remote API with the Java Client Library

You can call the remote API directly from a Java client application using a library from the Java SDK. This configures the Java API to use the remote API handler for your application for all service calls, so you can use the service APIs as you would from a request handler directly in your client apps.

The client relies on two JARs provided with the App Engine SDK: impl/appengine-api.jar and appengine-remote-api.jar. If you installed the App Engine Java package via Cloud SDK, you can find these under *google-cloud-sdk/platform/appengine-java-sdk/lib*. When installed via the Eclipse plugin, they're in *eclipse/plugins/com.google.appengine.eclipse.sdkbundle_1.9.18/appengine-java-sdk-1.9.18/lib* (where 1.9.18 is the SDK version). In Eclipse, create a Java project, then in the new project wizard, click the Next button, select the Libraries tab, then click Add External JARs… to add each of these.

Here's a simple console application that connects to a proxy with a developer account email address and password, then performs a datastore query:

```
package myclient;

import java.io.IOException;

import com.google.appengine.api.datastore.DatastoreService;
import com.google.appengine.api.datastore.DatastoreServiceFactory;
import com.google.appengine.api.datastore.Entity;
import com.google.appengine.api.datastore.PreparedQuery;
```

```java
import com.google.appengine.api.datastore.Query;
import com.google.appengine.tools.remoteapi.RemoteApiInstaller;
import com.google.appengine.tools.remoteapi.RemoteApiOptions;

public class TryRemoteClient {
    static final String username = "user.name@gmail.com";
    static final String password = "password";

    static final String hostname = "saucy-boomerang-123.appspot.com";
    static final int port = 443;

    // To test this with a development server:
    // static final String hostname = "localhost";
    // static final int port = 8888;

    public static void main(String[] args) throws IOException {

        RemoteApiOptions options = new RemoteApiOptions()
            .server(hostname, port)
            .credentials(username, password);
        RemoteApiInstaller installer = new RemoteApiInstaller();
        installer.install(options);

        try {
            DatastoreService ds = DatastoreServiceFactory.getDatastoreService();
            PreparedQuery pq = ds.prepare(new Query("Book"));
            for (Entity result : pq.asIterable()) {
                String title = (String) result.getProperty("title");
                System.out.println("Book: " + title);
            }
        } finally {
            installer.uninstall();
        }
    }
}
```

Replace username, password, and hostname as appropriate. If you are using two-factor authentication with the account, you must generate an app-specific password for this in your Google account settings (*https://myaccount.google.com/*). You can test this in a development server by setting hostname to "localhost" and port to 8888.

The RemoteApiOptions instance contains the connection parameters for the proxy. The RemoteApiInstaller configures all of the App Engine service APIs to use the remote proxy for the current thread. If you use multiple threads, be sure to create a new RemoteApiInstaller for each thread, and call the install() and uninstall() methods appropriately.

With the remote proxy client installed, all of the App Engine APIs work as they do when running on App Engine. The datastore code in this example is identical to the equivalent code for a server-side application. This allows you to share code between the server app and client-side tools as needed.

Remember that every call to an App Engine library that performs a service call does so over the network via an HTTP request to the application. This is inevitably slower than running within the live application. It also consumes application resources like web requests do, including bandwidth and request counts, which are not normally consumed by service calls in the live app.

On the plus side, because your code runs on your local computer, it is not constrained by the App Engine runtime sandbox or the 30-second request deadline. You can run long jobs and interactive applications on your computer without restriction, using any libraries you like—at the expense of consuming app resources to marshal service calls over HTTP.

CHAPTER 10

The Java Persistence API

The App Engine Java SDK includes implementations of two data access interface standards: the Java Persistence API (JPA) and Java Data Objects (JDO). These interfaces provide two essential features.

For one, these interfaces define a mechanism for describing the structure of data objects in terms of Java classes. You can use them to define and enforce consistent data schemas on top of App Engine's schemaless datastore, and take advantage of type safety in the Java language. These interfaces serve as a data modeling layer.

The interfaces also serve as a portability layer to other data storage solutions. Relational databases and other key-value stores support these interface standards, in varying degrees. Because the standards were developed with SQL-based relational databases in mind, the App Engine datastore can only be said to support a portion of the standard, and it is often easier to port away from App Engine than to it. But this alone adds value, as you can reserve the right to move your app to your company's own servers at any time.

The App Engine SDK uses an open source product called DataNucleus Access Platform as the basis for its implementations of JDO and JPA. Access Platform uses an adapter layer that translates both standards to an underlying implementation. The App Engine SDK includes an Access Platform adapter based on its low-level datastore API.

The JDO and JPA standards are similar, and share similar roots. The concepts that apply to the App Engine datastore have similar interfaces in both standards but with different terminology and minor behavioral differences. Which one you choose may depend on how familiar you are with it, or how well it is implemented for your most likely porting target, if you have one in mind.

In this chapter, we look at how to use JPA version 1.0 with App Engine. If you'd prefer to use JPA 2.0 or JDO, check out the official documentation for App Engine.

 A quick note on terminology: JPA refers to data objects as "entities." This similarity to datastore entities is convenient in some ways, and not so convenient in others. For this chapter, we'll refer to JPA entities as "data objects" (or just "objects") to avoid confusion with datastore entities.

Setting Up JPA

To use JPA, you must perform a few steps to set up the library.

JPA needs a configuration file that specifies that you want to use the App Engine implementation of the interface. This file is named *persistence.xml*, and should appear in your WAR's *WEB-INF/classes/META-INF/* directory. If you're using Eclipse, you can create this file in the *src/META-INF/* directory, and Eclipse will copy it to the final location automatically. It should look like this:

```xml
<?xml version="1.0" encoding="UTF-8" ?>
<persistence xmlns="http://java.sun.com/xml/ns/persistence"
  xmlns:xsi="http://www.w3.org/2001/XMLSchema-instance"
  xsi:schemaLocation="http://java.sun.com/xml/ns/persistence
      http://java.sun.com/xml/ns/persistence/persistence_1_0.xsd" version="1.0">
    <persistence-unit name="transactions-optional">
        <provider>
          org.datanucleus.api.jpa.PersistenceProviderImpl
        </provider>
        <properties>
            <property name="datanucleus.NontransactionalRead" value="true"/>
            <property name="datanucleus.NontransactionalWrite" value="true"/>
            <property name="datanucleus.ConnectionURL" value="appengine"/>
        </properties>
    </persistence-unit>
</persistence>
```

This configuration tells Access Platform to use the "appengine" adapter. It also says to allow reads and writes outside of transactions (NontransactionalRead and Non transactionalWrite are true), which fits the semantics of the datastore that we described earlier. We named this configuration set "transactions-optional" to match.

Your application uses an EntityManager object to perform a set of datastore operations. The application creates an EntityManager, using an EntityManagerFactory. The factory loads the configuration file and uses it for subsequent datastore interactions. You get an instance of the factory by calling a static method and passing it the name of the configuration set ("transactions-optional"):

```
import javax.persistence.EntityManagerFactory;
import javax.persistence.Persistence;

// ...
    EntityManagerFactory emfInstance =
        Persistence.createEntityManagerFactory("transactions-optional");
```

The `createEntityManagerFactory()` static method performs a nontrivial amount of work. You can think of the factory as a connection pool, and each `EntityManager` as an individual connection. Because you only need one factory for the entire existence of the application, a best practice is to call the method only once, store the factory in a static member, and reuse it for multiple web requests:

```
package myapp;  // where "myapp" is your app's package

import javax.persistence.EntityManagerFactory;
import javax.persistence.Persistence;

public final class EMF {
    private static final EntityManagerFactory emfInstance =
        Persistence.createEntityManagerFactory("transactions-optional");

    private EMF() {}

    public static EntityManagerFactory get() {
        return emfInstance;
    }
}
```

Access Platform hooks up the persistence plumbing to your JPA data classes in a post-compilation process that it calls "enhancement." If you are using Eclipse with the Google Plugin, the plugin performs this step automatically. If you are not using Eclipse, you must add the enhancement step to your build process. See the official documentation for information about performing this build step with Apache Ant.

Entities and Keys

In JPA, you define data classes as plain old Java objects (POJOs). You use annotations to tell JPA which classes to persist to the datastore, and how to store its members. Defining your data exclusively in terms of the Java classes your application uses makes it easy to manipulate your persistent data. It also makes it easy to test your application, because you can create mock data objects directly from the classes.

JPA also lets you use an XML file instead of annotations to describe how to persist data classes. We'll only cover the annotation style here, but if you are familiar with the XML file mechanism, you can use it with Access Platform.

Here's a simple example of a data class:

```
import java.util.Date;
import javax.persistence.Entity;
import javax.persistence.Id;

@Entity(name = "Book")
public class Book {
    @Id
    private String isbn;

    private String title;
    private String author;
    private int copyrightYear;
    private Date authorBirthdate;

    // ... constructors, accessors ...
}
```

JPA knows instances of the Book class can be made persistent (saved to the datastore) because of the @Entity annotation. This annotation takes a name argument that specifies the name to be used in JPA queries for objects of this class. The name must be unique across all data classes in the application.

By default, the name of the datastore kind is derived from the name of the class. Specifically, this is the simple name of the class, without the package path (everything after the last ., e.g., "Book"). If you have two data classes with the same simple name in different packages, you can specify an alternative kind name by using the @Table annotation. (JPA was designed with tabular databases in mind, but the concept is equivalent.)

```
import javax.persistence.Entity;
import javax.persistence.Table;

@Entity(name = "Book")
@Table(name = "BookItem")
public class Book {
    // ...
}
```

The Book class has five members. Four of these members are stored as properties on the datastore entity: title, author, copyrightYear, and authorBirthdate. The fifth member, isbn, represents the key name for the entity. JPA knows this because the member has the @Id annotation, and because the type of the member is String.

Every data class needs a member that represents the object's primary key, annotated with @Id. If the type of this member is String and it has no other annotations, then the key has no ancestors, and the value of the member is the string key name. The application must set this field before saving the object for the first time.

To tell JPA to let the datastore assign a unique numeric ID instead of using an app-provided key name string, you declare the member with a type of Long and give it the annotation @GeneratedValue(strategy = GenerationType.IDENTITY), like so:

```
import javax.persistence.Entity;
import javax.persistence.GeneratedValue;
import javax.persistence.GenerationType;
import javax.persistence.Id;

@Entity(name = "Book")
public class Book {
    @Id
    @GeneratedValue(strategy = GenerationType.IDENTITY)
    private Long id;

    // ...
}
```

The member is set with the system-assigned ID when the object is saved to the datastore for the first time.

These simple key member types are sufficient for entities without ancestors. Together with the entity kind ("Book"), the member represents the complete key of a root entity. If an instance of the class may represent an entity with ancestors, the key member must be able to represent the full key path. There are two ways to do this.

One way is to declare the type of the key member to be the com.google.appengine.api.datastore.Key class:

```
import javax.persistence.Entity;
import javax.persistence.Id;
import com.google.appengine.api.datastore.Key;

@Entity(name = "Book")
public class Book {
    @Id
    private Key id;

    // ...
}
```

You can use this key member type to create a complete Key with a string name. You can also use system-assigned numeric IDs with ancestors by using the @Generated Value annotation, then assigning a Key value with neither the name nor the ID set.

If you'd prefer not to create a dependency on an App Engine–specific class, there is another way to implement a key with ancestors. Simply declare the ID field's type as String and use a DataNucleus JPA extension that encodes the complete key as a string value, like so:

```
import javax.persistence.Entity;
import javax.persistence.Id;
import org.datanucleus.api.jpa.annotations.Extension;

@Entity(name = "Book")
public class Book {
    @Id
    @Extension(vendorName = "datanucleus",
               key = "gae.encoded-pk",
               value = "true")
    private String id;

    // ...
}
```

You can convert between a `Key` and a string-encoded key using the `KeyFactory` class's `keyToString()` and `stringToKey()` methods. (Note that the `Key` class's `toString()` method returns something else.)

You can use a `Key` ID field or a string-encoded ID field in combination with the `@GeneratedValue` annotation to produce keys with ancestors and system-assigned numeric IDs.

Entity Properties

The fields of the object become the properties of the corresponding entity. The name of a field is used as the name of the property. The `@Id` field is not stored as a property value, only as the key.

JPA and App Engine support many types of fields. Any of the types mentioned in Table 6-1 can be used as a field type. A field can contain a serializable object, stored as a single property. A field can also be a collection of one of the core datastore types or a serializable class, to be stored as a multivalued property. Additionally, App Engine supports JPA embedded data objects and relationships between entities using fields.

In some cases, JPA must be told which fields to save to the datastore. For the Java standard types (such as `Long` or `String` or `Date`), JPA assumes that fields of those types should be saved. For other types, especially the datastore-specific classes such as `datastore.ShortBlob`, you must tell JPA to save the field by giving it the `@Basic` annotation. If you have a field that should not be saved to the datastore, give it the `@Transient` annotation:

```
import java.util.List;
import javax.persistence.Basic;
import javax.persistence.Id;
import javax.persistence.Transient;
import com.google.appengine.api.datastore.ShortBlob;

@Entity(name = "Book")
```

```
public class Book {
    // ...

    private String title;        // saved

    @Basic                       // saved
    private ShortBlob coverIcon;

    @Basic                       // saved
    private List<String> tags;

    @Transient                   // not saved
    private int debugAccessCount;
}
```

As with the low-level API, some types are widened before being stored. int and Integer are converted to Long, and float and Float become Double. With the JPA interface, these values are converted back to the declared field types when loaded into an object.

A Serializable class can be used as a field type, using the @Lob annotation. These values are stored in serialized form as datastore.Blob values. As such, these values are not indexed, and cannot be used in queries.

Collection types are stored as multivalued properties in iteration order. When loaded into the data class, multivalued properties are converted back into the specified collection type.

By default, the name of a field is used as the name of the corresponding property. You can override this by using the @Column annotation:

```
import javax.persistence.Column;
import javax.persistence.Entity;

@Entity(name = "Book")
public class Book {
    // ...

    @Column(name = "long_description")
    private String longDescription;
}
```

You can declare that the datastore property of a field should not be mentioned in indexes—the property of each entity should be created as a nonindexed property—using an @Extension annotation:

```
import org.datanucleus.api.jpa.annotations.Extension;

@Entity(name = "Book")
public class Book {
    // ...
```

```
        @Extension(vendorName = "datanucleus",
                   key = "gae.unindexed",
                   value = "true")
        private String firstSentence;
    }
```

Embedded Objects

App Engine supports JPA embedded classes by storing the fields of the embedded class as properties on the same datastore entity as the fields of the primary class. You must declare the class to embed using the @Embeddable annotation:

```
import javax.persistence.Embeddable;

@Embeddable
public class Publisher {
    private String name;
    private String address;
    private String city;
    private String stateOrProvince;
    private String postalCode;

    // ...
}
```

To embed the class, simply use it as a field type:

```
import javax.persistence.Entity;
import Publisher;

@Entity(name = "Book")
public class Book {
    // ...

    private Publisher publisher;
}
```

Because fields of embedded classes are stored as separate properties, they are queryable just like other properties. You can refer to an embedded field in a property with the name of the outer field with a dot-notation, such as publisher.name. The actual property name is just the name of the inner field, and you can change this if needed, using an @Column annotation.

Saving, Fetching, and Deleting Objects

To start a session with the datastore, you use the EntityManagerFactory to create an EntityManager. You must create a new EntityManager for each request handler, and close it when you're done:

```
import javax.persistence.EntityManager;
import javax.persistence.EntityManagerFactory;
import myapp.EMF;  // where "myapp" is your app's package

// ...
        EntityManagerFactory emf = EMF.get();
        EntityManager em = null;
        try {
            em = emf.createEntityManager();
            // ... do datastore stuff ...
        } finally {
            if (em != null)
                em.close();
        }
```

In order to create a new data object, you construct the data class and then call the EntityManager's `persist()` method with the object:

```
import myapp.Book;  // our data class

// ...
        EntityManager em = null;
        try {
            em = emf.createEntityManager();
            Book book = new Book();
            book.setTitle("The Grapes of Wrath");
            // ...
            em.persist(book);
        } finally {
            if (em != null)
                em.close();
        }
```

If you create an object with a complete key, and an entity with that key already exists in the datastore, saving the new object will overwrite the old one. In App Engine's implementation, JPA's `merge()` method is equivalent to `persist()` in this way. (Other implementations may do something different in this case.)

To fetch an entity with a known key, you use the `find()` method. This method takes the class of the object in which to load the entity, and the key of the object. The key can be any appropriate type: a string key name, a numeric ID, a `datastore.Key` object, or a string-encoded complete key. The method returns an object of the given class, or `null` if no object with that key is found:

```
        Book book = em.find(Book.class, "9780596156732");
        if (book == null) {
            // not found
        }
```

The ability of find() to accept all four key types is nonstandard. To make your code more portable, only call find(), using the type of key you used in the data class.

When you create or fetch an entity (or get an entity back from a query), the data object becomes "attached" to (or managed by) the entity manager. If you make changes to an attached object and do not save them by calling the persist() method explicitly, the object is saved automatically when you close the entity manager. As we'll see in the next section, if you need the entity to be updated in a transaction, you pass the updated object to the persist() method at the moment it needs to be saved.

To delete an entity, you call the remove() method. This method takes the data object as its sole argument. The object still exists in memory after it is removed from the datastore:

```
em.remove(book);
```

The remove() method requires a loaded data object. There is no way to delete an entity with this method without fetching its object first. (You can delete entities without fetching them by using a JPQL delete query. See the section "Queries and JPQL" on page 244.)

Remember to close the EntityManager by calling its close() method. If you don't, changes to objects will not be saved to the datastore. The best way to do this is in a finally block, as shown previously, so the manager still gets closed in the event of an uncaught exception.

Transactions in JPA

The API for performing transactions in JPA is similar to the low-level datastore API. You call a method on the entity manager to create a Transaction object, then call methods on the object to begin and commit or roll back the transaction:

```
import javax.persistence.EntityTransaction;

// ...
        EntityTransaction txn = em.getTransaction();
        txn.begin();
        try {
            Book book = em.find(Book.class, "9780596156732");
            BookReview bookReview = new BookReview();
            bookReview.setRating(5);
            book.getBookReviews().add(bookReview);
```

```
        // Persist all updates and commit.
        txn.commit();
    } finally {
        if (txn.isActive()) {
            txn.rollback();
        }
    }
}
```

The JPA transaction interface was designed for databases that support global transactions, so it knows nothing of App Engine's local transactions and entity groups. It's up to the application to know which operations are appropriate to perform in a single transaction. You can manage entity groups and ancestors by using App Engine's extensions to JPA.

One way to set up a data class that can represent entities with parents is to use either a datastore.Key or a string-encoded key for the @Id field. When you create a new object, you can construct the complete key, including ancestors, and assign it to this field.

Alternatively, you can establish a second field to contain the parent key as either a Key or string-encoded key, using an extension:

```
import javax.persistence.Basic;
import javax.persistence.Entity;
import javax.persistence.GeneratedValue;
import javax.persistence.GenerationType;
import javax.persistence.Id;

import org.datanucleus.api.jpa.annotations.Extension;

@Entity
public class BookReview {
    @Id
    @GeneratedValue(strategy = GenerationType.IDENTITY)
    @Extension(vendorName = "datanucleus",
               key = "gae.encoded-pk",
               value = "true")
    private String keyString;

    @Basic
    @Extension(vendorName = "datanucleus",
               key = "gae.parent-pk",
               value = "true")
    private String bookKeyString;
}
```

The parent key field makes it easier to port your application to another database at a later time. It declares a slot in the data class for the ancestor relationship that is separate from the entity's key name.

The parent key field is required if you want to perform queries with ancestor filters. As we'll see in the next section, JPA queries must refer to fields on the data class.

The App Engine implementation of JPA includes features for managing entity groups automatically using object relationships. We'll discuss relationships later in this chapter.

Queries and JPQL

JPA includes a SQL-like query language called JPQL. JPQL provides access to the underlying database's query functionality at the level of abstraction of JPA data objects. You form queries for data objects in terms of the data classes, and get objects as results.

To perform a query, you call the entity manager's `createQuery()` method with the text of the JPQL query. This returns a `Query` object. To get the results, you call `getResultList()` on the Query object:

```
import java.util.List;
import javax.persistence.Query;

// ...

    Query query = em.createQuery("SELECT b FROM Book b");

    @SuppressWarnings("unchecked")
    List<Book> results = (List<Book>) query.getResultList();
```

In this example, the cast to `List<Book>` generates a compiler warning, so we suppress this warning by using an `@SuppressWarnings` annotation.

JPA knows which class to use for each result from the `@Entity(name = "…")` annotation on the class. You can also use the full package path of the class in the query.

You can use parameters in your JPQL query, and replace the parameters with values by calling `setParameter()`:

```
    Query query = em.createQuery(
        "SELECT b FROM Book b WHERE copyrightYear >= :earliestYear");
    query.setParameter("earliestYear", 1923);
```

`getResultList()` returns a special App Engine–specific implementation of `List` that knows how to fetch results in batches. If you iterate over the entire list, the `List` implementation may make multiple calls to the datastore to fetch results.

If you are only expecting one result, you can call `getSingleResult()` instead. This gets the single result, or throws an exception if the query returns no results (`NoResultException`) or more than one result (`NonUniqueResultException`):

```
Book book = (Book) query.getSingleResult();
```

You can fetch a range of results by setting an offset and a maximum number of results, using the `setFirstResult()` and `setMaxResults()` methods before calling `getResultList()`:

```
// Get results 5-15.
query.setFirstResult(4);
query.setMaxResults(10);

@SuppressWarnings("unchecked")
List<Book> results = (List<Book>) query.getResultList();
```

The syntax of JPQL is straightforward, and similar to SQL. JPQL keywords can be all uppercase or all lowercase, and are shown as uppercase here, as is tradition. Class and field names are case-sensitive. The query begins by identifying the simple name of the class of objects to query, corresponding to the kind of the entities:

```
SELECT b FROM Book b
```

This query returns all `Book` data objects, where `Book` is the value of the `name` argument to the `@Entity` annotation on the data class (which happens to also be named `Book`). The class name is followed by an identifier (b); stating that identifier after the word `SELECT` tells JPA to return objects of that class as results.

To perform a keys-only query, give the name of the key field instead of the class identifier. The methods that return results return values of the type used for the `@Id` field in the data class:

```
Query query = em.createQuery("SELECT isbn FROM Book");

@SuppressWarnings("unchecked")
List<String> results = (List<String>) query.getResultList();
```

The App Engine implementation of JPQL supports queries for specific fields, although perhaps not in the way you'd expect. For a query for specific fields, the datastore returns the complete data for each entity to the application, and the interface implementation selects the requested fields and assembles the results. This is only true if one of the requested fields is a datastore property, and is not true if the only field is a key field (`@Id`).

If the query is for one field, each result is a value of the type of that field. If the query is for multiple fields, each result is an `Object[]` whose elements are the field values in the order specified in the query:

```
Query query = em.createQuery("SELECT isbn, title, author FROM Book");

// Fetch complete Book objects, then
// produce result objects from 3 fields
// of each result
@SuppressWarnings("unchecked")
List<Object[]> results = (List<Object[]>) query.getResultList();
for (Object[] result : results) {
    String isbn = (String) result[0];
    String title = (String) result[1];
    String author = (String) result[2];

    // ...
}
```

You specify filters on fields by using a WHERE clause and one or more conditions:

```
SELECT b FROM Book b WHERE author = "John Steinbeck"
                     AND copyrightYear >= 1940
```

To filter on the entity key, refer to the field that represents the key in the data class (the @Id field):

```
SELECT b FROM Book b WHERE author = "John Steinbeck"
                     AND isbn > :firstKeyToFetch
```

You can perform an ancestor filter by establishing a parent key field (as we did in the previous section) and referring to that field in the query:

```
SELECT br FROM BookReview br WHERE bookKey = :pk
```

As with find(), you can use any of the four key types with parameterized queries, but the most portable way is to use the type used in the class.

You specify sort orders by using an ORDER BY clause. Multiple sort orders are comma-delimited. Each sort order can have a direction of ASC (the default) or DESC:

```
SELECT b FROM Book b ORDER BY rating DESC title
```

The App Engine implementation of JPQL includes a couple of additional tricks that the datastore can support natively. One such trick is the string prefix trick:

```
SELECT b FROM Book b WHERE title LIKE 'The Grape%'
```

The implementation translates this to WHERE title >= 'The Grape', which does the same thing: it returns all books with a title that begins with the string The Grape, including "The Grape", "The Grapefruit", and "The Grapes of Wrath".

This trick only supports a single wildcard at the end of a string. It does not support a wildcard at the beginning of the string.

Another trick App Engine's JPQL implementation knows how to do is to translate queries on key fields into batch gets. For example:

```
SELECT b FROM Book b WHERE isbn IN (:i1, :i2, :i3)
```

This becomes a batch get of three keys, and does not perform a query at all.

In addition to these SELECT queries, App Engine's JPA implementation supports deleting entities that meet criteria with JPQL. A DELETE query can include filters on keys and properties to specify the entities to delete:

```
DELETE FROM Book b WHERE isbn >= "TEST_000" AND isbn <= "TEST_999"
```

To execute a DELETE query, call the Query object's executeUpdate() method. This method returns the number of entities deleted.

As with other mechanisms for modifying data, if you perform a delete query outside of a transaction, it is possible for a delete of one entity to fail while the others succeed. If you perform it inside a transaction, it'll be all or nothing, but all entities must be in the same entity group, and the delete query must use an ancestor filter.

 The JPA specification supports many features of queries that are common to SQL databases, but are not supported natively in the App Engine datastore. With a SQL database, using one of these features calls the database directly, with all the performance implications (good and bad) of the datastore's implementation.

When an app uses a feature of JPQL that the underlying database does not support, DataNucleus Access Platform tries to make up the difference using its own in-memory query evaluator. It attempts to load all the information it needs to perform the query into memory, execute the nonnative operations itself, then return the result.

Because such features are potential scalability hazards—an AVG() query would require fetching every entity of the kind, for example—the App Engine implementation disables the Access Platform in-memory query evaluator.

Relationships

Most useful data models involve relationships between classes of data objects. Players are members of guilds, book reviews are about books, messages are posted to message boards, customers place orders, and orders have multiple line items. For logical reasons or architectural reasons, two concepts may be modeled as separate but related classes. Those relationships are as much a part of the data model as the data fields of the objects.

In the App Engine datastore (and most databases), one easy way to model a relationship between two objects is to store the entity key of one object as a property of the other, and (if needed) vice versa. The datastore supports Key values as a native property value type, and also provides a way to encode key values as strings. You don't need any help from JPA to model relationships this way.

But relationships are so important to data modeling that JPA has a family of features to support them. In JPA, you can define *owned relationships* in the data model that enforce constraints by managing changes. With owned relationships, you can say that a book has zero or more book reviews, and JPA ensures that you can't have a book review without a book. If you delete a `Book` object, JPA knows to also delete all its `BookReview` objects. In the Java code, the relationship is represented by a field whose type is of the related data class, ensuring that only the appropriate classes are used on either side of the relationship.

The App Engine implementation of JPA supports one-to-one and one-to-many relationships. It does not yet support JPA's notion of many-to-many relationships.

An *unowned relationship* is a relationship without these constraints. App Engine supports unowned relationships through the storing of literal key values, but does not yet support them through JPA. You can use multivalued properties of `Key` values to model unowned one-to-one, one-to-many, and many-to-many relationships.

To completely support the semantics of JPA owned relationships, App Engine stores objects with owned relationships in the same entity group. It's easy to see why this has to be the case. If one object is deleted within a transaction, the relationship says the related object must also be deleted. But to do that in the same transaction requires that both objects be in the same entity group. If one object is deleted outside of a transaction, then the other object must be deleted in a separate operation, and if one delete or the other fails, an object remains that doesn't meet the relationship requirement.

While the use of entity groups may sound constraining, it's also a powerful feature. You can use JPA owned relationships to perform transactions on related entities, and the JPA implementation will manage entity groups for you automatically.

You specify an owned one-to-one relationship by creating a field whose type is of the related class, and giving the field an `@OneToOne` annotation. For example, you could associate each book with a cover image, like so:

```
import javax.persistence.Entity;
import javax.persistence.OneToOne;
import bookstore.BookCoverImage;

@Entity(name = "Book")
public class Book {
    // ...

    @OneToOne(cascade=CascadeType.ALL)
    private BookCoverImage bookCoverImage;
}
```

This annotation declares a one-to-one relationship between the Book and BookCover
Image classes.

In every relationship, one class "owns" the relationship. The owner of a relationship is
responsible for propagating changes to related objects. In this example, the Book class
is the "owner" of the relationship.

The cascade=CascadeType.ALL argument annotation says that all kinds of changes
should propagate to related objects (including PERSIST, REFRESH, REMOVE, and MERGE).
For example:

```
// EntityManager em;
// ...

Book book = new Book();
book.setBookCoverImage(new BookCoverImage());

book.setTitle("The Grapes of Wrath");
book.bookCoverImage.setType("image/jpg");

EntityTransaction txn = em.getTransaction();
txn.begin();
try {
    em.persist(book);
    txn.commit();
} finally {
    if (txn.isActive()) {
        txn.rollback();
    }
}
em.close();
```

This code creates a Book and a related BookCoverImage. When it makes the Book persistent, the BookCoverImage is made persistent automatically (the PERSIST action cascades). Similarly, if we were to delete the Book, the BookCoverImage would also be
deleted (the DELETE action cascades). Cascading actions follow all ownership paths
from "owner" to "owned," and do the right thing if the objects they find have changed
since they were loaded from the datastore.

You can have JPA populate a field on the "owned" class that points back to the owner
automatically, like so:

```
import javax.persistence.Entity;
import javax.persistence.OneToOne;
import bookstore.Book;

@Entity(name = "BookCoverImage")
public class BookCoverImage {
    // ...

    @OneToOne(mappedBy="bookCoverImage")
```

```
        private Book book;
    }
```

The `mappedBy` argument tells JPA that the book field refers to the `Book` object that is related to this object. This is managed from the "owner" side of the relationship: when the `BookCoverImage` is assigned to the `Book`'s field, JPA knows that the back-reference refers to the `Book` object.

To specify a one-to-many relationship, you use a field type that is a `List` or `Set` of the related class, and use the `@OneToMany` annotation on the "one" class, with a `mappedBy` argument that refers to the property on the entities of the "many" class:

```
import java.util.List;
import javax.persistence.CascadeType;
import javax.persistence.Entity;
import javax.persistence.OneToMany;
import bookstore.BookReview;

@Entity(name = "Book")
public class Book {
    // ...

    @OneToMany(cascade=CascadeType.ALL, mappedBy="book")
    private List<BookReview> bookReviews = null;
}
```

To create a back-reference from the "many" class to the "one" class, you use an `@Many ToOne` annotation, with no arguments:

```
// BookReview.java
@Entity(name = "BookReview")
public class BookReview {
    // ...

    @ManyToOne()
    private Book book;
}

// Book.java
@Entity(name = "Book")
public class Book {
    // ...

    @OneToMany(cascade=CascadeType.ALL,
            mappedBy="book")
    private List<BookReview> bookReviews;
}
```

In a one-to-many relationship, the "one" is always the owner class, and the "many" is the owned class. In a one-to-one relationship, JPA knows which is the "owned" class

by the absence of a back-reference field, or a back-reference field mentioned by a map
pedBy annotation argument: the side with the mappedBy is the owned class.

When you fetch a data object that has a relationship field, JPA does not fetch the
related objects right away. Instead, it waits until you access the field to fetch the object
(or objects). This is called "lazy" fetching, and it saves your app from unnecessary
datastore operations. The App Engine implementation of JPA only supports lazy
fetching (FetchType.LAZY), and does not yet support its opposite, "eager" fetching
(FetchType.EAGER). Note that you must access related objects prior to closing the
EntityManager, so they are fetched into memory:

```
// Fetch a Book, but not its BookCoverImage.
Book book = em.find(Book.class, "9780596156732");
// ...

// The BookCoverImage is fetched when it is first accessed.
resp.setContentType(book.bookCoverImage.type);
```

In the datastore, the relationship is represented using ancestors. The owner object is
the parent, and all owned objects are children. When you access the relationship field
on the owner object, the interface uses an ancestor query to get the owned objects.
When you access a back-reference to the owner from the owned object, the interface
parses the owned object's key to get the parent.

Related objects are created in the same entity group, so they can all be updated within
the same transaction if necessary. The owner's entity is created first (if necessary) and
becomes the parent of the owned objects' entities. If you declare a back-reference by
using mappedBy, no property is stored on the owned object's entity. Instead, when the
field is dereferenced, the implementation uses the owned object's key path to determine the owner's key and fetches it.

The App Engine implementation does not support many-to-one relationships where
the "many" is the owner. That is, it does not support a one-to-many relationship
where actions cascade from the many to the one.

Creating new relationships between existing data classes can be tricky, because the
entity group requirements must be met in the migrated data. Adding a relationship to
the owner class is like adding a field: the entities that represent instances of the owner
class must be updated to have appropriate key properties. The "owned" side is trick-
ier: because an owned object's entity must have the owner as its parent, if the owned
object already exists in the datastore, it must be deleted and re-created with the new
parent. You can't change an entity's parent after the entity has been created.

This use of datastore ancestors means you cannot reassign an owned object to
another owner after it has been saved to the datastore. This also means that one
object cannot be on the "owned" side of more than one relationship, as the entity can
have only one parent.

Relationships and cascading actions imply that an operation on a data object can translate to multiple datastore operations on multiple entities, all in the same entity group. If you want these operations to occur in a single transaction, you must perform the initial operation (such as em.merge(...)) within an explicit transaction.

If you perform a cascading action outside of an explicit transaction, each of the datastore operations performed by JPA occurs in a separate operation. Some of these operations may fail while others succeed. As such, it's a best practice to perform all JPA updates within explicit transactions, so there is no confusion as to what succeeded and what failed.

You can perform queries on relationship fields in JPQL by using key values. For a query on the owner class, the query is a simple key property query:

```
SELECT FROM Book b WHERE bookCoverImage = :bci AND publishDate > :pdate
```

For a query on an owned class, a query on the back-reference field becomes an ancestor filter:

```
SELECT FROM BookCoverImage bci WHERE book = :b
```

You cannot refer to properties of the related entity in the query filter. App Engine does not support join queries.

For More Information

The JDO and JPA interfaces have many useful features that work with the App Engine implementation. One excellent source of documentation on these interfaces is the DataNucleus Access Platform website:

http://www.datanucleus.org/products/accessplatform/

The App Engine implementation is an open source project hosted on Google Code. The source includes many unit tests that exercise and demonstrate many features of JDO and JPA. You can browse the source code at the project page:

http://code.google.com/p/datanucleus-appengine/

To read the unit tests, click the Source tab, then click Browse in the navigation bar. The path is *svn/trunk/tests/com/google/appengine/datanucleus/*.

CHAPTER 11

Using Google Cloud SQL with App Engine

A sizable portion of this book is dedicated to Google Cloud Datastore, a schemaless persistent object store designed for applications that scale to arbitrary sizes. Those automatic scaling capabilities come at the expense of features common to relational databases such as MySQL, PostgreSQL, and Oracle Database. While many common tasks of web application programming are well suited, or even better suited, for a scalable datastore, some cases call for a real relational database, with normalized entries, real-time join queries, and enforced and migratable data schemas. And sometimes you just want to run third-party software that expects you to have a SQL database on hand.

For those cases, there's Google Cloud SQL. A feature of Google Cloud Platform, Cloud SQL gives you a straight-up no-nonsense MySQL relational database, designed for ease of use from Cloud Platform runtime environments like App Engine. Your database lives on a Cloud SQL *instance,* a virtual machine of a particular size that runs for as long as you need the database to be available. Your app code connects to the instance to execute SQL statements and queries using a standard database interface. You can also configure an IP address for the instance and connect to it with any MySQL client.

Naturally, Cloud SQL is the opposite of Cloud Datastore when it comes to scaling. Each SQL instance has a large but limited capacity for concurrent connections, CPU, and data. If you need more capacity than a single instance can provide, it's up to you to start new instances, divide traffic, and shard or replicate data. Cloud SQL includes special support (currently in a beta release) for *read replicas,* special instances in a read-only mode that copy all of the updates from a master instance. You manage Cloud SQL instances just like you would a fleet of MySQL machines, with all of the flexibility and overhead that comes with it. Cloud SQL offers many instance types, and for many applications you can upgrade a single instance quite far before you have to worry about scaling.

In this chapter, we'll give a brief overview of how to get started with Cloud SQL, and how to develop App Engine applications that use it. We won't cover every feature of MySQL, as there is plenty of documentation online and many excellent books on the subject. For information on advanced subjects like read replicas, see the official documentation (*https://cloud.google.com/sql/*).

Choosing a Cloud SQL Instance

With Cloud SQL, as with all of Google Cloud Platform, you only pay for the resources you use. Cloud SQL's billable resources include instance hours, storage, I/O operations to storage, and outbound network bandwidth. Network traffic between App Engine and Cloud SQL is free. Every instance gets a free externally visible IPv6 address, and inbound network traffic is also free of charge. You can pay a little more for an IPv4 address for the instance if you have a client on a network that doesn't issue global IPv6 addresses.

Like App Engine instances, Cloud SQL instances are available in multiple sizes: D0, D1, D2, D4, D8, D16, and D32. The instance tiers mainly differ in RAM, ranging from 0.125 gigabytes for a D0 to 16 gigabytes for a D32, and the maximum number of concurrent connections, from 250 to 4,000.

Storage is billed per gigabyte used per month, and you only pay for the disk space used by MySQL over time. This includes storage for system tables and logs, as well as your app's table schemas and rows. You don't need to specify (or pay for) a maximum size. An instance of any tier can grow its data up to 250 gigabytes by default, and you can raise this limit to 500 gigabytes by purchasing a Google Cloud support package at the "silver" level.

There are two billing plans for Cloud SQL: per use billing, and package billing. With per use billing, you are billed for each hour an instance runs, with a minimum of one hour each time you enable an instance, rounded to the nearest hour. You can start and stop the instance as needed, and the database persists when the instance is stopped, with storage billed at the usual storage rate. This is useful for single user sessions or applications that only need the database during a fixed window of time, where the instance does not need to run continuously.

If you intend to keep the instance running over a sustained period of multiple days, such as to keep it available for a web application, you can claim a substantial discount by selecting package billing. With package billing, you are billed for each day that the instance exists. You can keep the instance running continuously for no additional charge. The package price also includes an amount of storage and I/O, and you aren't charged for these resources until usage exceeds the bundled amount.

As with App Engine instances, the rate differs by instance tier, with D0 being the least expensive. You can change an instance's tier at any time. Doing so results in only a few seconds of downtime.

As usual, prices change frequently enough that we won't bother to list specific numbers here. See the official documentation (*https://cloud.google.com/sql/pricing*) for the latest pricing information.

 When you first sign up for Cloud SQL, or other Cloud Platform services such as Compute Engine, you may be eligible for a free trial of the Platform. The free trial gives you a starting budget of free resources so you can try out Cloud SQL without charge. This is a one-time trial budget for you to spend on these services. (This is different from App Engine's free quotas, which refresh daily.) Go to the Cloud Platform website (*https://cloud.google.com/*) and look for the Free Trial button to get started.

Installing MySQL Locally

While developing and maintaining an app that uses Cloud SQL, you will use a MySQL administrative client to connect to the Cloud SQL instance from your local machine. In addition, you will probably want to run a MySQL server locally to test your application without connecting to Cloud SQL. You can download and install MySQL Community Edition from Oracle's website to get both the client and the server tools for Windows, Mac OS X, or Linux. MySQL Community Edition is free.

To download MySQL, visit the MySQL Community Downloads page (*http://dev.mysql.com/downloads/*). Be sure to get the version of MySQL that matches Cloud SQL. Currently, this is version 5.5.

Linux users can install MySQL using `apt-get` like so:

```
sudo apt-get install mysql-server mysql-client
```

Once you have MySQL server installed, the server is running locally and can accept local connections. If the installation process did not prompt you to set a password for the root account, set one using the `mysqladmin` command, where `new-password` is the password you wish to set:

```
mysqladmin -u root password "new-password"
```

Try connecting to the server using the `mysql` command:

```
mysql -u root -p
```

Enter the password when prompted. When successful, you see a `mysql>` prompt. You can enter SQL statements at this prompt to create and modify databases. The `root` account has full access, and can also create new accounts and grant privileges.

See the MySQL documentation (*http://dev.mysql.com/doc/refman/5.5/en/*) for more information about setting up the local server.

 While you're at the MySQL website, you might also want to get MySQL Workbench, a visual client for designing and managing databases. You can download MySQL Workbench Community Edition for free.

Creating a Cloud SQL Instance

Open a browser and visit the Cloud Console (*https://console.developers.google.com/*). Create a new project, or select an existing project, in the usual way. In the sidebar navigation, expand Storage, then select Cloud SQL. If this is your first Cloud SQL instance, you see a "Create an instance" button. Click it.

The form for creating a new Cloud SQL instance appears short and simple, asking for an instance ID, region, and tier. Click "Show advanced options…" to see the full list of capabilities. A portion of the full screen is shown in Figure 11-1.

The instance ID is a unique name for the Cloud SQL instance. It always begins with the project ID that "owns" the instance, followed by a colon and the name that you specify.

The region is the major geographical region where the instance lives. When using Cloud SQL with App Engine, this must be set to United States. In the future, when App Engine is available in other regions, the SQL instance and the App Engine app must be hosted in the same region.

The tier is the tier for this instance. The database version selects a version of MySQL to use; version 5.5 is fine. Below that, you can select the billing plan for this instance, either the per use plan or the package plan. Adjusting the tier changes the pricing information displayed in this section.

The "Preferred location" is more specific than the region. For an App Engine app, you want to set this to Follow App Engine App to minimize the latency between the app and the database. Set the App Engine app ID (the project ID) to tell it to follow this app. You can adjust this if you have more than one distinct app using the same database instance, and you want the database to follow a specific app that isn't in this project.

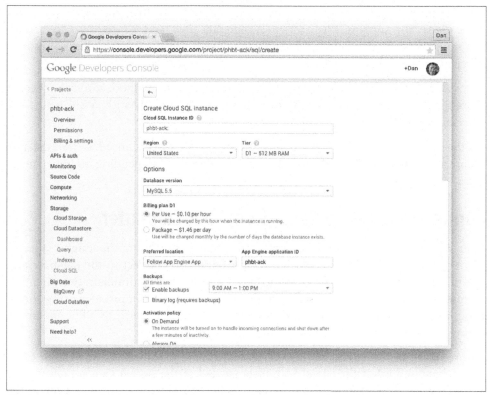

Figure 11-1. The "Create Cloud SQL instance" form with advanced options shown (excerpt)

Cloud SQL can do automatic daily backups of the database. This increases storage costs, but is likely to be less expensive than backing up to an external repository (which consumes outgoing bandwidth). If you want backups, make sure "Enable backups" is checked, and adjust the time range if needed. You can optionally store a MySQL binary log in addition to backups. The binary log contains every change event to the database, which is useful for restoring changes that were made since the last backup.

The "Activation policy" determines how the instance responds to usage. If you set this to On Demand, it will attempt to limit the instance running time by activating the instance for traffic then shutting it down after a few minutes without a connection. You can pair this with a per use billing plan and allow Cloud SQL to activate the instance as needed. The "Always On" option activates the instance as soon as you create it, and leaves it running even when idle. You might as well choose this option if you've selected package billing and expect the database to be used at least once a day. The "Never" option leaves the instance disabled, and only activates it in response to administrative commands.

If you intend to connect to this database with an external client and that client's network does not support IPv6, select "Assign an IPv4 address to my Cloud SQL instance." With an IPv4 address assigned, you are charged a small amount of money every hour the instance is idle.

Advanced options let you adjust the filesystem replication method, authorize specific IP ranges for clients, and set MySQL server flags for the instance. We'll adjust the external authorization settings in the next section.

Set the options as you like them, then click Save. When the instance has been created, it appears with a status of either "Runnable" or "Running," depending on how you set the activation policy.

Connecting to an Instance from Your Computer

Your new instance is ready to accept connections from your App Engine app. In theory, you could use code deployed to App Engine to connect to the database and create tables. More likely, you'll want to do this with an administrative client or another tool running on your local computer. To connect to an instance using something other than App Engine, you must configure the instance to allow incoming connections from a specific IP address or address range.

Before doing anything else, set a root password for the instance. In the Cloud Console, locate and select the Cloud SQL instance. Select the Access Control tab. Under Set Root Password, enter a password, then click Set. You will use this password when connecting with the `root` account.

Next, you need to authorize incoming connections from your computer to the instance. You can configure the instance to accept connections from specific IP addresses or network ranges, using either IPv6 addresses or IPv4 addresses. You can only connect to the instance via its IPv6 address if your network has assigned a public IPv6 address to your computer. If your computer does not have an IPv6 address, you must request an IPv4 address for the instance, then authorize your computer's IPv4 address to connect to it. There is an hourly charge to reserve an IPv4 address, but only if you leave it idle.

The easiest way to determine whether your computer has an IPv6 address is to visit the What's My Web IP website (*http://whatsmywebip.appspot.com*) using your browser. If this displays an IPv6 address, such as `fba2:2c26:f4e4:8000:abcd:1234:b5ef:7051`, then your computer connected to the site with an IPv6 address. You can confirm that this is your address using your computer's Network settings panel, or by running the `ipconfig` command on Windows or the `ifconfig` command on Mac OS X or Linux.

If this displays an IPv4 address, such as 216.123.55.120, then your computer connected to the site with an IPv4 address. Even if your network assigned an IPv6 address to your computer, that address is only used locally and won't be used to make the final connection to the Cloud SQL instance. You must request an IPv4 address for the instance in order to connect to it from your computer's network.

If you need an IPv4 address, click Request an IP Address. An address is assigned to the instance and displayed.

To authorize your network to connect to the instance, click the Add Authorized Network button. Copy and paste your computer's address into the form field, then click Add.

Finally, use the mysql command to connect to the instance. You can find the instance's IPv6 address on the Overview tab, or use the IPv4 address you requested. Specify the address as the --host=… parameter:

```
# Using the IPv6 address of the instance:
mysql --host=2001:4860:4864:1:9e4a:e5a2:abcd:ef01 --user=root --password

# Or with an IPv4 address:
mysql --host=173.194.225.123 --user=root --password
```

When using an IPv6 address, you may get a message such as this:

```
ERROR 2013 (HY000): Lost connection to MySQL server at
'reading initial communication packet', system error: 22
```

If you do, try authorizing a wider portion of your network's address space. For example, if your computer's address is fba2:2c26:f4e4:8000:abcd:1234:b5ef:7051, take the first four groups, then add ::/64, like this: fba2:2c26:f4e4:8000::/64. Authorize that network, then try the mysql command again with the instance's IPv6 address.

A successful connection results in a mysql> prompt. You can enter SQL commands at this prompt. For example, the show databases; command lists the databases currently on the instance. MySQL always starts with several databases it uses for maintenance and configuration:

```
mysql> SHOW DATABASES;
+--------------------+
| Database           |
+--------------------+
| information_schema |
| mysql              |
| performance_schema |
+--------------------+
3 rows in set (0.07 sec)
```

Type quit to terminate the connection and close the client.

If you requested an IPv4 address and do not intend to connect remotely on a regular basis, you can remove the IP address to save on costs. Click Remove next to the IP address in the Access Control tab. Removing the address abandons it, and you may not get the same address the next time you request one.

If your network assigns IP addresses dynamically or you change networks, you may need to authorize a new address the next time you connect.

 Cloud SQL supports secure connections over SSL. You can set up SSL certificates from the "Access Control" tab for the instance. This is only needed if you want external clients to connect with SSL. Traffic between App Engine and Cloud SQL is always secure.

Setting Up a Database

Your Cloud SQL instance begins life with MySQL's initial databases, but no database for your app to use. The next step is to create a database for the app, then create one or more accounts with passwords and appropriate privileges to access the new database.

We'll continue using the mysql command-line client, but you might also use MySQL Workbench or some other tool to create the database and users. Remember that you will need to replicate these steps for your local server as well as the Cloud SQL instance, and possibly create more than one database with the same tables so you can use one for testing and another for the live app. Some web application frameworks have features to automate and replicate databases and tables for this purpose.

Set up a new connection with the mysql command as in the previous section, repeating the network authorization step if necessary. Use the root account and password. At the mysql> prompt, create a new database:

    CREATE DATABASE mmorpg;

(As is traditional with SQL, we will capitalize SQL keywords, but you can type these in lowercase. Names and values are case sensitive. And don't forget the semicolon.)

You must enter another command to tell the MySQL client to use the new database for subsequent commands in this session. For subsequent sessions, you can give the database name as an argument to the mysql command, or just type this as the first SQL command in the session:

    USE mmorpg;

The root account you are currently using has maximum privileges across the Cloud SQL instance, including the powers to create and delete entire databases. It's a good practice to use a separate account with limited privileges when connecting from your app. If a coding error in the app accidentally allows an attacker to run arbitrary SQL commands (a *SQL injection* attack), you can limit the damage to just the privileges granted to the app's account. Most apps need permission to DELETE rows from a table, but few apps need to be able to DROP databases, GRANT privileges to other accounts, or SHUTDOWN the server.

Some web application frameworks automate the management of tables, and need an account with wider privileges to create and delete tables than would normally be used by the app while handling user requests. If your framework allows it, you can create a separate account specifically for these management tools, and use a more limited account within the app itself.

To create a user, enter the CREATE USER command. The following command creates a user named app with the password p4$$w0rd:

```
CREATE USER 'app' IDENTIFIED BY 'p4$$w0rd';
```

You can change the password for this account later (as root) with the SET PASSWORD command:

```
SET PASSWORD FOR 'app' = PASSWORD('new-p4$$w0rd');
```

App Engine does not need a password to connect to a Cloud SQL instance, even when the account has a password set. You only need the password for connecting to the Cloud SQL instance from outside of App Engine. Your app code does need a password when connecting to your local development database if the local account has a password.

A new account starts with no privileges. To grant the app account the ability to SELECT, INSERT, UPDATE, and DELETE rows in all tables in the mmorpg database:

```
GRANT SELECT, INSERT, UPDATE, DELETE ON mmorpg.* TO 'app';
```

For accounts that need to create and drop tables, the CREATE, DROP, and ALTER privileges are also needed. GRANT ALL ON mmorpg.* will give the account complete access to the database. See the documentation on the GRANT statement (*http://dev.mysql.com/doc/refman/5.5/en/grant.html*) for more information about privileges.

We won't go into detail about how to create tables here. For now, here is a simple example of creating a table with a few columns in the mmorpg database:

```
CREATE TABLE guild (id VARCHAR(20) PRIMARY KEY, title VARCHAR(50),
                    created_date DATETIME, min_level INT);
```

You can test the app account by disconnecting (type quit) then reconnecting using the app username and password:

```
mysql --host=... --user=app -p
```

Use the `mmorpg` database, then list the tables:

```
USE mmorpg;
SHOW TABLES;
```

The list of tables includes the `guild` table we created:

```
mysql> show tables;
+------------------+
| Tables_in_mmorpg |
+------------------+
| guild            |
+------------------+
1 row in set (0.07 sec)
```

Still using the app account, try inserting a row:

```
INSERT INTO guild VALUES ('superawesomes', 'The Super Awesomes', NOW(), 7);
```

Select the rows of the table to see the newly added row:

```
SELECT * FROM guild;
```

Setting Up JDBC

App Engine and Cloud SQL support the JDBC API standard for Java database connectivity. You can use this API directly, or you can use any of the database frameworks built on JDBC, even JPA implementations like Hibernate or DataNucleus, with Cloud SQL databases.

Underneath JDBC, your app uses a component called MySQL Connector/J to connect to MySQL instances. The App Engine runtime provides a special version of this component automatically, on request. To enable the connector on App Engine, edit your *appengine-web.xml* file, then add `<use-google-connector-j>` to `<appengine-web-app>`, like so:

```
<appengine-web-app>
  <!-- ... -->
  <use-google-connector-j>true</use-google-connector-j>
</appengine-web-app>
```

When running on your local development server, your app uses MySQL Connector/J to connect to your local database instance. This component is not distributed with the App Engine SDK, so you must download and install it locally. This is only needed when running locally, as the configuration change tells App Engine to provide this to the running app.

Download MySQL Connector/J from the MySQL website:

http://dev.mysql.com/downloads/connector/j/

Expand the archive, then locate the JAR file, named something like *mysql-connector-java-5.1.34-bin.jar*.

This JAR must be added to the class path when running locally. An easy way to do this is to copy this file to your project's *war/WEB-INF/lib/* directory. If you're using Eclipse, you can drag this file directly into this location in the Package Explorer. All JARs in this directory are added to the class path automatically.

Doing it this way also uploads the JAR when you deploy your app. This is harmless, but it wastes space. You can avoid uploading the spurious copy of MySQL Connector/J by adding the JAR to your project's class path when running locally. In Eclipse, edit your run configuration, select the "Classpath" tab, then add the JAR.

Connecting to the Database from App Engine

It's time to try connecting to the database from App Engine code. With JDBC, you use the Cloud SQL instance as you would any other database. The only difference is the initial connection: App Engine provides a named socket based on the name you provided when you created the instance. You use this name as part of the JDBC URL for the connection.

Unlike the App Engine services and Cloud Datastore, the App Engine development server does not attempt to emulate the presence of Cloud SQL on your local computer. You must add code to your app that detects whether it is running in the development server and react accordingly. It's up to you whether you want the development server to connect to your local MySQL database, to a Cloud SQL instance or database reserved for testing, or to the Cloud SQL instance and database used by the live app. It's a good idea to use some kind of test database that is separate from the live database for your regular development, regardless of whether it lives on a separate Cloud SQL instance or your local machine.

What follows is a simple example that reads and displays the guild table, and prompts the user to add a row. We'll use a minimum of features to highlight the JDBC connection code. In a real app, you might use a framework to manage the SQL statements and form handling.

A file named *src/myapp/GuildServlet.java* contains all of the code for connecting to the database, reading and displaying all rows in the table, and inserting a new row based on submitted form data:

```
package myapp;

import java.io.IOException;
import java.sql.DriverManager;
import java.sql.PreparedStatement;
import java.sql.ResultSet;
import java.sql.SQLException;
```

```java
import javax.servlet.RequestDispatcher;
import javax.servlet.ServletException;
import javax.servlet.http.*;

import com.google.appengine.api.utils.SystemProperty;

import java.sql.Connection;
import java.util.ArrayList;
import java.util.Date;
import java.util.List;
import java.util.regex.Pattern;

@SuppressWarnings("serial")
public class GuildServlet extends HttpServlet {
    private static final String INSTANCE_ID = "saucy-boomerang-123:mydb";
    private static final String DATABASE = "mmorpg";
    private static final String DB_USER = "app";
    private static final String DB_PASSWORD = "p4$$w0rd";

    public class Guild {
        public String id;
        public String title;
        public Date createdDate;
        public int minLevel;

        Guild(String id, String title, Date createdDate, int minLevel) {
            this.id = id;
            this.title = title;
            this.createdDate = createdDate;
            this.minLevel = minLevel;
        }

        public String getId() { return id; }
        public String getTitle() { return title; }
        public Date getCreatedDate() { return createdDate; }
        public int getMinLevel() { return minLevel; }
    }

    private static Connection getDb(
            String instanceId, String database,
            String user, String password)
        throws ClassNotFoundException, SQLException {

        Connection conn = null;
        String url = null;

        if (SystemProperty.environment.value() ==
                SystemProperty.Environment.Value.Production) {
            // This is App Engine.
            Class.forName("com.mysql.jdbc.GoogleDriver");
            url = "jdbc:google:mysql://" + instanceId + "/" +
```

```java
            database + "?user=" + user;
        conn = DriverManager.getConnection(url);

    } else {
        // This is a development server.
        Class.forName("com.mysql.jdbc.Driver");
        url = "jdbc:mysql://127.0.0.1:3306/" + database;
        conn = DriverManager.getConnection(url, user, password);
    }

    return conn;
}

public void doGet(HttpServletRequest req, HttpServletResponse resp)
    throws IOException, ServletException {

    List<Guild> guilds = new ArrayList<Guild>();

    Connection conn = null;
    try {
        conn = getDb(INSTANCE_ID, DATABASE, DB_USER, DB_PASSWORD);
        try {
            PreparedStatement stmt = conn.prepareStatement(
                    "SELECT id, title, created_date, " +
                    "min_level FROM guild;");
            ResultSet result = stmt.executeQuery();
            while (result.next()) {
                guilds.add(new Guild(
                        result.getString("id"),
                        result.getString("title"),
                        result.getDate("created_date"),
                        result.getInt("min_level")));
            }

        } finally {
            if (conn != null) {
                conn.close();
            }
        }
    } catch (SQLException e) {
        e.printStackTrace();
    } catch (ClassNotFoundException e) {
        e.printStackTrace();
    }

    req.setAttribute("guilds", guilds);

    resp.setContentType("text/html");
    RequestDispatcher jsp =
        req.getRequestDispatcher("/WEB-INF/guilds.jsp");
    jsp.forward(req, resp);
}
```

```
    public void doPost(HttpServletRequest req, HttpServletResponse resp)
        throws IOException {

        String title = req.getParameter("title");
        String id =
            Pattern.compile("\\W").matcher(title).replaceAll("_");
        String minLevelStr = req.getParameter("min_level");
        int minLevel = new Integer(minLevelStr).intValue();

        Connection conn = null;
        try {
            conn = getDb(INSTANCE_ID, DATABASE, DB_USER, DB_PASSWORD);
            try {
                PreparedStatement stmt = conn.prepareStatement(
                        "INSERT INTO guild VALUES (?, ?, NOW(), ?);");
                stmt.setString(1, id);
                stmt.setString(2, title);
                stmt.setInt(3, minLevel);
                stmt.executeUpdate();

            } finally {
                if (conn != null) {
                    conn.close();
                }
            }
        } catch (SQLException e) {
            e.printStackTrace();
        } catch (ClassNotFoundException e) {
            e.printStackTrace();
        }

        resp.sendRedirect("/");
    }
}
```

The file *war/WEB-INF/guilds.jsp* contains the JSP template for the list and form:

```
<%@ taglib uri="http://java.sun.com/jsp/jstl/core" prefix="c" %>
<!doctype html>
<html>
  <head>
    <title>Guild List</title>
  </head>
  <body>
    <c:choose>
    <c:when test="${not empty guilds}">
    <p>Guilds:</p>
    <ul>
      <c:forEach var="guild" items="${guilds}">
      <li>
        ${guild.title},
        minimum level: ${guild.minLevel},
```

```
    created ${guild.createdDate}
      </li>
      </c:forEach>
    </ul>
    </c:when>
    <c:otherwise>
    <p>There are no guilds.</p>
    </c:otherwise>
    </c:choose>

    <p>Create a guild:</p>
    <form action="/" method="post">
      <label for="title">Title:</label>
      <input type="text" id="title" name="title" /><br />
      <label for="min_level">Minimum level:</label>
      <input type="text" id="min_level" name="min_level" /><br />
      <input type="submit" name="Create Guild" />
    </form>
  </body>
</html>
```

The *war/WEB-INF/web.xml* for the app routes all requests to the app:

```
<?xml version="1.0" encoding="utf-8"?>
<web-app xmlns:xsi="http://www.w3.org/2001/XMLSchema-instance"
  xmlns="http://java.sun.com/xml/ns/javaee"
  xmlns:web="http://java.sun.com/xml/ns/javaee/web-app_2_5.xsd"
  xsi:schemaLocation="http://java.sun.com/xml/ns/javaee
  http://java.sun.com/xml/ns/javaee/web-app_2_5.xsd" version="2.5">
  <servlet>
    <servlet-name>Guild</servlet-name>
    <servlet-class>myapp.GuildServlet</servlet-class>
  </servlet>
  <servlet-mapping>
    <servlet-name>Guild</servlet-name>
    <url-pattern>/</url-pattern>
  </servlet-mapping>
</web-app>
```

The *war/WEB-INF/appengine-web.xml* requests the MySQL Connector/J component:

```
<?xml version="1.0" encoding="utf-8"?>
<appengine-web-app xmlns="http://appengine.google.com/ns/1.0">
  <application>saucy-boomerang</application>
  <version>1</version>
  <threadsafe>true</threadsafe>

  <use-google-connector-j>true</use-google-connector-j>
</appengine-web-app>
```

In this example, we define the static method `getDb()` to prepare the database connection based on whether the app is running in a development server or on App Engine.

We test for this using `SystemProperty.environment.value()`, whose value says which environment we're in:

```
if (SystemProperty.environment.value() ==
        SystemProperty.Environment.Value.Production) {
    // This is App Engine.
    Class.forName("com.mysql.jdbc.GoogleDriver");
    url = "jdbc:google:mysql://" + instanceId + "/" + database +
        "?user=" + user;
    conn = DriverManager.getConnection(url);

} else {
    // This is a development server.
    Class.forName("com.mysql.jdbc.Driver");
    url = "jdbc:mysql://127.0.0.1:3306/" + database;
    conn = DriverManager.getConnection(url, user, password);
}
```

We use a `Class.forName()` call to load the class that will be invoked by the JDBC URL. For App Engine's MySQL Connector/J, this is `com.mysql.jdbc.GoogleDriver`. On the development server, this is simply `com.mysql.jdbc.Driver`.

The JDBC URL tells the connector the location and parameters for connecting to the database. From App Engine to Cloud SQL, this uses a `jdbc:google:mysql://` prefix, followed by the instance ID (including the project ID), a slash, and the name of the database. We also include the database username, forming a complete URL like this:

```
jdbc:google:mysql://project-id:instance-name/database?user=username
```

The `DriverManager.getConnection()` call makes the connection. On App Engine, this only needs the URL, which includes the database username. App Engine does not need a password when connecting to the instance, as it is specially authorized to do so. You still need to provide a username, which determines the database privileges for the app.

Locally, and for regular MySQL connections in general, the `jdbc:mysql://` URL includes the host name or IP address, the port (3306 is the default port for MySQL), a slash, and the database name. This connection does require a password, so we provide the username and password as arguments to `DriverManager.getConnection()` instead of on the URL. The local URL looks like this:

```
jdbc:mysql://127.0.0.1:3306/database
```

The `doGet()` and `doPost()` handlers for the servlet call `getDb()` to make the connection. Once the connection is made, subsequent statements are executed in a `try { ... } finally { ... }` block, so regardless of what happens, the servlet closes the connection. It is important to close connections because each app instance has a limited number of connections it can keep open at a time:

```
Connection conn = null;
try {
    conn = getDb(INSTANCE_ID, DATABASE, DB_USER, DB_PASSWORD);
    try {
        // ...

    } finally {
        if (conn != null) {
            conn.close();
        }
    }
} catch (SQLException e) {
    e.printStackTrace();
} catch (ClassNotFoundException e) {
    e.printStackTrace();
}
```

One way to perform a query in JDBC is to call the `Connection`'s `prepareStatement()` method with the SQL statement as a string. For query statements (SELECT), we can call the `PreparedStatement`'s `executeQuery()` method, and get back a streaming `ResultSet`. In this example, we loop over the result set, and use the typed field accessors (`getString(…)`) to process each row into a data structure that we can pass to the JSP. (If this is really all we want to do, we could just make the query and iterate over the result set directly from the JSP.)

```
PreparedStatement stmt = conn.prepareStatement(
        "SELECT id, title, created_date, " +
        "min_level FROM guild;");
ResultSet result = stmt.executeQuery();
while (result.next()) {
    guilds.add(new Guild(
            result.getString("id"),
            result.getString("title"),
            result.getDate("created_date"),
            result.getInt("min_level")));
}
```

When using values derived from an external source, such as data submitted by the user via a form, use parameter substitution: use a ? character in the SQL string for each value, then set the values using typed setters on the `PreparedStatement`:

```
PreparedStatement stmt = conn.prepareStatement(
        "INSERT INTO guild VALUES (?, ?, NOW(), ?);");
stmt.setString(1, id);
stmt.setString(2, title);
stmt.setInt(3, minLevel);
stmt.executeUpdate();
```

Parameter substitution prevents the data from being misconstrued as SQL statement syntax. This is especially important because it prevents *SQL injection attacks* from malicious users. (See "xkcd: Exploits of a Mom," by Randall Munroe (*http://xkcd.com/327/*).)

Instead of `executeQuery()`, we call `executeUpdate()`, which is more appropriate for statements that change the database. We're ignoring the return value, which is the number of entities updated. This connection is in auto-commit mode by default, so we do not need an explicit call to the `Connection`'s `commit()` method.

For more information about JDBC, see Oracle's JDBC Basics tutorial (*http://docs.oracle.com/javase/tutorial/jdbc/basics/*).

Backup and Restore

If you opted for backups when you created the instance, Cloud SQL performs regular backups of your database automatically. You can enable and disable backups at a later time from the Cloud Console by editing the instance configuration. You can also adjust the time of day during which backups occur.

To restore from a recent backup via the Cloud Console, select your Cloud SQL instance, then scroll down to Backups. Recent backups are listed by timestamp. Find the backup you want to restore, then click Restore.

Backups are intended for convenient and automatic recovery of the Cloud SQL instance. If you want to copy data out of Cloud Platform for archival storage or off-line processing, you must export the data. (We'll cover this in the next section.)

Exporting and Importing Data

The Cloud Console provides a convenient way to import and export data from your database. The format for this data is a text file containing SQL statements, equivalent to using the `mysqldump` command.

Exports and imports use Google Cloud Storage for the data file. This can save you the cost of external bandwidth if you intend to manipulate the data file further using Google Cloud Platform, such as with a batch job running on App Engine or Compute Engine.

Each Cloud Storage object has a name (like a filename) and belongs to a *bucket* (like a directory). The path to a Cloud Storage object consists of `gs://`, the bucket name, a slash, and the object name:

```
gs://bucket-name/object-name
```

Bucket names must be unique across all of Cloud Storage, much like usernames. Cloud Storage reserves bucket names that look like domain names (containing dots) for the owners of the domains, so if you have verified ownership of your domain using Google Webmaster Tools (*https://www.google.com/webmasters/tools*), you can use your domain name as your bucket name. Otherwise, you can register any bucket name that hasn't already been registered by someone else.

You must create a Cloud Storage bucket before you can export Cloud SQL data. To create the bucket, go to the Cloud Console, then navigate to Storage, Cloud Storage, "Storage browser." Click "Create bucket" (or "Add bucket"), then enter a name for the bucket and click the Create button.

To export one or more databases from the Cloud Console, navigate to the Cloud SQL instance, then click the Export… button. In the dialog, enter a Cloud Storage path using the bucket you just created, followed by a filename. A file of that name must not already exist in the bucket. Optionally, click "Show advanced options…" then enter the names of the databases to export. By default, all databases are exported. Click OK. The export takes a few moments to complete.

To access the exported data, return to the Storage browser, then select the bucket. The bucket contains the exported file you requested, as well as a log file. You can select these files in the Cloud Console to download them via your browser.

Importing data via the Cloud Console is similar. Go to the Storage browser, select the bucket, then click the "Upload files" button. Follow the prompts to select the data file on your local computer and upload it to the bucket. Next, navigate to the Cloud SQL instance, then click Import…. Enter the Cloud Storage path to the file you uploaded, then click OK. The import process reads the data file and executes the SQL statements inside it.

The file generated by an export includes SQL statements to drop tables before re-creating them. Importing such a file effectively resets the tables to the state they were in at the time of export. It does not merge old data with new, nor does it result in duplicate rows.

Because exported data is a file of SQL statements, you can save space and bandwidth by compressing the file. To export data compressed using the gzip file format, specify a file path that ends in .gz. To import a gzip-compressed file, make sure the path ends in .gz.

The gcloud sql Commands

All of the administrative features for Cloud SQL instances that you see in the Cloud Console are also available from the command line. The gcloud sql family of commands can create, delete, restart, and clone instances, as well as import and export data. These commands are an alternative to the Cloud Console for some interactive actions, and can also be used in scripts for automation.

Make sure `gcloud` is configured to use your project, you are signed in, and you have the `sql` component installed:

```
gcloud config set project project-id
gcloud auth login
gcloud components update sql
```

To list the current Cloud SQL instances for the project:

```
gcloud sql instances list
```

To get detailed information about the instance in YAML format:

```
gcloud sql instances describe instance-name
```

To get a list of automatic backups for the instance, each identified by a timestamp:

```
gcloud sql backups list --instance instance-name
```

To restore a backup from this list:

```
gcloud sql instances restore-backup --instance instance-name --due-time timestamp
```

You can initiate exports and imports from the command line as well. As with doing this from the Cloud Console, exports and imports use Cloud Storage for storing or reading data. To initiate an export of all databases on the instance to a given Cloud Storage path:

```
gcloud sql instances export instance-name gs://bucket-name/object-name
```

You can narrow the export to specific databases or tables using the `--database` and `--table` flags.

The command to import a file from Cloud Storage is similar:

```
gcloud sql instances import instance-name gs://bucket-name/object-name
```

Naturally, you can upload and download files to and from Cloud Storage from the command line as well. For this, you use the `gsutil` command. Make sure you have this command installed:

```
gcloud components update gsutil
```

To download a file from Cloud Storage:

```
gsutil cp gs://bucket-name/object-name .
```

Just like the `cp` command, `gsutil cp` takes a path to the file to copy, and a destination path. If the destination path is a directory path (like . for the current directory), the file is copied using its original filename.

To upload a file to Cloud Storage, use the `gsutil cp` command with a `gs://` path as the second argument:

```
gsutil cp filename.gz gs://bucket-name/object-name
```

The Cloud SDK command-line interface has many features for fetching SQL status and configuration as structured data, as well as for waiting for initiating operations asynchronously and waiting for operations to complete. You can use the `gcloud help` command to browse information on these features. For example, to learn about creating Cloud SQL instances from the command line:

```
gcloud help sql instances create
```

CHAPTER 12

The Memory Cache

Durable data storage requires a storage medium that retains data through power loss and system restarts. Today's medium of choice is the hard drive, a storage device composed of circular platters coated with magnetic material on which data is encoded. The platters spin at a constant rate while a sensor moves along the radius, reading and writing bits on the platters as they travel past. Reading or writing a specific piece of data requires a *disk seek* to position the sensor at the proper radius and wait for the platter to rotate until the desired data is underneath. All things considered, hard drives are astonishingly fast, but for web applications, disk seeks can be costly. Fetching an entity from the datastore by key can take time on the order of tens of milliseconds.

Most high-performance web applications mitigate this cost with a *memory cache*. A memory cache uses a volatile storage medium, usually the RAM of the cache machines, for very fast read and write access to values. A *distributed memory cache* provides scalable, consistent temporary storage for distributed systems, so many processes on many machines can access the same data. Because memory is volatile—it gets erased during an outage—the cache is not useful for long-term storage, or even short-term primary storage for important data. But it's excellent as a secondary system for fast access to data also kept elsewhere, such as the datastore. It's also sufficient as global high-speed memory for some uses.

The App Engine distributed memory cache service, known as *memcache* in honor of the original memcached system that it resembles, stores key-value pairs. You can set a value with a key, and get the value given the key. A value can be up to a megabyte in size. A key is up to 250 bytes, and the API accepts larger keys and uses a hash algorithm to convert them to 250 bytes.

The memcache does not support transactions like the datastore does, but it does provide several atomic operations. Setting a single value in the cache is atomic: the key either gets the new value or retains the old one (or remains unset). You can tell memcache to set a value only if it hasn't changed since it was last fetched, a technique known as "compare and set" in the API. The App Engine memcache also includes the ability to increment and decrement numeric values as an atomic operation.

A common way to use the memcache with the datastore is to cache datastore entities by their keys. When you want to fetch an entity by key, you first check the memcache for a value with that key, and use it if found (known as a *cache hit*). If it's not in the memcache (a *cache miss*), you fetch it from the datastore, then put it in the memcache so future attempts to access it will find it there. At the expense of a small amount of overhead during the first fetch, subsequent fetches become much faster.

If the entity changes in the datastore, you can attempt to update the memcache when the entity is updated in the datastore, so subsequent requests can continue to go to the cache but see fresh data. This mostly works, but it has two minor problems. For one, it is possible that the memcache update will fail even if the datastore update succeeds, leaving old data in the cache. Also, if two processes update the same datastore entity, then update the memcache, the datastore will have correct data (thanks to datastore transactions), but the memcache update will have the value of whichever update occurs last. Because of this possibility, it's somewhat better to just delete the memcache key when the datastore changes, and let the next read attempt to populate the cache with a current value. Naturally, the delete could also fail.

Because there is no way to update both the datastore and the memcache in a single transaction, there is no way to avoid the possibility that the cache may contain old data. To minimize the duration that the memcache will have a stale value, you can give the value an expiration time when you set it. When the expiration time elapses, the cache unsets the key, and a subsequent read results in a cache miss and triggers a fresh fetch from the datastore.

Of course, this caching pattern works for more than just datastore entities. You can use it for datastore queries, web service calls made with URL Fetch, expensive calculations, or any other data that can be replaced with a slow operation, where the benefits of fast access outweigh the possibility of staleness.

This is so often the case with web applications that a best practice is to cache aggressively. Look through your application for opportunities to make this trade-off, and implement caching whenever the same value is needed an arbitrary number of times, especially if that number increases with traffic. Site content such as an article on a news website often falls into this category. Caching speeds up requests and saves CPU time.

The APIs for the memcache service are straightforward. Let's look at each of the memcache features.

Calling Memcache from Java

App Engine supports two Java APIs to memcache. The first is a proprietary interface, which will be the subject of the Java portions of this chapter. App Engine also includes an implementation of JSR 107, known as JCache, an interface standard for memcache services. You can find the JCache interface in the package `net.sf.jsr107cache`.

The Java API to the memcache service is in the `com.google.appengine.api.memc` `ache` package. As with the other service APIs, you get a service implementation by calling a static method on the `MemcacheServiceFactory` class, then interact with the service by calling methods on this instance.

To make synchronous calls to the memcache service, you use an implementation of the `MemcacheService` interface, which you get by calling the `getMemcacheService()` method of the factory:

```
import com.google.appengine.api.memcache.MemcacheService;
import com.google.appengine.api.memcache.MemcacheServiceFactory;

// ...
        MemcacheService memcache = MemcacheServiceFactory.getMemcacheService();
```

To make asynchronous calls, you need to use an implementation of the `AsyncMemcacheService` interface, obtained by calling the `getAsyncMemcache.Service()` method. For more information about asynchronous service calls, see "Calling Services Asynchronously" on page 362.

Memcache values can be partitioned into namespaces. To use a namespace, provide the namespace as a `String` argument to the factory method. All calls to the resulting service implementation will use the namespace.

Here's a simple example that fetches a web feed by using the URL Fetch service, stores it in the memcache, and uses the cached value until it expires five minutes (300 seconds) later. The key is the feed URL, and the value is the raw data returned by URL Fetch:

```
import java.net.URL;

import com.google.appengine.api.memcache.Expiration;
import com.google.appengine.api.memcache.MemcacheService;
import com.google.appengine.api.memcache.MemcacheServiceFactory;
import com.google.appengine.api.urlfetch.URLFetchService;
import com.google.appengine.api.urlfetch.URLFetchServiceFactory;

// ...
    public byte[] getFeed(URL feedUrl) {
        MemcacheService memcache = MemcacheServiceFactory.getMemcacheService();
        byte[] feedData = (byte[]) memcache.get(feedUrl);
```

```
    if (feedData == null) {
        URLFetchService urlFetch =
            URLFetchServiceFactory.getURLFetchService();
        try {
            feedData = urlFetch.fetch(feedUrl).getContent();
            memcache.put(feedUrl, feedData,
                        Expiration.byDeltaSeconds(300));
        } catch (Exception e) {
            return null;
        }
    }
    return feedData;
}
```

Keys and Values

The memcache service stores key-value pairs. To store a value, you provide both a key and a value. To get a value, you provide its key, and memcache returns the value.

Both the key and the value can be data of any type that can be serialized. The key and value can be of any class that implements the `java.io.Serializable` interface, which includes the (auto-boxed) primitive types.

The key can be of any size. App Engine converts the key data to 250 bytes by using a hash algorithm, which makes for a number of possible unique keys larger than a 1 followed by 600 zeroes. You generally don't have to think about the size of the key.

The value can be up to 1 megabyte in its serialized form. In practice, this means that pretty much anything that can fit in a datastore entity can also be a memcache value.

Setting Values

The simplest way to store a value in memcache is to set it. If no value exists for the given key, setting the value will create a new value in memcache for the key. If there is already a value for the key, it will be replaced with the new value.

In Java, you call the `put()` method of the service implementation. When called with just the key and value, this method sets the key-value pair, and the method has no return value:

```
memcache.put(key, value)
```

Setting Values That Expire

By default, a memcache value stays in the memcache until it is deleted by the app with a service call, or until it is evicted by the memcache service. The memcache service will evict a value if it runs out of space, or if a machine holding a value goes down or is turned down for maintenance.

When you set a value, you can specify an optional expiration time. If provided, the memcache service will make an effort to evict the value when the expiration time is reached. The timing may not be exact, but it'll be close. Setting an expiration time encourages a cache-backed process to refresh its data periodically, without the app having to track the age of a cached value and forcibly delete it.

You set the expiration as an optional third argument to the put() method. This value is an instance of the Expiration class, which you construct by calling a static class method. In order to set an expiration time in the future relative to the current time, you call Expiration.byDeltaSeconds(int). You can also specify this time in milliseconds using Expiration.byDeltaMillis(int); this value will be rounded down to the nearest second. To set an expiration time as an absolute date and time, you call Expiration.onDate(java.util.Date):

```
memcache.put(key, value, Expiration.byDeltaSeconds(300));
```

A value's expiration date is updated every time the value is updated. If you replace a value with an expiration date, the new value does not inherit the old date. There is no way to query a key for "time until expiration."

Adding and Replacing Values

There are two subtle variations on setting a value: adding and replacing.

When you add a value with a given key, the value is created in memcache only if the key is not already set. If the key is set, adding the value will do nothing. This operation is atomic, so you can use the add operation to avoid a race condition between two request handlers doing related work.

Similarly, when you replace a value with a given key, the value is updated in memcache only if the key is set. If the key is not set, the replace operation does nothing, and the key remains unset. Replacing a value is useful if the absence of the value is meaningful to another process, such as to inspire a refresh after an expiration date. Note that, as with replacing values with set, the replaced value will need its own expiration date if the previous value had one, and there is no way to preserve the previous expiration after a replacement.

In Java, the distinction between set, add, and replace is made using a fourth argument to put(). This argument is from the enum MemcacheService.SetPolicy, and is either SET_ALWAYS (set, the default), ADD_ONLY_IF_NOT_PRESENT (add), or REPLACE_ONLY_IF_PRESENT (replace). If you want to add or replace but do not want to set an expiration, you can set the third argument to null. The four-argument form of put() returns `true` on success, so you can test whether the add or replace failed, possibly due to the existence or absence of the key:

```
boolean success = memcache.put(key, value, null,
    MemcacheService.SetPolicy.ADD_ONLY_IF_NOT_PRESENT);
```

Getting Values

You can get a value out of the memcache by using its key. To do so, call the `get()` method of the service implementation. Its return value is of type `Object`, so you'll need to cast it back to its original type. If the key is not set, the method returns `null`:

```
String value = (String) memcache.get(key);
if (value == null) {
    // The key was not set...
}
```

Deleting Values

An app can force an eviction of a value by deleting its key. The deletion is immediate, and atomic. To delete a value, call the `delete()` method with the key to delete. This method returns `true` if the key was deleted successfully or if it was already unset, or `false` if the service could not be reached:

```
boolean success = memcache.delete(key);
```

Locking a Deleted Key

When you delete a value, you can tell memcache to lock the key for a period of time. During this time, attempts to add the key will fail as if the key is set, while attempts to get the value will return nothing. This is sometimes useful to give mechanisms that rely on an add-only policy some breathing room, so an immediate reading of the key doesn't cause confusion.

Only the add operation is affected by a delete lock. The set operation will always succeed, and will cancel the delete lock. The replace operation will fail during the lock period as long as the key is not set; it otherwise ignores the lock.

To lock the key when deleting in Java, pass a second argument to `delete()`. Its value, a `long`, is a number of milliseconds in the future. (You can't set an absolute date and time for a delete lock in Java.)

```
boolean success = memcache.delete(key, 20000);
```

Atomic Increment and Decrement

Memcache includes special support for incrementing and decrementing numeric values as atomic operations. This allows for multiple processes to contribute to a shared value in the cache without interfering with each other. With just the get and set operations we've seen so far, this would be difficult: incrementing a value would involve reading then setting the value with separate operations, and two concurrent processes might interleave these operations and produce an incorrect result. The atomic increment operation does not have this problem.

When considering using memcache for counting, remember that memcache is nondurable storage. Your process must be resilient to the counter value being evicted at any time. But there are many forms this resilience can take. For instance, the app can periodically save the counter value to the datastore, and detect and recover if the increment fails due to the key being unset. In other cases, the counter may be helpful but not strictly necessary, and the work can proceed without it. In practice, unexpected cache evictions are rare, but it's best to code defensively.

You can use the increment and decrement operations on any unsigned integer value. Memcache integers are 64 bits in size. Incrementing beyond the maximum 64-bit integer causes the value to wrap around to the minimum signed 64-bit integer value (negative 2 to the 63rd power), and decrementing has the same behavior in reverse. If the value being incremented is not an integer, nothing changes.

When you call the increment operation, you can specify an optional initial value. Normally, the increment does nothing if the key is not set. If you specify an initial value and the key being incremented is not set, the key is set to the initial value, and the initial value is returned as the result of the operation.

The Java API uses one method for both increment and decrement, called simply `increment()`. It takes as arguments the key and the amount of change, which can be negative. An optional third argument specifies an initial value, which sets the value if the key is unset. The method returns a `java.lang.Long` equal to the new value, or `null` if the increment does not occur:

```
// Increment by 1, if key is set. v = v + 1
Long result = memcache.increment(key, 1L);
if (result == null) {
    // The key is not set, or another error occurred...
}

// Increment by 9, or initialize to 0 if not set.
result = memcache.increment(key, 9L, 0L);

// Decrement by 3, if key is set. v = v + (-3)
result = memcache.increment(key, -3L);
```

Compare and Set

While memcache does not support general-purpose transactions across multiple values, it does have a feature that provides a modest amount of transactionality for single values. The "compare and set" primitive operation sets a value if and only if it has not been updated since the last time the caller read the value. If the value was updated by another process, the caller's update does not occur, and the operation reports this condition. The caller can retry its calculation for another chance at a consistent update.

This is a simpler version of the optimistic concurrency control we saw with datastore transactions, with some important differences. "Compare and set" can only operate on one memcache value at a time. Because the value is retained in fast nondurable storage, there is no replication delay. Read and write operations occur simply in the order they arrive at the service.

The API for this feature consists of two methods: a different get operation that returns both the value and a unique identifier (the compare-and-set ID, or CAS ID) for the value that is meaningful to the memcache, and the compare-and-set operation that sends the previous CAS ID with the updated value. The CAS ID for a key in memcache changes whenever the key is updated, even if it is updated to the same value as it had before the update. The memcache service uses the provided CAS ID to decide whether the compare-and-set operation should succeed.

To get a CAS ID, call the `getIdentifiable()` method. The method accepts a key, and returns the value and its CAS ID wrapped in an instance of the `MemcacheService.IdentifiableValue` class. You can access the value with its `getValue()` method. To perform a compare-and-set update, you call the `putIfUntouched()` method with the key, the original `MemcacheService.IdentifiableValue` instance, the new value, and an optional `Expiration` value. This method returns `true` on success:

```
MemcacheService.IdentifiableValue idValue;
int retries = 3;

// Attempt to append a string to a memcache value.
while (retries-- > 0) {
    idValue = memcache.getIdentifiable(key);
    String value = "";
    if (idValue != null) {
        value = (String) idValue.getValue();
    }
    value += "MORE DATA!\n";
    if (memcache.putIfUntouched(key, idValue, value)) {
        break;
    }
}
```

Batching Calls to Memcache

The memcache service includes batching versions of its API methods, so you can combine operations in a single remote procedure call. As with the datastore's batch API, this can save time in cases where the app needs to perform the same operation on multiple independent values. And as with the datastore, batching is not transactional: some operations may succeed while others fail. The total size of the batch call parameters can be up to 32 megabytes, as can the total size of the return values.

The `<T> putAll()` method takes a `java.util.Map` of keys and values, where `T` is the key type. As with `put()`, other forms of this method accept optional `Expiration` and `SetPolicy` values. The three-argument form of this method returns a `java.util.Set<T>` containing all the keys set by the call. The returned set may omit a provided key if the policy disallows setting keys that already exist. (Without both an `Expiration` and the `SetPolicy` arguments, the method's return type is `void`.) Here's a simple example using the default options:

```java
import java.util.HashMap;
import java.util.Map;

// ...
        Map<String, String> valueMap = new HashMap<String, String>();
        memcache.putAll(valueMap);
```

The `getAll()` method takes a `java.util.Collection<T>` of keys, and returns a `Map<T, Object>` of keys and values that are set. If a provided key is not set, then it is omitted from the result `Map`:

```java
        Map<String, Object> values = memcache.getAll(keys);
```

The `incrementAll()` method takes a `java.util.Collection<T>` of keys and an amount to change each value (a positive or negative `long`). Another form of the method takes an initial value as a third argument, which is used for all keys. The method returns a `Map<T, Long>` containing keys and updated values for all keys set or incremented successfully:

```java
        Map<String, Long> newValues = memcache.incrementAll(keys, 1L);

        newValues = memcache.incrementAll(keys, 10L, 0L);
```

To get multiple values that can be used with "compare and set" in a batch, you call the `getIdentifiables()` method (with the plural s at the end of the method name). It takes a `Collection` of keys and returns a `Map` of keys to `MemcacheService.IdentifiableValue` instances:

```java
        Map<String, MemcacheService.IdentifiableValue> values;
        values = memcache.getIdentifiables(keys);
```

```
// Get a value for key k from the result map.
String v = (String) (values.get(k).getValue());
```

The `putIfUntouched()` method has a batch calling form for performing a "compare and set" with multiple values. It takes a `Map` of keys to instances of the wrapper class `MemcacheService.CasValues`, each of which holds the original `MemcacheService.IdentifiableValue`, the new value, and an optional `Expiration`. You can also provide an optional `Expiration` to `putIfUntouched()`, which applies to all values in the batch. The return value is the `Set` of keys that was stored successfully:

```
MemcacheService.IdentifiableValue oldIdentValue1;
// ...

Map<String, MemcacheService.CasValues> updateMap =
    new HashMap<String, MemcacheService.CasValues>();
updateMap.put(key1,
            new MemcacheService.CasValues(oldIdentValue1,
                                          newValue1));
// ...

Set<String> successKeys = memcache.putIfUntouched(updateMap);
```

Memcache and the Datastore

The most common use of the memcache on App Engine is as a fast access layer in front of the datastore. We've discussed the general pattern several times already: when the app needs to fetch an entity by key, it checks the cache first, and if it's not there, it fetches from the datastore and puts it in the cache for later. This exchanges potential update latency (cached data may be old) for access speed. The memcache is well suited for this purpose: it can use datastore entity keys as keys, and serialized datastore entity structures as values.

In Java, caching a datastore entity is a simple matter of making sure your entity class is `Serializable`. The `Entity` class of the low-level datastore API is already `Serializable`, as are all property value types. If you're using JPA, you can usually just declare that your model class `implements Serializable`. The resulting memcache value contains the data in the properties of your entity, or the fields of your model class:

```
// String userId = ...;

DatastoreService datastore =
    DatastoreServiceFactory.getDatastoreService();
MemcacheService memcache =
    MemcacheServiceFactory.getMemcacheService();

Key userPrefsKey = KeyFactory.createKey("UserPrefs", userId);
Entity userPrefs = (Entity) memcache.get(userPrefsKey);
```

```
if (userPrefs == null) {
    try {
        userPrefs = datastore.get(userPrefsKey);
        memcache.put(userPrefsKey, userPrefs);
    } catch (EntityNotFoundException e) {
        // not in the datastore either, leave null
    }
}
```

Handling Memcache Errors

By default, if the memcache service is unavailable or there is an error accessing the service, the memcache API behaves as if keys do not exist. Attempts to set, add, or replace values report failure as if the put failed due to the set policy. Attempts to get values will behave as cache misses.

In the Java API, you can change this behavior by installing an alternative error handler. The `setErrorHandler()` method of `MemcacheService` takes an object that implements the `ConsistentErrorHandler` interface. Two such implementations are provided: `ConsistentLogAndContinueErrorHandler` and `StrictErrorHandler`. The default is `ConsistentLogAndContinueErrorHandler` with its log level set to `FINE` (the "debug" level in the Cloud Console). `StrictErrorHandler` throws `MemcacheServiceException` for all transient service errors:

```
import com.google.appengine.api.memcache.StrictErrorHandler;

// ...
        memcache.setErrorHandler(new StrictErrorHandler());
```

Error handlers can have custom responses for invalid values and service errors. Other kinds of exceptions thrown by the API behave as usual.

Memcache Administration

With the memcache service playing such an important role in the health and well-being of your application, it's important to understand how your app is using it under real-world conditions. App Engine provides a Memcache Viewer in the Cloud Console (Compute, App Engine, Memcache), which shows you up-to-date statistics about your app's memcache data, and lets you query values by key. You can also delete the entire contents of the cache from this panel, a drastic but sometimes necessary act.

The viewer displays the number of hits (successful attempts to get a value), the number of misses (attempts to get a value using a key that was unset), and the ratio of these numbers. The raw numbers are roughly over the lifetime of the app, but it's the ratio that's the more useful number: the higher the hit ratio, the more time is being saved by using a cached value instead of performing a slower query or calculation.

Also shown is the total number of items and the total size of all items. These numbers mostly serve as vague insight into the overall content of the cache. They don't apply to any fixed limits or billable quotas, and there's no need to worry if these numbers are large. Understanding the average item size might be useful if you're troubleshooting why small items used less frequently than very large items are getting evicted.

A particularly interesting statistic is the "oldest item age." This is a bit of a misnomer: it's actually the amount of time since the last access of the least recently accessed item, not the full age of that item. Under moderate load, this value approximates the amount of time a value can go without being accessed before it is evicted from the cache to make room for hotter items. You can think of it as a lower bound on the usefulness of the cache. Note that more popular cache items live longer than less popular ones, so this age refers to the least popular item in the cache.

You can use the Memcache Viewer to query, create, and modify a value in the memcache, if you have the key. The API lets you use any serializable data type for keys, and the Viewer can't support all possible types, so this feature is only good for some key types. String keys are supported, as well as several Java primitive types, such an integers. Similarly, updating values from the Viewer is limited to several data types, including bytestrings, Unicode text strings, Booleans, and integers.

Lastly, the Memcache Viewer has a big scary button to flush the cache, evicting (deleting) all of its values. Hopefully you've engineered your app to not depend on a value being available in the cache, and clicking this button would only inconvenience the app while it reloads values from primary storage or other computation. But for an app of significant size under moderate traffic with a heavy reliance on the cache, flushing the cache can be disruptive. You may need this button to clear out data inconsistencies caused by a bug after deploying a fix (for example), but you may want to schedule the flush during a period of low traffic.

Cache Statistics

The memcache statistics shown in the Cloud Console are also available to your app through a simple API.

You fetch memcache statistics with the `getStatistics()` service method. This returns an instance of the `Stats` class, a read-only object with getters for each of the statistics:

```
MemcacheService memcache =
    MemcacheServiceFactory.getMemcacheService();

long totalCacheSize =
    memcache.getStatistics().getTotalItemBytes();
```

Available statistics include the following:

`getHitCount()`
> The number of cache hits counted

`getMissCount()`
> The number of cache misses counted

`getItemCount()`
> The number of items currently in the cache

`getTotalItemBytes()`
> The total size of items currently in the cache

`getBytesReturnsForHits()`
> The total number of bytes returned in response to cache hits, including keys and values

`getMaxTimeWithoutAccess()`
> The amount of time since the last access of the least recently accessed item in the cache, in milliseconds

Flushing the Memcache

You can delete every item in the memcache for your app, using a single API call. Just like the button in the Cloud Console, this action is all or nothing: there is no way to flush a subset of keys, beyond deleting known keys individually or in a batch call.

If your app makes heavy use of memcache to front-load datastore entities, keep in mind that flushing the cache may cause a spike in datastore traffic and slower request handlers as your app reloads the cache.

To flush the cache, you call the `clearAll()` service method. This method has no return value:

```
memcache.clearAll();
```

CHAPTER 13

Fetching URLs and Web Resources

An App Engine application can connect to other sites on the Internet to retrieve data and communicate with web services. It does this not by opening a connection to the remote host from the application server, but through a scalable service called the URL Fetch service. This takes the burden of maintaining connections away from the app servers, and ensures that resource fetching performs well regardless of how many request handlers are fetching resources simultaneously. As with other parts of the App Engine infrastructure, the URL Fetch service is used by other Google applications to fetch web pages.

The URL Fetch service supports fetching URLs using the HTTP protocol as well as HTTP with SSL (HTTPS). Other methods sometimes associated with URLs (such as FTP) are not supported.

Because the URL Fetch service is based on Google infrastructure, the service inherits a few restrictions that were put in place in the original design of the underlying HTTP proxy. The service supports the five most common HTTP actions (GET, POST, PUT, HEAD, and DELETE) but does not allow for others or for using a non-standard action. Also, it can only connect to TCP ports in several allowed ranges: 80–90, 440–450, and 1024–65535. By default, it uses port 80 for HTTP, and port 443 for HTTPS. The proxy uses HTTP 1.1 to connect to the remote host.

The outgoing request can contain URL parameters, a request body, and HTTP headers. A few headers cannot be modified for security reasons, which mostly means that an app cannot issue a malformed request, such as a request whose `Content-Length` header does not accurately reflect the actual content length of the request-body. In these cases, the service uses the correct values, or does not include the header.

Request and response sizes are limited, but generous. A request can be up to 10 megabytes in size (including headers), and a response can be up to 32 megabytes in size.

The service waits for a response up to a time limit, or "deadline." The default fetch deadline is 5 seconds, but you can increase this on a per-request basis. The maximum deadline is 60 seconds during a user request, or 10 minutes during a task queue or scheduled task or from a backend. That is, the fetch deadline can be up to the request handler's own deadline, except for backends (which have none).

The Java runtime environment offers implementations of standard classes used for fetching URLs that call the URL Fetch service behind the scenes. This is the `java.net.URLConnection` set of APIs, including `java.net.URL`. These implementations give you a reasonable degree of portability and interoperability with other libraries.

Naturally, the standard interfaces do not give you complete access to the service's features. When using the standard libraries, the service uses the following default behaviors:

- If the remote host doesn't respond within 5 seconds, the request is canceled and a service exception is raised.

- The service follows HTTP redirects up to 5 times before returning the response to the application.

- Responses from remote hosts that exceed 32 megabytes in size are truncated to 32 megabytes. The application is not told whether the response is truncated.

- HTTP over SSL (HTTPS) URLs will use SSL to make the connection, but the service will not validate the server's security certificate. (The App Engine team has said certificate validation will become the default for the standard libraries in a future release, so check the App Engine website.)

All of these behaviors can be customized when calling the service APIs directly. You can increase the fetch response deadline, disable the automatic following of redirects, cause an exception to be thrown for responses that exceed the maximum size, and enable validation of certificates for HTTPS connections.

The development server simulates the URL Fetch service by making HTTP connections directly from your computer. If the remote host might behave differently when your app connects from your computer rather than from Google's proxy servers, be sure to test your URL Fetch calls on App Engine.

In this chapter, we introduce the standard-library and direct interfaces to the URL Fetch service. We also examine several features of the service, and how to use them from the direct APIs.

Fetching resources from remote hosts can take quite a bit of time. Like several other services, the URL Fetch service offers a way to call the service asynchronously, so your application can issue fetch requests and do other things while remote servers take their time to respond. See Chapter 17 for more information.

Fetching URLs

The direct URL Fetch service API is provided by the com.google.appengine.api.urlfetch package. You can also use standard java.net calls to fetch URLs. The Java runtime includes a custom implementation of the URL Connection class in the java.net package that calls the URL Fetch service instead of making a direct socket connection. As with the other standard interfaces, you can use this interface and rest assured that you can port your app to another platform easily.

Example 13-1 shows a simple example of using a convenience method in the URL class, which in turn uses the URLConnection class to fetch the contents of a web page. The openStream() method of the URL object returns an input stream of bytes. As shown, you can use an InputStreamReader (from java.io) to process the byte stream as a character stream. The BufferedReader class makes it easy to read lines of text from the InputStreamReader.

Example 13-1. Using java.net.URL to call the URL Fetch service

```
import java.net.URL;
import java.net.MalformedURLException;
import java.io.IOException;
import java.io.InputStream;
import java.io.InputStreamReader;
import java.io.BufferedReader;

// ...

    try {
        URL url = new URL("http://ae-book.appspot.com/blog/atom.xml/");
        InputStream inStream = url.openStream();

        InputStreamReader inStreamReader = new InputStreamReader(inStream);
        BufferedReader reader = new BufferedReader(inStreamReader);
        // ... read characters or lines with reader ...
        reader.close();

    } catch (MalformedURLException e) {
        // ...
    } catch (IOException e) {
        // ...
    }
```

Note that the URL Fetch service has already buffered the entire response into the application's memory by the time the app begins to read. The app reads the response data from memory, not from a network stream from the socket or the service.

You can use other features of the `URLConnection` interface, as long as they operate within the functionality of the service API. Notably, the URL Fetch service does not maintain a persistent connection with the remote host, so features that require such a connection will not work.

By default, the URL Fetch service waits up to 5 seconds for a response from the remote server. If the server does not respond by the deadline, the service throws an `IOException`. You can adjust the amount of time to wait using the `setConnectTimeout()` method of the `URLConnection`. (The `setReadTimeout()` method has the same effect; the service uses the greater of the two values.) The deadline can be up to 60 seconds during user requests, or up to 10 minutes (600 seconds) for task queue and scheduled tasks and when running on a backend.

When using the `URLConnection` interface, the URL Fetch service follows HTTP redirects automatically, up to five consecutive redirects. The app does not see the intermediate redirect responses, only the last one. If there are more than five redirects, the service returns the fifth redirect response to the app.

The low-level API for the URL Fetch service lets you customize several behaviors of the service. Example 13-2 demonstrates how to fetch a URL with this API with options specified. As shown, the `FetchOptions` object tells the service not to follow any redirects, and to throw a `ResponseTooLargeException` if the response exceeds the maximum size of 32 megabytes instead of truncating the data.

Example 13-2. Using the low-level API to call the URL Fetch service, with options

```
import java.net.URL;
import java.net.MalformedURLException;
import com.google.appengine.api.urlfetch.FetchOptions;
import com.google.appengine.api.urlfetch.HTTPMethod;
import com.google.appengine.api.urlfetch.HTTPRequest;
import com.google.appengine.api.urlfetch.HTTPResponse;
import com.google.appengine.api.urlfetch.ResponseTooLargeException;
import com.google.appengine.api.urlfetch.URLFetchService;
import com.google.appengine.api.urlfetch.URLFetchServiceFactory;

// ...
        try {
            URL url = new URL("http://ae-book.appspot.com/blog/atom.xml/");

            FetchOptions options = FetchOptions.Builder
                .doNotFollowRedirects()
                .disallowTruncate();
            HTTPRequest request = new HTTPRequest(url, HTTPMethod.GET, options);
```

```
        URLFetchService urlfetch = URLFetchServiceFactory.getURLFetchService();
        HTTPResponse response = urlfetch.fetch(request);
        // ... process response.getContent() ...

    } catch (ResponseTooLargeException e) {
        // ...
    } catch (MalformedURLException e) {
        // ...
    } catch (IOException e) {
        // ...
    }
```

You use the `FetchOptions` class to adjust many of the service's features. You get an instance of this class by calling a static method of `FetchOptions.Builder`, and then set options by calling methods on the instance. For convenience, there is a static method for each option, and every method returns the instance, so your code can build the full set of options with a single statement of chained method calls.

We will use the direct `urlfetch` API for the remainder of this chapter.

Outgoing HTTP Requests

An HTTP request can consist of a URL, an HTTP method, request headers, and a payload. Only the URL and HTTP method are required, and the API assumes you mean the HTTP GET method if you only provide a URL.

To make a request, you prepare an instance of the `HTTPRequest` class from the `com.google.appengine.api.urlfetch` package with the URL as a `java.net.URL` instance, then you pass the request object to the service's `fetch()` method. (Notice that this `HTTPRequest` class is different from the J2EE class you use with your request handler servlets.)

```
import java.net.URL;
import com.google.appengine.api.urlfetch.HTTPRequest;
import com.google.appengine.api.urlfetch.HTTPResponse;
import com.google.appengine.api.urlfetch.URLFetchService;
import com.google.appengine.api.urlfetch.URLFetchServiceFactory;

// ...
        HTTPRequest outRequest =
            new HTTPRequest(new URL("http://www.example.com/feed.xml"));

        URLFetchService urlfetch = URLFetchServiceFactory.getURLFetchService();
        HTTPResponse response = urlfetch.fetch(outRequest);
```

The URL

The URL consists of a scheme, a domain, an optional port, and a path. For example:

```
https://www.example.com:8081/private/feed.xml
```

In this example, `https` is the scheme, `www.example.com` is the domain, `8081` is the port, and `/private/feed.xml` is the path.

The URL Fetch service supports the `http` and `https` schemes. Other schemes, such as `ftp`, are not supported.

If no port is specified, the service will use the default port for the scheme: port 80 for HTTP, and port 443 for HTTPS. If you specify a port, it must be within 80–90, 440–450, or 1024–65535.

As a safety measure against accidental request loops in an application, the URL Fetch service will refuse to fetch the URL that maps to the request handler doing the fetching. An app can make connections to other URLs of its own, so request loops are still possible, but this restriction provides a simple sanity check.

As just shown, the Java API accepts a `java.net.URL` object as an argument to the `HTTPRequest` constructor.

The HTTP Method and Payload

The HTTP method describes the general nature of the request, as codified by the HTTP standard. For example, the GET method asks for the data associated with the resource identified by the URL (such as a document or database record). The server is expected to verify that the request is allowed, then return the data in the response, without making changes to the resource. The POST method asks the server to modify records or perform an action, and the client usually includes a payload of data with the request.

The URL Fetch service can send requests using the GET, POST, PUT, HEAD, and DELETE methods. No other methods are supported.

You set the method by passing an optional second argument to the `HTTPRequest` constructor. Its value is from the enum `HTTPMethod`, whose values are named `GET`, `POST`, `PUT`, `HEAD`, and `DELETE`. To add a payload, you call the `setPayload()` method of the `HTTPRequest`, passing in a `byte[]`:

```
import com.google.appengine.api.urlfetch.HTTPMethod;

// ...
        byte[] profileData = profile.getFieldData();
        HTTPRequest request = new HTTPRequest(url, HTTPMethod.POST);
        request.setPayload(profileData);
```

Request Headers

Requests can include headers, a set of key-value pairs distinct from the payload that describe the client, the request, and the expected response. App Engine sets several headers automatically, such as `Content-Length`. Your app can provide additional headers that may be expected by the server.

You set a request header by calling the `setHeader()` method on the `HTTPRequest`. Its sole argument is an instance of the `HTTPHeader` class, whose constructor takes the header name and value as strings:

```
import com.google.appengine.api.urlfetch.HTTPHeader;

// ...
        HTTPRequest request =
            new HTTPRequest(
                new URL("http://www.example.com/article/roof_on_fire"));
        request.setHeader(new HTTPHeader("Accept-Charset", "utf-8"));
```

Some headers cannot be set directly by the application. This is primarily to discourage request forgery or invalid requests that could be used as an attack on some servers. Disallowed headers include `Content-Length` (which is set by App Engine automatically to the actual size of the request), `Host`, `Vary`, `Via`, `X-Forwarded-For`, and `X-ProxyUser-IP`.

The `User-Agent` header, which most servers use to identify the software of the client, can be set by the app. However, App Engine will append a string to this value identifying the request as coming from App Engine. This string includes your application ID. This is usually enough to allow an app to coax a server into serving content intended for a specific type of client (such as a specific brand or version of web browser), but it won't be a complete impersonation of such a client.

HTTP over SSL (HTTPS)

When the scheme of a URL is `https`, the URL Fetch service uses HTTP over SSL to connect to the remote server, encrypting both the request and the response.

The SSL protocol also allows the client to verify the identity of the remote host, to ensure it is talking directly to the host and traffic is not being intercepted by a malicious host (a "man in the middle" attack). This protocol involves security certificates and a process for clients to validate certificates.

By default, the URL Fetch service does *not* validate SSL certificates. With validation disabled, traffic is still encrypted, but the remote host's certificates are not validated before sending the request data. You can tell the URL Fetch service to enable validation of security certificates.

To enable certificate validation in Java, you use a `FetchOptions` instance with the request, and call its `validateCertificate()` option. Its antonym is `doNotValidate Certificate()`, which is the default:

```
FetchOptions options = FetchOptions.Builder
    .validateCertificate();
HTTPRequest request = new HTTPRequest(
    new URL("https://secure.example.com/profile/126542"),
    HTTPMethod.GET, options);
```

The standard libraries use the default behavior and do not validate certificates. If you need to validate certificates, you must use the `urlfetch` API.

Request and Response Sizes

The request can be up to 10 megabytes in size, including the headers and payload. The response can be up to 32 megabytes in size.

The URL Fetch service can do one of two things if the remote host returns a response larger than 32 megabytes: it can truncate the response (delete everything after the first 32 megabytes), or it can raise an exception in your app. You control this behavior with an option.

The `FetchOptions` method `allowTruncate()` enables truncation. `disallowTruncate()` tells the service to throw a `ResponseTooLargeException` if the response is too large:

```
FetchOptions options = FetchOptions.Builder
    .allowTruncate();
HTTPRequest request = new HTTPRequest(
    new URL("http://www.example.com/firehose.dat"),
    HTTPMethod.GET, options);
```

The standard libraries tell the URL Fetch service to allow truncation. This ensures that the standard libraries won't raise an unfamiliar exception when third-party code fetches a URL, at the expense of returning unexpectedly truncated data when responses are too large.

Request Deadlines

The URL Fetch service issues a request, waits for the remote host to respond, and then makes the response available to the app. But the service won't wait on the remote host forever. By default, the service will wait 5 seconds before terminating the connection and raising an exception with your app.

You can adjust the amount of time the service will wait (the "deadline") as an option to the fetch call. You can set a deadline up to 60 seconds for fetches made during user requests, and up to 10 minutes (600 seconds) for requests made during tasks. That is,

---

you can wait up to the maximum amount of time your request handler can run. Typically, you'll want to set a fetch deadline shorter than your request handler's deadline, so it can react to a failed fetch.

To set the fetch deadline, you call the setDeadline() method of the FetchOptions class, which takes a java.lang.Double. The Builder static method is slightly different, named withDeadline() and taking a double. The value is a number of seconds:

```
FetchOptions options = FetchOptions.Builder
    .withDeadline(30);
HTTPRequest request = new HTTPRequest(
    new URL("http://www.example.com/users/ackermann"),
    HTTPMethod.GET, options);
```

Handling Redirects

You can tell the service to follow redirects automatically, if HTTP redirect requests are returned by the remote server. The server will follow up to five redirects, then return the last response to the app (regardless of whether the last response is a redirect or not).

The FetchOptions.Builder has a followRedirects() method, and its opposite doNotFollowRedirects(). The default is to not follow redirects. When using java.net.URLConnection, redirects are followed automatically, up to five times:

```
FetchOptions options = FetchOptions.Builder
    .followRedirects();
HTTPRequest request = new HTTPRequest(
    new URL("http://www.example.com/bounce"),
    HTTPMethod.GET, options);
```

When following redirects, the service does not retain or use cookies set in the responses of the intermediate steps. If you need requests to honor cookies during a redirect chain, you must disable the automatic redirect feature, and process redirects manually in your application code.

Response Objects

The fetch() service method returns an HTTPResponse instance, with getter methods for the response data.

The response fields are as follows:

getContent()
    The response body, as a byte[].

getResponseCode()
    The HTTP status code. An int.

getHeaders()

The response headers. This is a List<HTTPHeader>, where each header has get
Name() and getValue() methods (returning strings).

getFinalUrl()

The URL that corresponds to the response data. If automatic redirects were
enabled and the server issued one or more redirects, this is the URL of the final
destination, which may differ from the request URL. A Java java.net.URL.

CHAPTER 14

Sending and Receiving Email Messages

While today's Internet offers many modes of communication, one of the oldest modes is still one of the most popular: email. For web applications, email is the primary mechanism for representing and validating identity, and managing access to application-specific accounts. Email is how your app reaches out to your users when they are not on your website and signed in.

An App Engine app can send email messages by calling the Mail service API. An app might send email to notify users of system events or the actions of other users (such as to send social networking invitations), confirm user actions (such as to confirm an order), follow up on long-term user actions (such as to send a shipping notice for an order), or send system notifications to administrators. The app can send email on behalf of itself or the app's administrators. The app can also send email on behalf of the currently signed-in user, during the request handler.

Sending email messages is similar to initiating HTTP requests: the app calls a service by using an API, and the service takes care of making remote connections and managing the appropriate protocols. Unlike the URL Fetch service, the Mail service does not return a response immediately. Instead, messages are enqueued for delivery, and errors are reported via "bounce" email messages to the sender address.

An app can also receive email messages sent to specific addresses. This might allow an app to provide an email interface to the application, or to moderate or monitor email discussions. The app can reply to the email immediately, or set up work that causes a reply to be sent later.

Receiving email messages is also similar to receiving HTTP requests. In fact, this uses the same mechanism: request handlers. When a service receives an email message intended for your app, the Mail service sends an HTTP request to the app using a specified URL with the message in the HTTP payload. The app processes incoming messages, using request handlers mapped to the specified URLs. The service ignores the response for the request; if the app needs to reply to the user, it can send a message using the API.

Figure 14-1 illustrates the flow of incoming email messages.

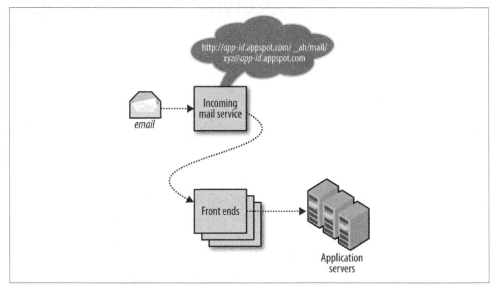

Figure 14-1. Architecture of incoming email messages, calling web hooks in response to incoming message events

Each app has its own set of incoming email addresses, based on its application ID. For email, the app can receive messages at addresses of these forms:

`app-id@appspotmail.com`

`anything@app-id.appspotmail.com`

App Engine does not support receiving email at an address on an app's custom domain name. However, you can use an email address on your custom domain as a "From" address by setting it up as a Google account, and then making that account a "developer" of the app in the Cloud Console. You can further configure automatic forwarding of replies to that address by using Gmail.

In this chapter, we discuss the APIs for sending and receiving email messages, and language-specific tools for creating and processing those messages.

Sending Email Messages

To send an email message, you call the API of the Mail service. The outgoing message has a sender address ("From"), one or more recipients ("To," "Cc," or "Bcc"), a subject, a message body, and optional file attachments.

An email message can contain a limited set of message headers, which are understood by mail servers and clients. The headers an app can set are restricted to prevent the service from being abused to send forged messages. (See the official documentation for the current list of allowed headers.) The Mail service attaches additional headers to the message, such as the date and time the message is sent.

You can specify a multipart message body, such as to include both plain-text and HTML versions of the message, and to include attachments. The total size of the message, including all headers and attachments, cannot exceed 10 megabytes.

The call to the Mail service is asynchronous. When your application calls the Mail service to send a message, the message is enqueued for delivery, and the service call returns. If there is a problem delivering the message, such as if the remote mail server cannot be contacted or the remote server says the address is invalid, an error message is sent via email to the sender address. The app is not notified of the failure by the service directly. If the app must be notified of a message send failure, you can use an incoming email address for the app as the sender address. The app will have to parse the message sent by the remote server for an error.

When running on App Engine, outgoing email counts toward your outgoing bandwidth quota, as well as the quota for the total number of email recipients. You can increase these quotas by adjusting your billing settings. Email messages sent to the application administrators use a separate limit (Admins Emailed in the Quotas display of the Cloud Console) to allow for apps that send maintenance reports and alerts to administrators but do not need to send email to arbitrary recipients.

App Engine gives special treatment to the limit on email recipients to prevent abuse of the system, such as sending junk or scam email (which is against the terms of service and an all-around lousy thing to do). New apps are only allowed a small number of email recipients per month under the free plan. When you activate billing for an app for the first time, this limit is not raised until the first charge to your billing account succeeds. This is intended to discourage abusers from activating billing with invalid payment details just to temporarily raise the recipient limit.

If your app relies on sending email to many users (such as for registration confirmation), be sure to activate billing and test your email features two weeks in advance of launching your website.

Logging Sent Mail in the Development Server

When your app runs in the development server, sending a message causes the server to print information about the message to the logs, and no message is sent. The server logs the message at the "info" log level. You can adjust the level at which outgoing mail messages are logged by running the development server with the `mail.log_mail_level` property set to a value such as `WARNING`. You can also tell the development server to log the body of the message by setting the `mail.log_mail_body` system property to `true`. From the command line:

```
dev_appserver.sh \
    --jvm_flag=-Dmail.log_mail_level=WARNING \
    --jvm_flag=-Dmail.log_message_body=true \
    appdir
```

From Eclipse, select the Run menu, Debug Configurations, and then select your app's configuration. Select the Arguments tab, then in the "VM arguments" section, set VM properties like this:

```
-Dmail.log_mail_level=WARNING -Dmail.log_mail_body=true
```

Sender Addresses

The sender ("From") address on an outgoing email message must be one of the allowed addresses:

- The Google Account address of one of the application administrators
- The address of the user currently signed in to the app with Google Accounts (during the request handler that is sending the message)
- A valid incoming email address for the application

Replies to messages sent by the app go to the sender address, as do error messages sent by the outgoing mail server (such as "Could not connect to remote host") or the remote mail server (such as "User not found").

You can use an application developer's Google Account address as the sender address. To add accounts as application administrators, go to the Developers section of the Cloud Console. If you do not want to use the account of a specific developer as the sender address, you can create a new Google Account for a general-purpose address, then add it as a developer for the app: in the Console, select Permissions, then invite the user account. Be sure to select the Viewer role, so if someone gets the account's password, that person cannot make changes to the app. You can use Gmail to monitor the account for replies, and you can set up automatic email forwarding in Gmail to relay replies to specific administrators or a mailing list (or Google Group) automatically.

A Google account can use a Gmail address or a Google Apps domain address. If your app has a custom domain, you can create a new Google account with an address on the domain (such as `sup port@example.com`), give the account Viewer permissions for the app, and use the address for outgoing mail.

If you don't have a Google Apps domain, you can create a Gmail account, using the application ID, and add `app-id@gmail.com` as a developer. Note that if you create the Gmail account before you register the application ID, you must be signed in using the Gmail account when you register the application ID. App Engine won't let you register an app ID that matches a Gmail account name unless you are signed in with that account.

You can use the email address of a user as the sender address if and only if the address is of a registered Google Account, the user is signed in, and the user initiated the request whose handler is sending the email. That is, you can send email on behalf of the "current" user. This is useful if the email is triggered by the user's action and if replies to the message ought to go to the user's email address. The Google Accounts API does not expose the user's human-readable name, so you won't be able to provide that unless you get it from the user yourself.

As we mentioned earlier, an application can receive email messages at addresses of the form `app-id@appspotmail.com` or `anything@app-id.appspotmail.com`, where `app-id` is your application ID and `anything` can be any string that's valid on the left side of the email address (it can't contain an @ symbol). You can use an incoming email address as the sender of an email message to have replies routed to a request handler.

The "anything" lets you create custom sender addresses on the fly. For example, a customer support app could start an email conversation with a unique ID and include the ID in the email address (`support+ID@app-id.appspotmail.com`), and save replies for that conversation in the datastore so the entire thread can be viewed by customer service personnel.

Note that the sender address will also receive error ("bounce") messages. If you use an incoming mail address as the sender, you could have the app process error messages to remove invalid email addresses automatically. Note that different remote email servers may use different formatting for error messages.

Any email address can also have a human-friendly name, such as `"The Example Team <admin@example.com>"`. How you do this is specific to the interface; we'll look at the interfaces in a moment.

You can include a separate "Reply-to" address in addition to the sender ("From") address. Most mail readers and servers will use this address instead of the sender address for replies and error messages. The "Reply-to" address must meet the same requirements as the sender address.

The development server does not check that the sender address meets these conditions because it doesn't know who the app's developers are. Be sure to test features that send email while running on App Engine.

Recipients

An outgoing email message can use any address for a recipient, and can have multiple recipients.

A recipient can be a primary recipient (the "To" field), a secondary or "carbon-copied" recipient (the "Cc" field), or a "blind carbon-copied" recipient ("Bcc"). The "To" and "Cc" recipients are included in the content of the message, so a reply intended for all recipients can be sent to the visible addresses. The "Bcc" recipients receive the message, but their addresses are not included in the content of the message, and so are not included in replies.

The "Bcc" recipient type is especially useful if you want a single message to go to multiple recipients, but you do not want any recipient to know who received the message. You can use this technique to send an email newsletter to users without exposing the users' email addresses. A common technique for newsletters is to use the sender address as the sole "To" recipient, and make everyone else a "Bcc" recipient.

The number of recipients for an email message counts toward an email recipient quota. This quota is initially small to prevent unsolicited email advertisers from abusing the system. You can raise this quota by allocating part of your budget toward email recipients.

When you enable billing in your app for the first time, the email recipients quota will not increase from the free level until your first payment is processed. This is one of several measures to prevent spammers from abusing the service.

Attachments

An app can attach files to an email message. One good use of attachments is to include images for rich HTML email messages.

For security reasons (mostly having to do with insecure email clients), some file types are not allowed as email attachments. A file's type is determined by its filename extension. For example, files that represent executable programs (such as *.exe*, *.bat*, or *.sh*) are not allowed. Some file archive types like *.zip* are allowed, but the archive cannot contain files that are executable programs.

The MIME content type of each attachment is derived from the filename extension. If a filename extension is not recognized, the content type is set to `application/octet-stream`.

See the official documentation for the complete list of disallowed attachment types, as well as a list of mappings from extensions to MIME content types.

 If you want to deliver files to users that are not allowed as attachments, one option is to send a link to a request handler that delivers the file through the browser. The link can be personalized with a temporary unique ID, or restricted using Google Accounts authentication.

Sending Email

The Java interface to the Mail service is the JavaMail standard interface (`javax.mail.*`). There is also a low-level interface, although you can access every feature of the service through the JavaMail implementation. (As such, we'll only discuss the JavaMail interface here.)

To use JavaMail, you first create a JavaMail "session." The `Session` object usually contains information needed to connect to a mail server, but with App Engine, no configuration is needed. You prepare the message as a `MimeMessage` object, then send it using the `send()` static method of the `Transport` class. The `Transport` class uses the most recently created session to send the message:

```
import java.util.Properties;
import javax.mail.Message;
import javax.mail.MessagingException;
import javax.mail.Session;
import javax.mail.Transport;
import javax.mail.internet.AddressException;
import javax.mail.internet.InternetAddress;
import javax.mail.internet.MimeMessage;

import com.google.appengine.api.users.User;
import com.google.appengine.api.users.UserServiceFactory;

// ...
        User user = UserServiceFactory.getUserService().getCurrentUser();
        String recipientAddress = user.getEmail();

        Properties props = new Properties();
        Session session = Session.getDefaultInstance(props, null);

        String messageBody =
            "Welcome to Example!  Your account has been created. " +
            "You can edit your user profile by clicking the " +
```

```
            "following link:\n\n" +
            "http://www.example.com/profile/\n\n" +
            "Let us know if you have any questions.\n\n" +
            "The Example Team\n";

    try {
        Message message = new MimeMessage(session);
        message.setFrom(new InternetAddress("admin@example.com",
                                            "The Example Team"));
        message.addRecipient(Message.RecipientType.TO,
                        new InternetAddress(recipientAddress));
        message.setSubject("Welcome to Example.com!");
        message.setText(messageBody);
        Transport.send(message);

    } catch (AddressException e) {
        // An email address was invalid.
        // ...
    } catch (MessagingException e) {
        // There was an error contacting the Mail service.
        // ...
    }
```

As shown here, you call methods on the MimeMessage to set fields and to add recipients and content. The simplest message has a sender (setFrom()), one "To" recipient (addRecipient()), a subject (setSubject()), and a plain-text message body (set Text()).

The setFrom() method takes an InternetAddress. You can create an InternetAddress with just the email address (a String) or the address and a human-readable name as arguments to the constructor. The email address of the sender must meet the requirements described earlier. You can use any string for the human-readable name.

The addRecipient() method takes a recipient type and an InternetAddress. The allowed recipient types are Message.RecipientType.TO ("To," a primary recipient), Message.RecipientType.CC ("Cc" or "carbon-copy," a secondary recipient), and Message.RecipientType.BCC ("Bcc" or "blind carbon-copy," where the recipient is sent the message but the address does not appear in the message content). You can call addRecipient() multiple times to add multiple recipients of any type.

The setText() method sets the plain-text body for the message. To include an HTML version of the message body for mail readers that support HTML, you create a MimeMultipart object, then create a MimeBodyPart for the plain-text body and another for the HTML body and add them to the MimeMultipart. You then make the MimeMultipart the content of the MimeMessage:

```
import javax.mail.Multipart;
import javax.mail.internet.MimeBodyPart;
```

```
import javax.mail.internet.MimeMultipart;

// ...
        String textBody = "...text...";
        String htmlBody = "...HTML...";

        Multipart multipart = new MimeMultipart();

        MimeBodyPart textPart = new MimeBodyPart();
        textPart.setContent(textBody, "text/plain");
        multipart.addBodyPart(textPart);

        MimeBodyPart htmlPart = new MimeBodyPart();
        htmlPart.setContent(htmlBody, "text/html");
        multipart.addBodyPart(htmlPart);

        message.setContent(multipart);
```
You attach files to the email message in a similar way:

```
        Multipart multipart = new MimeMultipart();
        // ...

        byte[] fileData = getBrochureData();
        String fileName = "brochure.pdf";
        String fileType = "application/pdf";

        MimeBodyPart attachmentPart = new MimeBodyPart();
        attachmentPart.setContent(fileData, fileType);
        attachmentPart.setFileName(fileName);
        multipart.addBodyPart(attachmentPart);

        // ...
        message.setContent(multipart);
```

You can add multiple MimeBodyPart objects to a single MimeMultipart. The plain-text body, the HTML body, and the file attachments are each part of a MIME multipart message.

When using a MimeMultipart, you must include a text/plain part to be the plain-text body of the message. The multipart object overrides any plain-text content set on the MimeMessage with setText().

App Engine's implementation of the JavaMail interface includes a shortcut for sending an email message to all of the app's administrators. To send a message to all administrators, use a recipient address of "admins", with no @ symbol or domain name.

Receiving Email Messages

To receive incoming email messages, you must first enable the feature in your app's configuration. Incoming email is disabled by default, so unwanted messages are ignored and do not try to contact your app or incur costs.

To enable inbound services, you add a section to the app's *appengine-web.xml* configuration file, anywhere inside the root element:

```
<inbound-services>
  <service>mail</service>
</inbound-services>
```

Once your app is deployed, you can confirm that the incoming mail service is enabled from the Cloud Console, under Application Settings. If your app does not appear to be receiving HTTP requests for incoming email messages, check the Console and update the configuration if necessary.

With the `mail` inbound service enabled in configuration, an application can receive email messages at any of several addresses. An incoming mail message is routed to the app in the form of an HTTP request.

Email sent to addresses of the following forms are routed to the default version of the app:

app-id@appspotmail.com

anything@*app-id*.appspotmail.com

The HTTP request uses the POST action, and is sent to the following URL path:

/_ah/mail/to-address

The recipient email address of the message is included at the end of the URL path, so the app can distinguish between different values of "anything."

The body content of the HTTP POST request is the complete MIME email message, including the mail headers and body. It can be parsed by any library capable of parsing MIME email messages.

The development server console (*http://localhost:8080/_ah/admin/*) includes a feature for simulating incoming email by submitting a web form. The development server cannot receive actual email messages.

 If the app has the incoming mail service enabled but does not have a request handler for the appropriate URL, or if the request handler returns an HTTP response code other than 200 for the request, the message gets "bounced" and the sender receives an error email message.

To receive email, you map the incoming email URL path to a servlet with an entry in the deployment descriptor (*web.xml*):

```
<servlet>
  <servlet-name>mailreceiver</servlet-name>
  <servlet-class>myapp.MailReceiverServlet</servlet-class>
</servlet>
<servlet-mapping>
  <servlet-name>mailreceiver</servlet-name>
  <url-pattern>/_ah/mail/*</url-pattern>
</servlet-mapping>
```

The JavaMail and servlet APIs provide everything we need to parse the MIME multipart message in the HTTP POST request. The `MimeMessage` class (in the `javax.mail.internet` package) has a constructor that accepts a `java.io.Input Stream`, which we can get from the `HttpServletRequest` by using its `getInput Stream()` method. The `MimeMessage` constructor also needs a JavaMail `Session`, which, as with sending email, can use the default empty configuration:

```
import java.io.IOException;
import java.util.Properties;
import javax.mail.Session;
import javax.mail.MessagingException;
import javax.mail.Multipart;
import javax.mail.Part;
import javax.mail.internet.MimeMessage;
import javax.servlet.http.*;

public class MailReceiverServlet extends HttpServlet {
    public void doPost(HttpServletRequest req,
                       HttpServletResponse resp)
            throws IOException {
        Properties props = new Properties();
        Session session = Session.getDefaultInstance(props, null);

        try {
            MimeMessage message = new MimeMessage(session, req.getInputStream());
            String contentType = message.getContentType();
            Object content = message.getContent();
            if (content instanceof String) {
                // A plain-text body.
                // ...

            } else if (content instanceof Multipart) {
                // A multipart body.
                for (int i = 0; i < ((Multipart) content).getCount(); i++) {
                    Part part = ((Multipart) content).getBodyPart(i);
                    // ...

                }
            }
```

```
        } catch (MessagingException e) {
            // Problem parsing the message data.
            // ...

        }
    }
}
```

If the incoming message is a MIME multipart message (such as a message with an HTML body, or attachments), the getContent() method of the MimeMessage returns an object that implements the Multipart interface. You can use this interface to get a count of the parts (getCount()) and select parts by index (getBodyPart(int index), which returns a BodyPart).

CHAPTER 15

Sending and Receiving Instant Messages with XMPP

So far, we've seen two mechanisms an app can use to communicate with the outside world. The first and most prominent of these is HTTP: an app can receive and respond to HTTP requests, and can send HTTP requests to other hosts and receive responses with the URL Fetch service. The second is email: an app can send email messages by using the Mail service, and can receive messages via a proxy that calls a request handler for each incoming email message.

In this chapter, we introduce a third method of communication: XMPP, also known as "instant messages," or simply "chat." An app can participate in a chat dialogue with a user of any XMPP-compatible chat service. The XMPP service is useful for chat interfaces, such as a chat-based query engine, or a customer service proxy. App Engine does not act as an XMPP service itself. Instead, it connects to Google's own XMPP infrastructure to participate as a chat user.

Sending and receiving XMPP messages works similarly to email messages. To send a message, an app calls the XMPP service API. To receive a message, the app declares that it accepts such messages in its configuration, and then handles HTTP requests sent by the XMPP service to special-purpose URLs. Figure 15-1 illustrates the flow of incoming XMPP messages.

Each participant in an XMPP communication has an address similar to an email address, known as a *JID*. (JID is short for "Jabber ID," named after the Jabber project, where XMPP originated.) A JID consists of a username, an "at" symbol (@), and the domain name of the XMPP server. A JID can also have an optional "resource" string, which is used to identify specific clients connected to the service with the username. A message sent to the ID without the resource goes to all connected clients:

username @ domain / resource

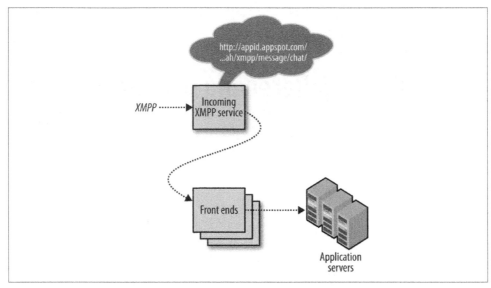

Figure 15-1. Architecture of incoming XMPP messages, calling web hooks in response to incoming message events

To send a message, a chat participant sends an XMPP message to its own XMPP server. The participant's chat service contacts the recipient service's host by using the domain name of the JID and a standard port, then delivers the message. If the remote service accepts messages for the JID and someone is connected to the service with a chat client for that JID, the service delivers the message to the client.

As with email, each app has its own set of JIDs, based on its application ID. For XMPP chat, the app can receive messages at addresses of these forms:

    app-id@appspot.com

    anything@*app-id*.appspotchat.com

(Notice the differences in the domain names from the options available for incoming email.)

App Engine does not support XMPP addresses on a custom domain. This is one of only a few cases where exposing your application ID to users cannot be avoided.

Let's take a look at the features and API of the XMPP service.

Inviting a User to Chat

Before a user of an XMPP-compatible instant messaging service will see any messages your app sends, the service needs to know that the user is expecting your messages.

This can happen in two ways: either the user explicitly adds your app's JID to her contact list, or she accepts an invitation to chat sent by the app.

An app can send an invitation to chat by calling the XMPP service API. For apps, it's polite to get the user's permission to do this first, so the complete workflow looks something like this:

1. The user visits the website, and activates the chat-based feature of the service, providing a JID.
2. The app sends an invitation to chat to the user's JID.
3. The user accepts the invitation in her chat client.
4. The user and app exchange chat messages.

The alternative where the user adds the app's JID to her contact list is usually equivalent to sending an invitation to the app. App Engine accepts all such invitations automatically, even if the app does not accept chat messages.

An accepted invitation entitles both parties to know the other party's *presence* status, whether the party is connected and accepting messages. This includes the ability to know when an invitation is accepted. (For more information, see "Managing Presence" on page 319.)

In the development server, inviting a user to chat emits a log message, but otherwise does nothing.

In Java, each JID is represented by an instance of the JID class, in the package com.google.appengine.api.xmpp. You create this by passing the address as a string to the JID constructor. To send an invitation, you call the sendInvitation() method with either one or two arguments:

```java
import com.google.appengine.api.xmpp.JID;
import com.google.appengine.api.xmpp.XMPPService;
import com.google.appengine.api.xmpp.XMPPServiceFactory;

// ...
    XMPPService xmpp = XMPPServiceFactory.getXMPPService();

    // From saucy-boomerang-123@appspot.com:
    xmpp.sendInvitation(new JID("juliet@example.com"));

    // From a custom JID:
    xmpp.sendInvitation(
        new JID("juliet@example.com"),
        new JID("support@saucy-boomerang-123.appspotchat.com"));
```

Sending Chat Messages

An XMPP message includes a sender address, one or more recipient addresses, a message type, and a message body.

The sender address must be one of the app's incoming XMPP addresses. These are of the form *app-id*@appspot.com or *anything*@*app-id*.appspotchat.com, where *app-id* is your application ID and *anything* can be any string that's valid on the left side of a JID (it can't contain an @ symbol). Unlike incoming email addresses, it's not as convenient to use the "anything" form for creating IDs on the fly, because the recipient needs to accept an invitation from that ID before receiving messages. But it can still be useful for sessions that begin with an invitation, or addresses that represent specific purposes or users of the app (support@app-id.appspotchat.com).

If the version of the app that is sending an XMPP message is not the default version, App Engine modifies the sender address to a version-specific address, so replies go directly to the correct version: either *anything*@*version*.*app-id*.appspotchat.com or *app-id*@*version*.*app-id*.appspotchat.com.

App Engine adds a "resource" to the end of the sender JID (after the domain name) that looks like this: /bot. This is mostly just to comply with the best practice of sending messages using JIDs with resources. It isn't noticed by chat users, and is not needed when a user wishes to send a message to the app. You'll see it in log messages.

The message type can be any of the types in the XMPP standard, including chat, error, groupchat, headline, and normal. An app can only receive messages of the types chat, normal, and error, and so cannot participate in group chats. For straightforward communication between an app and a chat user, you usually want to send chat messages. For an app and a custom client, you can do what you like.

Messages are sent asynchronously. The service call returns immediately, and reports success only if the XMPP service enqueued the message successfully. You can configure the app to receive error messages, such as to be notified if a sent message was not received because the user went offline. (See "Handling Error Messages" on page 318.)

When an app is running in the development server, sending an XMPP chat message or invitation causes the server to print the message to the console. The development server does not contact the XMPP service or send messages.

Each action is a method of an `XMPPService` object, which you get from `XMPPServiceFactory.getXMPPService()`. You send a message by calling the `sendMessage()` method. The method takes a `Message` object, which you build with a `MessageBuilder` object. `sendMessage()` returns a `SendResponse` object, which contains status codes for each intended recipient of the message:

```
import com.google.appengine.api.xmpp.JID;
import com.google.appengine.api.xmpp.Message;
import com.google.appengine.api.xmpp.MessageBuilder;
import com.google.appengine.api.xmpp.SendResponse;
import com.google.appengine.api.xmpp.XMPPService;
import com.google.appengine.api.xmpp.XMPPServiceFactory;

// ...
    XMPPService xmpp = XMPPServiceFactory.getXMPPService();

    JID recipient = new JID("juliet@example.com");
    Message message = new MessageBuilder()
        .withRecipientJids(recipient)
        .withBody("Your dog has reached level 12!")
        .build();

    SendResponse success = xmpp.sendMessage(message);
    if (success.getStatusMap().get(recipient)
        != SendResponse.Status.SUCCESS) {
        // ...
    }
```

You use the `MessageBuilder` class to assemble the (immutable) `Message` object. You can chain its methods to construct a complete message in a single statement. Relevant methods include:

withBody(String body)
> Sets the message body.

asXml(boolean asXml)
> Declares that the body contains a well-formed XML stanza (and not plain text).

*keep-together*withFromJid(JID jid)
> Sets the sender JID.

withRecipientJids(JID jid1, …)
> Adds one or more recipient JIDs.

withMessageType(MessageType type)
> Sets the message type.

build()
> Returns the finished `Message`.

Message types are represented by the `MessageType` enum: `MessageType.CHAT`, `MessageType.ERROR`, `MessageType.GROUPCHAT`, `MessageType.HEADLINE`, and `Message Type.NORMAL`.

The `sendMessage()` method returns a `SendResponse` object. Calling this object's `get StatusMap()` method returns a `Map<JID, SendResponse.Status>`, a map of recipient

JIDs to status codes. The possible status codes are `SendResponse.Status.SUCCESS`, `SendResponse.Status.INVALID_ID`, and `SendResponse.Status.OTHER_ERROR`.

Receiving Chat Messages

As with email, to receive incoming XMPP messages, you must first enable the feature by adding the XMPP inbound services to your app's configuration. Add a similar section to the *appengine-web.xml* file, anywhere inside the root element:

```
<inbound-services>
  <service>xmpp_message</service>
</inbound-services>
```

This is the same configuration list as the `mail` inbound service. If you're enabling both email and XMPP, you provide one list of inbound services with all the items.

Deploy your app, and confirm that incoming XMPP is enabled using the Cloud Console, under Application Settings. If your app does not appear to be receiving HTTP requests for incoming XMPP messages, check the Console and update the configuration if necessary.

The `xmpp_message` inbound service routes incoming XMPP messages of the types chat and normal to your app.

An app receives XMPP messages at several addresses. Messages sent to addresses of these forms are routed to the default version of the app:

   `app-id@appspot.com`

   `anything@app-id.appspotchat.com`

Messages sent to addresses of this form are routed to the specified version of the app, useful for testing:

   `anything@version.app-id.appspotmail.com`

Each message is delivered to the app as an HTTP POST request to a fixed URL path. Chat messages (both chat and normal) become POST requests to this URL path:

   `/_ah/xmpp/message/chat/`

(Unlike incoming email, the sender JID is not included in these URL paths.)

The body content of the HTTP POST request is a MIME multipart message, with a part for each field of the message:

`from`
   The sender's JID

`to`
   The app JID to which this message was sent

---

body
: The message body content (with characters as they were originally typed)

stanza
: The full XML stanza of the message, including the previous fields (with XML special characters escaped); useful for communicating with a custom client using XML

The API includes classes for parsing the request data into objects. (See the sections that follow.)

The development server console (*http://localhost:8080/_ah/admin/*) includes a feature for simulating incoming XMPP messages by submitting a web form. The development server cannot receive actual XMPP messages.

 When using the development server console to simulate an incoming XMPP message, you must use a valid JID for the app in the "To:" field, with the application ID that appears in the app's configuration. Using any other "To:" address in the development server is an error.

Receiving Chat Messages in Java

In Java, you process incoming XMPP messages by mapping a servlet to the URL path called by the XMPP service, in the deployment descriptor. You can restrict the URL path by using a `<security-constraint>` to ensure only the XMPP service can access it:

```
<servlet>
  <servlet-name>xmppreceiver</servlet-name>
  <servlet-class>myapp.XMPPReceiverServlet</servlet-class>
</servlet>
<servlet-mapping>
  <servlet-name>xmppreceiver</servlet-name>
  <url-pattern>/_ah/xmpp/message/chat/</url-pattern>
</servlet-mapping>

<security-constraint>
  <web-resource-collection>
    <url-pattern>/_ah/xmpp/message/chat/</url-pattern>
  </web-resource-collection>
  <auth-constraint>
    <role-name>admin</role-name>
  </auth-constraint>
</security-constraint>
```

The `XMPPService` object includes a `parseMessage()` method that knows how to parse the incoming request data into a `Message` object. You access the data by using the `Message`'s methods:

```
import java.io.IOException;
import javax.servlet.http.*;

import com.google.appengine.api.xmpp.Message;
import com.google.appengine.api.xmpp.XMPPService;
import com.google.appengine.api.xmpp.XMPPServiceFactory;

public class XMPPReceiverServlet extends HttpServlet {
    public void doPost(HttpServletRequest req,
                       HttpServletResponse resp)
            throws IOException {
        XMPPService xmpp = XMPPServiceFactory.getXMPPService();
        Message message = xmpp.parseMessage(req);
        // ...
    }
}
```

You access the fields of a `Message` using methods:

getFromJid()
: The sender JID

getMessageType()
: The `MessageType` of the message: `MessageType.CHAT` or `MessageType.NORMAL`

getRecipientJids()
: The app JID used, as a single-element JID[ ]

getBody()
: The `String` content of the message

getStanza()
: The `String` raw XML of the message

Handling Error Messages

When an app calls the XMPP service to send a message, the message is queued for delivery and sent asynchronously with the call. The call will only return with an error if the message the app is sending is malformed. If the app wants to know about an error during delivery of the message (such as the inability to connect to a remote server), or an error returned by the remote XMPP server (such as a nonexistent user), it can listen for error messages.

Error messages are just another type of chat message, but the XMPP service separates incoming error messages into a separate inbound service. To enable this service, add the `xmpp_error` inbound service to the app's *appengine-web.xml* configuration file:

```
<inbound-services>
  <service>xmpp_message</service>
  <service>xmpp_error</service>
</inbound-services>
```

Error messages arrive as POST requests at this URL path:

```
/_ah/xmpp/error/
```

You handle an error message just as you would a chat message: create a request handler, map it to the URL path, and parse the POST request for more information.

The API doesn't provide any assistance parsing incoming error messages. While XMPP error messages are similar in structure to chat messages (with a type of `error`), minor differences are not recognized by the message parsers provided. You can examine the XML data structure in the POST message body, which conforms to the XMPP message standard. (See the XMPP specification (*http://xmpp.org/*) for details.)

Managing Presence

After the user accepts an app's invitation to chat, both parties are able to see whether the other party is available to receive chat messages. In XMPP RFC 3921 (*http://xmpp.org/rfcs/rfc3921.html*), this is known as *presence*. The process of asking for and granting permission to see presence is called *subscription*. For privacy reasons, one user must be successfully subscribed to the other before she can send messages, see presence information, or otherwise know the user exists.

When a user accepts an app's invitation to chat (subscription request), the user's client sends a "subscribed" message to the app, to confirm that the app is now subscribed. If, later, the user revokes this permission, the client sends an "unsubscribed" message. While the app is subscribed to a user, the user's client will send all changes in presence to the app as another kind of message.

Conversely, a user can also send "subscribe" and "unsubscribe" messages to the app. It's the app's responsibility to maintain a list of subscribed users to use when sending presence updates.

If you'd like to receive these new message types (and be billed for the bandwidth), you must enable these as separate inbound services. Subscription information (invitation responses and subscription requests) use the `xmpp_subscribe` service, and presence updates use the `xmpp_presence` service.

Here's the configuration for *appengine-web.xml* that does enables all four XMPP inbound message types:

```
<inbound-services>
  <service>xmpp_message</service>
  <service>xmpp_error</service>
  <service>xmpp_subscribe</service>
  <service>xmpp_presence</service>
</inbound-services>
```

 If you want to know when a user accepts or revokes your app's chat invitation, but otherwise do not need to see the user's presence updates, you can enable the xmpp_subscribe service without the xmpp_presence service. This can save on costs associated with the incoming bandwidth of changes in the user's presence, which can be frequent.

As with chat messages, you can simulate incoming subscription and presence messages in the development server by using the development server console. Outgoing subscription and presence messages in the development server are logged to the console, but not actually sent.

Managing Subscriptions

An app subscribes to a user when it sends an invitation to chat, with the sendInvitation() method. An app cannot send an explicit "unsubscribe" message, only "subscribe."

When the user accepts the invitation, her chat client sends a subscribed message to the app. If the user later revokes the invitation, the client sends an unsubscribed message.

These messages arrive via the xmpp_subscribe inbound service as POST requests on the following URL paths:

```
/_ah/xmpp/subscription/subscribed/
/_ah/xmpp/subscription/unsubscribed/
```

A user can send an explicit subscription request (invitation to chat) to the app by sending a subscribe message. Similarly, the user can explicitly unsubscribe from presence updates by sending an unsubscribe message. These arrive at the following URL paths:

```
/_ah/xmpp/subscription/subscribe/
/_ah/xmpp/subscription/unsubscribe/
```

The subscription process typically happens just once in the lifetime of the relationship between two chat users. After the users are successfully subscribed, they remain subscribed until one party explicitly unsubscribes from the other (`unsubscribe`), or one party revokes the other party's invitation (`unsubscribed`).

If you intend for your app to have visible changes in presence, the app must maintain a roster of subscribers based on `subscribe` and `unsubscribe` messages, and send updates only to subscribed users.

Incoming subscription-related requests include form-style fields in the POST data, with the following fields:

`from`

> The sender's JID

`to`

> The app JID to which this message was sent

`stanza`

> The full XML stanza of the subscription message, including the previous fields

Because the POST data for these requests does not contain a body field, you cannot use the SDK's `Message` class to parse the data. You access these fields simply as POST form fields in the request.

The app gets the subscription command from the URL path.

As with chat messages, the `XMPPService` class includes a facility for parsing subscription messages out of the incoming HTTP request. The `parseSubscription()` method takes the `HttpServletRequest` and returns a `Subscription` object:

```
import com.google.appengine.api.xmpp.JID;
import com.google.appengine.api.xmpp.Subscription;
import com.google.appengine.api.xmpp.SubscriptionType;
import com.google.appengine.api.xmpp.XMPPService;
import com.google.appengine.api.xmpp.XMPPServiceFactory;

// ...
public class SubscriptionServlet extends HttpServlet {
    public void doPost(HttpServletRequest req,
                       HttpServletResponse resp)
        throws IOException, ServletException {

        XMPPService xmpp = XMPPServiceFactory.getXMPPService();
        Subscription sub = xmpp.parseSubscription(req);
        JID userJID = sub.getFromJid();

        if (sub.getSubscriptionType() == SubscriptionType.SUBSCRIBED) {
            // User accepted a chat invitation.
            // ...

        } else if (sub.getSubscriptionType() == SubscriptionType.UNSUBSCRIBED) {
```

```
            // User revoked a chat invitation.
            // ...

        } else if (sub.getSubscriptionType() == SubscriptionType.SUBSCRIBE) {
            // User wants presence updates from the app.
            // ...

        } else if (sub.getSubscriptionType() == SubscriptionType.UNSUBSCRIBE) {
            // User no longer wants presence updates from the app.
            // ...

        }
    }
}
```

You can access the fields of a `Subscription` message, using methods:

getFromJid()
> The sender's JID

getToJid()
> The app's recipient JID used in the message

getSubscriptionType()
> The type of the subscription message: `SubscriptionType.SUBSCRIBED`, `SubscriptionType.UNSUBSCRIBED`, `SubscriptionType.SUBSCRIBE`, or `SubscriptionType.UNSUBSCRIBE`

getStanza()
> The `String` raw XML of the message

An app sends a subscription request (`'subscribe'`) to a user by calling the `sendInvitation(jid)` method of the `XMPPService`. There is no way to send an `'unsubscribe'` message from an app. If the app no longer cares about a user's presence messages, the only choice is to ignore the incoming presence updates from that user.

Managing Presence Updates

While an app is subscribed to a user, the user sends changes in presence to the app. If the app is configured to receive inbound presence messages via the `xmpp_presence` service, these messages arrive as POST requests on one of these URL paths:

```
/_ah/xmpp/presence/available/
/_ah/xmpp/presence/unavailable/
```

Chat clients typically send an `available` message when connecting, and an `unavailable` message when disconnecting (or going "invisible").

A presence message can also contain additional status information: the *presence show* ("show me as") value and a *status message*. Most chat clients represent the show value as a colored dot or icon, and may display the status message as well. And of course, most chat clients allow the user to change the show value and the message. The possible show values, along with how they typically appear in chat clients, are as follows:

chat
> The user is available to chat. Green, "available."

away
> The user is away from her computer temporarily and not available to chat. Yellow, "away." A typical chat client switches to this presence show value automatically when the user is away from the keyboard.

dnd
> "Do not disturb": the user may be at her computer, but does not want to receive chat messages. Red, "busy."

xa
> "Extended away": the user is not available to chat and is away for an extended period. Red.

In XMPP, availability and the presence show value are distinct concepts. For a user to appear as "busy," the user must be available. For example, a red-colored "busy" user is available, with a show value of "dnd." Chat clients represent unavailable users either with a grey icon or by showing the user in another list.

An incoming presence update request includes form-style fields in the POST data, with the following fields:

`from`
> The sender's JID

`to`
> The app JID to which this message was sent

`show`
> One of several standard presence show values; if omitted, this implies the "chat" presence

`status`
> A custom status message; only present if the user has a custom status message set, or is changing her status message

`stanza`
> The full XML stanza of the subscription message, including the previous fields

An app can notify users of its own presence by sending a presence message. If the app's presence changes, it should attempt to send a presence message to every user known to be subscribed to the app. To support this, the app should listen for "subscribe" and "unsubscribe" messages, and keep a list of subscribed users, as described in "Managing Subscriptions" on page 320.

An app should also send a presence message to a user if it receives a *presence probe* message from that user. (See "Probing for Presence" on page 326.)

As with chat and subscription messages, the development server can simulate incoming presence messages. However, it cannot include presence show and status strings in these updates.

The XMPPService class can parse incoming presence update messages. The parsePresence() method takes the HttpServletRequest and returns a Presence object:

```java
import com.google.appengine.api.xmpp.JID;
import com.google.appengine.api.xmpp.Presence;
import com.google.appengine.api.xmpp.PresenceShow;
import com.google.appengine.api.xmpp.PresenceType;
import com.google.appengine.api.xmpp.XMPPService;
import com.google.appengine.api.xmpp.XMPPServiceFactory;

// ...
public class PresenceServlet extends HttpServlet {
    public void doPost(HttpServletRequest req,
                       HttpServletResponse resp)
        throws IOException, ServletException {

        XMPPService xmpp = XMPPServiceFactory.getXMPPService();
        Presence presence = xmpp.parsePresence(req);
        JID userJID = presence.getFromJid();

        if (presence.getPresenceType() == PresenceType.AVAILABLE) {
            // The user is available.

            PresenceShow show = presence.getPresenceShow();
            String status = presence.getStatus();
            // ...

        } else if (presence.getPresenceType() == PresenceType.UNAVAILABLE) {
            // The user is not available (disconnected).
            // ...

        }
    }
}
```

You can access the fields of a Presence message, using methods:

getFromJid()

The sender `JID`.

getToJid()

The app's recipient `JID` used in the message.

getPresenceType()

The type of the presence message: `PresenceType.AVAILABLE`, `Presence Type.UNAVAILABLE`, or `PresenceType.PROBE` (see later).

isAvailable()

A convenience method for testing whether the presence type is "available." Returns `true` or `false`.

getPresenceShow()

The presence show value: `PresenceShow.NONE`, `PresenceShow.AWAY`, `Presence Show.CHAT`, `PresenceShow.DND`, or `PresenceShow.XA`. This returns `null` if no value was present in the message.

getStatus()

A custom status message, if the user has one set.

getStanza()

The `String` raw XML of the message.

To send a presence update to a single user, call the `sendPresence()` method of the `XMPPService`:

```
xmpp.sendPresence(new JID("arthur@example.com"),
                  PresenceType.AVAILABLE,
                  PresenceShow.CHAT,
                  null);
```

This takes as arguments a `JID`, a `PresenceType`, a `PresenceShow`, and a `String` custom status message. You can set the show value or status message to `null` if no value is appropriate.

When the app wishes to broadcast a change in presence, it must call `sendPresence()` once for each user currently subscribed to the app. Unlike `sendMessage()`, you can't pass a list of JIDs to `sendPresence()` to send many updates in one API call. A best practice is to use task queues to query your data for subscribed users and send presence updates in batches. (See Chapter 16 for more information on task queues.)

Probing for Presence

Chat services broadcast presence updates to subscribed users as a user's presence changes. But this is only useful while the subscribed users are online. When a user comes online after a period of being disconnected (such as if her computer was turned off or not on the Internet), the user's client must *probe* the users in her contact list to get updated presence information.

When a user sends a probe to an app, it comes in via the xmpp_presence inbound service, as a POST request to this URL path:

    /_ah/xmpp/presence/probe/

The POST data contains the following fields:

from
> The sender's JID

to
> The app JID to which this message was sent

stanza
> The full XML stanza of the subscription message, including the previous fields

If your app receives this message, it should respond immediately by sending a presence update just to that user.

An app can send a presence probe message to a user. If the app is subscribed to the user, the user will send a presence message to the app in the usual way.

In the development server, outgoing probe messages are logged to the console, and not actually sent. There is currently no way to simulate an incoming probe message in the development server console.

An incoming presence probe message is just another type of Presence message. You can map a separate servlet to the /_ah/xmpp/presence/probe/ URL path, or just test the PresenceType of the parsed message in a servlet that handles all /_ah/xmpp/presence/* requests:

```
XMPPService xmpp = XMPPServiceFactory.getXMPPService();
Presence presence = xmpp.parsePresence(req);
JID userJID = presence.getFromJid();

if (presence.getPresenceType() == PresenceType.PROBE) {
    xmpp.sendPresence(userJID,
                      PresenceType.AVAILABLE,
                      PresenceShow.CHAT,
                      null);
}
```

Similarly, to send a presence probe to a user, you call the sendPresence() method with a presence type of PresenceType.PROBE:

```
xmpp.sendPresence(jid, PresenceType.PROBE, null, null);
```

The reply comes back as a presence update message.

CHAPTER 16

Task Queues and Scheduled Tasks

The App Engine architecture is well suited for handling web requests, small amounts of work that run in a stateless environment with the intent of returning a response to the user as fast as possible. But many web applications have other kinds of work that need to get done, work that doesn't fit in the fast response model. Instead of doing the work while the user waits, it's often acceptable to record what work needs to get done, respond to the user right away, then do the work later, within seconds or minutes. The ability to make this trade-off is especially useful with scalable web applications that use a read-optimized datastore, because updating an element of data may require several related but time-consuming updates, and it may not be essential for those updates to happen right away.

Consider a simple example. You're the leader of your guild, and you're scheduling a raid on the Lair of the Basilisk for next Thursday. When you post the invitation, two things need to happen: the raid is recorded on the guild calendar, and an invitation is sent to each member of the guild by email. If the app tries to do all of this in a single request handler, you might be staring at the browser's spinning wheel for a while as the app calls the Mail API for each member of the guild. For a particularly large guild, the request handler might not even finish within 60 seconds, you'll see a server error, and only some members will see the invitation. How do we fix this?

What we need is a way to do work outside of a user-facing request handler. By "outside," we mean code that is run separately from the code that evaluates a request from a user and returns a response to the user. This work can run in parallel to the user-facing request handler, or after the request handler has returned a response, or completely independently of user requests. We also need a way to request that this work be done.

App Engine has two major mechanisms for initiating this kind of work: *task queues* and *scheduled tasks*. A *task* is simply a request that a unit of work be performed separately from the code requesting the task. Any application code can call the task queue service to request a task, and the task queue manages the process of driving the task to completion. Scheduled tasks are tasks that are invoked on a schedule that you define in a configuration file, separately from any application code or queue (although a scheduled task is welcome to add other tasks to a queue, as is any other task running on App Engine).

In the terminology of task queues, a *producer* is a process that requests that work be done. The producer *enqueues* a task that represents the work onto a queue. A *consumer* is a process, separate from the producer, that *leases* tasks on the queue that it intends to perform. If the consumer performs a task successfully, it deletes the task from the queue so no other consumer tries to perform it. If the consumer fails to delete the task, the queue assumes the task was not completed successfully, and after an amount of time, the lease expires and becomes available again to other consumers. A consumer may also explicitly revoke the lease if it can't perform the task.

Task queues are a general category for two mechanisms for driving work to completion: *push queues* and *pull queues*. With push queues, App Engine is the consumer: it executes tasks on the queues at configurable rates, and retries tasks that return a failure code. With pull queues, you provide the consumer mechanism that leases task records off of a queue, does the work they represent, and then deletes them from the queue. Your custom mechanism can run on App Engine, or it can run on your own infrastructure and pull tasks, using a REST API.

To perform a task on a push queue, App Engine does what it does best: it invokes a request handler! You can configure a URL path in your app per queue, or specify a specific URL path when you enqueue a task. To implement the task, you simply implement a request handler for requests sent to that URL. Naturally, you can secure these URLs against outside requests, so only tasks can trigger that logic. This is why we've been making a distinction between "user-facing" request handlers and other handlers. All code on App Engine runs in a request handler, and typically code for handling user requests is distinct from code for performing tasks.

Scheduled tasks also run on App Engine, and also use request handlers. You configure a schedule of URL paths and times, and App Engine calls your application at those URL paths at the requested times. Scheduled tasks are not retried to completion, but you can achieve this effect by having a scheduled task enqueue a task on a queue.

All of these mechanisms support a major design goal for App Engine applications: do as much work outside of user-facing requests as possible, so user-facing requests are as fast as possible. Task queues allow your code to request that work be done separately from the current unit of work. Scheduled tasks initiate computation on a predefined schedule, independently of other code. The results of this work can be stored in the datastore, memcache, and Cloud Storage, so user-facing request handlers can retrieve and serve it quickly, without doing the work itself.

Enqueueing a task is fast, about three times faster than writing to the datastore. This makes tasks useful for pretty much anything whose success or failure doesn't need to be reported to the user in the response to the user request that initiates the work. For example, an app can write a value to the memcache, then enqueue a task to persist that value to the datastore. This saves time during the user request, and allows the task to do bookkeeping or make other time-consuming updates based on the change (assuming it meets the application's needs that the bookkeeping happens later than the initial update).

App Engine invokes a request handler for a push queue task or scheduled task in the same environment as it does a handler for a user request, with a few minor differences. Most notably, a task handler can run continuously for up to 10 minutes, instead of 60 seconds for user-facing request handlers. In some cases, it can be better to implement task handlers with short running times, then split a batch of work over multiple tasks, so the tasks can be executed in parallel with multiple instances. But 10 minutes of headroom let you simplify your code for work that can or must take its time on an instance.

Figure 16-1 illustrates how task queues and scheduled tasks take advantage of the request handler infrastructure.

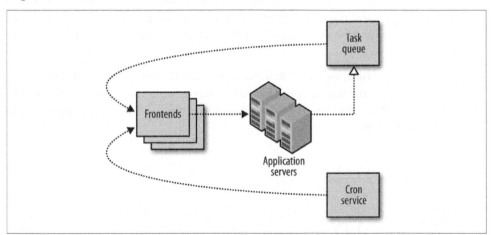

Figure 16-1. Architecture of push queues and scheduled tasks ("cron")

The development server maintains push and pull queues, and can run push queues in the background and simulate their timing and throttling behaviors. Of course, it won't be as fast as running on App Engine, but it's enough to test the behavior. You can use the development server console to inspect the configured queues, check their contents, and delete individual tasks or all tasks on a queue ("Purge Queue"). With push queues, you can also force a task to run from the console.

Basilisk raid invitations are now easy. When you submit the raid event creation form, a single request handler stores the event information in the datastore, initiates a task, then returns a success code. Later, possibly mere seconds later, App Engine pops the task off the task queue and calls the "send email" handler. This task can run for up to 10 minutes, so it can just iterate over all of the guild members and send an email for each one. If there are so many members that 10 minutes isn't enough, the handler can enqueue another task, storing a datastore query cursor with the task data to mark where it left off. Everyone shows up, and the raid is a smashing success.

Task queues are an important part of App Engine, with several powerful features for structuring your work and optimizing your application's behavior. Not the least of these features is how task queues integrate with the App Engine datastore transactions. In this chapter, we describe the concepts of task queues and scheduled tasks, and how to use them in applications. We take a brief look at pull queues and consider how they are useful. We cover using tasks and datastore transactions to achieve special effects, especially eventually consistent data operations and task chaining. And finally, we review the queue-related features of the Cloud Console.

Configuring Task Queues

Every app has one default push queue with default settings. You can use a configuration file to change the settings of the default push queue, create new named push and pull queues each with their own settings, and set global parameters for task queues in general.

To configure task queues, create a file named *queue.xml* in your *war/WEB-INF/* directory. This is an XML file whose root element is `<queue-entries>`. Here is an example file that updates the rate of the default queue, and defines a new named push queue with its own configuration:

```
<queue-entries>
  <queue>
    <name>default</name>
    <rate>10/s</rate>
  </queue>
  <queue>
    <name>attack_effects</name>
    <rate>100/s</rate>
    <bucket-size>20</bucket-size>
  </queue>
</queue-entries>
```

(We'll see what these settings do in a moment.)

Task queues contain durable data, and this storage counts toward your billable storage quota, just like data in the datastore. You can set a total limit for the amount of task queue data to store with configuration. In *queue.xml*, this setting is named `total-storage-limit`:

```
<queue-entries>
  <total-storage-limit>200M</total-storage-limit>

  <!-- ... -->
</queue-entries>
```

Its value is a number followed by a unit of storage measurement, such as M for megabytes, G for gigabytes, or T for terabytes.

The default mode for a queue is to be a push queue. To declare a queue a pull queue, you set the `mode` of the queue to `pull`:

```
<queue-entries>
  <queue>
    <name>process_images</name>
    <mode>pull</mode>
  </queue>
</queue-entries>
```

We'll mention additional configuration options when we discuss push queues and pull queues in more detail.

Task queue configuration is uploaded when you deploy your application. You can upload new task queue configuration separately from the rest of your app with the AppCfg tool's `update_queues` command:

```
appcfg update_queues appdir
```

 Task queue configuration is distinct from application configuration (*appengine-web.xml*), and is kept in a separate file. Unlike application configuration, task queue configuration modifies the behavior of task queues for the entire application. All application versions use the same task queue configuration.

Enqueuing a Task

Your app adds a task to a queue (it *enqueues* the task) by calling the task queue service API with appropriate arguments. Some arguments are specific to push queues or pull queues, but the main API is the same for both.

The task queue API is provided by the `com.google.appengine.api.taskqueue` package. You manipulate a queue via a `Queue` instance, which you get from the

QueueFactory static methods getDefaultQueue(), which returns the default queue, and getQueue(name), which returns the queue of the given name:

```
import com.google.appengine.api.taskqueue.Queue;
import com.google.appengine.api.taskqueue.QueueFactory;

// ...
        Queue defaultQueue = QueueFactory.getDefaultQueue();
        Queue queue = QueueFactory.getQueue("reward_players");
```

To add a task to a queue, you call its add() method. With no arguments, add() puts a task onto the queue with default options. add() returns a TaskHandle, which describes the task just added, including fields filled in by the system (such as get QueueName()):

```
        TaskHandle handle = defaultQueue.add();
```

The default queue is a push queue, so App Engine will process this task by invoking a request handler at a URL path. The default URL path for the default queue is:

```
/_ah/queue/default
```

If you need them, the default queue name and URL path are available as the constants Queue.DEFAULT_QUEUE and Queue.DEFAULT_QUEUE_PATH.

You map a servlet to the URL in the usual way, with *web.xml*. You can restrict access to the URL so that only App Engine can call it (and outsiders can't), using a security-constraint with the admin role:

```
<servlet>
  <servlet-name>defaultqueue</servlet-name>
  <servlet-class>app.DefaultQueueServlet</servlet-class>
</servlet>
<servlet-mapping>
  <servlet-name>defaultqueue</servlet-name>
  <url-pattern>/_ah/queue/default</url-pattern>
</servlet-mapping>

<security-constraint>
  <web-resource-collection>
    <web-resource-name>defaultqueue</web-resource-name>
    <url-pattern>/_ah/queue/default</url-pattern>
  </web-resource-collection>
  <auth-constraint>
    <role-name>admin</role-name>
  </auth-constraint>
</security-constraint>
```

Adding an empty task record to a queue can be quite useful, as the task handler can do anything you want. You can further control the behavior of the task and how it interacts with the queue, using options. To set options for a task, you build and pass a TaskOptions instance to the add() method. This is a Builder-based API, where you can start a new instance with a static method and chain additional options to the same statement. `TaskOptions.Builder.withDefaults()` returns a `TaskOptions` with all default settings, which is useful in cases where a `TaskOptions` is required but no options need to be changed. (`add()` with no arguments is equivalent to `add(TaskOptions.Builder.withDefaults())`.)

```
queue.add(TaskOptions.Builder
    .withParam("player_id", playerId)
    .param("achievement", "paid_in_full"));
```

We'll discuss some of the available options in the next section and elsewhere in this chapter.

You can add multiple tasks to a single queue in a single service call (a batch call) by passing an `Iterable<TaskOptions>`. This form of the method returns a `List<TaskHandle>`, whose members correspond directly with the inputs:

```
TaskOptions t1, t2, t3;
// ...

List<TaskHandle> handle = queue.add(Arrays.asList(t1, t2, t3));
```

 Tasks are routed and handled by the app like any other request. If you want a task queue task (or cron job) to be processed by a module other than the default module, use a *dispatch.xml* file to route requests for a URL path to the module, then assign that URL to the tasks. (Refer back to Chapter 5.)

Task Parameters

A task record on a queue carries two kinds of parameters: parameters that are passed on to the code or system performing the task, and parameters that affect how the task is managed on the queue. You set these parameters when you enqueue the task. After the task is enqueued, the parameters can't be changed, although you can delete and re-create a task, as needed.

The following sections describe task parameters common to both push queues and pull queues. We'll look at mode-specific options later.

Payloads

A task's *payload* is a set of data intended for the system performing the task. You don't need a payload if the task handler already knows what to do, but it's useful to write task handling code in a general way, and parameterize its behavior with a payload.

For example, you could have a task that performs a transformation on a datastore entity, such as to update its property layout to a new schema. The task handler would take the ID of an entity to transform, and perform one transformation. You'd then have a process (possibly also managed with task queues) that traverses all the entities that need transformation with a datastore query, and it creates a task for each entity, using the task handler and a payload.

For convenience, the task API has two ways to set a payload: as a byte string, or as a set of named parameters with byte string values. When you set a payload as a set of parameters, the data is formatted like a web form (`application/x-www-form-urlencoded`), so the task handler can parse the payload into parameters, using typical web request handling code. Payloads and parameters are mutually exclusive: you set one or the other, not both.

You set a payload for a task by using the `payload()` method or the `param()` method of `TaskOptions`, or the corresponding starter methods `withPayload()` or `withParam()` of the `TaskOptions.Builder` class. `payload()` sets or overrides the payload. `param()` sets a named parameter, and can be called multiple times in a builder chain to set multiple parameters. A payload or parameter value can be a `String` or a `byte[]`:

```
// byte[] imgData = ...;
queue.add(TaskOptions.Builder.withPayload(imgData));

queue.add(TaskOptions.Builder
        .withParam("entity_key", KeyFactory.keyToString(entity.getKey()))
        .param("version", "7"));
```

The `payload(byte[])` form can take an optional second argument to specify the MIME content type of the data. The `payload(String)` form can take an optional second argument to specify a character set. These arguments affect how the payload is converted into an HTTP request when managed by a push queue.

Task Names

Every task has a unique name. By default, App Engine will generate a unique name for a task when it is added to a queue. You can also set the task name in the app. A task name can be up to 500 characters, and can contain letters, numbers, underscores, and hyphens.

If an app sets the name for a task and another task already exists for that name on a given queue, the API will raise an exception when the app adds the task to the queue. Task names prevent the app from enqueuing the same task more than once on the same queue. App Engine remembers in-use task names for a period of time after the task completes, on the order of days. (The remembered names are called *tombstones* or *tombstoned tasks*.)

This is especially useful when enqueuing a task from within a push task handler. Consider the datastore entity transformation example again. A master task performs a datastore query, then creates a transformation task for each entity in the results, like so:

```
import com.google.appengine.api.taskqueue.Queue;
import com.google.appengine.api.taskqueue.QueueFactory;
import com.google.appengine.api.taskqueue.TaskOptions;

// ...
    public void doPost(HttpServletRequest req, HttpServletResponse resp)
        throws IOException, ServletException {
        DatastoreService datastore =
            DatastoreServiceFactory.getDatastoreService();
        Queue taskQueue = QueueFactory.getDefaultQueue();
        for (Entity entity :
            datastore.prepare(new Query("MyKind")).asQueryResultIterable()) {
                taskQueue.add(TaskOptions.Builder
                    .withParam("entity_key",
                            KeyFactory.keyToString(entity.getKey()))
                    .param("version", Integer.valueOf(7).toString()));
        }
    }
```

If there is a datastore error while the master task is fetching results, the datastore raises an exception, which bubbles up, and the request handler returns an HTTP 500 server error. The push queue sees the error, then retries the master task from the beginning. If the first run of the master task successfully enqueued some tasks for entities to the 'upgrade' queue, those entities will be added to the queue again, wasting work.

The master task handler can guard against this by using a task name for each task that uniquely represents the work. In the preceding example, a good task name might be the entity's key concatenated with the upgrade version (the two parameters to the task):

```
String taskName = KeyFactory.keyToString(entity.getKey()) + "7";
taskName = taskName.replaceAll("[^a-zA-Z0-9_-]", "_");
taskQueue.add(TaskOptions.Builder
    .withTaskName(taskName)
    .param("entity_key", KeyFactory.keyToString(entity.getKey()))
    .param("version", "7"));
```

 Take care when using datastore keys, query cursors, and other values as parts of task names that the resulting name meets the requirements of task names. A task name can contain letters, numbers, underscores, and hyphens. Base64-encoded values (such as string-ified datastore keys) use this alphabet, but may use equal-sign (=) characters for padding. The preceding examples use a regular expression to substitute characters outside of this alphabet with underscores.

Countdowns and ETAs

By default, a task is made available to run immediately. A push queue can execute an available task whenever it is ready (subject to its rate limiting configuration, which we'll see later). The consumer of a pull queue sees only available tasks when it requests a lease.

You can delay the availability of a task when you add it, so it doesn't become available until a later time. You specify this as either a number of seconds into the future from the time of the enqueue operation (a countdown), or an explicit date and time in the future (an earliest time of availability, or ETA). Delaying the availability of a task can be a useful way to slow down a complex multistage process, such as to avoid hitting a remote server too often.

To use these features, you use the countdownMillis() (withCountdownMillis()) or etaMillis() (withEtaMillis()) builder methods with TaskOptions. countdownMillis() takes a number of milliseconds in the future. etaMillis() takes a date and time in the future, as a Unix epoch date-time in milliseconds:

```
// Execute no earlier than 5 seconds from now.
queue.add(TaskOptions.Builder
    .withParam("url", nextUrl)
    .countdownMillis(5000));

// Execute no earlier than December 31, 2012, midnight Pacific Time.
queue.add(TaskOptions.Builder
    .withParam("url", nextUrl)
    .etaMillis(1356940800000L));
```

 Countdowns and ETAs specify the earliest time the task will be available, not the exact time the task will be performed. Do not rely on ETAs as exact timers.

Push Queues

Push queues are queues of tasks that are performed automatically by App Engine at a configurable rate. App Engine performs a task by invoking a request handler of your app. It forms an HTTP request based on the contents of the task record, and issues the request to a URL path associated with the task. App Engine uses the HTTP status code of the response to decide whether the task was completed successfully and should be deleted from the queue. Unsuccessful tasks are retried again later.

Because tasks on push queues are just requests to your app, they use the same infrastructure as any other request handler. You implement tasks by implementing request handlers mapped to URLs, using your web application framework of choice. Tasks are executed in threads of instances, and use the same automatic scaling mechanism as user requests. A queue with multiple tasks will distribute the tasks to multiple threads and instances to be performed in parallel, based on the availability of instances and the processing rate of the queue.

You can control aspects of the HTTP request for a task by setting task options. You can also configure aspects of how push queues process tasks, and how tasks are retried.

Task Requests

You can set various aspects of the HTTP request issued for a task using task options, including the URL, the HTTP method, and request headers. The payload for the task also becomes part of the request, depending on the method.

By default, the URL path for a task is based on the queue name, in this format:

```
/_ah/queue/queue_name
```

You can override the URL path for an individual task. This is the `url()` (`withUrl()`) builder method on `TaskOptions`:

```
queue.add(TaskOptions.Builder
    .withUrl("/admin/tasks/persist_scores"));
```

If there is no request handler mapped to the URL for a task (or the task's queue, if no custom URL is specified), the invocation of the task will return a 404 status code. This is interpreted by the push queue as task failure, and the task is added back to the queue to be retried. You can delete these tasks by flushing the queue in the Cloud Console, or by pushing a software version that supplies a successful handler for the task URL.

By default, the HTTP request uses the POST method. You can change this with the `method()` (`withMethod()`) `TaskOptions` builder method, which takes a value from the `TaskOptions.Method` enum: `GET`, `POST`, `PUT`, `PULL`, `HEAD`, or `DELETE`.

You can set HTTP headers on the task's request. You can set an individual header with the `header()` (`withHeader()`) builder method of `TaskOptions`, passing it a string name and a string value. Alternatively, you can set multiple headers in one call with the `headers()` (`withHeaders()`) builder method, which takes a `Map<String, String>`.

Task queues have special behavior with regard to app versions. If the version of the app that enqueued a task was the default version, then the task uses the default version of the app when it executes—even if the default version has changed since the task was enqueued. If the version of the app that enqueued the task was not the default version at the time, then the task uses that version specifically when it executes. This allows you to test nondefault versions that use tasks before making them the default.

App Engine adds the following headers to the request automatically when invoking the request handler, so the handler can identify the task record:

X-AppEngine-QueueName
> The name of the queue issuing the task request

X-AppEngine-TaskName
> The name of the task, either assigned by the app or assigned by the system

X-AppEngine-TaskRetryCount
> The number of times this task has been retried

X-AppEngine-TaskETA
> The time this task became available, as the number of microseconds since January 1, 1970; this is set when the app specifies a countdown or an ETA, or if the task was retried with a delay

Incoming requests from outside App Engine are not allowed to set these headers, so a request handler can test for these headers to confirm the request is from a task queue.

Task requests are considered to be from an administrator user for the purposes of the URL access control in *web.xml*. You can restrict task URLs to be administrator-only, and then only task queues (and actual app administrators) can issue requests to the URL.

The body of a response from a task's request handler is ignored. If the task needs to store or communicate information, it must do so by using the appropriate services or by logging messages.

A call to a task handler appears in the request log, just like a user-initiated web request. You can monitor and analyze the performance of tasks just as you would user requests.

Processing Rates and Token Buckets

The processing rate for a queue is controlled using a "token bucket" algorithm. In this algorithm, a queue has a number of "tokens," and it spends a token for each task it executes. Tokens are replenished at a steady rate up to a maximum number of tokens (the "bucket size"). Both the replenishment rate and the bucket size are configurable for a queue.

If a queue contains a task and has a token, it usually executes the task immediately. If a queue has many tasks and many available tokens, it executes as many tasks as it can afford, immediately and in parallel. If there are tasks remaining, the queue must wait until a token is replenished before executing the next task. The token bucket algorithm gives a queue the flexibility to handle bursts of new tasks, while still remaining within acceptable limits. The larger the bucket, the more tasks an idle queue will execute immediately when the tasks are enqueued all at once.

I say it *usually* executes the tasks immediately because App Engine may adjust the method and rate of how it executes tasks based on the performance of the system. In general, task queue schedules are approximate, and may vary as App Engine balances resources.

A queue does not wait for one task to finish before executing the next task. Instead, it initiates the next task as soon as a token is available, in parallel with any currently running tasks. Tasks are not strictly ordered, but App Engine makes an effort to perform tasks in the order they are enqueued. Tasks must not rely on being executed serially or in a specific order.

Each task queue has a name and processing rate (token replenishment rate and bucket size). Every app has a queue named `default` that processes 5 tasks per second, with a bucket size of 5. If you don't specify a queue name when enqueueing a task, the task is added to the default queue. You can adjust the rate and bucket size of the default queue, and can set the rate to 0 to turn it off. Tasks enqueued to a paused queue remain on the queue until you upload the new configuration with a positive rate.

Task queues and token buckets help you control how tasks are executed so you can plan for maximizing throughput, making the most efficient use of system resources to execute tasks in parallel. Tasks inevitably share resources, even if the resource is just the pool of warmed-up application servers. Executing a bunch of tasks simultaneously may not be the fastest way to complete all the tasks, because App Engine may need to start up new instances of the application to handle the sudden load. If multiple tasks operate on the same entity groups in the datastore, it may be faster to perform only a few tasks at a time and let datastore retries sort out contention, instead of relying on task retries to drive in all the changes. Limiting the execution rate with token buckets can actually result in faster completion of multiple tasks.

Queue processing rates are configured using the queue configuration file (*queue.xml*). You specify the rate of bucket replenishment using the `rate` option for a queue. Its value is a number, a slash (/), and a unit of time (s for seconds), such as `20/s` for 20 tokens per second.

You specify the size of the token bucket with the `bucket-size` element. Its value is a number:

```
<queue-entries>
  <queue>
```

```
    <name>fast_queue</name>
    <rate>20/s</rate>
    <bucket-size>10</bucket-size>
  </queue>
</queue-entries>
```

In addition to the rate and bucket size, you can set a maximum number of tasks from the queue that can be executed at the same time, with the `max-concurrent-requests` option. Its value is the number of tasks. If this many task requests are in progress, the queue will wait to issue another task even if there are tokens in the bucket. This allows for large bucket sizes but still prevents bursts of new tasks from flooding instances. It also accommodates tasks that take a variable amount of time, so slow tasks don't take over your instances.

Together, these options control the flow of tasks from the push queue into the request queue for the application. If a given queue is processing tasks too quickly, you can upload a new temporary configuration for the queue that tells it to run at a slower rate, and the change will take effect immediately. You can experiment with different rates and token bucket sizes to improve task throughput.

Retrying Push Tasks

To ensure that tasks get completed in a way that is robust against system failure, a task queue will retry a task until it is satisfied the task is complete.

A push queue retries a task if the request handler it invokes returns an HTTP response with a status code other than a "success" code (in the range 200–299). It retries the task by putting it back on the queue with a countdown, so it'll wait a bit before trying again in the hopes that the error condition will subside. You can configure the retry behavior for every queue in a task by using the queue configuration, and you can override this configuration on a per-task basis with task options.

Under very rare circumstances, such as after a system failure, a task may be retried even if it completed successfully. This is a design trade-off that favors fast task creation over built-in, once-only fault tolerance. A task that can be repeated without changing the end result is called *idempotent*. Whether a task's code must be strictly idempotent depends on what the task is doing and how important it is that the calculation it is performing be accurate. For instance, a task that deletes a datastore entity can be retried because the second delete fails harmlessly.

Because a task on a push queue is retried when its handler returns anything other than a successful HTTP status code, a buggy handler that always returns an error for a given input will be retried indefinitely, or until the retry limit is reached if a retry limit was specified.

If a task needs to abort without retrying, it must return a success code.

There are five parameters that control how push queues retry a given task. We'll define these parameters first. Then we'll see how to set defaults for these parameters in queue configuration, and how to override them for a specific task.

The `task-retry-limit` is the maximum number of times a failing task is retried before it is deleted from the queue. If you do not specify a retry limit, the task is retried indefinitely, or until you flush the cache or delete the task by some other means. A retry limit is a good guard against perpetual failure (such as a bug in a task), and in some cases it makes sense to abort a task in transient but long-lasting failure conditions. Be sure to set it high enough so that tasks can accommodate brief transient failures, which are to be expected in large distributed systems.

The `task-age-limit` calls for automatic deletion of an incomplete task after a period of time on the queue. If not specified, the task lives until it succeeds, hits its retry limit, or is deleted by other means. Its value is a number followed by a unit of time: s for seconds, m for minutes, h for hours, d for days. For example, 3d is three days.

When a task fails, it is added back to the queue with a countdown. The duration of this countdown doubles each time the task is retried, a method called *exponential backoff*. (The queue is "backing off" the failing task by trying it less frequently with each failure.) Three settings control the backoff behavior. `min-backoff-seconds` is the minimum countdown, the countdown of the first retry. `max-backoff-seconds` is the maximum; retries will increase the countdown up to this amount. These values are an amount of time, as a number of seconds. Finally, the `max_doublings` setting lets you set the number of times the countdown doubles. After that many retries, the countdown stays constant for each subsequent retry.

To set any of these retry options as the default for all tasks added to a queue, you add them to the queue configuration file, in a `retry-parameters` subsection of the queue's configuration. Here's an example of retry configuration in *queue.xml*:

```
<queue-entries>
  <queue>
    <name>respawn_health</name>
    <rate>2/s</rate>
    <retry-parameters>
      <task-retry-limit>10</task-retry-limit>
      <max-doublings>3</max-doublings>
```

```
          </retry-parameters>
        </queue>
  </queue-entries>
```

To override these settings for a task, you call the `TaskOptions` builder method `retryOptions()` (`withRetryOptions()`), which takes an instance of the `RetryOptions` class. This class also uses the builder pattern with methods for each setting: `taskRetryLimit()`, `taskAgeLimitSeconds()`, `minBackoffSeconds()`, `maxBackoffSeconds()`, and `maxDoublings()` (and their `withXXX()` starter equivalents):

```
Queue queue = QueueFactory.getQueue("respawn_health");
queue.add(TaskOptions.Builder.withRetryOptions(
    RetryOptions.Builder
        .withTaskRetryLimit(10)
        .maxDoublings(3)));
```

Pull Queues

In our initial definition of a task queue, we said that a queue has a producer and a consumer. With push queues, the producer is application code running in an App Engine request handler, and the consumer is the App Engine push queue mechanism, which calls request handlers to do the actual work of the task. With pull queues, you provide the consumer logic. The consumer calls the pull queue to lease one or more tasks, and the queue ensures that a task is leased to only one consumer at a time. Typically, the consumer deletes the task from the queue after performing the corresponding work, so no other consumer sees it. If the consumer fails to delete it, eventually the lease expires and the pull queue makes the task available to consumers again.

A pull queue is useful when you want to customize the consumer logic. For example, the push queue driver consumes one task at a time, executing a separate request handler for each task. With a pull queue, a custom consumer can lease multiple related tasks at once, and perform them together as a batch. This might be faster or more productive than doing it one at a time. For example, each task might represent an update to an entity group in the datastore. If a pull queue consumer sees multiple updates in the queue, it can lease them all in a batch, and make a single transactional update to the entity group for all of them. This is likely to be faster than multiple push queue tasks each trying to make their own transactional update to the same data.

You can build pull queue consumers on App Engine, using request handlers (such as a scheduled task that processes the queue periodically), or using a long-running process on a backend that polls for new tasks on a recurring basis. You can also build a consumer that runs on a remote system, using the task queue web service REST API. With a remote consumer, your app can enqueue tasks that trigger behavior in separate systems. The REST API also allows you to build remote producers that add tasks to pull queues. (A remote producer can't add to push queues directly, but a local con-

---

sumer running on App Engine could periodically convert remotely added tasks to push queue tasks.)

To create a pull queue, you add it to the queue configuration file. A pull queue must have a name, and must have its mode set to pull. In *queue.xml*:

```
<queue-entries>
  <queue>
    <name>update_leaderboard</name>
    <mode>pull</mode>
  </queue>
</queue-entries>
```

Enqueuing Tasks to Pull Queues

You enqueue a task on a pull queue similarly to how you enqueue a task on a push queue, using a named queue whose mode is pull. As with push queues, a task on a pull queue can have a payload, a task name, and a countdown or ETA.

A task added to a pull queue must have a method set to PULL. This tells the queue that the task is only compatible with the queue when it is in the pull queue mode. You call the method() (withMethod()) builder method on TaskOptions with the value TaskOptions.Method.PULL:

```
Queue queue = QueueFactory.getQueue("update_leaderboard");
queue.add(TaskOptions.Builder
    .withMethod(TaskOptions.Method.PULL));
```

Leasing and Deleting Tasks

A pull queue consumer running on App Engine can use the task queue service API to lease and delete tasks.

A lease is a guarantee that the consumer that acquired the lease has exclusive access to a task for a period of time. During that time, the consumer can do whatever work corresponds with that task record. The consumer is expected to delete the task at the end.

To lease tasks from a pull queue, you call a method of the queue specifying the duration of the lease and the maximum number of tasks. The service reserves up to that many tasks currently available on the queue for the requested amount of time, then returns identifiers for each of the successfully leased tasks. You can use these identifiers to delete the tasks, or update leases.

You construct the Queue object for the named pull queue, then call the leaseTasks() method. This method takes a LeaseOptions instance, built from LeaseOptions.Builder builder methods. The leasePeriod() (withLeasePeriod()) builder method takes a long and a java.util.concurrent.TimeUnit, which together specify the duration of the lease. The countLimit() (withCountLimit()) builder method sets the maximum number of tasks to lease. leaseTasks() returns a List<TaskHandle>, which may be empty:

```
import java.util.concurrent.TimeUnit;

// ...
        // Lease 5 tasks from update_leaderboard for up to 20 seconds.
        Queue queue = QueueFactory.getQueue("update_leaderboard");
        List<TaskHandle> tasks = queue.leaseTasks(
            LeaseOptions.Builder
                .withLeasePeriod(20, TimeUnit.SECONDS)
                .countLimit(5));

        for (TaskHandle task : tasks) {
            // Read task.getPayload() and do the corresponding work...
        }
```

Once the consumer has executed the work for a task successfully, it must delete the task to prevent it from being re-leased to another consumer. You call the delete Task() method of the Queue. The single-task form takes either a TaskHandle or a String task name, and returns true on success. The batch form takes a List<TaskHandle>, and returns a corresponding List<Boolean>:

```
// ...
List<Boolean> success = queue.deleteTask(tasks);
```

 Each of the examples shown here leases a batch of tasks, does the work for all the tasks, and then deletes them all with another batch call. When using this pattern, make sure the lease duration is long enough to accommodate all the work in the batch. Even if you delete each task as it finishes, the last task must wait for all of the others.

If the consumer needs more time, you can renew the lease without relinquishing it to another consumer. The Queue method modifyTaskLease() takes a TaskHandle, a long, and a TimeUnit, and returns the new TaskHandle.

Retrying Pull Queue Tasks

When a lease duration on a task expires, the task becomes available on the pull queue. When another consumer leases tasks from the queue, it may obtain a lease on the task and start the work again. This is the pull queue equivalent of a "retry": if the first consumer failed to delete the task before the lease expired, then the task is assumed to have failed and needs to be tried again.

You can set a limit to the number of times a task is retried. This can be a default for all tasks added to a queue, in the queue configuration. You can also set this for an individual task, overriding the queue default. If the lease for a task is allowed to expire as many times as the limit for the task, the task is deleted automatically.

To configure a retry limit for a queue in *queue.xml,* you provide a retry-parameters element in the queue's configuration, with a task-retry-limit value:

```
<queue-entries>
  <queue>
    <name>update_leaderboard</name>
    <retry-parameters>
      <task-retry-limit>10</task-retry-limit>
    </retry-parameters>
  </queue>
</queue-entries>
```

To set the limit for an individual task, call the TaskOptions builder method retryOptions() (withRetryOptions()), which takes an instance of the RetryOptions class, and using the taskRetryLimit() (withTaskRetryLimit()) builder method to set the limit:

```
Queue queue = QueueFactory.getQueue("update_leaderboard");
queue.add(TaskOptions.Builder.withRetryOptions(
    RetryOptions.Builder
      .withTaskRetryLimit(10)));
```

Transactional Task Enqueueing

Task queues are an essential reliability mechanism for App Engine applications. If a call to enqueue a task is successful, and the task can be completed, the task is guaranteed to be completed, even given the possibility of transient service failure. It is common to pair the reliability of task queues with the durability of the datastore: tasks can take datastore values, act on them, and then update the datastore.

To complete this picture, the task queue service includes an extremely useful feature: the ability to enqueue a task as part of a datastore transaction. A task enqueued within a transaction is only enqueued if the transaction succeeds. If the transaction fails, the task is not enqueued.

This opens up a world of possibilities for the datastore. Specifically, it enables easy transactions that operate across an arbitrary number of entity groups, with eventual consistency.

Consider the message board example from Chapter 8. To maintain an accurate count of every message in each conversation, we have to update the count each time a message is posted. To do this with strong consistency, the count and the message have to be updated in the same transaction, which means they have to be in the same entity group—and therefore every message in the thread has to be in the same entity group. This might be acceptable for a count of messages per conversation, as it's unlikely that many users will be posting to the same conversation simultaneously, and even so, the delay for resolving concurrency failures might not be noticed.

But what if we want a count of every message on the website? Putting every message in a single entity group would be impractical, as it would effectively serialize all updates to the entire site. We need a way to update the count reliably without keeping everything in one entity group.

Transactional task enqueueing lets us update the count reliably without concern for entity groups. To post a message, we use a transaction to create the message entity and enqueue a task that will update the count. If the transaction fails, the task is not enqueued, so the count remains accurate. The task is performed outside of the transaction, so the count does not need to be in the same entity group as the message, but transactional enqueueing and task retries ensure that the count is updated, but only under the proper circumstances.

Of course, this comes with a trade-off: it must be acceptable for the count to be inaccurate between the time the message entity is created and the time the count is updated. In other words, we must trade strong consistency for *eventual consistency*. Transactional task enqueueing gives us a simple way to implement eventually consistent global transactions.

You might think that eventual consistency is suitable for the global message count, because who cares if the message count is accurate? But eventual consistency is useful for important data as well. Say the user Alicandria posts a quest with a bounty of 10,000 gold, and a guild of 20 players completes the quest, claiming the bounty. Because any player can trade gold with any other player, it is impractical to put all players in the same entity group. A typical person-to-person exchange can use a cross-group transaction, but this can only involve up to five entity groups. So to distribute the bounty, we use transactional task enqueueing: the app deducts 10,000 gold pieces from Alicandria's inventory, then enqueues a task to give 500 gold pieces to each member of the guild, all in a transaction. We use task names and memcache locks to ensure the system doesn't accidentally create new gold pieces if it retries the task. Also, because the guild might get angry if they don't get their money quickly, we configure the gold transfer queue to execute at a fast rate and with a large token bucket.

You can enqueue up to five tasks transactionally. In a typical case, it's sufficient to start a master task within the transaction, then trigger additional tasks as needed, and let the queue-retry mechanism drive the completion of the work.

Only the task enqueuing action joins the datastore transaction. The task itself is executed outside of the transaction, either in its own request handler (push queues) or elsewhere (pull queues). Indeed, by definition, the task is not enqueued until the transaction is committed, so the task itself has no way to contribute further actions to the transaction.

The API for transactional task enqueuing is simple, and typically just means calling the task queue API during an active transaction.

When we discussed the datastore API in Chapter 8, we saw that you start a datastore transaction with the `beginTransaction()` service method. This method returns a `Transaction` object. You perform a datastore operation within the transaction by passing the `Transaction` object to the operation's method. Alternatively, if you configured the service instance with `ImplicitTransactionManagementPolicy.AUTO`, you can call an operation's method without the transaction instance, and it will join the most recently created (and not committed) transaction.

The task queue API works the same way. The `add()` method of a `Queue` accepts an optional `Transaction` instance as its first argument. If you're using `ImplicitTransactionManagementPolicy.AUTO`, calling the `add()` method without this argument while an uncommitted transaction is open will cause the enqueue operation to join the transaction. The task is enqueued when the transaction is committed, if and only if the `txn.commit()` method is successful.

Here's an example of transferring gold from one player to many other players in a single transaction:

```
import java.util.List;
import com.google.appengine.api.datastore.DatastoreService;
import com.google.appengine.api.datastore.DatastoreServiceFactory;
import com.google.appengine.api.datastore.Entity;
import com.google.appengine.api.datastore.Key;
import com.google.appengine.api.datastore.Transaction;
import com.google.appengine.api.taskqueue.Queue;
import com.google.appengine.api.taskqueue.QueueFactory;
import com.google.appengine.api.taskqueue.TaskOptions;

// ...
    void payQuestBounty(Key questMasterKey,
                        List<String> guildMemberKeyStrs,
                        long amount) {
        DatastoreService datastore =
            DatastoreServiceFactory.getDatastoreService();
        Transaction txn = datastore.beginTransaction();

        Entity questMaster = datastore.get(questMasterKey);
        // ... Handle the case where questMaster == null...
```

```
Long gold = (Long) questMaster.getProperty("gold");
gold -= amount;
questMaster.setProperty("gold", gold);
datastore.put(questMaster);

Queue queue = QueueFactory.getDefaultQueue();
TaskOptions task =
    TaskOptions.Builder.withUrl("/actions/payment/bounty");
for (String userKeyStr : guildMemberKeyStrs) {
    task = task.param("user_key", userKeyStr);
}
task = task.param("total_amount", Long.toString(amount));
queue.add(task);

txn.commit();
}
```

Task Chaining

A single task performed by a push queue can run for up to 10 minutes. There's a lot you can get done in 10 minutes, but the fact that there's a limit at all raises a red flag: a single task does not scale. If a job uses a single task and the amount of work it has to do scales with a growing factor of your app, the moment the amount of work exceeds 10 minutes, the task breaks.

One option is to use a master task, a task whose job is to figure out what work needs to be done, and then create an arbitrary number of tasks to do fixed-size units of the work. For example, the master task could fetch a feed URL from a remote host, and then create a task for each entry in the feed to process it. This goes a long way to doing more work within the 10-minute limit, and is useful to parallelize the units of work to complete the total job more quickly. But it's still a fixed capacity, limited to the number of child tasks the master task can create in 10 minutes.

For jobs of arbitrary size, another useful pattern is a *task chain*. The idea is straightforward: complete the job with an arbitrary number of tasks, where each task is responsible for creating the subsequent task, in addition to doing a fixed amount of work. Each task must be capable of performing its own amount of work in a fixed amount of time, as well as determining what the next unit of work ought to be.

Task chains are especially useful when combined with datastore query cursors, which meet these exact requirements. A task that ought to update every entity of a kind (possibly those that match other query criteria) can use the following steps:

1. Start a query for entities of the kind. If the task payload includes a cursor, set the query to start at the cursor location.

2. Read and process a fixed number of entities from the query results.

3. Take the cursor after the last query result. If there are any results after the cursor, create a new task with the new cursor as its payload.

4. Return a success code.

This produces the simple task chain shown in Figure 16-2. Each new task starts just as the previous task finishes.

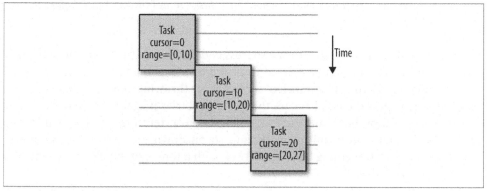

Figure 16-2. A simple task chain, where each task does a fixed amount of work, then creates the next task

If the work for the next task can be determined before performing the work for the current task, and the next task does not depend upon the completion of the current task, we can improve the performance of this job by creating the next task before we begin the work. In the case of iterating over every result of a query, we can get the next cursor immediately after performing the query:

1. Start a query for entities of the kind. If the task payload includes a cursor, set the query to start at the cursor location.

2. Read a fixed number of entities from the query results.

3. Take the cursor after the last query result. If there are any results after the cursor, create a new task with the new cursor as its payload.

4. Process the results from the query.

5. Return a success code.

This technique compresses the timeline so the work of each task is performed concurrently. App Engine will perform the tasks up to the capacity of the queue, and will utilize instances based on your app's performance settings, so you can create tasks aggressively and throttle their execution to your taste. Figure 16-3 shows the timeline of the compressed behavior.

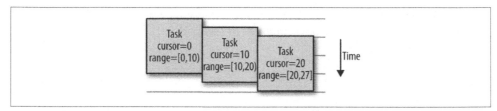

Figure 16-3. An improved task chain, where each task creates the next task before doing its own work

The last step of each task is to return a success code. This tells the push queue that the task was successful and can be deleted from the queue. If the task does not return a success code, such as due to a transient service error throwing an uncaught exception, the push queue puts the task back on the queue and tries it again. As we've described it so far, this is a problem for our task chain, because retrying one task will create another task for the next unit of work, and so on down the rest of the chain. We might end up with something like Figure 16-4, with a ton—potentially an exponential amount—of wasted work.

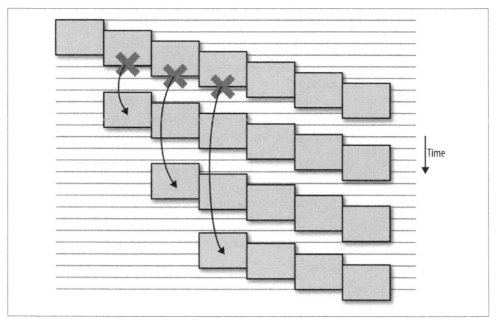

Figure 16-4. A transient error in a naive task chain explodes into many chains of wasted work, as links in the chain are retried

You might think the solution is to go back to the previous version of the task, where the work is performed before the next task is enqueued. This would reduce the likelihood that a transient service error occurs after the next link in the chain is created, but this doesn't eliminate the possibility. Even with no lines of code following the task enqueue operation in the handler, a failure on the app instance might still cause an error condition, and a fork in the chain.

The real solution is to use task names. As we saw earlier, every task has a unique name, either specified by the app or by the system. A given task name can only be used once (within a reasonably long period of time, on the order of days). When a named task finishes, it leaves behind a "tombstone" record to prevent the name from being reused right away.

A task name can be any string that identifies the next unit of work, and that the current task can calculate. In the datastore traversal example, we already have such a value: the query cursor. We can prepend a *nonce value* that identifies the job, to distinguish the query cursor for this job from a similar cursor of a job we might run later.

Our resilient task routine is as follows:

1. Start a query for entities of the kind. If the task payload includes a cursor, set the query to start at the cursor location.

2. Read a fixed number of entities from the query results.

3. Take the cursor after the last query result. If there are any results after the cursor, prepare to create a new task. If the task payload contains a nonce value for the job, use it, otherwise generate a new one. Generate the next task name based on the nonce value and the new query cursor. Create a new task with the task name, and the nonce value and the new cursor as its payload.

4. Process the results from the query.

5. Return a success code.

Transient errors no longer bother us, resulting in a pattern like Figure 16-5. Tasks that fail due to transient errors are retried and may cause their units of work to complete later, but they no longer cause the rest of the chain to be re-created for each failure.

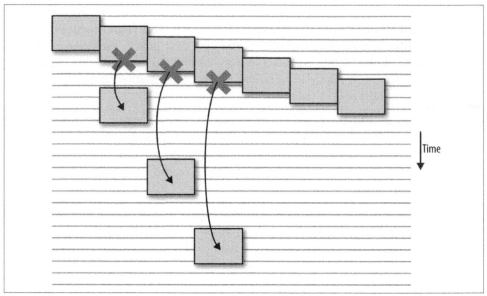

Figure 16-5. Named tasks prevent an exploding chain during a transient error

We close this discussion of task chains with an example implementation:

```java
package messages;

import java.io.IOException;
import java.util.Date;

import javax.servlet.ServletException;
import javax.servlet.http.*;

import com.google.appengine.api.datastore.Cursor;
import com.google.appengine.api.datastore.DatastoreService;
import com.google.appengine.api.datastore.DatastoreServiceFactory;
import com.google.appengine.api.datastore.Entity;
import com.google.appengine.api.datastore.FetchOptions;
import com.google.appengine.api.datastore.PreparedQuery;
import com.google.appengine.api.datastore.Query;
import com.google.appengine.api.datastore.QueryResultList;
import com.google.appengine.api.taskqueue.Queue;
import com.google.appengine.api.taskqueue.QueueFactory;
import com.google.appengine.api.taskqueue.TaskOptions;

@SuppressWarnings("serial")
public class MessagesServlet extends HttpServlet {
    private static final int TASK_SIZE = 10;

        public void doPost(HttpServletRequest req, HttpServletResponse resp)
                throws IOException, ServletException {
            DatastoreService datastore =
```

```
DatastoreServiceFactory.getDatastoreService();
    PreparedQuery pq = datastore.prepare(new Query("Quest"));

    String cursorStr = req.getParameter("cursor");
    FetchOptions options = FetchOptions.Builder.withLimit(TASK_SIZE);
    if (cursorStr != null) {
            Cursor cursor = Cursor.fromWebSafeString(cursorStr);
            options = options.startCursor(cursor);
    }

    QueryResultList<Entity> results = pq.asQueryResultList(options);

    Cursor newCursor = results.getCursor();
    String newCursorStr = null;
    if (results.size() == TASK_SIZE) {
            newCursorStr = newCursor.toWebSafeString();
            Queue taskQueue = QueueFactory.getDefaultQueue();

            String jobId = req.getParameter("job_id");
            String taskName = jobId + "_" + newCursorStr;
taskName = taskName.replaceAll("[^a-zA-Z0-9_-]", "_");
            taskQueue.add(TaskOptions.Builder
                            .withTaskName(taskName)
                            .url("/admin/jobs/upgradequests/task")
                            .param("job_id", jobId)
                            .param("cursor", newCursorStr));
    }

    // Do the work.
    for (Entity questEntity : results) {
            Long timestamp =
(Long) questEntity.getProperty("end_timestamp");
            questEntity.setProperty("end_datetime",
                                new Date(timestamp));
    }
    datastore.put(results);
  }
}
```

Task Queue Administration

The Cloud Console provides a great deal of information about the current status of
your task queues and their contents. The Task Queues panel lists all the queues you
have configured, with their rate configurations and current running status. You can
click on any queue to get more information about individual tasks, such as their calling parameters and how many times they have been retried. You can also delete tasks
or force tasks to run, pause and restart the queue, or purge all tasks.

The features of this panel are intuitive, so we'll just add one comment on a common
use of the panel: finding and deleting stuck tasks. If a queue has a task that is failing

and being retried repeatedly, the Oldest Task column may have a suspiciously old date. Select the queue, then browse for a task with a large number in the Retries column. You can trace this back to logs from an individual attempt by copying the URL from the Method/URL column, then going to the Logs panel to do a search for that path. You may need to force a run of the task by clicking the Run Now button to get a recent entry to show up in the logs.

How you fix the problem depends on how important the data in the task record is. If the task is failing because of an error in the code that can be fixed, you can leave the task in the queue, fix the bug in the code, and then deploy new code to the target version of the task. When the task is retried, it'll use the new code, and proceed to completion. If the task is failing because the task record is incompatible with a recent change to the code, you can try to rescue the task record with a code change, or just delete the task record. It's often easier to delete old task records and re-create the activity they represent than to figure out how to usher them to completion.

Deferring Work

The task queue library includes a handy utility that makes it easy to throw work into a task without writing a custom task handler. The utility uses a prepackaged general-purpose task handler to process deferred work.

The mechanism for deferring work is based on the `DeferredTask` interface. This interface describes a class which is both `java.lang.Runnable` and `java.io.Serializable`. You provide an implementation of this interface, with a `run()` method that does the work. To defer a call to this code, you add an instance of your class to a push queue, using a special form of the `withPayload()` builder method to `TaskOptions`. This method serializes the instance and puts it on the queue, to be executed by the deferred task handler provided by the runtime environment. No further setup is required, making this a convenient way to run code in the future:

```
import com.google.appengine.api.taskqueue.DeferredTask;
import com.google.appengine.api.taskqueue.Queue;
import com.google.appengine.api.taskqueue.QueueFactory;
import com.google.appengine.api.taskqueue.TaskOptions;

public class MyWork implements DeferredTask {
    String arg;

    public MyWork(String arg) {
        this.arg = arg;
    }

    public void run() {
        // Do something with arg...
    }
}
```

```
// ...
        Queue queue = QueueFactory.getDefaultQueue();
        queue.add(TaskOptions.Builder.withPayload(new MyWork("my arg")));
```

Within the `run()` method, your deferred task can access basic information about the request handler in which it is running by using static methods of the `DeferredTask Context` class. The `getCurrentServlet()` method returns the servlet, and `getCurrentRequest()` and `getCurrentResponse()` return the request and response, respectively.

By default, an unchecked exception thrown by the `run()` method causes the task to be retried. You can disable this behavior by calling the `DeferredTaskContext.setDo NotRetry(true)` method within the `run()` method. With retries disabled, any uncaught exception will be treated as a clean exit, and the task will be deleted from the queue.

 The serialized version of the instance of your deferred task is stored as data in the task record. If you upload a new version of your application code and serialized data cannot be deserialized into an instance by using the new code, the task will fail perpetually. Take care to either clear deferred work from task queues before uploading new code, or only make serialization-compatible changes to the code while deferred work is in a task queue.

Scheduled Tasks

Applications do work in response to external stimuli: user requests, incoming email and XMPP messages, HTTP requests sent by a script on your computer. And while task queues can be used to trigger events across a period of time, a task must be enqueued by application code before anything happens.

Sometimes you want an application to do something "on its own." For instance, an app may need to send nightly email reports of the day's activity, or fetch news headlines from a news service. For this purpose, App Engine lets you specify a schedule of tasks to perform on a regular basis. In the App Engine API, scheduled tasks are also known as "cron jobs," named after a similar feature in the Unix operating system.

A scheduled task consists of a URL path to call and a description of the recurring times of the day, week, or month at which to call it. It can also include a textual description of the task, which is displayed in the Cloud Console and other reports of the schedule.

To execute a scheduled task, App Engine calls the URL path by using an empty GET request. A scheduled task cannot be configured with parameters, headers, or a different HTTP method. If you need something more complicated, you can do it in the code for the request handler mapped to the scheduled task's URL path.

As with task queue handlers, you can secure the URL path by restricting it to application developers in the frontend configuration. The system can call such URL paths to execute scheduled tasks.

The HTTP request includes the header `X-AppEngine-Cron: true` to differentiate it from other App Engine–initiated requests. Only App Engine can set this header. If an external request tries to set it, App Engine removes it before it reaches your app. You can use the header to protect against outside requests triggering the job. Scheduled task requests are also treated like requests from an administrator user (similarly to push queue tasks), so you can guard task URLs by using a login requirement in *web.xml*.

Just like tasks in push queues, scheduled tasks have a request deadline of 10 minutes, so you can do a significant amount of computation and service calls in a single request handler. Depending on how quickly the task needs to be completed, you may still wish to break work into small pieces and use task queues to execute them on multiple instances in parallel.

Unlike push queues, scheduled tasks that fail are not retried. If a failed schedule task should be retried immediately, the scheduled task should put the work onto a push queue.

The development server does not execute scheduled tasks automatically. If you need to test a scheduled task, you can visit the task URL path while signed in as an administrator.

If you have enabled billing for your application, your app can have up to 100 task schedules. At the free billing tier, an app can have up to 20 task schedules.

Configuring Scheduled Tasks

The schedule is a configuration file in the *WEB-INF/* directory named *cron.xml*. A `<cronentries>` element contains zero or more `<cron>` elements, one for each schedule. The `<url>`, `<description>`, `<schedule>`, and `<timezone>` elements define the scheduled task:

```
<cronentries>
  <cron>
    <url>/cron/reports</url>
    <description>Send nightly reports.</description>
    <schedule>every day 23:59</schedule>
    <timezone>America/Los_Angeles</timezone>
  </cron>
  <cron>
    <url>/cron/getnews</url>
```

```
        <description>Refresh news.</description>
        <schedule>every 1 hours</schedule>
      </cron>
    </cronentries>
```

As with other service configuration files, the scheduled task configuration file applies to the entire app, and is uploaded along with the application. You can also upload it separately:

```
    appcfg update_cron war
```

You can validate your task schedule and get a human-readable description of it by using appcfg cron_info war. The report includes the exact days and times of the next few runs, so you can make sure that the schedule is what you want.

These are the possible fields for each scheduled task:

description
  A textual description of the scheduled task, displayed in the Cloud Console

url
  The URL path of the request handler to call for this task

schedule
  The schedule on which to execute this task

timezone
  The time zone for the schedule, as a standard "zoneinfo" time zone descriptor (such as America/Los_Angeles); if omitted, the schedule times are interpreted as UTC time

target
  The ID of the app version to use for the task; if omitted, App Engine calls the version that is the default at the time the task executes

 If you choose a time zone identifier where Daylight Saving Time (DST) is used and have a task scheduled during the DST hour, your task will be skipped when DST advances forward an hour, and run twice when DST retreats back an hour. Unless this is desired, pick a time zone that does not use DST, or do not schedule tasks during the DST hour. (The default time zone UTC does not use DST.)

Specifying Schedules

The value for the schedule element uses a simplified English-like format for describing the recurrence of the task. It accepts simple recurrences, such as:

```
    every 30 minutes
    every 3 hours
```

The minimum interval is every 1 minutes. The parser's English isn't that good: it doesn't understand every 1 minute or every minute. It does understand every day, as an exception.

The interval every day accepts an optional time of day, as a 24-hour hh:mm time. This runs every day at 11:59 p.m.:

```
every day 23:59
```

You can have a task recur weekly using the name of a weekday, as in every tuesday, and can also include a time: every tuesday 23:59. In another English parsing foible, day names must use all lowercase letters. You can abbreviate day names using just the first three letters, such as every tue 23:59.

You can have a task recur monthly or on several days of a given month by specifying a comma-delimited list of ordinals (such as 2nd, or first,third) and a comma-delimited list of weekday names (monday,wednesday,friday or sat,sun). You can also include a time of day, as earlier. This occurs on the second and fourth Sunday of each month:

```
2nd,4th sunday
```

You can have a task recur yearly by including the word "of" and a comma-delimited list of lowercase month names (january,july, or oct,nov,dec). This schedule executes at 6 p.m. on six specific days of the year:

```
3rd,4th tue,wed,thu of march 18:00
```

You can specify recurrences to occur between two times of the day. This executes the task every 15 minutes between 3 a.m. and 5 a.m. every day:

```
every 15 mins from 03:00 to 05:00
```

By default, when a schedule uses a time interval without an explicit start time, App Engine will wait for the previous task to complete before restarting the timer. If a task runs every 15 minutes and the task takes 5 minutes to complete, each task's start time begins 20 minutes apart. If you'd prefer the next task to start at a specific interval from the previous start time regardless of the time taken to complete the previous task (or whether the previous task has finished), use the synchronized keyword:

```
every 15 mins synchronized
```

CHAPTER 17

Optimizing Service Calls

Handlers for user-facing requests spend most of their time calling App Engine services, such as the datastore or memcache. As such, making user-facing requests fast requires understanding how your application calls services, and applying techniques to optimize the heaviest uses of calls.

We've seen three optimization techniques already, but they're worth reviewing:

- Store heavily used results of datastore queries, URL fetches, and large computations in memcache. This exchanges expensive operations (even simple datastore gets) for fast calls to the memcache in the vast majority of cases, at the expense of a potentially stale view of the data in rare cases.

- Defer work outside of the user-facing request by using task queues. When the work to prepare results for users occurs outside of the user-facing request, it's easy to see how user-facing requests are dominated by requests to the datastore or memcache.

- Use the datastore and memcache batch APIs when operating on many independent elements (when batch size limitations are not an issue). Every call to the service has remote procedure call overhead, so combining calls into batches saves overhead. It also reduces clock time spent on the call, because the services can perform the operations on the elements in parallel.

Another important optimization technique is to call services *asynchronously*. When you call a service asynchronously, the call returns immediately. Your request handler code can continue executing while the service does the requested work. When your code needs the result, it calls a method that waits for the service call to finish (if it hasn't finished already), and then returns the result. With asynchronous calls, you can get services and your app code doing multiple things at the same time, so the user response is ready sooner.

App Engine supports asynchronous service APIs to the datastore, memcache, and URL Fetch services. Support for asynchronous calls is also currently supported in a few other places.

All of these optimization techniques require understanding your application's needs and recognizing where the benefits of the technique justify the added code complexity. App Engine includes a tool called AppStats to help you understand how your app calls services and where you may be able to optimize the call patterns. AppStats hooks into your application logic to collect timing data for service calls, and reports this data visually in a web-based interface.

In this chapter, we demonstrate how to call services using the asynchronous APIs. We also walk through the process of setting up and using AppStats, and see how it can help us understand our application's performance.

Calling Services Asynchronously

Consider the following call to the URL Fetch service:

```
import java.net.URL;

import com.google.appengine.api.urlfetch.HTTPResponse;
import com.google.appengine.api.urlfetch.URLFetchService;
import com.google.appengine.api.urlfetch.URLFetchServiceFactory;

// ...
        URLFetchService urlfetch = URLFetchServiceFactory.getURLFetchService();
        HTTPResponse response = urlfetch.fetch(
                new URL("http://store.example.com/products/molasses"));

        processData(response);
```

When execution of the request handler reaches this line, a sequence of events takes place. The app issues a remote procedure call to the URL Fetch service. The service prepares the request, then opens a connection with the remote host and sends it. The remote host does whatever it needs to do to prepare a response, invoking handler logic, making local connections to database servers, performing queries, and formatting results. The response travels back over the network, and the URL Fetch service concludes its business and returns the response data to the app. Execution of the request handler continues with the next line.

From the point when it makes the service call to the point it receives the response data, the app is idle. If the app has multithreading enabled in its configuration, the handler's instance can use the spare CPU to handle other requests. But no further progress is made on this request handler.

In the preceding case, that's the best the request handler can do: it needs the response in order to proceed to the next line of execution. But consider this amended example:

```
HTTPResponse ingred1 = urlfetch.fetch(
        new URL("http://store.example.com/products/molasses"));
HTTPResponse ingred2 = urlfetch.fetch(
        new URL("http://store.example.com/products/sugar"));
HTTPResponse ingred3 = urlfetch.fetch(
        new URL("http://store.example.com/products/flour"));

combine(ingred1, ingred2, ingred3)
```

Here, the request handler issues the first request, then waits for the first response before issuing the second request. It waits again for the second response before issuing the third. The total running time of just these three lines is equal to the sum of the execution times of each call, and during that time the request handler is doing nothing but waiting. Most importantly, the code does not need the data in the first response in order to issue the second or third request. In fact, it doesn't need any of the responses until the fourth line.

These calls to the URL Fetch service are *synchronous*: each call waits for the requested action to be complete before proceeding. With synchronous calls, your code has complete results before it proceeds, which is sometimes necessary, but sometimes not. Our second example would benefit from service calls that are *asynchronous*, where the handler can do other things while the service prepares its results.

When your app makes an asynchronous service call, the call returns immediately. Its return value is not the result of the call (which is still in progress). Instead, the call returns a special kind of object called a *future*, which represents the call and provides access to the results when you need them later. A future is an I.O.U., a promise to return the result at a later time. Your app is free to perform additional work while the service does its job. When the app needs the promised result, it calls a method on the future. This call either returns the result if it's ready, or waits for the result.

A synchronous call can be thought of as an asynchronous call that waits on the future immediately. In fact, this is precisely how the App Engine synchronous APIs are implemented.

Here is the asynchronous version of the second example:

```
import java.util.concurrent.Future;

// ...
        Future<HTTPResponse> ingred1Future = urlfetch.fetchAsync(
                new URL("http://store.example.com/products/molasses"));
        Future<HTTPResponse> ingred2Future = urlfetch.fetchAsync(
                new URL("http://store.example.com/products/sugar"));
        Future<HTTPResponse> ingred3Future = urlfetch.fetchAsync(
                new URL("http://store.example.com/products/flour"));

        try {
            combine(ingred1Future.get(),
```

```
                    ingred2Future.get(),
                    ingred3Future.get());
        } catch (InterruptedException | ExecutionException e) {
            // ...
        }
```

The fetchAsync() method calls each issue their request to the service, then return immediately. The requests execute in parallel. The total clock time of this code, including the get() calls, is equal to the longest of the three service calls, not the sum. This is a potentially dramatic speed increase for our code.

Figure 17-1 illustrates the difference between a synchronous and an asynchronous call, using the URL Fetch API as an example.

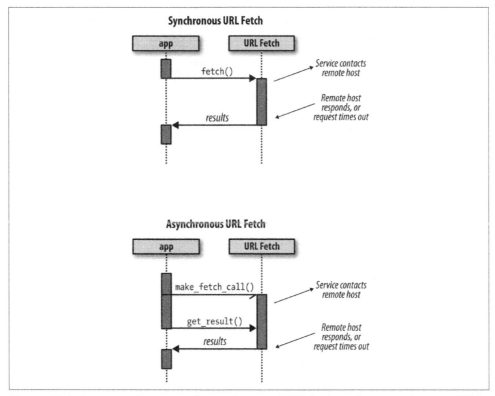

Figure 17-1. Sequence diagrams of a synchronous URL fetch and an asynchronous URL fetch

The preceding example was trivial: we could determine an obvious optimization just from looking at the code, and the change was not complicated. In a real app, reordering your code and data dependencies to best exploit asynchronous calls can add complexity. Like most optimization, it's an investment to gain performance.

The service APIs have their own particular ways of making asynchronous calls. Furthermore, not every service has an official asynchronous API in every runtime environment. Let's take a look at what's available.

The Asynchronous Call API

The Java runtime environment includes asynchronous APIs for the datastore, memcache, and URL Fetch. The location of these methods differs slightly from service to service, but they all use the same standard mechanism for representing results: `java.util.concurrent.Future<T>`.

For each synchronous method that returns a value of a particular type, the asynchronous equivalent for that method returns a `Future<T>` wrapper of that type. The method invokes the service call, then immediately returns the `Future<T>` to the app. The app can proceed with other work while the service call is in progress. When it needs the result, the app calls the `get()` method of the `Future<T>`, which waits for the call to complete (if needed) and then returns the result of type `T`:

```
import java.util.concurrent.Future;
import com.google.appengine.api.urlfetch.URLFetchService;
import com.google.appengine.api.urlfetch.URLFetchServiceFactory;
import com.google.appengine.api.urlfetch.HTTPResponse;

// ...
        URLFetchService urlfetch = URLFetchServiceFactory.getURLFetchService();
        Future<HTTPResponse> responseFuture =
            urlfetch.fetchAsync(
                new URL("http://store.example.com/products/molasses"));

        // ...
        HTTPResponse response = responseFuture.get();
```

The `get()` method accepts optional parameters that set a maximum amount of time for the app to wait for a pending result. This amount is specified as two arguments: a `long` and a `java.util.concurrent.TimeUnit` (such as `TimeUnit.SECONDS`). This timeout is separate from any deadlines associated with the service itself; it's just how long the app will wait on the call.

The `Future<T>` has a `cancel()` method, which cancels the service call. This method returns `true` if the call was canceled successfully, or `false` if the call had already completed or was previously canceled. The `isCancelled()` method (note the spelling) returns `true` if the call has been canceled in the past. `isDone()` returns `true` if the call is not in progress, including if it succeeded, failed, or was canceled.

Service calls that don't return values normally have a `void` return type in the API. The asynchronous versions of these return a `Future<java.lang.Void>`, so you can still wait for the completion of the call. To do so, simply call the get() method in a void context.

Datastore

To call the datastore asynchronously in Java, you use a different service class: AsyncDatastoreService. You get an instance of this class by calling Data storeServiceFactory.getAsyncDatastoreService(). Like its synchronous counterpart, this factory method can take an optional DatastoreServiceConfig value.

The methods of AsyncDatastoreService are identical to those of DatastoreService, except that return values are all wrapped in Future<T> objects.

There are no explicit asynchronous methods for fetching query results. Instead, the PreparedQuery methods asIterable(), asIterator(), and asList() always return immediately and begin prefetching results in the background. (This is true even when using the DatastoreService API.)

Committing a datastore transaction will wait for all previous asynchronous datastore calls since the most recent commit. You can commit a transaction asynchronously using the commitAsync() method of the Transaction. Calling get() on its Future will block similarly.

When using AsyncDatastoreService with transactions, you must provide the Transaction instance explicitly with each call. Setting the implicit transaction management policy to AUTO (in DatastoreServiceConfig) will have no effect. This is because the automatic policy sometimes has to commit transactions, and this would block on all unresolved calls, possibly unexpectedly. To avoid confusion, AsyncDatastoreService does not support implicit transactions.

 The cancel() method of a datastore Future<T> may return true even if the service call has already modified data. Canceling a data change in progress does not roll back changes.

Memcache

To call the memcache asynchronously in Java, you use the AsyncMemcacheService service class. You get an instance of this class by calling MemcacheServiceFactory.getAsyncMemcacheService(). The methods of AsyncMemcacheService are identical to those of MemcacheService, except that return values are all wrapped in Future<T> objects.

URL Fetch

The Java URL Fetch API has one asynchronous method: `fetchAsync()`, of the URL `FetchService` class. This method is equivalent to the `fetch()` method, except it returns a `Future<HTTPResponse>`.

Visualizing Calls with AppStats

AppStats is a tool to help you understand how your code calls services. After you install the tool in your application, AppStats records timing data for requests, including when each service call started and ended relative to the request running time. You use the AppStats Console to view this data as a timeline of the request activity.

Let's take another look at our contrived URL Fetch example from earlier in this chapter:

```
HTTPResponse ingred1 = urlfetch.fetch(
        new URL("http://store.example.com/products/molasses"));
HTTPResponse ingred2 = urlfetch.fetch(
        new URL("http://store.example.com/products/sugar"));
HTTPResponse ingred3 = urlfetch.fetch(
        new URL("http://store.example.com/products/flour"));

combine(ingred1, ingred2, ingred3)
```

Figure 17-2 is the AppStats timeline for this code. It's clear from this graph how each individual call contributes to the total running time. In particular, notice that the Grand Total is as large as the RPC Total.

Here's the same example using asynchronous calls to the URL Fetch service:

```
Future<HTTPResponse> ingred1Future = urlfetch.fetchAsync(
        new URL("http://store.example.com/products/molasses"));
Future<HTTPResponse> ingred2Future = urlfetch.fetchAsync(
        new URL("http://store.example.com/products/sugar"));
Future<HTTPResponse> ingred3Future = urlfetch.fetchAsync(
        new URL("http://store.example.com/products/flour"));

try {
    combine(ingred1Future.get(),
            ingred2Future.get(),
            ingred3Future.get());
} catch (InterruptedException | ExecutionException e) {
    // ...
}
```

Figure 17-3 shows the new chart, and the difference is dramatic: the URL Fetch calls occur simultaneously, and the Grand Total is not much larger than the longest of the three fetches.

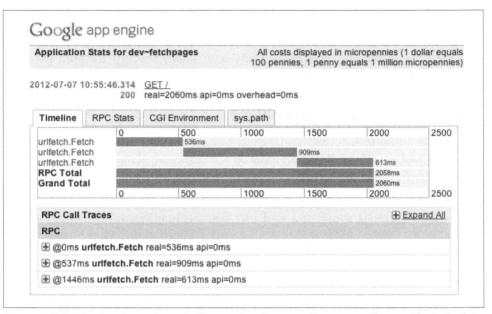

Figure 17-2. The AppStats Console illustrating three synchronous calls to urlfetch.fetchA-sync

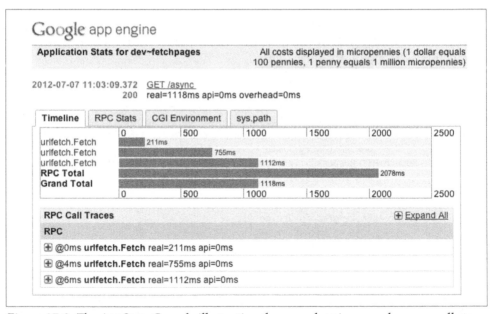

Figure 17-3. The AppStats Console illustrating three overlapping asynchronous calls to urlfetch.Fetch

AppStats has two parts: the event recorder and the AppStats Console. Both parts live within your app, and are included in the runtime environment.

Once installed, you can use AppStats in both the development server and your live app. Running in the development server can give you a good idea of the call patterns, although naturally the timings will not match the live service.

The event recorder hooks into the serving infrastructure for your app to start recording at the beginning of each request, and store the results at the end. It records the start and end times of the request handler, and the start and end times of each remote procedure call (RPC) to the services. It also stores stack traces at each call site.

The recorder uses memcache for storage, and does not use the datastore. It stores two values: a short record and a long record. The short record is used by the AppStats Console to render a browsing interface for the long records. Only the most recent 1,000 records are retained. Of course, memcache values may be evicted more aggressively if your app uses memcache heavily. But in general, AppStats is able to show a representative sample of recent requests.

The performance overhead of the recorder is minimal. For typical user-facing requests, you can leave the recorder turned on for live traffic in a popular app. If necessary, you can limit the impact of the recorder by configuring it to only record a subset of traffic, or traffic to a subset of URLs. AppStats records and reports its own overhead.

 AppStats accrues its timing data in instance memory during the request, and then stores the result in memcache at the end of the request handler's lifetime. This works well for user-facing requests, even those that last many seconds. For non-user-facing task handlers that last many minutes and make many RPC calls, App Engine may kill the task (and log a critical error) due to excess memory consumption. AppStats can be useful for optimizing batch jobs, but you may want to watch carefully for memory overruns, and disable it for large task handlers when you're not testing them actively.

In the next few sections, we'll walk through how to install the event recorder and the Console. Then we'll take a closer look at the AppStats Console.

Installing AppStats

The AppStats event recorder is a servlet filter. You install the filter by editing your deployment descriptor (*web.xml*) and adding lines such as the following:

```
<filter>
  <filter-name>appstats</filter-name>
```

```
  <filter-class>
    com.google.appengine.tools.appstats.AppstatsFilter
  </filter-class>
</filter>

<filter-mapping>
  <filter-name>appstats</filter-name>
  <url-pattern>/*</url-pattern>
</filter-mapping>
```

The `url-pattern` controls which requests get recorded, based on the URL. As before, the /* pattern matches all requests. Adjust this pattern if needed.

The AppStats Console is a web servlet, like any other. Add the following lines to *web.xml* to install the Console at the path `/_ah/stats/`, restricted to app administrators:

```
<servlet>
  <servlet-name>appstats</servlet-name>
  <servlet-class>
    com.google.appengine.tools.appstats.AppstatsServlet
  </servlet-class>
</servlet>

<servlet-mapping>
  <servlet-name>appstats</servlet-name>
  <url-pattern>/_ah/stats/*</url-pattern>
</servlet-mapping>

<security-constraint>
  <web-resource-collection>
    <url-pattern>/_ah/stats/*</url-pattern>
  </web-resource-collection>
  <auth-constraint>
    <role-name>admin</role-name>
  </auth-constraint>
</security-constraint>
```

Using the AppStats Console

The AppStats Console is your window to your app's service call behavior. To open the Console, visit `/_ah/stats/` in your app, or if you configured it, use the link you added to the Cloud Console sidebar. AppStats works in your development server as well as your live app.

Figure 17-4 shows an example of the AppStats Console. (A very small app is shown, to limit the size of the example.)

Figure 17-4. The AppStats Console front page for a small app

The front page of the Console shows a summary of recent service calls. RPC Stats is a summary of calls by service, with the most popular service at the top. Click to expand a service to see which recent request URLs called the service. Path Stats shows the same information organized by path, with the URL with the heaviest total number of calls at the top. Click to expand a path to see a summary of the path's calls per service. The Most Recent Requests column references the Requests History table at the bottom of the screen.

The Requests History table at the bottom lists all recent requests for which AppStats has data, up to 1,000 recent requests, with the most recent request on top. Click the + to expand the tally of service calls made during the request.

To view the complete data for the request, click the blue request date and path in the Requests History table. Figure 17-5 shows an expanded version of an example we saw earlier.

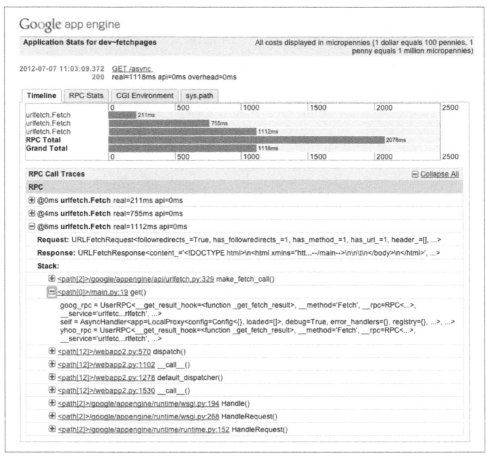

Figure 17-5. The AppStats Console request details page, with stack trace

The centerpiece of the request details page is the timeline. The timeline shows the history of the entire request, with a separate line for each service call. From this you can see when each service call began and ended in the lifetime of the request, the total (aggregate) time of all service calls (the RPC Total), and the actual amount of time spent handling the request (Grand Total). As we saw earlier, the Grand Total can be less than the RPC Total if you use simultaneous asynchronous requests.

When running on App Engine (not the development server), the timeline also includes red bars on top of the blue ones. This represents an estimate of the monetary costs of the call, including API and bandwidth costs. (The unit, "API milliseconds," is not always useful, except in comparison to other red bars in the graph.)

The RPC Call Traces table below the timeline lets you examine each RPC call to find out where in the code it occurred. The request details page includes another tab that shows the service call tallies (RPC Stats).

The interface to the datastore is a library built on top of a more rudimentary service interface. The correspondence between library calls and datastore RPCs is fairly intuitive, but you'll notice a few differences.

The most notable difference is how the datastore libraries fetch query results. Some features of the query APIs, such as the != operator, use multiple datastore queries behind the scenes. Also, when results are fetched using iterator-based interfaces, the libraries use multiple datastore RPCs to fetch results as needed. These will appear as `RunQuery` and `Next` calls in AppStats.

Also, the local development server uses the RPC mechanism to update index configuration, so it'll sometimes show `CreateIndex` and `UpdateIndex` calls that do not occur when running on App Engine.

You can use stack traces to find where in the datastore library code each call is being made.

CHAPTER 18

Managing Request Logs

Activity and message logs are an essential part of a web application. They are your view into what happens with your application over time as it is being used, who is using it and how, and what problems, if any, your users are having.

App Engine logs all incoming requests for your application, including application requests, static file requests, and requests for invalid URLs (so you can determine whether there is a bad link somewhere). For each request, App Engine logs the date and time, the IP address of the client, the URL requested (including the path and parameters), the domain name requested, the browser's identification string (the "user agent"), the referring URL if the user followed a link, and the HTTP status code in the response returned by the app or by the frontend.

App Engine also logs several important statistics about each request: the amount of time it took to handle each request, the amount of "CPU time" that was spent handling the request, and the size of the response. The CPU time measurement is particularly important to watch because requests that consistently consume a large amount of CPU may be throttled, such that the CPU use is spread over more clock time.

Your application code can log the occurrence of notable events and data by using a logging API. Logging a message associates a line of text with the request that emitted it, including all the data logged for the request. Each message has a *log level* indicating the severity of the message to make it easier to find important messages during analysis. App Engine supports five log levels: debug, info, warning, error, and critical.

You can browse your application's request and message logs, using the Cloud Console, under Monitoring, Logs. You can also download your log data for offline analysis and recordkeeping. An app can query log data programmatically using the log service API.

In this brief but important chapter, we'll look at all of these features of the logging system.

 If you're new to web programming, you can ignore the advanced features of the logging system for now. But be sure to read the first couple of sections right away. Writing log messages and finding them in the Cloud Console are important methods for figuring out what's going on in a web application.

Writing to the Log

App Engine writes information about every request to the application log automatically. The app can write additional messages during the request to note application-specific details about what happened during the request handler.

An application log message has a *log level* that indicates the importance of the message. App Engine supports five levels: debug, info, warning, error, and critical. These are in order of "severity," where "debug" is the least severe. When you browse or query log data, you can filter for messages above a given log level, such as to see just the requests where an error condition occurred.

App Engine will occasionally write its own messages to the log for a request. Uncaught application exceptions are written to the log as errors, with traceback information. When a handler exceeds its request deadline, App Engine writes an explicit message stating this fact. App Engine may also write informational messages, such as to say that the request was the first request served from a newly started instance, and so may have taken more time than usual.

In the development server, log messages are printed to the terminal (if run in a terminal window) or the Eclipse Console window. During development, you can use log messages to see what's going on inside your application, even if you decide not to keep those log messages in the live version of the app.

App Engine supports the `java.util.logging` library from the JRE. App Engine recognizes log levels of messages logged using this library. Example 18-1 illustrates the use of the `Logger` class and its convenience methods.

Example 18-1. The use of the java.util.logging package to emit messages at different log levels

```
import java.io.IOException;
import javax.servlet.http.*;

import java.util.logging.Logger;

public class LoggingServlet extends HttpServlet {
```

```
    private static final Logger log =
        Logger.getLogger(LoggingServlet.class.getName());

    public void doGet(HttpServletRequest req, HttpServletResponse resp)
            throws IOException {
        log.finest("finest level");    // DEBUG
        log.finer("finer level");      // DEBUG
        log.fine("fine level");        // DEBUG
        log.config("config level");    // DEBUG
        log.info("info level");        // INFO
        log.warning("warning level");  // WARNING
        log.severe("severe level");    // ERROR

        System.out.println("stdout level");  // INFO
        System.err.println("stderr level");  // WARNING
    }
}
```

The seven log levels of `java.util.logging` correspond to four of App Engine's log levels: "finest," "finer," "fine," and "config" all correspond to the App Engine debug level; "info" is info, "warning" is warning, and "severe" is error. The "critical" log level is reserved for exceptions that are not caught by the servlet; when this happens, the runtime environment logs a message at this level.

If the application writes any data to the standard output or error streams (`System.out` and `System.err`), App Engine adds that data to the log. Each line of text written to standard output becomes a log message at the "info" level, and each line written to standard error is logged at the "warning" level.

You can control which level of message should be written to the log by using configuration for `java.util.logging`. This allows you to leave detailed low-level logging statements in your code without having all that information clutter up the logs unnecessarily in a high-traffic app.

Configuring the log level requires two things: a configuration file and a system property that identifies the configuration file. For the configuration, create a resource file, such as *war/WEB-INF/logging.properties*, containing a line like this:

```
.level=INFO
```

You can configure the log level on a per-class basis by adding lines like this with the package path before the `.level`. This allows you to turn on fine-grained messaging for some components without turning it on for all components. For example, the Google Plugin for Eclipse creates a *logging.properties* configuration file with per-component settings for DataNucleus, the JDO/JPA interface package, so you can use verbose logging for your app code without cluttering up your output with messages from the DataNucleus component.

Be sure to use the logging level name (such as FINEST) and not the App Engine level name for values in *logging.properties*. App Engine log levels only affect how messages are represented in the Admin Console.

Next, set a system property telling the logging library where to find its configuration file. You do this by including a `<system-properties>` element in your *appengine-web.xml* file, like so:

```
<system-properties>
  <property name="java.util.logging.config.file"
            value="WEB-INF/logging.properties" />
</system-properties>
```

If you created your Java project using the Google Plugin for Eclipse, your app already has this configuration file and this system property. This configuration comes preloaded with log levels for the DataNucleus interface (an interface for the datastore), so you can leave those set to the "warning" level while the rest of your app uses another level.

The `java.util.logging` library and the standard output and error streams are the only ways to log messages at specific log levels. If you or a component of your app prefers a different logging library, such as log4j, messages emitted by that library will work as long as the library can write to the standard streams. If you want to be able to use the Cloud Console to filter logs by levels other than "info" and "warning," you will need an adapter of some kind that calls `java.util.logging` behind the scenes. You get complete log messages when you download log data, so you can always analyze alternative log formats in downloaded data.

When running in the development web server, log messages are written to the console, and text written to the standard streams is written to the corresponding streams for the server. In Eclipse, these messages appear in the Console pane.

Viewing Recent Logs

You can browse and search your application's request logs and messages from the Cloud Console. Open the Monitoring top-level section, then select the Logs panel. Figure 18-1 shows the Logs panel with a request opened to reveal the detailed request data.

The Logs panel features a rich dynamic interface for browsing and searching recent log data. You can load more results in real time by scrolling to the ends of the list. You can filter this display by module, version, and log level.

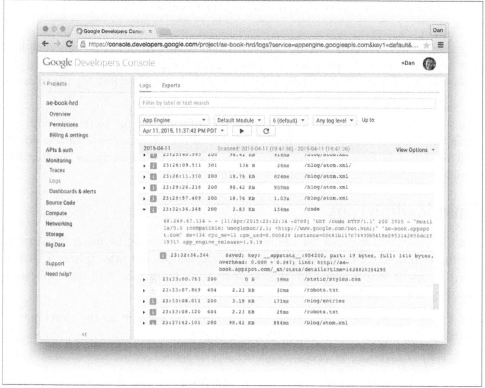

Figure 18-1. The Logs panel in the Cloud Console

You can also apply textual filters to labels and other request metadata. There are two ways to specify a filter: as a regular expression, or as a set of labels and patterns. When you specify just a regular expression, the Logs panel shows all requests where any field or application log message matches the expression.

You can use labels and patterns to match more specific fields of the request. Each field filter is the field name followed by a colon, then the regular expression for the pattern. Field filters are delimited by spaces. Some useful examples of fields are `path` (the URL path, starting with a slash) and `user` (a user signed in with a Google Account; the pattern matches the Google username). For example, this query shows requests by the user `dan.sanderson` for paths beginning with `/admin/`:

```
path:/admin/.* user:dan\.sanderson
```

The Logs panel shows log data for the application version currently selected in the drop-down menus. If you're having a problem with a live app, a useful technique is to deploy a separate version of the app with additional logging statements added to the code near the problem area, and then reproduce the issue using the version-specific URL (or temporarily make the new version the default, then switch it back). Then you can view and search the logs specific to the version with the added logging messages.

If a specific long-running instance appears to be having trouble, you can view logs just for that instance. Open the Compute top-level section, App Engine, then the Instances panel, then find the Logs column and click the View link for the instance you wish to inspect.

The Logs panel is useful for digging up more information for problems with the application code. For broader analysis of traffic and user trends, you'll want to download the log data for offline processing, or use a web traffic analytics product like Google Analytics (*http://www.google.com/analytics/*).

Downloading Logs

You can download log data for offline analysis and archiving by using the AppCfg command-line tool. (The Google Plugin for Eclipse does not offer this as a UI feature.) To use it, run `appcfg` with the `request_logs` command, with the application directory and log output filename as arguments.

The following command downloads request logs for the app in the development directory *clock*, and saves them to a file named *logs.txt*:

```
appcfg request_logs clock logs.txt
```

This command takes many of the same arguments as `appcfg update`, such as those used for authentication.

The command fetches log data for the application ID and version described in the application config file. As with `appcfg update`, you can override these with the `--application=…` and `--version=…` arguments, respectively.

By default, this command downloads request data only. To download log messages emitted by the application, include a minimum severity level specified as a number, where 0 is all log messages ("debug" level and up) and 5 is only "critical" messages, using the `--severity` argument:

```
appcfg request_logs clock logs.txt --severity=1
```

Application messages appear in the file on separate lines immediately following the corresponding request. The format for this line is a tab, the severity of the message as a number, a colon, a numeric timestamp for the message, then the message:

```
1:1246801590.938119 get_published_entries cache HIT
```

Log data is ordered chronologically by request, from earliest to latest. Application messages are ordered within each request by their timestamps.

Request data appears in the file in a common format known as the Apache Combined (or "NCSA Combined") logfile format, one request per line (shown here as two lines to fit on the page):

```
127.0.0.1 - - [05/Jul/2009:06:46:30 -0700] "GET /blog/ HTTP/1.1" 200 14598 -
"Mozilla/5.0 (Macintosh; U; Intel Mac OS X 10_5_8; en-us)...,gzip(gfe)"
```

From left to right, the fields are:

- The IP address of the client
- A - (an unused field retained for backward compatibility)
- The email address of the user who made the request, if the user is signed in using Google Accounts; otherwise a - appears here
- The date and time of the request
- The HTTP command string in double quotes, including the method and URL path
- The HTTP response code returned by the server
- The size of the response, as a number of bytes
- The "Referrer" header provided by the client, usually the URL of the page that linked to this URL
- The "User-Agent" header provided by the client, usually identifying the browser and its capabilities

By default, the command fetches the last calendar day's worth of logs, back to midnight, Pacific Time. You can change this with the `--num_days=…` argument. Set this to 0 to get all available log data. You can also specify an alternative end date with the `--end_date=…` option, whose value is of the form YYYY-MM-DD (such as 2009-11-04).

You can specify the `--append` argument to extend the log data file with new data, if the logfile exists. By default, the command overwrites the file with the complete result of the query. The append feature is smart: it checks the data file for the date and time of the most recent log message, then only appends messages from after that time.

Logs Retention

By default, App Engine stores up to 1 gigabyte of log data, or up to 90 days worth of messages, whichever is less. Once the retention limit is reached, the oldest messages are dropped in favor of new ones.

You can increase the maximum amount and maximum age in the Compute, App Engine, Settings panel of the Cloud Console. Locate the Logs Retention setting, enter new values, and then click Save Settings.

The first gigabyte and 90 days of retention are included with the cost of your application. Additional storage and retention time is billed at a storage rate specific to logs. See the official website for the latest rates. If you're paying for log storage, you can retain logs for up to 365 days (one year).

Querying Logs from the App

App Engine provides a simple API for querying log data directly from the application. With this API, you can retrieve log data by date-time ranges, filter by log level and version ID, and page through results. You can use this API to build custom interactive log data inspectors for your app, or implement log-based alerts.

This is the same API that the Cloud Console uses to power the Logs panel. You'll notice that the API does not include filters based on regular expressions. Instead, the Logs panel simply pages through unfiltered results, and only displays those that match a given pattern. Your app can use a similar technique.

You fetch log data by building a `LogQuery` object, then passing it to the `fetch()` method of a `LogService` instance. These classes are provided by the package `com.google.appengine.api.log`.

You get a `LogQuery` by calling `LogQuery.Builder.withDefaults()`. You can then call builder methods to specify the query parameters. Each method returns the `LogQuery` instance, so you can stack calls:

`includeAppLogs(boolean)`
> `true` if the log records returned should include application messages.

`minLogLevel(LogService.LogLevel)`
> The minimum severity a request's application log messages should have to be a result. The value is an enum constant from `LogService.LogLevel`, one of `DEBUG`, `INFO`, `WARN`, `ERROR`, or `FATAL` (critical). The default is to return all requests; specifying a log level limits the results to just those requests with application log messages at or above the specified level.

`startTimeUsec(long)`
> The earliest timestamp to consider as a Unix epoch time. If not specified, there is no starting bound.

`endTimeUsec(long)`
> The latest timestamp to consider as a Unix epoch time. If not specified, there is no ending bound.

`majorVersionIds:` *a* `java.util.List<String>`

A list of version IDs whose logs to fetch. If not specified, this fetches the calling app's version.

`includeIncomplete(boolean)`

If `true`, include incomplete requests in the results. (See below.)

`batchSize(int)`

The number of results to fetch per service call when iterating over results.

`offset(String)`

The offset of the last-seen result, for paging through results. The next result returned follows the last-seen result.

You get a `LogService` instance by calling `LogServiceFactory.getLogService()`. The instance's `fetch()` method takes the `LogQuery` as an argument, and returns an iterable of `RequestLogs` objects, one for each request that matches the query. `RequestLogs` has getters for each request data field, such as `getMethod()`, `getResource()`, and `getEndTimeUsec()`. See the official documentation for the complete list of fields.

If application log messages are requested (`includeAppLogs(true)`), the `getAppLog Lines()` method of a `RequestLogs` returns a `List` of zero or more `AppLogLine` objects, one for each log message. `AppLogLine` has the getter methods `getLogLevel()` (returns a `LogService.LogLevel`), `getLogMessage()`, and `getTimeUsec()`.

Here's a simple example:

```
import com.google.appengine.api.log.AppLogLine;
import com.google.appengine.api.log.LogQuery;
import com.google.appengine.api.log.LogService;
import com.google.appengine.api.log.LogServiceFactory;
import com.google.appengine.api.log.RequestLogs;
import java.util.Calendar;

// ...
        LogQuery query = LogQuery.Builder.withDefaults();
        query.includeAppLogs(true);

        Calendar cal = Calendar.getInstance();
        int count = 0;

        LogService logSvc = LogServiceFactory.getLogService();
        for (RequestLogs reqLog : logSvc.fetch(query)) {
            count++;
            if (count > 20) {
                break;
            }

            cal.setTimeInMillis(reqLog.getEndTimeUsec() / 1000);
```

```
resp.getOutputStream().println(
    cal.getTime().toString() + " " +
    reqLog.getMethod() + " " +
    reqLog.getResource());

for (AppLogLine appLog : reqLog.getAppLogLines()) {
    cal.setTimeInMillis(appLog.getTimeUsec() / 1000);
    resp.getOutputStream().println(
        "   " +
        cal.getTime().toString() + " " +
        appLog.getLogLevel() + " " +
        appLog.getLogMessage());
}
}
```

Each result includes a getOffset() method, which returns a web-safe string you can use to make a "next page" button in a paginated display. Simply add the offset string of the last result on a page as the offset() parameter of the query, and the first result returned will be the next result in the sequence.

In the log fetch API, an "incomplete request" is a request that has not yet finished, but may have written some messages to the log. The API lets you optionally fetch log data for incomplete requests, such as to include the logged activity of a long-running task in the log data.

CHAPTER 19

Deploying and Managing Applications

Uploading your application to App Engine is as easy as clicking a button or running a command. All your application's code, configuration, and static files are sent to App Engine, and seconds later your new app is running.

Easy deployment is one of App Engine's most useful features. You don't have to worry about which servers have which software, how servers connect to services, or whether machines need to be rebooted or processes restarted. Other than your developer account, there are no database passwords to remember, no secret keys to generate, and no need to administer and troubleshoot individual machines. Your application exists as a single logical entity, and running it on large-scale infrastructure is as easy as running it on your local computer.

App Engine includes features for testing a new version of an app before making it public, reverting to a previous version quickly in case of a problem, and migrating the datastore and service configuration for the app from one version to another. These features let you control how quickly changes are applied to your application: you can make a new version public immediately to fix small bugs, or you can test a new version for a while before making it the version everyone sees.

Service configuration is shared across all versions of an app, including datastore indexes, task queues, and scheduled tasks. When you upload the app, the service configuration files on your computer are uploaded as well, and take effect immediately for all app versions. You can also upload each configuration file separately. This is especially useful for datastore indexes, as new indexes based on existing entities take time to build before they are ready to serve datastore queries.

Notice that service configuration is separate from the application configuration, which includes URL mappings, runtime environment selection, and inbound service activation. Application configuration is bound to a specific app version.

App Engine provides rich facilities for inspecting the performance of an app while it is serving live traffic. Most of these features are available in the Cloud Console, including analytic graphs of traffic and resource usage, and browsable request and message logs. You can also use the Console to inspect and make one-off changes to datastore entities.

You also use the Cloud Console to perform maintenance tasks, such as giving other developers access to the Console, changing settings, and setting up a billing account.

In this chapter, we discuss how to upload a new app, how to update an existing app, and how to use App Engine's versioning feature to test a new version of an app on App Engine while your users continue to use the previous version. We look at how to migrate the datastore and service configuration from one version to another. We also look at features of the SDK and the Cloud Console for inspecting, troubleshooting, and analyzing how your live application is running. And finally, we discuss other application maintenance tasks, billing, and where to get more information.

Uploading an Application

We introduced uploading an application way back in Chapter 2, but let's begin with a brief review.

If you're developing an app with Eclipse and the Google Plugin, you can deploy your app by clicking on the Deploy App Engine Project button in the Eclipse toolbar (the one that looks like the App Engine logo, a gray airplane engine with blue wings). It prompts for your developer account email address and password. The upload begins, and an Eclipse progress window reports on the status.

You can also upload the app with the AppCfg command-line tool from the SDK. The tool takes the update action and a path to the WAR directory:

```
appcfg update clock/war
```

Using Versions

The upload tool determines the application ID from the appropriate configuration file. This is the <application> element in the *appengine-web.xml* file.

The tool also uses this file to determine the version ID to use for this upload, from the version element. If App Engine does not yet have a version of this app with this ID, then it creates a new version with the uploaded files. If App Engine does have such a version, then it replaces the existing version. The replacement is total: no remnants of the previous version's code or static files remain. The new app has only the files present in the project directory on your computer at the time of the upload. Of course, data stored by the services for the app remain, including the datastore, memcache, log data, and enqueued tasks.

The version of the app that is visible on your app's primary domain name—either app-id.appspot.com or your custom domain—is known as the *default version*. When you upload your app for the first time, the initial version becomes the default version automatically. If you subsequently upload a version with a different version ID, the original version remains the default until you change the default using the Cloud Console.

Recall from Chapter 3 that each version has its own appspot.com URL that includes the version ID as well as the application ID:

    version-id.app-id.appspot.com

 Remember that there are no special protections on the version URLs. If the app does not restrict access by using code or configuration, then anyone who knows an unrestricted URL can access it. If you don't want a user to be able to access a version other than the default, you can check the Host header in the app and respond accordingly. You can also upload the nondefault version with configuration that restricts all URLs to administrators. Be sure to upload it again with the real configuration before making it the default version.

When you replace an existing version by uploading the app with that version ID, App Engine starts using the uploaded app for requests for that version within seconds of the upload. It is not guaranteed that every request after a particular time will use the new code and static files, but it usually doesn't take more than a few seconds for the App Master to update all the frontend servers. (It can take longer for apps with many instances and long warmup requests, as App Engine waits for new instances to be ready before diverting traffic from the previous version.) The App Master ensures that all the files are in place on a frontend server before using the new files to handle requests.

If you upload the app with the same version ID as that of the version that's currently the default, your users will start seeing the updated app within a few seconds of uploading. This is fine for small, low-risk changes that don't depend on changes to your data schemas or datastore indexes.

For larger changes, it's better to upload the app with a new version ID (in the application configuration file), test the app with the version URL, then switch the default version to direct traffic to the new version. To switch the default version, go to the Cloud Console, Compute, App Engine, then select the Versions panel. Select the radio button next to the desired version, and then click the "Make default" button. This is shown in Figure 19-1.

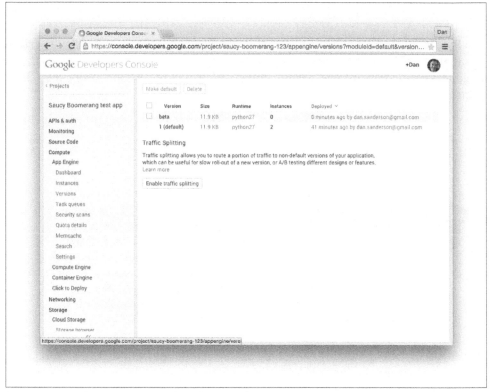

Figure 19-1. The Versions panel in the Cloud Console

App Engine can host up to 60 different version IDs per app at one time, across all modules. You can delete unused versions from the Cloud Console by clicking the Delete button on the appropriate row.

Many actions in the Cloud Console refer to a specific version of the app, including usage statistics and the log viewer. You can control which version you're looking at by selecting it from the drop-down menu in the top-left corner of the screen, next to the application ID. The version ID only appears as a drop-down menu if you have more than one version of the app.

Instead of updating the default version in Cloud Console, you can do this via the `appcfg set_default_version` command. This makes it easy to include this last step in your automated deployment workflows:

```
appcfg set_default_version --application=myapp --version=rel-20141231
```

Managing Service Configuration

All versions of an application use the same services. Service configuration and application data are shared across all versions of the app.

An app can have several service-related configuration files:

datastore-indexes.xml
A description of all the required datastore indexes

queue.xml
Configuration for task queues

cron.xml
The schedule for scheduled tasks (cron jobs)

Whenever you upload the app, these configuration files are uploaded from your computer to the services and take effect for the entire app, replacing any configuration that was once there. This is true regardless of whether the app version ID is new or already exists, or whether the version ID is the default.

You can update the configuration for each service without uploading the entire app by using the AppCfg tool. To update just the index configuration, use the `update_indexes` action, with the project directory (e.g., `app-dir`):

```
appcfg update_indexes app-dir
```

To update just the task queue configuration, use `update_queues`:

```
appcfg update_queues app-dir
```

And to update just the pending task schedule, use `update_cron`:

```
appcfg update_cron app-dir
```

App Engine Settings

There are various App Engine–specific settings for projects that are important but don't justify their own entry in the sidebar nav. You can find these in the Settings panel, under Compute, App Engine. This panel has multiple tabs to further organize these settings.

Under the Application Settings tab, you'll find your daily budget. This is where you set the maximum daily expenditure that you want to allow for the application. If the app ends up consuming resources whose cost is covered by the full amount, App Engine stops serving the app to avoid charging you more than you're willing to spend. This is a safety catch. Once you have an idea of how much your app's resource usage costs during a typical day, it's best to add a significant amount to this for your budget to accommodate unexpected traffic.

The "Google login cookie expiration" time is the amount of time a user signed in with a Google account will remain signed in. If the user signs in to your app, he will not have to sign in again from the computer he is using until the expiration time elapses.

The "Google authentication" setting refers to how Google account authentication works for apps running on a Google Apps domain. When set to "Google Accounts API," all Google users can sign in, and and it's up to the app to decide which user is authorized to perform certain actions. When set to "Google Apps domain," only Google accounts on the domain are allowed to sign in, and other domain account management policies apply.

This is also where you set the amount of log data to retain for the app. If you retain more than the default 1 GB, you may be billed for additional storage. See Chapter 18.

The Settings panel also provides the Custom Domains tab, which you can use for setting up a domain name for the app. (Refer back to "Domain Names" on page 65.)

Managing Developers

When you register an application ID, you become a developer for the application automatically. You can invite other people to be developers for the application from the Permissions section of the Cloud Console. (This is a project-wide panel, under the project name.)

To invite a developer, click the Add Member button, then enter the person's email address in the dialog that opens. You can select from several levels of access, including ownership, edit-only privileges, or read-only privileges.

App Engine sends an email to the developer inviting her to set up an account. If the email address you invited is for a Google account, the developer can use the existing account to access App Engine, although she must still accept the invitation by clicking on a link in the invitation email message. If the email address does not have a corresponding Google account, the developer can create a Google account for that address by following the instructions in the message. The developer cannot accept the invitation from a Google account with a different address; you must invite the alternative address explicitly.

An invited developer who has not yet accepted the invitation appears in the list with a status of "Pending." After the developer accepts the invitation, she appears with a status corresponding to her level of access.

You can remove any developer from the list by clicking the Remove button for the developer. The developer loses all access immediately. You can also adjust the permission level from this screen.

Developers with view permissions can see the Console for the project, but cannot make changes or deploy code. Developers with edit permissions can do everything except manage project permissions for other people, billing, and disabling or deleting the app. Edit access includes deploying new versions, changing the default version, accessing logs, and inspecting and tweaking the datastore. All developers, including read-only developers, can access application URLs configured as administrator-only, and are recognized by the Users API as adminsitrators.

Quotas and Billing

The Cloud Console provides a detailed summary of the App Engine resources your project is using via the App Engine "dashboard." You can locate this dashboard in the sidebar navigation: Compute, App Engine, Dashboard. This handy screen provides a visual overview of your app's traffic, resource usage, and errors.

The topmost chart displays time-based data over the past 24 hours. You can select from several data sets to view via the drop-down menu, including requests per second, clock time or CPU time per request, bandwidth, errors, and quota denials. You can adjust the period for this chart by clicking on the buttons (such as "6 hr").

Below the chart is a graph showing how much of the billable quotas have been consumed for the calendar day, and how much of your daily budget has been spent for each quota. A message at the upper-right of the chart indicates how much of the calendar day is remaining. If any of the bars look like they might fill up before the next reset, you may need to increase your budget for that quota to avoid quota denials.

Near the bottom of the dashboard are lists of popular URL paths and URLs that are returning errors. You can click on a URL to view the detailed request logs for that URL path.

The dashboard's time-based chart and URL traffic lists show data for the version of the app selected by the drop-down menu in the upper-left corner of the screen. When you first sign in to the Console, the default version is selected. To view data for a different version of the app, select it from the drop-down menu.

You can view a more comprehensive chart of how the app is consuming resources with quotas from the Quota Details section of the Cloud Console. This chart shows billable quotas as well as several fixed quotas, such as API calls and service bandwidth. If your app is having quota-denial errors, check this screen for information on how the app is consuming resources.

The resource usage chart on the dashboard and the quota details screen show the total of all resource usage for all versions of the app. All versions of an app share the same budget and quotas.

When your app is ready to outgrow the free quotas, you can set a budget for additional resources. App Engine allocates more resources as needed according to the budget you establish, and you are only billed for the resources actually consumed.

You probably set up a billing account when you created the project. If you need to adjust which account is associated with the project select the Billing & Settings panel in the Cloud Console. The owner of the billing account is solely responsible for setting the budget and paying for resources consumed.

Getting Help

If you have questions not answered by this book, you may find your answers in the official documentation on Google's website:

https://cloud.google.com/appengine/

The documentation includes complete references for the APIs and tools for the Java runtime environment; a list of frequently asked questions and answers (the FAQ); and a large collection of articles describing best practices, interesting features, and complete working examples.

You may also want to browse the contents of the SDK, as installed by the Eclipse plugin and also available as a ZIP archive from the website. The SDK also includes a set of functional example applications.

All App Engine developers should subscribe to Google's App Engine downtime mailing list. This low-traffic, announcement-only list is used by the App Engine team to announce scheduled times when services are taken down for maintenance, and also to report the status of unexpected problems:

http://groups.google.com/group/google-appengine-downtime-notify

You can check the current and past health of App Engine and its services by consulting the system status site:

http://code.google.com/status/appengine

By far the best place to ask questions about Google App Engine is Stack Overflow. Post your question with the google-app-engine tag, and it'll be seen by the App Engine developer community, as well as the App Engine team at Google. As you learn more, you can answer other people's questions and build your reputation as an App Engine expert. You can also use Google to search through past answers, which may have what you're looking for:

http://stackoverflow.com/questions/tagged/google-app-engine

If you believe you have found a bug in App Engine, the SDK, or the Cloud Console, or if you have a feature you'd like to request, you can post to the App Engine issue tracker. You can also see features others have requested, and vote for your favorites. (The App Engine team does indeed consider the highly requested features in this list when determining the product road map.)

http://code.google.com/p/googleappengine/issues/list

Google has a general discussion group for App Engine developers and an IRC channel, and also does regular live-streamed video question-and-answer sessions with the team. This page has more information on community resources:

https://cloud.google.com/appengine/community

Index

read replicas, 253
registering applications, 48
regular expressions, 58
relational databases, 134, 136, 151, 233
relationships, in JPA, 247
remote controls, 229-232
    benefits of, 229
    Java client library and, 230
    setting up, 229
request forgery attacks, 295
request handlers, 81-93
    configuring, 60
    definition of term, 25
    dispatching requests to modules, 124
    overview of, 53, 81
    push queues and, 330, 338
    request handler abstraction, 90
    runtime environment and, 82-90
    scheduled tasks and, 330
    startup requests, 115
    stateless behavior of, 134
    traffic splitting, 102
request headers, 295, 339
request logs, 375-384
    downloading logs, 380
    items included, 375
    querying from apps, 382
    retention of, 381
    statistics included, 375
    viewing logs, 378
    writing to logs, 376
request scheduling, 96
request timers, 84
resident instances, 98, 106, 115
resource budget, setting, 87
resource files, 62
resources, accessing, 392
response objects, 297
REST (Representational State Transfer), 12
roll-forward mechanism, 211
root entities, 201
RPC (remote procedure call), 362
runtime environment, 81-90
    App Engine architecture and, 55
    as abstraction, 4
    choices, 3
    documentation, 392
    functions of, 82
    Java runtime environment, 89

overview of, 2, 81
quotas and limits, 84-89
using different simultaneously, 120
versions of, 82

S

sandboxing, 3, 82-84
scalability
    automatic scaling feature, 96, 105
    definition of term, 1
    manual vs. basic scaling, 105, 113
    need for, xi
    solutions for, xi
    transactions and, 198
scam email, 301
scheduled tasks
    architecture of, 331
    benefits of, 357
    configuring, 358
    definition of term, 330
    execution of, 357
    parts of, 357
    vs. push queues, 358
    request handlers and, 330
    specifying schedules, 359
    validating, 359
SDK Shell, 19
Search service, 10
Secure Socket Layer (SSL), 72, 295
security
    connections in modules, 123
    connections with custom domains, 72
    data sharing during multithreading, 60
    request forgery attacks, 295
    restricting app access, 59, 387
    SSL/TLS connections, 68, 70
self-invitation maneuver, 70
Server Name Indication (SNI), 73
service call optimization, 361-373
    asynchronous vs. synchronous calls, 363
    techniques for, 361
    visualizing calls with AppStats, 367-373
service configuration, 389
service limits, 85
servlet classes, 26
sharding, 201
shutdown hooks, 116, 128
sort order, 164, 168, 177, 184
SQL injection attacks, 260

SQL instances, 10
SQL-based relational databases, 233
SSL (Secure Socket Layer), 72, 295
SSL/TLS connections, 68, 70
start cursors, 189
StartSSL, 73
startup requests, 115, 128
stateless vs. stateful, 133
static files
    configuring, 62-65
    overview of, 4
statistics, querying, 224
status messages, 323
strong consistency, 198
subscription, 319
synchronous calls, to memcache service, 277
system IDs, 148

T

task chains, 350
task names, 336
task parameters
    countdowns/ETAs, 338
    payloads, 335
    task names, 336
    types of, 335
task queues
    adding tasks to (enqueuing), 333
    administration of, 355
    architecture of, 331
    benefits of, 329, 332
    billable storage quota, 333
    configuring, 332
    deferring work, 356
    example of, 329
    mechanisms of, 330
    overview of, 12
    producers/consumers in, 330
    pull queues, 344-347
    push queues, 338-344
    specifying alternate modules, 335
    task chaining, 350
    task parameters, 335-338
    transactional task enqueuing, 347
tasks, definition of term, 330
TCP port 443, 71
templating systems, 32
testing applications, 50
text searches, 10

text strings, 140, 140
third-party libraries, 86
threads, background, 117, 128
    (see also multithreading)
threadsafe declaration, 60
throughput, 198
TLS (Transport Layer Security), 72
token buckets, 340
tombstones, 336
traffic splitting, 102
transactional reads, 204
transactional task enqueueing, 347
transactions, 8, 197
    (see also datastore transactions)
Transport Layer Security (TLS), 72

U

unowned relationships, 248
unset properties, 142, 176
upload tool, 386
uploading applications, 48
URL Fetch service
    accidental request loop prevention in, 294
    calling, 291
    customizing behaviors, 292
    default behavior, 290
    handling redirects, 297
    HTTP method and payload, 294
    HTTP over SSL (HTTPS), 295
    outgoing HTTP requests, 293
    overview of, 10, 289
    request and response sizes, 296
    request deadlines, 296
    response objects, 297
    restrictions on, 289
    service call optimization, 362
    using Java.net package, 291
URL mapping, explicit vs. default, 37
URL paths, 61, 294
URLConnection interface, 292
user account systems, 26
user preferences pattern, 25
utilization, 99

V

value types, 177
values
    adding and replacing, 279
    atomic increment and decrement, 281

About the Author

Dan Sanderson is a technical writer and software engineer at Google. He has worked in the web industry for over 15 years as a software engineer and technical writer for Google, Amazon, and the Walt Disney Internet Group. He lives in Seattle, Washington. For more information about Dan, visit his website at *http://www.dansanderson.com*.

Colophon

The animal on the cover of *Programming Google App Engine with Java* is a Comoro cuckoo roller (*Leptosomus gracilis*). This medium-sized bird is widespread throughout the tropical forests of Madagascar and the neighboring Comoro Islands.

At roughly 40 centimeters long, the Comoro cuckoo roller is the smallest of the three named subspecies of *Leptosomus*. It is distinguished by its large, round head, short legs, and zygodactyl feet, with two forward-pointing and two backward-pointing toes on each foot.

The cuckoo roller hunts for prey—mostly insects (particularly caterpillars) and small reptiles—in the forest canopy. Often seen in pairs, they nest in natural tree cavities, typically laying four eggs per clutch.

Many of the animals on O'Reilly covers are endangered; all of them are important to the world. To learn more about how you can help, go to *animals.oreilly.com*.

The cover image is from *Cassell's Natural History*. The cover fonts are URW Typewriter and Guardian Sans. The text font is Adobe Minion Pro; the heading font is Adobe Myriad Condensed; and the code font is Dalton Maag's Ubuntu Mono.

Have it your way.

Get even more for your money.

Join the O'Reilly Community, and register the O'Reilly books you own. It's free, and you'll get:

- $4.99 ebook upgrade offer
- 40% upgrade offer on O'Reilly print books
- Membership discounts on books and events
- Free lifetime updates to ebooks and videos
- Multiple ebook formats, DRM FREE
- Participation in the O'Reilly community
- Newsletters
- Account management
- 100% Satisfaction Guarantee

Signing up is easy:

1. Go to: oreilly.com/go/register
2. Create an O'Reilly login.
3. Provide your address.
4. Register your books.

Note: English-language books only

To order books online:
oreilly.com/store

For questions about products or an order:
orders@oreilly.com

To sign up to get topic-specific email announcements and/or news about upcoming books, conferences, special offers, and new technologies:
elists@oreilly.com

For technical questions about book content:
booktech@oreilly.com

To submit new book proposals to our editors:
proposals@oreilly.com

O'Reilly books are available in multiple DRM-free ebook formats. For more information:
oreilly.com/ebooks

O'REILLY®

CPSIA information can be obtained at www.ICGtesting.com
Printed in the USA
BVOW09s0342010715

406906BV00002B/3/P